MW01257045

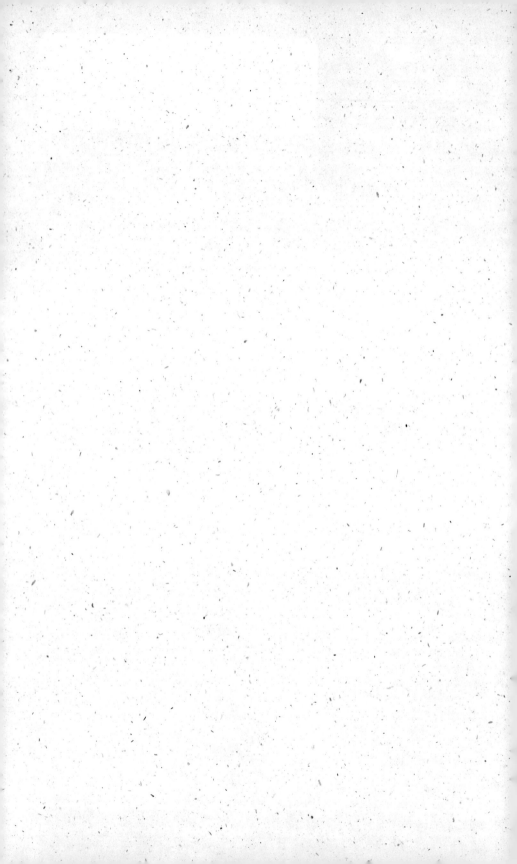

Scripture and the
People of God

Scripture and the People of God

Essays in Honor of Wayne Grudem

Edited by John DelHousaye,
John J. Hughes, and Jeff T. Purswell

Foreword by John M. Frame

WHEATON, ILLINOIS

Scripture and the People of God: Essays in Honor of Wayne Grudem
Copyright © 2018 by John DelHousaye, John J. Hughes, and Jeff T. Purswell
Published by Crossway
  1300 Crescent Street
  Wheaton, Illinois 60187

All rights reserved. No part of this publication may be reproduced, stored in a retrieval system, or transmitted in any form by any means, electronic, mechanical, photocopy, recording, or otherwise, without the prior permission of the publisher, except as provided for by USA copyright law. Crossway® is a registered trademark in the United States of America.

Cover design: Jordan Singer

First printing 2018

Printed in the United States of America

Unless otherwise indicated, Scripture quotations are from the ESV® Bible (The Holy Bible, English Standard Version®), copyright © 2001 by Crossway, a publishing ministry of Good News Publishers. Used by permission. All rights reserved.

For other Scripture versions cited, please see the appendix.

All italics in Scripture quotations have been added by the authors.

Hardcover ISBN: 978-1-4335-5857-3
epub ISBN: 978-1-4335-5860-3
PDF ISBN: 978-1-4335-5858-0
Mobipocket ISBN: 978-1-4335-5859-7

Library of Congress Cataloging-in-Publication Data
Names: Grudem, Wayne A., honoree. | DelHousaye, John, editor.
Title: Scripture and the people of God: essays in honor of Wayne Grudem / edited by John DelHousaye, John J. Hughes, and Jeff T. Purswell; foreword by John M. Frame.
Description: Wheaton: Crossway, 2018. | Includes bibliographical references and index.
Identifiers: LCCN 2018035155 (print) | LCCN 2018038215 (ebook) | ISBN 9781433558580 (pdf) | ISBN 9781433558597 (mobi) | ISBN 9781433558603 (epub) | ISBN 9781433558573 (hc)
Subjects: LCSH: Bible—Criticism, interpretation, etc.
Classification: LCC BS511.3 (ebook) | LCC BS511.3 .S369 2018 (print) | DDC 220.6—dc23
LC record available at https://lccn.loc.gov/2018035155

Crossway is a publishing ministry of Good News Publishers.

SH		28	27	26	25	24	23	22	21	20	19	18
15	14	13	12	11	10	9	8	7	6	5	4	3	2	1

The law of the LORD is perfect,
reviving the soul;
the testimony of the LORD is sure,
making wise the simple;
the precepts of the LORD are right,
rejoicing the heart;
the commandment of the LORD is pure,
enlightening the eyes;
the fear of the LORD is clean,
enduring forever;
the rules of the LORD are true,
and righteous altogether.
More to be desired are they than gold,
even much fine gold;
sweeter also than honey
and drippings of the honeycomb.
Moreover, by them is your servant warned;
in keeping them there is great reward.

Psalm 19:7–11

Contents

PART 1 SYSTEMATIC THEOLOGY

PART 2 BIBLICAL STUDIES

PART 3 PASTORAL MINISTRY

Tribute to Wayne Grudem

Lane T. Dennis

It is a privilege for me to add my voice to the authors of this book in tribute to Wayne Grudem. Like each of the contributors, I too have a long relationship with Wayne—one that has given me an enormous appreciation for the man and his ministry.

This volume has been appropriately titled *Scripture and the People of God*, as faithfulness to Scripture has been at the heart of all of Wayne's work throughout his life. I often think of Wayne as uniquely exemplifying the apostle Paul's admonition to Timothy to "guard the deposit entrusted to you" (1 Tim. 6:20).

First, it is a great privilege to have Wayne as a founding member of the Translation Oversight Committee (TOC) for the English Standard Version of the Bible and to benefit from Wayne's invaluable contribution on the TOC. What precious memories we have of working together in remarkable unity among the fourteen TOC members—seeking to render every word and phrase as transparently and faithfully as the Lord would enable. Thus we give all glory to God alone for the ESV, "with ongoing wonder that our God should ever have entrusted to us so momentous a task" (as the ESV preface concludes).

Second, I would mention the creation of the *ESV Study Bible* (*ESVSB*). I remember well how my wife, Ebeth, and I sought the Lord's leading for the best person to be entrusted with the enormous theological and spiritual responsibility of serving as general editor for the *ESVSB*. Having worked together with Wayne on the translation of the ESV Bible, and given his invaluable *Systematic Theology*, we were convinced that Wayne was the person that the Lord had uniquely equipped and called for this purpose—a call that Wayne graciously accepted after much prayer. Again we give all glory to God for what he has accomplished—for the provision of Wayne, for the provision of the ninety-five contributors who created the *ESVSB* under Wayne's general editorship, and now to see the Lord's extraordinary hand of blessing on the publication and distribution of the *ESVSB* in more than seventy countries worldwide.

Lastly, I would mention the recent publication of Wayne's *Christian Ethics* (just a few days ago as of this writing). *Christian Ethics* beautifully represents Wayne's lifelong calling to apply Scripture to "the people of God" in all of life.

It is with much joy and delight, then, that Ebeth and I express our great appreciation to Wayne and Margaret Grudem—for their dear friendship, their faithfulness to God's Word and the gospel, and the tremendous legacy that Wayne has provided throughout his life of teaching, writing, mentoring, and ministry. We would not be surprised to hear Wayne rejoicing with the apostle Paul: "I am not ashamed, for I know whom I have believed, and I am convinced that he is able to guard until that day what has been entrusted to me. . . . By the Holy Spirit who dwells within us, guard the good deposit entrusted to you" (2 Tim. 1:12, 14).

Foreword

John M. Frame

I have written elsewhere[1] about the exciting period 1964–1974, when
Westminster Theological Seminary experienced a major theological
transition. From 1961 to 1964, I had studied under the "old faculty,"
the "boys" that J. Gresham Machen had brought with him when he left
Princeton in 1929 to found Westminster. Those boys—John Murray,
Cornelius Van Til, Ned B. Stonehouse, and Paul Woolley, joined later
by several others, including Edward J. Young, Meredith G. Kline, and
Edmund P. Clowney—gave the school a formidable reputation for
scholarship and consistent Reformed orthodoxy. But in the late sixties
and early seventies, deaths, retirements, and other departures neces-
sitated replacements. As a teacher, I joined a group of new professors,
including Jay E. Adams, C. John Miller, D. Clair Davis, Raymond B.
Dillard, and later Harvie M. Conn.

And God also brought to Westminster during this time a group
of students with remarkable theological gifts, many of whom would
go on to write significant theological works and join the faculties of
Westminster and other schools, becoming leaders in various fields of
evangelical theology. In that group were William Edgar, James Hurley,
David Clowney, Willem VanGemeren, Moisés Silva, Alan Groves,

---

1. John Frame, *Theology of My Life: A Theological and Apologetic Memoir* (Eugene, OR:
Cascade, 2017), 88–122; Frame, foreword to *Redeeming the Life of the Mind: Essays in Honor of
Vern Poythress*, ed. John M. Frame, Wayne Grudem, and John J. Hughes (Wheaton, IL: Crossway,
2017); Frame, "Backgrounds to My Thought," in *Speaking the Truth in Love: The Theology of
John M. Frame*, ed. John J. Hughes (Phillipsburg, NJ, P&R, 2009), 9–30.

Susan Foh, Dennis Johnson, Greg Bahnsen, Paul Wells, Tiina Allik, John Hughes, Vern Poythress, and Wayne Grudem, whom we honor in this volume.

Westminster had been known not only for its high level of scholarship and Reformed orthodoxy but also for its creativity—creativity, of course, within the bounds of orthodoxy. The Westminster faculty was committed to the church's creeds and the Reformed confessions; but it had never been content with simply repeating and emphasizing those formulations. Rather, faculty members had a strong motivation toward rethinking their tradition—in order both to apply it to new questions and to verify its biblical basis. That was true of the Old Princeton tradition: one thinks, for example, of the development by the Hodges and Warfield of the church's doctrine of biblical authority and inerrancy. At Westminster, Murray's systematic theology, unlike many previous Reformed syntheses, was focused almost entirely on the exegesis of biblical texts, with minimal (though expert when necessary) interaction with the history of doctrine. Stonehouse and Young, like Machen, dug deep into Scripture to respond in depth to the objections of modern critics of biblical teaching. Kline developed original responses to exegetical issues, such as the "framework hypothesis" in Genesis 1–2. Clowney built on the "redemptive-historical" emphasis of Geerhardus Vos to develop a view of preaching that sought above all to preach Christ from all the Bible. Van Til rejected the dominant apologetic traditions of the church, seeking a more biblical way of defending the faith. Jay Adams, similarly, rejected the traditional accommodation of Christian counseling to secular psychology, developing a new system of "nouthetic" or "biblical" counseling. Harvie Conn insisted on the importance of "contextualization" in missions: presenting biblical truth in the language of those to whom the gospel comes. C. John Miller insisted on evangelism with a deep understanding of grace, overcoming the self-defensiveness of the church's "ingrown" traditions. And Vern Poythress and John Frame became known for something called "perspectivalism," the habit of looking at theological questions from many different angles. The pattern was this: at Old Princeton and Westminster there was a special passion to dig more deeply into what Scripture says, together with a creative independence from past historical formulations.

Of this group, Wayne Grudem may be the best known to the theological public, because of his wonderful *Systematic Theology: An Introduction to Biblical Doctrine*.[2] This best-selling, influential volume is often described as representative of the conservative Reformed tradition. But, like the other theologians I have mentioned, Grudem is far more than a mere representative. He too is an original thinker of the first order.

After his studies at Harvard and Westminster, Grudem earned his doctorate in New Testament at Cambridge University under C. F. D. Moule, writing a dissertation on the nature of prophecy in the New Testament, especially 1 Corinthians.[3] In his argument, he rejected the Reformed tradition of "cessationism," the view that God had removed the gift of prophecy from the church at the end of the apostolic age. But he nevertheless defended the Reformed understanding of the sufficiency of Scripture, by making a sharp distinction between the authority of scriptural revelation and the authority of New Testament (and contemporary) prophecy. Prophecy in the Old Testament, he argued, was identical with God's own word and therefore of ultimate and permanent authority for the church. But prophecy in the New Testament consisted of less authoritative utterances, lacking the ultimacy and permanence of the biblical canon. Therefore in Grudem's view, as in traditional Reformed theology, Scripture alone is our final authority, inerrant and infallible, a suitable starting point for the development of Christian doctrine.

His *Systematic Theology*, then, incorporates his highly unusual view of prophecy, together with an emphasis on *sola Scriptura*, an intention (no less than John Murray's) to derive all doctrinal conclusions from biblical exegesis. His argument gives a certain level of support for the charismatic movement while insisting on a rigorous exegetical basis for all his theological positions. His view of prophecy is certainly creative, while his view of biblical sufficiency is deeply conservative.

At other points as well, Grudem differs from traditional Reformed thinking while basing his ideas on a deep study of Scripture. He

---

2. Leicester, UK: Inter-Varsity Press; Grand Rapids, MI: Zondervan, 1994. Grudem has also published portions and abbreviations of this volume, with applications of its teaching to different topics.

3. For a revised version of his dissertation, see Grudem, *The Gift of Prophecy in the New Testament and Today*, rev. ed. (Wheaton, IL: Crossway, 2000).

advocates believer's baptism and premillennialism—views never entirely absent from the Reformed tradition, but not typical of it.

But he has also put a huge effort into defending a very traditional Reformed and evangelical view: that the relation of men and women in the church is "complementarian" rather than "egalitarian." With John Piper, Grudem edited *Recovering Biblical Manhood and Womanhood: A Response to Evangelical Feminism.*[4] This book of essays argues comprehensively that although men and women are equal in dignity before God, the Scriptures do not prescribe for them identical roles in the family, society, and church. So Grudem opposes the evangelical feminists' movement to open the church's offices to women.

In the course of this debate, Grudem entered the controversy as to whether the term *kephalē* (translated "head"), used to describe the relation of husband to wife in 1 Corinthians 11:3 and Ephesians 5:23, means "authority over" or "source." He argued the first alternative from a remarkably comprehensive examination of the term and the literature about it.[5]

So Grudem's concern with the theology of gender entailed a concern with Bible translations. His book with Vern Poythress *The Gender-Neutral Bible Controversy: Muting the Masculinity of God's Words*[6] and their later *The TNIV and the Gender-Neutral Bible Controversy*[7] argued that some recent translations have distorted the biblical text to make it support egalitarianism. He and Poythress worked with the team of translators that produced and edited the English Standard Version,[8] an "essentially literal" translation of Scripture that seeks to avoid theological, philosophical, and political bias, including gender ideology.

More recently, Grudem, who was an economics major at Harvard, has produced works in the economic and political spheres: *Politics—*

---

4. Wheaton, IL: Crossway, 1991. See also Grudem, *Evangelical Feminism and Biblical Truth: An Analysis of Over One Hundred Disputed Questions* (Wheaton, IL: Crossway, 2012). Grudem is also a cofounder of the Council on Biblical Manhood and Womanhood, which promotes the complementarian position.

5. Wayne Grudem, "Does Κεφαλή ('Head') Mean 'Source' or 'Authority Over' in Greek Literature? A Survey of 2,336 Examples," *TJ* 6, no. 1 (Spring 1985): 38–59. Grudem updated and supplemented his article in *Recovering Biblical Manhood and Womanhood*, ed. Wayne Grudem and John Piper (Wheaton, IL: Crossway, 1991), appendix I, 425–68.

6. Nashville: Broadman & Holman, 2000.

7. Nashville: Broadman & Holman, 2004.

8. Wheaton, IL: Crossway, 2001, and in many editions since. From 2005 to 2008, Grudem served as general editor of the *ESV Study Bible*.

according to the Bible: A Comprehensive Resource for Understanding Modern Political Issues in Light of Scripture[9] and (with Barry Asmus) *The Poverty of Nations: A Sustainable Solution.*[10] These books do not mark any departure from Grudem's general theological emphasis or his direct engagement with the Bible. Indeed, these arguments for Christian political engagement reinforce his commitment to the Reformed tradition, as in Puritanism and Dutch neo-Calvinism.[11] In the 2016 election, Grudem was a supporter of Donald Trump, with qualifications.

There has been controversy between Grudem and some other writers about the doctrine of the Trinity.[12] The church confesses that there is one God in three persons, and that Scripture names those persons as Father, Son, and Holy Spirit. Scripture is clear both as to God's oneness and as to the deity of the three persons, but beyond those affirmations much is mysterious. It is not immediately obvious how God can be both one and three, or how a "person" of God is different from other persons or from the singular divine nature. Traditional theology confesses that the three persons may be distinguished from one another by their "personal properties": the Father is unbegotten, eternally generates the Son, and eternally sends forth the Spirit; the Son is eternally begotten and eternally sends forth the Spirit; the Spirit eternally proceeds from the Father and the Son.[13] But it is unclear what these personal properties tell us about the persons beyond the names Father, Son, and Spirit, and, if the properties are more than elaborations of these names, how their meanings can be established from Scripture.

Clearly there are differences among the three persons beyond those implied by their personal properties. It was the Son who became incarnate, not the Father or the Holy Spirit. And this fact was not an accident. In God's plan nothing is inappropriate, and so there evidently

---

9. Grand Rapids, MI: Zondervan, 2010.
10. Wheaton, IL: Crossway, 2013.
11. Some Reformed theologians press Luther's "two kingdoms" distinction to argue that Scripture deals only with salvation from sin and not with politics or the general culture. Grudem, of course, is on the other side of this debate. His writings contain the best resolution of the controversy, showing how there are in Scripture solutions for specific social issues.
12. This controversy goes back to the formulations of Grudem's *Systematic Theology* and his differences with evangelical feminism, but it was reignited at the 2016 annual meeting of the Evangelical Theological Society.
13. Whether the Spirit proceeds from the Father *and* the Son (*filioque*) or proceeds only from the Father is disputed between the Eastern and the Western churches. My formulation of the personal properties reflects the Western understanding.

was a reason why only the Son became incarnate.[14] So the history of redemption reveals to us some truths about the eternal distinctions between the Trinitarian persons, however difficult it may be for us to understand them.

In Grudem's *Systematic Theology*, he maintains that although the three persons are equal in their being, deity, nature, power, and glory, there are some differences in "role" among them,[15] differences that exist through all eternity. Particularly, Grudem stresses that the Father has the distinctive role of being supreme authority, so that even the Son and the Spirit are eternally subordinate to the Father's eternal plan.

Other theologians, particularly evangelical feminists, have taken issue with Grudem here as elsewhere. Evangelical feminists have invoked the equality of the persons of the Trinity as a model for egalitarian marriage among human beings, and they have charged Grudem (wrongly, in my view) with holding to a subordinationism like that of the heretic Arius.[16] The 2016 annual meeting of the Evangelical Theological Society featured a number of lectures on the Trinity, and the views of Grudem and Bruce Ware (who holds essentially the same position) came up for scrutiny.

For the details of the controversy, consult the essay by Bruce Ware in this volume. For what it's worth, I would argue the following: (1) It is wrong for either side to use the classic doctrine of the Trinity as a model for human marriage. A biblical view of marriage ought to focus not on the doctrine of the Trinity, difficult as that is to formulate, but on the passages of Scripture that address human marriage specifically, such as Genesis 1:24 and Ephesians 5:22–33. (2) It is misleading to speak of "subordination" of the Son to the Father, since the Arian controversy gave that term a specific meaning that is hard to avoid and confusing to introduce into other contexts. And (3) it is nevertheless quite legitimate for theologians to venture beyond the classic creedal statements, seeking better to understand the distinctions among the persons of the Trinity from the roles they play in the history of redemption.

---

14. To cite a statement Einstein made in a different context, "God does not throw dice" (Letter to Max Born, December 4, 1926, in *The Born-Einstein Letters*, trans. Irene Born [New York: Walker and Company, 1971]).

15. Grudem, *Systematic Theology*, 248–52.

16. In my view, it was a mistake on Grudem's part to use the term "subordination" here, even in his highly qualified way ("functional," not "ontological" subordination), since theological critics often attend to words without paying due attention to their contexts and qualifications.

In summary, I see Wayne Grudem as an excellent representative of the Westminster tradition in theology. He exhibits the Old Princeton/ Westminster passion to honor the authority and inerrancy of Scripture, and to bring all theological controversies directly to Scripture for their resolution.[17] At the same time, like many representatives of Old Princeton and Westminster, he is not bound by tradition but applies the Bible creatively to many areas of human life.

Alongside my theological admiration of him, I would express thanks to God for Wayne Grudem's friendship over many years and the example of his Christian life. The essay in this volume by his son Elliot testifies to Wayne Grudem's love of worship and praise. And his love of God motivates him to be gracious to his colleagues as well. He has always been willing to support the work of other evangelical theologians.[18] He gladly acknowledged his debt to a number of us on the dedication page of his *Systematic Theology*. Later, he wrote an article for my own Festschrift,[19] even though, as it turned out, we held different positions on the topic he chose to write on. When I published my own *Systematic Theology*[20] after many years of recommending Grudem's,[21] I would not have asked him to recommend mine; but P&R's editor did, and Wayne was willing to give my book a gracious endorsement.

Though Grudem is now afflicted with Parkinson's disease, he maintains an active work schedule and continues to bless the church and the world with the riches of God's Word. I hope that this Festschrift brings much further honor to his distinguished career and to the Lord Jesus whom he serves.

---

17. Grudem is knowledgeable and appreciative of the creeds and catechisms of the church. But his son Elliott Grudem, in this volume, explains interestingly why his father had his son memorize Scripture rather than catechism questions.

18. He has been a very active member of the Evangelical Theological Society for many years and served as president of the organization in 1999.

19. Wayne Grudem, "Why It Is Never Right to Lie: An Example of John Frame's Influence on My Approach to Ethics," in Hughes, *Speaking the Truth in Love*, 778–801. When Grudem began the article, he had the impression that his position on lying was the same as mine. After reading my *Doctrine of the Christian Life* (Phillipsburg, NJ: P&R, 2008) he realized that I had changed my position and we were in different camps! To Grudem's credit, however, he stuck by his guns and presented at great length and in great depth what he believed the Scriptures taught. I still disagree with him on this matter, but I deeply respect his allegiance to Scripture as he understands it.

20. John M. Frame, *Systematic Theology: An Introduction to Christian Belief* (Phillipsburg, NJ: P&R, 2013).

21. In fact, I still recommend it. The two books have some different features and serve different purposes. Grudem's is more complete than mine in many areas, and I love the study materials he places after each chapter. The hymns and memory passages and points of personal application he cites are immensely valuable.

Preface

John Calvin once referred to Holy Scripture as "God's scepter."[1] This evocative metaphor captures much of both the nature and function of God's written Word. Because God's Word originates with him, it partakes of his holy character. It carries his authority. It is the instrument of his rule in our lives. From it we learn his character, his plans, his purposes, and his will. As those who have come under God's saving reign through Christ, we are to treasure it, meditate upon it, view the world and all of life in light of it, and honor and obey it with all our hearts and in every area of our lives.

For those who know Wayne Grudem, this understanding of and posture toward the Bible will sound familiar. If there is a common factor that underlies Wayne's varied interests, unifies his academic pursuits, and governs his methodology, surely it is his unswerving allegiance to Scripture's authority and his resolve to bring Scripture's truth to bear upon all of life. The title of this book—*Scripture and the People of God*—alludes to the intersection between God's Word and God's people, which has animated Wayne's productive career as a theologian, teacher, and author, and marked his life as a husband, father, friend, and follower of Christ.

A devotion to the Bible was instilled in Wayne from his earliest years. Wayne Arden Grudem was born on February 11, 1948, in Chippewa Falls, Wisconsin, the oldest of three sons born to Arden and Jean (née Sheady) Grudem. Although he prayed with his mother to receive Christ at age twelve, he now sees evidence of his conversion at a much

---

1. The phrase comes from his "Prefatory Address to King Francis I of France," in John Calvin, *Institutes of the Christian Religion*, ed. John T. McNeill, trans. Ford Lewis Battles (Philadelphia: Westminster, 1960), 12.

earlier age, perhaps four or five. In the dedication to his *Systematic Theology*, he notes, "My parents . . . taught me to believe the Bible, to trust in God, and to speak and write clearly." He also credits the influence of "A. Kenneth Ham, my Baptist pastor, who awakened in me a love for systematic theology by teaching a class on Christian doctrine when I was thirteen years old, and who taught me by example to believe every word of Scripture." The blessings of a Christian home and a solid church proved formative for Wayne's future calling as a teacher of God's Word.

Wayne's love for biblical truth did not stifle but rather fueled a wide range of interests. An early fascination with politics led him to study economics at Harvard University, topics to which he has recently returned in his writing.[2] While he was at Harvard, his plans for law school were changed as a result of sitting under the preaching of Harold John Ockenga at Park Street Church in Boston. He was now on a course to serve the church with his gifts, and during his undergraduate years he was active (along with Vern Poythress) in the leadership of the Harvard-Radcliffe Christian Fellowship and the Collegiate Club at Park Street Church. Between his sophomore and junior years, he served as a summer intern for Harald Bredesen at the First Christian Reformed Church in Mount Vernon, New York, an experience that greatly strengthened his convictions concerning the power and presence of the Holy Spirit in ministry.

It was also during his Harvard years, on June 6, 1969, that he married Margaret White, whom he had known since middle school. Wayne and Margaret have three sons—Elliot (married Kacey), Oliver (married Sarah), and Alexander (married Lauren)—and three grandchildren.

After college Wayne and Margaret moved to California, where he would attend Fuller Theological Seminary. However, because of Fuller's evolving position on the doctrine of Scripture, he soon transferred to Westminster Theological Seminary, from which he graduated in 1973. His training at WTS had the single greatest impact upon his understanding of the Bible and theology, particularly through the teaching of Edmund Clowney and John Frame, along with his friendship with Vern Poythress, who was a student at WTS at the same time.

---

2. Wayne Grudem, *Politics according to the Bible: A Comprehensive Resource for Understanding Modern Political Issues in Light of Scripture* (Grand Rapids, MI: Zondervan, 2010); Wayne Grudem and Barry Asmus, *The Poverty of Nations: A Sustainable Solution* (Wheaton, IL: Crossway, 2013).

Wayne pursued doctoral work in New Testament studies at Cambridge University, England, under the supervision of C. F. D. Moule. One can detect in his dissertation, "The Gift of Prophecy in 1 Corinthians," the melding of a number of his interests: theological formulation based on rigorous exegesis, with a concern for the church to be empowered by the work of the Holy Spirit.[3]

Wayne's teaching career began when he left England for Bethel College in St. Paul, Minnesota, where he taught from 1977 to 1981. In 1981, he moved to Trinity Evangelical Divinity School in Deerfield, Illinois, where he would teach, write, and influence a generation of pastors and Christian leaders for the next twenty years. It was during his time at Trinity that Wayne gained prominence as one of the leading evangelical theologians in the English-speaking world. Beginning as a New Testament professor (during which time he produced a commentary on 1 Peter), he transitioned to the department of biblical and systematic theology in 1987.[4] This bridge between disciplines illuminates the exegetical emphasis in Wayne's theological methodology, most prominently exhibited in his *Systematic Theology*, a widely acclaimed and best-selling theology text.[5] The approach of the book, which stresses clarity and application to life, also illustrates his unflagging desire to make biblical teaching accessible to as many people as possible, regardless of their background or training.

Beyond his teaching and writing, Wayne also exerted much influence during these years through his energetic leadership in the evangelical world. In 1987, along with John Piper, he helped to found the Council on Biblical Manhood and Womanhood. CBMW produced "The Danvers Statement on Biblical Manhood and Womanhood," which has become the classic theological articulation of "complementarianism," the view that men and women are created equal before God in dignity and worth, and designed to complement each other in differing roles that together glorify him. Three years later, Piper and

---

3. Published as Wayne Grudem, *The Gift of Prophecy in 1 Corinthians* (Washington, DC: University Press of America, 1982). A popularized and expanded version of his dissertation appeared under the title *The Gift of Prophecy in the New Testament and Today* (Westchester, IL: Crossway, 1988); rev. ed. (Wheaton, IL: Crossway, 2000).

4. Wayne Grudem, *The First Epistle of Peter*, Tyndale New Testament Commentaries (Leicester, UK: Inter-Varsity Press; Grand Rapids, MI: Eerdmans, 1988).

5. Wayne Grudem, *Systematic Theology: An Introduction to Biblical Doctrine* (Leicester, UK: Inter-Varsity Press; Grand Rapids, MI: Zondervan, 1994).

Grudem edited *Recovering Biblical Manhood and Womanhood: A Response to Evangelical Feminism*, which provided extensive biblical and theological foundations for the complementarian position.[6] Wayne has also been active in the Evangelical Theological Society, serving as its president in 1999.

Perhaps the most enduring expression of Wayne's commitment to Scripture is his involvement with the English Standard Version (ESV) translation of the Bible, published in 2001 by Crossway. Wayne was involved in the original conception of the ESV as an updating and revision of the Revised Standard Version (RSV). He then participated in the process of revision and translation as a (continuing) member of the ESV Translation Oversight Committee, and later served as general editor of the *ESV Study Bible*.[7] In these ways Wayne has been a driving force behind a translation that is used by denominations, organizations, pastors, and Christians throughout the world.

Since 2001, Wayne has served as research professor of theology and biblical studies at Phoenix Seminary in Arizona. This transition was prompted by the hope that the desert climate would provide relief for Margaret's fibromyalgia. Although the move came as a surprise to many, Wayne's decision was wholly consistent with his allegiance to Christ, love for Margaret, and submission to Scripture (specifically in this case, Eph. 5:28).[8] His recently published *Christian Ethics*, a natural extension of his burden to connect God's Word with people's lives—and thus an appropriate bookend to *Systematic Theology*—will no doubt help countless others to apply Scripture to their daily lives in ways that are pleasing to God.[9]

As this brief survey illustrates, *Scripture and the People of God* is a title most befitting a book honoring Wayne's life and ministry. The book explores various dimensions of this topic, including the nature of Scripture, its reception, its translation, its use in doctrinal formula-

---

6. John Piper and Wayne Grudem, eds., *Recovering Biblical Manhood and Womanhood: A Response to Evangelical Feminism* (Wheaton, IL: Crossway, 1991). See also Grudem, ed., *Biblical Foundations for Manhood and Womanhood* (Wheaton, IL: Crossway, 2002); Grudem, *Evangelical Feminism and Biblical Truth: An Analysis of More Than One Hundred Disputed Questions* (Sisters, OR: Multnomah, 2004; repr., Wheaton, IL: Crossway, 2012).

7. *ESV Study Bible* (Wheaton, IL: Crossway, 2008).

8. Wayne's description of this decision can be found in Wayne Grudem, "Upon Leaving: Thoughts on Marriage and Ministry," *Trinity* (Summer 2001), http://www.waynegrudem.com/wp-content/uploads/2012/03/Upon-Leaving-Thoughts-on-Marriage-Ministry.pdf.

9. Wayne Grudem, *Christian Ethics: An Introduction to Biblical Moral Reasoning* (Wheaton, IL: Crossway, 2018).

tion, and its application to life and ministry. The essays are organized around three disciplines to which Wayne has made significant contributions: biblical studies, systematic theology, and pastoral ministry. The contributors are Wayne's colleagues, his former students, a former teacher, and his oldest son—all of them his friends.

Each of the editors of this book has his own experience of Wayne's biblically infused life and ministry. John Hughes was a fellow classmate of Wayne's at both WTS and Cambridge. Jeff Purswell was a student of Wayne's at TEDS and served as his teaching assistant from 1995 to 1997. John DelHousaye has been a colleague of Wayne's at Phoenix Seminary since they both joined the faculty in 2001. We are each marked by Wayne's example, indebted to him for his support, and enriched by his friendship. It is therefore our joy and honor to present this book to Wayne in celebration of his seventieth birthday. Wayne, we are deeply grateful to God for you, and we pray that you and Margaret will experience much joy together in the future and more years of fruitful ministry as you continue to serve God's people with God's Word. We conclude as you yourself closed the preface to your *Systematic Theology*: "Not to us, O LORD, not to us, but to your name give glory" (Ps. 115:1).

Jeff T. Purswell

John DelHousaye

John J. Hughes

Acknowledgments

It has been our pleasure to work with so many of Wayne's friends to produce this Festschrift as a tribute to him.

To this volume's many contributors, we express our thanks for their labors and contributions in Wayne's honor.

We would like to thank Corinne Bellars for creating the bibliography of Wayne's published writings.

We also would like to thank Justin Taylor at Crossway for supporting this project, for encouraging us, and for his gracious flexibility with the deadline.

Finally, we would like to thank Crossway's Thom Notaro for the professional copyediting skills he has brought to our project.

May our Trinitarian God be glorified by this book.

John DelHousaye
John J. Hughes
Jeff T. Purswell

Abbreviations

ASV	American Standard Version
BDAG	Walter Bauer, Frederick William Danker, William F. Arndt, and F. Wilbur Gingrich, *A Greek-English Lexicon of the New Testament and Other Early Christian Literature*, 3rd ed. (Chicago: University of Chicago Press, 2000)
BECNT	Baker Exegetical Commentary on the New Testament
Bruce, CPE	F. F. Bruce, *The Epistles to the Colossians, to Philemon, and to the Ephesians*, NICNT (Grand Rapids, MI: Eerdmans, 1984)
CBQ	*Catholic Biblical Quarterly*
CSB	Christian Standard Bible
EBC	The Expositor's Bible Commentary
ESV	English Standard Version
Fee, GEP	Gordon D. Fee, *God's Empowering Presence: The Holy Spirit in the Letters of Paul* (Peabody, MA: Hendrickson, 1994)
GNT	Good News Translation
HCSB	Holman Christian Standard Bible
JB	Jerusalem Bible
JBMW	*Journal for Biblical Manhood and Womanhood*
JETS	*Journal of the Evangelical Theological Society*
JTS	*Journal of Theological Studies*
KJV	King James Version

LXX	Septuagint (the Greek Old Testament)
NASB	New American Standard Bible
NEB	New English Bible
NICNT	New International Commentary on the New Testament
NIDNTT	*New International Dictionary of New Testament Theology*, ed. Colin Brown, 4 vols. (Grand Rapids, MI: Zondervan, 1975–1978)
NIGTC	New International Greek Testament Commentary
NIV	New International Version
NJB	New Jerusalem Bible
NKJV	New King James Version
NLT	New Living Translation
NovT	*Novum Testamentum*
NRSV	New Revised Standard Version
NTS	*New Testament Studies*
PNTC	Pillar New Testament Commentary
RSV	Revised Standard Version
SNTSMS	Society for New Testament Studies Monograph Series
TynBul	*Tyndale Bulletin*
TJ	*Trinity Journal*
UBS	United Bible Societies Greek New Testament
WBC	Word Biblical Commentary
WTJ	*Westminster Theological Journal*
WUNT	Wissenschaftliche Untersuchungen zum Neuen Testament

PART 1

SYSTEMATIC THEOLOGY

1

The Word of God and the People of God

The Mutual Relationship between Scripture and the Church

Gregg R. Allison

I love Wayne Grudem. As an incoming seminary student at Trinity Evangelical Divinity School, I took "suicide" Greek under his instruction in the summer of 1982. (Remember: Wayne began his teaching career in New Testament, the discipline in which he earned his doctorate from Cambridge.) Each day at noon, after four hours of class, Wayne would lead us in jogging for exercise while he quizzed us about our Greek paradigms, conjugations, and vocabulary. He rewarded Gummy Bears to students who did well—with Greek, not running. I took Wayne for several other classes during my three years of study, including Advanced Greek Exegesis, which featured seven weeks out of a total of ten on 1 Peter 1:3–9 as he familiarized us with grammar and syntax, the Greek of the early church fathers, the use of classical resources, and more.

After graduating with the MDiv and spending nearly four years working with Cru in Switzerland, I returned to TEDS with Wayne's encouragement and pursued a PhD in systematic theology. He supervised my dissertation on the perspicuity of Scripture, a doctrine and posture that I learned from and perceived in him. After completion of my doctorate, I joined the faculty of Western Seminary in Portland, Oregon. Shortly into my tenure there, I received a call from Wayne asking me if I saw a need for a book that would cover everything that his *Systematic Theology* volume does not—the historical development of those doctrines. The enthusiasm I expressed for the idea was met by this response: "Great, because you are going to write it!" Thirteen years later my *Historical Theology* was released as a complementary volume to Wayne's *Systematic Theology*. I am indebted to him for that opportunity.

From that first class until today, and for many years in the future if God so wills, I am thankful for Wayne's friendship. I am pleased to honor him by offering this chapter in the Festschrift dedicated to him.

Particularly because of Wayne's devotion to the Word of God and his involvement in several evangelical churches, I will look at the mutual relationship between the doctrine of Scripture and the doctrine of the church. My thesis is this: the triune God, through his mighty speech act of Scripture, the Word of God, reveals himself and his ways to the people whom he chooses, saves, and gathers into his church. Accordingly, there exists the strongest possible relationship between God, his Word, and his people.

Regarding my approach, I treat first the doctrine of Scripture. Specifically, I acquaint readers with (or review) speech act theory and demonstrate how viewing Scripture as divine speech act helps to emphasize the intimate relationship between God and his Word. Indeed, Scripture is Trinitarian communicative agency for the purpose of saving the people of God. Framing Scripture as Trinitarian communicative agency expressed as divine speech act has important implications for the doctrine of Scripture, which I treat briefly in regard to inerrancy, authority, sufficiency, and transformative power.

Second, I address the doctrine of the church. After defining the concept, I present Scripture as God's Word to his church in terms of inaugurating and standing at the center of the church. I then explore four implications of this point in regard to four identity markers of the church: as formed by the Word of God, the church is doxological, logocentric, confessional, and missional.

The Doctrine of Scripture

In his *Systematic Theology*, Wayne presents the doctrine of God-breathed, canonical Scripture under the attributes of authority, inerrancy, clarity, necessity, and sufficiency.[1] With this framework as background, I will consider the doctrine of Scripture from the perspective of speech act theory and Trinitarian communicative agency.

Scripture as Divine Speech Act

Let me first offer a brief introduction to (or review of) speech act theory: Every human utterance or communicative expression in social contexts consists of three aspects:[2] (1) A *locution*, or what is communicated (the content of the communication). For example, "Jesus Christ is coming again" addresses the return of the Lord. (2) An *illocution*, or the force with which the utterance is communicated (the type of communication). Speech act theory acknowledges some version of the following six illocutions: assertion, command, promise, declaration, exclamation, and warning. For example, "Jesus Christ is coming again" can be a promise or a warning. (3) A *perlocution*, or the intended or expected response on the part of the hearer (the anticipated or desired effect of the communication). With respect to the six illocutions, the perlocutionary effects are: for an assertion, acknowledgment or belief; for a command, obedience; for a promise, trust; for a declaration, a new state of affairs (e.g., "I now pronounce you husband and wife" joins a man and a woman in marriage); for an exclamation, joy or fear; and for a warning, action or avoidance. For example, "Jesus Christ is coming again" as a promise is intended to evoke hopeful trust in the Lord's return (e.g., John 14:1–3), but as a warning its goal is to stimulate attentiveness (e.g., Matt. 24:36–44).[3]

---

1. Wayne Grudem, *Systematic Theology: An Introduction to Biblical Doctrine* (Leicester, UK: Inter-Varsity Press; Grand Rapids, MI: Zondervan, 1994), chaps. 2–8.
2. The original advocates of speech act theory were John Austin and John Searle (J. L. Austin, *How to Do Things with Words* [Cambridge: Harvard University Press, 1962]; John R. Searle, *Speech Acts: An Essay in the Philosophy of Language* [Cambridge: Cambridge University Press, 1974]; Searle, *Expression and Meaning: Studies in the Theory of Speech Acts* [Cambridge: Cambridge University Press, 1986]).
3. For further discussion, see Gregg R. Allison, "Speech Act Theory and Its Implications for the Doctrine of the Inerrancy/Infallibility of Scripture," *Philosophia Christi* 18, no. (Spring 1995):1–23.

For several decades, theologians have sought to wed the doctrine of Scripture with speech act theory.[4] A key benefit of this approach is to underscore the fact that as human beings do things with words (beyond asserting, people promise, command, and so on), similarly God does things with his Word (beyond asserting, God promises, commands, and so on). Accordingly, speech act theory emphasizes the divine agency associated with the many-faceted utterances of Scripture: God himself is the agent who communicates through his Word, and God does more than merely state things, that is, make propositional statements.[5] Timothy Ward concisely expresses the nature of the relationship between God and his Word, Scripture, as divine speech act: "The words of the Bible are a significant aspect of *God's action* in the world."[6] God does things with words.

We may take divine commands and promises as illustrations of the close relationship of God with his Word: to obey God's words is to obey God, and to disobey God's words is to disobey God; to trust God's words is to trust God, and to mistrust God's words is to mistrust God. Again, as Ward underscores, "God has *invested* himself in his words, or . . . God has so *identified* himself with his words that whatever someone does to God's words . . . they do directly to God himself."[7]

In the rest of our discussion, I will consider Scripture as divine speech act.

Scripture as Trinitarian Communicative Agency

Building upon this idea, John Webster (along with others) encourages us to view Scripture as Trinitarian communicative agency for the pur-

---

4. Nicholas Wolterstorff, *Divine Discourse. Philosophical Reflections on the Claim That God Speaks* (Cambridge: Cambridge University Press, 1995); Kevin Vanhoozer, *Is There a Meaning in This Text? The Bible, the Reader, and the Morality of Literary Knowledge* (Grand Rapids, MI: Zondervan, 1998); Anthony C. Thiselton, *New Horizons in Hermeneutics: The Theory and Practice of Transforming Biblical Reading* (Grand Rapids, MI: Zondervan, 1992); Richard S. Briggs, *Words in Action: Speech Act Theory and Biblical Interpretation* (London: T&T Clark, 2001); Timothy Ward, *Word and Supplement: Speech Acts, Biblical Texts, and the Sufficiency of Scripture* (Oxford: Oxford University Press, 2002).

5. This affirmation should not be (mis)understood to be a criticism of the traditional evangelical insistence on the propositional nature of divine revelation. Propositions are (1) one type of speech act, in this essay referred to as *assertions*, in contrast with promises, commands, and more; and (2) the content of all types of communication, in this essay referred to as *locutions*. As I use "propositional statements" here, it is in the sense of propositions of the first kind. God does more than just communicate propositions. At the same time, I affirm the propositional nature of revelation; that is, revelation is not only personal in nature but also propositional in the second sense.

6. Timothy Ward, *Words of Life: Scripture as the Living and Active Word of God* (Downers Grove, IL: InterVarsity Press, 2009), 12.

7. Ward, *Words of Life*, 27.

pose of saving his people.[8] The triune God, Scripture as his Word or divine speech act, and his people are mutually related. I will treat each of these three elements in turn.

God is the author of Scripture: its origin is divine as the Holy Spirit moved the biblical authors so that their very words are the product of his creative breath (2 Tim. 3:16–17; 2 Pet. 1:19–21). As divinely authored speech act, Scripture communicates and effects whatsoever God wills to accomplish. Broadly speaking, a crucial aspect of this divine intention may be called salvation (more specific effects will be presented later): "For I am not ashamed of the gospel, for *it is the power of God for salvation* to everyone who believes, to the Jew first and also to the Greek" (Rom. 1:16–17).[9] God effects salvation through his Word. More broadly still, God accomplishes the entirety of his eternal purpose or plan through his Word:

> For as the rain and the snow come down from heaven
> and do not return there but water the earth,
> making it bring forth and sprout,
> giving seed to the sower and bread to the eater,
> so shall my word be that goes out from my mouth;
> it shall not return to me empty,
> but *it shall accomplish that which I purpose,*
> and shall succeed in the thing for which I sent it.
> (Isa. 55:10–11)

In summary, Scripture's origin, effect (salvation), and end are divine.

The divine authorship of Scripture is shorthand for the fact that Scripture is Trinitarian communication: the Father, the Son, and the Holy Spirit work inseparably to author the Word of God.[10] In the Gospel of John, Jesus presents the Trinitarian structure of divine revelation. Jesus affirms, "I do nothing on my own authority, but *speak just as the*

---

8. John Webster, *Holy Scripture: A Dogmatic Approach*, Current Issues in Theology (Cambridge: Cambridge University Press, 2003), chap. 1.

9. In the context of Paul's letter to the Romans, the referent of "the gospel" is the oral message of the good news of Jesus Christ. By extension, "the gospel" refers to the written message at the core of the New Testament. Since this New Testament was completed and added to the canon of Scripture, the church has known the gospel through these writings and has communicated it to people in accordance with this written formulation. This clarification applies to the other biblical passages cited in the following discussion.

10. For a discussion of the inseparable operations of the triune God, see Adonis Vidu, "Trinitarian Inseparable Operations and the Incarnation," *Journal of Analytic Theology* 4 (May 2016): 106–27.

Father taught me" (8:28). Again: "For I have not spoken on my own authority, but *the Father who sent me has himself given me a commandment—what to say and what to speak.* And I know that his commandment is eternal life. What I say, therefore, *I say as the Father has told me"* (12:49–50). Thus, the Father speaks, the Son hears, and the Son speaks what he has heard from the Father. To this communicative action, Jesus adds the Holy Spirit, whom he promises to the disciples:

> When the Spirit of truth comes, he will guide you into all the truth, for he will not speak on his own authority, but *whatever he hears he will speak*, and he will declare to you the things that are to come. He will glorify me, for *he will take what is mine and declare it to you.* All that the Father has is mine; therefore I said that *he will take what is mine and declare it to you.* (16:13–15)

Thus, the Father speaks and the Son hears; the Son speaks and the Holy Spirit hears; the Holy Spirit speaks and the apostles hear. This Trinitarian revelation is then communicated to the people of God, first through the apostles' oral teaching, then eventually through their written words, now our New Testament (1 Cor. 2:10–3:4; 2 Thess. 2:15).[11]

Thus, Scripture is Trinitarian communicative agency for the purpose of saving the people of God. Several specific examples of the divine saving activity through Scripture are the following: God *calls* his elect people to salvation through his Word: "God chose you as the firstfruits to be saved, through sanctification by the Spirit and belief in the truth. To this *he called you through our gospel*, so that you may obtain the glory of our Lord Jesus Christ" (2 Thess. 2:13–14). Additionally, *conviction of sin* comes through the Word of God, as illustrated by the response of Peter's listeners to his gospel message on the day of Pentecost: "Now when they heard this they were cut to the heart" (Acts 2:37; for the Spirit's role in convictions of sin, see John 16:7–11).

Moreover, God brings about the *regeneration* of his people through his Word: "You have been born again, not of perishable seed but of

---

11. Regarding the importance of the oral transmission of the teachings of the apostles, Papias offered: "Besides, if any man ever came who had been a follower of the elders [apostles], I would enquire about the sayings of the elders [apostles]; what Andrew said, or Peter, or Philip, or Thomas or James or John or Matthew or any other of the Lord's disciples. . . . For I did not consider that I got so much profit from the contents of books [collections of Jesus's sayings, or the Gospels] as from the utterances of a living and abiding voice" (Papias, *Expositions of the Oracles of the Lord*, 3.39.1, in Eusebius, *Historiae ecclesiasticae*, ed. and trans. G. A Williamson [New York: Dorset, 1984]).

imperishable, *through the living and abiding word of God. . . . And this word is the good news that was preached to you"* (1 Pet. 1:22–25). As a result of their regeneration, people respond with *conversion*, which involves both repentance and faith. *Repentance* from sin comes through the Word of God; for example, the Ephesians confessed their pagan practices, to the extent of burning their books of magic arts, as prompted by "the word of the Lord" (Acts 19:18–20). So also with *faith*: "So *faith* comes from hearing, and hearing *through the word of Christ"* (Rom. 10:17). God's ongoing work of *sanctification* is directly tied to the Word of God, in accordance with Jesus's prayer, "Sanctify them in the truth; your word is truth" (John 17:17). *Assurance of salvation* is given through the Word (1 John 5:11–13; for the Spirit's role, see Rom. 8:16).

In summary, God saves his people from distress through his Word:

Then they cried to the LORD in their trouble,
and he delivered them from their distress.
He sent out his word and healed them,
and delivered them from their destruction. (Ps. 107:19–20)

The people's response to the saving speech act of the triune God includes harkening to the divine call summoning them to salvation, begging the Lord for mercy, repenting from their sins and believing in Jesus Christ, yielding to his transformative work in their lives, believing the promise of assurance, and walking faithfully with God as his power protects them. In other words, God's people respond to his rescuing word by fleeing to him for salvation.

Accordingly, the triune God authored and now communicates his Word for the purpose of saving his people. The human response to Scripture should correspond to its divine origin, effect, and end. Webster insists that the church must always acknowledge Scripture and its reception to be subservient to the self-revelation of the triune God.[12] Scripture as the divine speech act is the means by which God reveals himself and his ways. In his speech act the triune God savingly engages

---

12. Webster, *Holy Scripture*, 6. Webster's concern is that the doctrine of Scripture becomes loosed from its proper moorings (as part of the doctrine of God, as well as the other theological loci) and floats about independently and hence improperly, for example, at the beginning of systematic theology, taking on the job of providing epistemological warrant for doctrines, that is, the *principium cognoscendi* in the realm of impartial reason (pp. 12–13).

his people through assertions, commands, promises, exclamations, declarations, and warnings, and their response must be fitting to this inscripturated Trinitarian communication.

In the rest of our discussion, I will consider Scripture as Trinitarian communicative agency.

Implications for the Doctrine of Scripture

Though space precludes me from developing fully the following areas, locating the doctrine of Scripture in its proper context has many implications for the attributes of Scripture that Wayne rehearses in his *Systematic Theology*. Four attributes of Scripture will serve as examples: inerrancy, authority, sufficiency, and power.

1. *The inerrancy of Scripture.* Jesus, as the one who hears and speaks the words of the Father, (at least) implies truthfulness for those words: "He [the Father] who sent me is *true*, and I declare to the world *what I have heard from him*," such that Jesus could say "[I] told you *the truth that I heard from God*" (John 8:26, 40; cf. 7:18). Furthermore, Jesus's promise to his disciples focuses on the truth-oriented Holy Spirit: "When the Spirit of truth comes, *he will guide you into all the truth*, for he will not speak on his own authority, but *whatever he hears he will speak*, and he will declare to you the things that are to come" (John 16:13; cf. 15:26). John, the writer of the Gospel, was one of the recipients of the truth-telling Spirit of truth and, appropriately, concludes his testimony, "This is the disciple who is bearing witness about these things, and who has written these things, and we know that *his testimony is true*" (John 21:24). Thus, the triune God is the true God, which means his revelation is true as well: The words the Father speaks and the Son hears are true words. The words the Son hears and speaks are true words. The words the Holy Spirit hears and speaks are true words. The words the apostles hear and speak are true words. And the words the people of God read and heed are the true words of Scripture. As Jesus himself expressed, "Your word is truth" (John 17:17).[13]

---

13. Of course, this discussion does not engage with the phenomenon of the human authorship of Scripture and its impact on the inerrancy of Scripture. For an extended treatment, see Henri A. G. Blocher, "God and the Scripture Writers: The Question of Double Authorship," in *The Enduring Authority of the Christian Scriptures*, ed. D. A. Carson (Grand Rapids, MI: Eerdmans, 2016), 497–541.

2. *The authority of Scripture.* I have written elsewhere:

> The authority of Scripture is its property whereby it possesses the prerogative to command what God's people are to believe, do, and be, and to prohibit what they are not to believe, do, and be. It is a subset of divine authority in general, the right that God possesses to establish laws, give orders, demand obedience, determine belief, and more.[14]

As already noted in the Gospel of John, Jesus links the transmission of the words of God with the respective economic authority of the triune persons: The Father, possessing paternal authority (as expressed in his sending the Son), speaks to the Son who in turn acknowledges, "I do nothing on my own authority, but speak just as the Father taught me" (John 8:28; cf. 12:49; 14:10). Moreover, the Son, possessing sonship authority (as expressed in his sending, together with the Father, the Holy Spirit), explains that the Spirit "will not speak on his own authority, but whatever he hears he will speak, and he will declare to you the things that are to come" (John 16:13; cf. 15:26). Thus, the authority of the triune God—from the Father, through the Son, by the Holy Spirit—grounds the authority of the Word of God. And thus, as noted above, to obey God's words is to obey God; to disobey God's words is to disobey God.[15]

3. *The sufficiency of Scripture.* Sufficiency is an attribute of Scripture whereby it provides everything that nonbelievers need to be saved and everything that believers need to please God fully. Such sufficiency is grounded properly in the sufficiency of God himself: as the completely self-sufficient and infinitely resourceful God, he alone is all that people need, whether they are non-Christians who need God to save them or Christians who need God to instruct, guide, equip, rebuke, and empower them.

Controversy surrounds this characteristic of Scripture, as illustrated by the debate over its sufficiency for providing care for people.[16]

---

14. Gregg R. Allison, *50 Core Truths of the Christian Faith: A Guide to Understanding and Teaching Theology* (Grand Rapids, MI: Baker, 2018), 24.

15. For recent evangelical treatments of biblical authority, see: Carson, *Enduring Authority*; Kevin Vanhoozer, *Biblical Authority after Babel: Retrieving the* Solas *in the Spirit of Mere Protestant Christianity* (Grand Rapids, MI: Brazos, 2016), especially chap. 3.

16. Eric L. Johnson, ed., *Psychology and Christianity: Five Views*, 2nd ed. (Downers Grove, IL: InterVarsity Press, 2010); Stuart Scott and Heath Lambert, eds., *Counseling the Hard Cases: True Stories Illustrating the Sufficiency of God's Resources in Scripture* (Nashville: B&H, 2015).

To oversimplify the issue, some proponents of the absolute sufficiency of Scripture reject, or at least question the advisability of, medical intervention and/or extrabiblical resources in cases of depression and personality disorders such as narcissism.[17] Their point: Scripture is sufficient for people who suffer from depression and are plagued by narcissistic personality disorder. On the other side of the debate are those who support the use of medication and extrabiblical resources to deal with such suffering. Their point: Scripture is sufficient for salvation and holy living, but not for all matters of physical and emotional distress.

By linking the sufficiency of Scripture and the self-sufficient, infinitely resourceful God, a way forward may be offered. Again, to oversimplify the issue, Scripture is sufficient for the salvation of non-believers and the godly living of believers so that they may fully please God. Moreover, this sufficiency is materially complete, for so-called "healthy" people as well as for people suffering from depression and personality disorders. However, the all-sufficiency of God, by which he has provided for the discovery and development of medical aid and extrabiblical resources for depression and narcissistic personality disorder, supplies relief from such suffering. Importantly, Scripture continues to be sufficient for people who avail themselves of such relief. They find themselves in a new state in which their depression and narcissism are moderated medically and through extrabiblical resources, and Scripture is materially sufficient for them in this new condition.[18]

4. *The transformative power of Scripture.* "The transformative power of Scripture is the multifaceted effect that God, its author, brings about through his Word."[19] This power is not the magical effect of the mere (written or spoken) words of Scripture. Sadly, superstitious

---

17. By "extrabiblical resources" I do not necessarily mean counseling that relies on resources from secular psychology, therapies, systems, and approaches. Rather, it stands in contrast with views of counseling that define it as assistance provided by one person with a particular focus on, and expertise in, Scripture to another person seeking wisdom from the Bible.

18. My friend and former colleague Eric Johnson has written two important books on soul care: *Foundations for Soul Care: A Christian Psychology Proposal* (Downers Grove, IL: InterVarsity Press, 2007); and *God and Soul Care: The Therapeutic Resources of the Christian Faith* (Downers Grove, IL: InterVarsity Academic, 2017). Heath Lambert has written a theological book on biblical counseling from a standpoint quite different from that of Eric Johnson: Heath Lambert, *A Theology for Biblical Counseling: The Doctrinal Foundation of Counseling Ministry* (Grand Rapids, MI: Zondervan, 2016).

19. Allison, *50 Core Truths*, 47.

Christians may view the Bible as a type of talisman bringing them luck or warding off evil. Moreover, this power is not humanly influenced in the sense of *quid pro quo*. Tragically, misguided Christians are caught up in the notion that if they just read their Bible and pray (that is, engage in daily devotions), then God will—indeed, must—bless them. They have done their part, so they expect God to do his part, per some kind of *tit-for-tat* arrangement. Accordingly, God's power becomes activated by human devotion, prayer, faith, fruitfulness, and so on; it is a humanly influenced power.

Furthermore, the transformative power of Scripture is not contingency destroying. Regretfully, well-meaning Christians may consider divine power to function in such a way that it minimizes or even destroys human response in terms of decisions and actions. But Scripture as divine speech act includes (in most cases) a perlocutionary aspect, an expected, appropriate response to him. God declares, and praise is voiced. He commands, and obedience is prompted. God promises, and faith is ignited. He affirms, and sound doctrine is confessed. God warns, and danger is avoided. He rebukes, and repentance is enacted. God corrects, and plans are changed. These contingent powers—the so-called "secondary causes"—are (in most cases) important and real factors in what transpires between God and his people. Indeed, his transformative power operating in their lives engages their faith, obedience, thanksgiving, and other human responses. Though God may will, and indeed sometimes chooses, to operate above and beyond these secondary causes, such miraculous interventions are not the norm. As Webster avers, "Talk of God's action does not compete with, suspend or obliterate talk of creaturely activity. Rather, it *specifies* or *determines* the character of creaturely activity."[20] God's transformative power expressed through his Word evokes and demands responsive human decisions and actions that are fitting for the particular kind of divine speech act.

In summary, the triune God, through his mighty speech act of Scripture, the Word of God, reveals himself and his ways to his people. This Trinitarian communicative agency has particular reference to those whom God has chosen, saved, and gathered into his church.

---

20. Webster, *Holy Scripture*, 92.

The Doctrine of the Church

In his *Systematic Theology*, Wayne presents ecclesiology under the topics of the nature, marks, and purpose of the church; its purity, unity,
and power (church discipline); church government; the means of grace;
the ordinances or sacraments of baptism and the Lord's Supper; worship; and the gifts of the Holy Spirit.[21]

Definition of the Church

I am building on my book *Sojourners and Strangers* and the definition
of the church offered in it:

> The church is the people of God who have been saved through re-
> pentance and faith in Jesus Christ and have been incorporated into
> his body through baptism with the Holy Spirit. It consists of two
> interrelated elements: the universal church is the fellowship of all
> Christians that extends from the day of Pentecost until the second
> coming, incorporating both the deceased believers who are pres-
> ently in heaven and the living believers from all over the world. This
> universal church becomes manifested in local churches character-
> ized by being doxological [oriented to the *doxa*, or glory of God],
> logocentric [centered on the Word of God, in two senses: the incar-
> nate Word, Jesus Christ, and the inspired Word, Scripture], pneu-
> madynamic [Spirit-activated], covenantal [gathered as members in
> new covenant relationship with God and in covenantal relationship
> with each other], confessional [united by both personal confession
> of faith in Christ and common confession of the historic Christian
> faith], missional [the body of divinely called and divinely sent min-
> isters proclaiming the gospel and advancing the kingdom of God],
> and spatio-temporal/eschatological [here, yet not here; already, but
> not yet]. Local churches are led by pastors (also called elders) and
> served by deacons [and deaconesses], possess and pursue purity and
> unity, exercise church discipline, develop strong connections with
> other churches, and celebrate the ordinances of baptism and the
> Lord's Supper. Equipped by the Holy Spirit with spiritual gifts for
> ministry, these communities regularly gather to worship the triune
> God, proclaim his Word, engage non-Christians with the gospel,

---

21. Grudem, *Systematic Theology*, chaps. 44–53.

disciple their members, care for people through prayer and giving, and stand both for and against the world.[22]

This definition of the church will be presupposed throughout the following discussion.

Scripture as God's Word to His Church

As I have underscored, God's operation through his Word is directed toward his people. This Trinitarian communicative agency, as divine speech act, forms the people of God as it effectively calls, convicts of sin, regenerates, prompts repentance and faith, sanctifies, grants assurance of salvation—as it effects salvation of those whom God has elected. Importantly, the formation of God's people does not have reference to them as individuals only, for the Word of God also forms them into the corporate, gathered people of God, the church. The Word both inaugurates and stands at the center of the church.

Indeed, the Word gave birth to the church, not vice versa. This position stands opposed to Roman Catholic theology's insistence that the church preceded Scripture; reasons for this view include Petrine authority (based on a misunderstanding of Matt. 16:13–20), the Christ-church interconnection (an axiom of Roman Catholic theology), and the claim (not backed by history) that the church was the determiner of the New Testament canon.[23] This position also stands opposed to the notion that the church generated itself. As Webster underscores, "Scripture is not the word of the church; the church is the church of the word. . . . The church exists in the space which is made by the Word. Accordingly, it is not a self-generated assembly."[24]

Two considerations provide the foundation for the view that Scripture inaugurated the church and not vice versa. First, Jewish Scripture was already in existence prior to the church (remember, the definition of the church places its beginning on the day of Pentecost),[25] and it was from this Scripture that the church arose. As (what Christians now

---

22. Gregg R. Allison, *Sojourners and Strangers: The Doctrine of the Church*, Foundations of Evangelical Theology (Wheaton, IL: Crossway, 2012), 29–30.

23. For discussion of these and other topics, see Gregg R. Allison, *Roman Catholic Theology and Practice: An Evangelical Assessment* (Wheaton, IL: Crossway, 2015).

24. Webster, *Holy Scripture*, 44.

25. On this point, Wayne and I disagree, in that he defines the church as "the community of all true believers for all time" (*Systematic Theology*, 853). See my *Sojourners and Strangers* (chap. 2) for arguments for placing the inauguration of the church at Pentecost.

call) the Old Testament pointed to and anticipated the coming of Jesus the Messiah, so also it pointed to and anticipated the inauguration of Messiah's people, the church. For example, Peter's confession of the identity of Jesus as "the Christ, the Son of the living God," summed up the Old Testament's hope of God's intervention through the second Adam / Son of Man / Son of God, precisely in line with the Father's revelation to Peter (Matt. 16:16–17). On the foundation of Peter and his confession, Jesus promises "I will build my church" (Matt. 16:18). This church is composed of the "brothers" of the One who, as "founder of their salvation, perfect[ed] through suffering," says about God (quoting Ps. 22:22),

> I will tell of your name to my brothers;
> in the midst of the congregation I will sing your praise.
> (Heb. 2:10–12)

Jesus taught and preached Hebrew Scripture, explaining that he himself is its fulfillment (Luke 4:16–21; John 5:37–47). Jesus's disciples, in turn, grounded their apostolic message on the Old Testament by quoting it, paraphrasing it, summarizing it, and alluding to it. From this ancient Scripture arose the church of Jesus Christ.

Second, the church is a covenantal people; specifically, it is the church of the new covenant. Like all biblical covenants, the new covenant was unilaterally established by God and is structured by a covenant document. In the case of the church, this document consists of two "covenants" or "testaments": from the outset of the church, the Old Testament and, through the addition of the apostolic writings later on, the New Testament. Though the completed covenant document required decades to expand in terms of its inspired writings and centuries to be collected in terms of its canon, it existed as the authoritative foundation for the church from the moment that community came into existence as the new covenant people of God. The inauguration of the church came about through the Word of God.

At the center of the church stands the Word of God, especially as it is preached. Indeed, Protestant churches are characterized by two historical marks, one of which is the preached Word. (The second is the proper administration of the sacraments of baptism and the Lord's Supper.) As the Reformers sought to locate the true church in the midst of the false church of the sixteenth century, they agreed with the four traditional attributes of the church: "We believe in one, holy, catholic, and apostolic church" (Apostles' Creed). At the same time, they considered the manifestation of the church in their day—the Roman Catholic Church—to have become so perverted in nature and derelict in ministry that it had forfeited the right to be called a church. For Martin Luther and John Calvin, the true church could be recognized by two marks, with the first being the Word of God. According to Luther, "Wherever this word is preached, believed, professed, and lived, do not doubt that the true, holy, catholic church must be there."[26] Calvin expressed something similar: "Wherever we see the Word of God purely preached and heard . . . there, it is not to be doubted, a church of God exists."[27]

Both expressions of this first mark of the true church recall our earlier discussion of Scripture as divine speech act. When pastors rightly preach the Word of God, their preaching has the three elements of a speech act: locution, illocution, and perlocution. For Luther, the perlocutions are summarized as belief, profession, and godly conduct: orthodoxy, orthoconfession, and orthopraxis. Certainly, these perlocutions are what Calvin simply referred to as "purely hearing" the purely preached Word. The preached Word of God, as the speech act of pastors, engages the church as assertion, command, promise, declaration, exclamation, or warning, with the corresponding prompt or demand for belief, obedience, trust, a new state of affairs, joy or fear, or action or avoidance.

The Word of God inaugurates and stands at the center of the church.

Implications for the Doctrine of the Church

Though space precludes me from developing fully the following areas, I draw implications for the church's essence as doxological, logocentric, confessional, and missional.[28]

First, the church is *doxological*, or oriented to the glory of God. The Word of God is central to this doxological orientation, especially

---

26. Martin Luther, *On the Councils of the Church*, in *Church and Ministry*, vol. 41 of *Luther's Works*, ed. Jaroslav Pelikan, Hilton C. Oswald, and Helmut T. Lehmann, 55 vols. (St. Louis: Concordia, 1955–1986), 150.

27. John Calvin, *Institutes of the Christian Religion*, ed. John T. McNeill, trans. Ford Lewis Battles (Philadelphia: Westminster, 1960), 4.1.9.

28. The following discussion is taken from Allison, *Sojourners and Strangers*, chaps. 3 and 4.

as that characteristic relates to the church's worship. In the first place, the Word qualifies the people of God as genuine worshipers. In his conversation with the woman of Samaria, Jesus clarified, "Woman, believe me, the hour is coming when neither on this mountain nor in Jerusalem will you worship the Father." He then rebuked both the false worship of the Samaritans on Mount Gerizim ("You worship what you do not know") and the proper but soon-to-be-obsolete worship of the Jews in the temple in Jerusalem ("we worship what we know, for salvation is from the Jews"). Proleptically, he added, "But the hour is coming, and is now here, when the true worshipers will worship the Father in spirit and truth, for the Father is seeking such people to worship him. God is spirit, and those who worship him must worship in spirit and truth" (John 4:21–24). Genuine worshipers are qualified to engage in genuine worship by living in the realm of "spirit and truth," (1) born again of the Holy Spirit so as to exist in "spirit" rather than in "flesh" (John 3:6), and (2) embracing the "truth," which has reference to Jesus, who is "the truth" (John 14:6), and (importantly for our discussion) embracing the Word of God ("your word is truth," John 17:17). The church is to engage in worship according to the way that God himself establishes, and he specifically directs his people how to ascribe glory to him in worship through his instruction in his Word.[29]

The Word of God orients the doxological church to the glory of God.

Second, the church is *logocentric*, or centered on the Word of God. This stands against the contemporary trend among evangelical churches to hold captive Scripture and twist it to promote their sub-Christian agendas—churches that endorse the prosperity gospel, churches that market their own brand, churches that advocate seriously compromised positions on critical moral issues, and more. I have noted elsewhere that the logocentricity of the church confronts such domestication of Scripture, as Scripture

> stands over the disobedience, faithlessness, pride, underdevelopment, legalism, selfishness, xenophobia, lethargy, and other sins of the church and its members. Appropriately, the Bible is "our adversary"; it always confronts with existential demands for ref-

---

29. Allison, *Sojourners and Strangers*, 424–33.

ormation. As John Webster notes, "Scripture is as much a desta-
bilizing feature of the church as it is a factor in its cohesion and
continuity."[30]

Certainly, the church gathers around the Word of God and finds its
unity in it. At the same time, the Word rebukes the church for its many
sins. "As the church is confronted by the Word of God, it should be
'destabilized' and then repent of such sins and embrace the way of
godliness."[31]

The Word of God is the heart of the logocentric church.

Third, the church is *confessional*, or united by common confession
of the historic Christian faith. That is, when it gathers together, the
church not only acknowledges but also publically professes "the faith
that was once for all delivered to the saints" (Jude 3), the sound doctrine it has always and everywhere believed. The Word of God itself
encourages such common confession, as exemplified in the following
snippet from an early creed that Paul highlights:

> Great indeed, we confess, is the mystery of godliness:
>
> > He was manifested in the flesh,
> >   vindicated by the Spirit,
> >   seen by angels,
> > proclaimed among the nations,
> >   believed on in the world,
> >   taken up in glory. (1 Tim. 3:16)[32]

From its articulation of its early "rule of faith" and "canon of
truth," through its formulation of its orthodox creeds (e.g., Nicene-
Constantinopolitan Creed, Chalcedonian Creed, Apostles' Creed),
to Protestant churches distinguishing their beliefs from those of the
Roman Catholic Church through the construction of the Protestant
statements of faith (e.g., Augsburg Confession, the Formula of Con-
cord, the Belgic Confession, the Thirty-Nine Articles, the Westminster
Confession of Faith, the London [Baptist] Confession of Faith), the
church has historically confessed its faith. Importantly, these creeds

---

30. Allison, *Sojourners and Strangers*, 115. The citation is from Webster, *Holy Scripture*, 46.
31. Allison, *Sojourners and Strangers*, 116.
32. Other examples of the New Testament's incorporation of (parts of) early church confessions include Phil. 2:5–11 and 1 Cor. 15:3–6 (or 7).

and confessions are grounded on the Word of God and express in summary form its affirmations on the cardinal doctrines—the Trinity, the deity and humanity of Christ, the gospel, salvation—that the church is bound to believe.

The Word of God directs the profession of the confessional church.

Fourth, the church is *missional*, or the body of divinely called and divinely sent ministers proclaiming the gospel and advancing the kingdom of God. Jesus himself addressed the missional nature of his church in his instruction to his disciple: "Peace be with you. As the Father has sent me, even so I am sending you" (John 20:21). As we read in the book of Acts, the Spirit-filled disciples carried out their mission by proclaiming the gospel, giving birth to scores of new churches. Thus, they began to fulfill the Great Commission of Jesus (Matt. 28:19–20). Specifically, the mission of the church is the "ministry" or "message" (Gr. *logos*, or "word") of reconciliation.

> All this is from God, who through Christ reconciled us to himself and gave us the ministry of reconciliation; that is, in Christ God was reconciling the world to himself, not counting their trespasses against them, and entrusting to us the message of reconciliation. Therefore, we are ambassadors for Christ, God making his appeal through us. We implore you on behalf of Christ, be reconciled to God. (2 Cor. 5:18–20)

The church expresses its missional character by proclaiming the Word of God in an ever-expanding movement (Acts 1:8), which saves the elect people of God and forms them into new churches, and the missional cycle continues.

The Word of God produces and propels the missional church.

Conclusion

The thesis of this chapter, in tribute to Wayne Grudem, is that the triune God, through his mighty speech act of Scripture, the Word of God, reveals himself and his ways to the people whom he chooses, saves, and gathers into his church. Accordingly, there exists the strongest possible relationship between God, his Word, and his people.

From the divine aspect of this relationship, the letter to the Hebrews underscores that "the word of God is living and active, sharper than any two-edged sword, piercing to the division of soul and of spirit, of joints and of marrow, and discerning the thoughts and intentions of the heart" (Heb. 4:12). Scripture, as Trinitarian communicative agency, effectively accomplishes the divine purpose, uninterruptedly and infallibly (Isa. 55:10–11). From the human side of this relationship, we may be tempted to despair as disobedience, faithlessness, rebellion, lukewarmness, self-centeredness, and many more failings continue to grip the church. But this persistent sinful state (from which one day the church will be delivered!) should never be blamed on a failure of Scripture. As Ward emphasizes, the words of Scripture do not obscure a relationship with God; on the contrary, God communicates with his human creatures by means of his Word as divine speech act given to save and gather his people into the church.[33] As the church, which is "'worded' all the way down,"[34] let us give greater heed to the Word of God "as to a lamp shining in a dark place" (2 Pet. 1:19).

---

33. Ward, *Words of Life*, 31–32.
34. Michael S. Horton, *People and Place: A Covenant Ecclesiology* (Louisville: Westminster John Knox, 2008), 44.

2

Is Scripture's Self-Attestation Sufficient?

John M. Frame

Wayne Grudem, a former student of mine and for many years a respected friend, is one of few recent theologians who has defended without apology the full authority of Scripture, along with its inerrancy. My contribution to his Festschrift will carry forward this shared conviction and deal with some issues of importance to both of us.

Reformed Christians (and some other Christians) have often referred to Scripture as *self-attesting*. But, understandably, some have asked how any book can authenticate itself. As John Murray once posed the question, "It might seem analogous to the case of a judge who accepts the witness of the accused in his own defense rather than the evidence derived from all the relevant facts in the case."[1] Initially, at least, to say that a book is self-attesting would seem to mean that its content is a sufficient basis for affirming its truth, that its authority is not based on anything beyond its own words, and that its own words are a sufficient reason for affirming its authority. But such claims

---

1. Murray, "The Attestation of Scripture," in *The Infallible Word*, ed. Ned B. Stonehouse and Paul Woolley (Grand Rapids, MI: Eerdmans, 1946), 5. Apparently this sentence was edited out of the 1967 edition.

seem to be inherently problematic. Who would argue that a book of mathematics or physics or history is true just because it claims to be?

But there is more to be said. In this chapter, I hope to deal with some theological confusions over the concept of self-attestation applied to Scripture,[2] and over the claim that Scripture does indeed authenticate its own content. This discussion will lead to considerations relevant to general epistemology and apologetics, as well as theology.

I will focus on the following statements from chapter 1 of the Westminster Confession of Faith, generally understood as an authoritative summary of the Reformed doctrine of Scripture's self-attestation:[3]

4. The authority of the Holy Scripture, for which it ought to be believed, and obeyed, depends not upon the testimony of any man, or Church; but wholly upon God (who is truth itself) the author thereof: and therefore it is to be received, because it is the Word of God.

5. We may be moved and induced by the testimony of the Church to an high and reverent esteem of the Holy Scripture. And the heavenliness of the matter, the efficacy of the doctrine, the majesty of the style, the consent of all the parts, the scope of the whole (which is, to give all glory to God), the full discovery it makes of the only way of man's salvation, the many other incomparable excellencies, and the entire perfection thereof, are arguments whereby it does abundantly evidence itself to be the Word of God: yet notwithstanding, our full persuasion and assurance of the infallible truth and divine authority thereof, is from the inward work of the Holy Spirit bearing witness by and with the Word in our hearts.

6. The whole counsel of God concerning all things necessary for His own glory, man's salvation, faith and life, is either expressly set down in Scripture, or by good and necessary consequence may be deduced from Scripture: unto which nothing at any time is to be added, whether by new revelations of the Spirit, or traditions of men. Nevertheless, we acknowledge the inward illumination of the Spirit of God to be necessary for the saving understanding of such things as are revealed in the Word: and that there are some

---

2. For my purposes, I will use *self-attestation* interchangeably with such terms as *self-authentication*, *self-witness*, and *autopistia*.

3. Here and in my discussion I will show paragraph numbers from the confession as arabic rather than roman numerals.

circumstances concerning the worship of God, and government of
the Church, common to human actions and societies, which are to
be ordered by the light of nature, and Christian prudence, according
to the general rules of the Word, which are always to be observed.

The Source of Scripture's Authority

The first quoted paragraph (4) says that God is the source of Scripture's
authority, and we are to believe Scripture *because* God is its author and
therefore because Scripture is his Word. First, we should note that God
is the source not only of Scripture's authority but of all authority. It
is he who grants authority to human beings over the rest of creation,
to civil rulers, to heads of households, to husbands in the home, and
so on. None of these forms of authority depends on the testimony of
man alone, but they all depend on God, who grants that authority. In
this respect, the authority of Scripture is no different from that of any
other legitimate authority.

But there are other considerations. In some ways, the authority of
Scripture is different from other authorities. Particularly, not all forms
of authority confer infallibility and inerrancy. A civil ruler, for example,
has genuine authority, given by God, and he should be obeyed because of
that divine authority. But that authority is not absolute: the ruler is not
the Lord of all things in heaven and earth, as God is. The civil ruler can
violate the law and therefore be sanctioned by a higher authority. And
he is not, because of his authority, infallible in his beliefs or statements.

What, then, is the difference between the authority of Scripture
and the authority of civil rulers? In the case of Scripture, God (who
is truth itself) is its *author*, according to the confession: and therefore
Scripture "is to be received, because it is the Word of God." Scripture
is not distinctive in having authority from God; rather, it is distinctive
because God is its "author."

Scripture describes this "authorship" in different ways. When Israel
met God at Mount Sinai, God gave them the Ten Commandments:
"And he gave to Moses, when he had finished speaking with him on
Mount Sinai, the two tablets of the testimony, tablets of stone, written with the finger of God" (Ex. 31:18). In this passage, we learn that
God spoke these specific words to his people and wrote them down as
well—directly, with his own "finger." Similarly, the apostle Paul says,

"All Scripture is breathed out by God and profitable for teaching, for reproof, for correction, and for training in righteousness, that the man of God may be complete, equipped for every good work" (2 Tim. 3:16–17). The divine "breathing" here is his *speaking*. And since the divine speech here results in written words ("Scripture"), it is equivalent to the writing of the divine finger in Exodus 31:18.

Authorship is not synonymous with publication. A publisher may or may not agree with the content of a book he produces and sells. But the author of that book necessarily agrees with that content. It is the author's own writing, his own speech, his own viewpoint. So to agree with the book is to agree with the author, and to disagree with it is to disagree with the author. So to say that God is the "author" of Scripture implies that if one disagrees with the content of Scripture, one disagrees with God.

Here already we are moved to confess the *sufficiency* of Scripture, or *sola Scriptura*. The point is not that Scripture is the only authority over our lives. It is not. But it is the only written language of which God is the author, the only language that is "the Word of God."

So paragraph 4 concludes by saying that we are to receive Scripture "because it is the Word of God." That is what cannot be said of any other kind of authoritative speech. The speech or writing of a civil official ought in most cases to be obeyed; but God is not its author, and it is not the Word of God in the confession's sense. If the confession, here based on passages like Exodus 31:18 and 2 Timothy 3:16–17, is right, then Scripture is the *only* written document in this category.

That is the meaning of *sola Scriptura*. The *sola* simply means that alongside all the other authorities God has given us, this is the only written document that has the authority of God himself. Therefore, it is the only *ultimate* authority, the only authority that takes precedence over all other authorities.

Does this doctrine of Scripture's authority imply that Scripture is self-attesting? To "attest" in this context means to give reasons for believing something. We have seen that one thing Scripture does is to give reasons why we should believe it, as in Exodus 31:18 and 2 Timothy 3:16–17. Those reasons are God's reasons. They are his bearing witness to the truth of his own Word. Certainly they are sufficient: we may not demand any higher reasons than God's own reasons. We may not demand that God's reasons be validated by reasons of a higher authority, for there are no reasons with a higher authority. To demand higher evidence is in effect to tell God that we are unsatisfied with his own evidence, and we demand evidence from a source higher than him. But to even consider that there might be such a source is to violate the first commandment. There is only one God, one Lord, and he is above all other sources of truth.

This is to say that God's attestation of his Word is sufficient. And therefore Scripture's attestation of its own authority is sufficient reason for us to accept it.

Why We Should Believe in Scripture's Authority

But we need to pursue our question further. For even granting that Scripture's own self-testimony is the Word of God, we need to ask how we can best appropriate that self-testimony in our thinking and living. How does one come to believe that Scripture attests itself? With that question in view, let us look at the confession again, this time paragraph 5 of chapter 1.

First, paragraph 5 recommends that we consider "the testimony of the Church" so that we can gain a "high and reverent esteem of the Holy Scripture." Since the earliest days of the church, it has appealed to Scripture (i.e., the books of Scripture extant at each period) as its supreme doctrinal authority. The church as a body has never been critical of Scripture, and it has accepted as true Scripture's accounts of the history of redemption.

But the confession does not see the testimony of the church as itself self-attesting. The testimony of the church is, for all its value, a *human* testimony. Human testimony, even at its best, is not infallible; it can be wrong. We should remember too that the Westminster Confession emerges out of the Protestant Reformation, in which the authority of the church in its official hierarchy, particularly the authority of the pope, came under severe critique. One of the main themes of the confession is that the Roman Catholic tradition and teaching magisterium are deeply flawed.

So the testimony of the church is persuasive but not the absolute basis of faith in Scripture. Of course, it could not be, even if it were without flaws. For only Scripture itself is self-attesting.

So paragraph 5 moves on to consider the *evidences* of Scripture's authority:

> . . . the heavenliness of the matter, the efficacy of the doctrine, the majesty of the style, the consent of all the parts, the scope of the whole (which is, to give all glory to God), the full discovery it makes of the only way of man's salvation, the many other incomparable excellencies, and the entire perfection thereof . . .

Much can be said about these evidences, but the main thrust of this discussion seems to be this: that reading Scripture brings you into a different world. It is a "heavenly" place, where God is executing his eternal plan of redemption. He participates in a context of spiritual warfare but carries out his will in overwhelming power, love, and grace. Although much of this story takes place on the earth, we normally have a very clouded view of what is happening. But when we read Scripture (directly and through accurate expositors), we are overwhelmed by the glory of it all.[4] Scripture's account of this story is immediately persuasive.

The individual evidences in the confession's list contribute to this heavenly vision set forth specifically in the first evidence. The second, "the efficacy of the doctrine," alludes to the *power* of the biblical content, stressed for example in Hebrews 4:12, its power to convict of sin and to arouse faith. The third, "the majesty of the style" raises questions: Parts of Scripture are in a common style, not a high literary style, as that is understood by linguists. But the confession sees this "majesty" as a spiritual quality, not primarily as a literary one. A high form of literary style would not be impressive to one who is seeking God. But when one looks at Scripture with illumined eyes (see below, p. 62), it seems to the writers of the confession that even the common words open our eyes to reveal something of the greatness of God himself.

The fourth evidence is "the consent of all the parts." This consent includes logical consistency, but it is a broader concept. It is the reader's amazement that this book, written by scores of authors over thousands

---

4. I have great admiration for John Piper's recent book *A Peculiar Glory: How the Christian Scriptures Reveal Their Complete Truthfulness* (Wheaton, IL: Crossway, 2016), which sets forth this point most eloquently.

of years, tells a single story: that something written in AD 60 can furnish a resolution of tensions created in 723 BC.

The fifth evidence is "the scope of the whole," defined as giving all glory to God. The Scriptures, as we shall see in paragraph 6, are not limited to a narrow subject matter (see p. 60, "How to Find God's Will"). Rather, they stretch over all reality and find God's glory in every aspect of creation and redemption. Then, sixth, there is "the full discovery it makes of the only way of man's salvation." Without this full discovery, we would perish at Scripture's revelation of the glory of God. But instead of condemnation, Scripture provides for everything we need to live and flourish in the presence of a glorious God. Scripture addresses all our needs: for righteousness (justification), for a divine family (adoption), for holiness (sanctification), for final perfection (glorification).

Perhaps we have left something out. The confession speaks also of "the many other incomparable excellencies." And, lest we worry that God gives us too few of these excellencies, the confession finds in Scripture "the entire perfection thereof."

The confession here presents the evidences in a highly positive way. It does not say only that the evidences are probable, or even highly probable. Many apologists are content with that sort of modest claim. But the confession itself says that the evidences are "arguments whereby [Scripture] does abundantly evidence itself to be the Word of God." It is not that the evidences are 85 percent or 90 percent credible. They are 100 percent cogent. Of course, the confession makes this claim for the evidences themselves, not for every writing or speech by a human apologist. Many apologetic presentations of the evidence are less credible than the evidence itself, and those presentations should legitimately be made in modest terms. But the content of Scripture itself "abundantly evidences" that it is the Word of God so that once that evidence is presented, the case should be settled.

Evidently, the logic of the confession's apologetic is rather different from the usual modern way of assessing the evidences for Scripture's truth. The evidences listed in the confession are not easily assessed by the methods of empirical science. The "heavenliness of the matter," for example, is not a quality capable of scientific measurement. How does one compare the relative heavenliness of two documents—say, the

Bible and the Qur'an? The confession assumes that readers have some ability to measure these qualities and to derive the right conclusion from them. But this ability is not simply the ability to make use of sense experience and logic. In an argument over the relative heavenliness of two books, it is not clear what considerations would resolve it. The same is true of the other excellencies listed in paragraph 5. There is evidently something intuitive about the process of reasoning. But the confession says that the evidence is abundant and immediately certain.

Yet, of course, for many people it is not. Many have read through the Bible many times and remain indifferent to its message. They entertain doubts.

In epistemology it is important to remember that a good argument has three features: logic (validity), evidence (soundness), and persuasion. An argument with good logic is an argument from which the conclusion validly follows from the premises. An argument with good evidence is an argument in which the premises are true and therefore (given the good logic) the conclusion is true. But many arguments are both valid and sound, yet not persuasive, at least to some hearers. For example,

> PREMISE: Scripture, as God's Word, is true.
> PREMISE: Scripture teaches that Jesus worked miracles.
> CONCLUSION: Jesus worked miracles.

I believe both premises, and so I regard the conclusion as certain. But some doubt one or both of the premises and therefore doubt the conclusion. For them the argument lacks *persuasiveness*.[5]

In the confession, this problem is based on the fact that some lack spiritual perception; they lack ears to hear (Jer. 25:4; Matt. 11:15; Rom. 11:8). Our fall into sin affected our thinking, so that people "by their unrighteousness suppress the truth" (Rom. 1:18). Fallen people "exchanged the truth about God for a lie" (Rom. 1:25). They "did not see fit to acknowledge God" (Rom. 1:28). The problem is not any defect in the evidence or in the logical argument from the evidences to

---

5. Of course, their doubt of the conclusion presupposes doubt of the premises and perhaps of the validity of the logic as well. In my understanding, the three elements validity, soundness, and persuasiveness are "perspectivally related," so that the lack of one imperils the others. See my *Doctrine of the Knowledge of God* (Phillipsburg, NJ: P&R, 1987) and my *Apologetics: A Justification of Christian Belief* (Phillipsburg, NJ: P&R, 2015).

the truth of Scripture. Rather, the problem is that in the face of perfect evidence and good logic, sinful people refuse to acknowledge Scripture's conclusions.

The remedy, according to paragraph 5: "Our full persuasion and assurance of the infallible truth and divine authority thereof, is from the inward work of the Holy Spirit bearing witness by and with the Word in our hearts." Persuasion comes not from additional evidence or more powerful logic but from a personal encounter with God, the Holy Spirit. As such, it is a subjective event. We need no more objective evidence; rather something needs to happen inside us. As Jesus said, "Unless one is born again he cannot see the kingdom of God" (John 3:3).

The Spirit must give us a desire to believe. The desire to believe is not a sufficient reason for believing. Wanting to believe something doesn't make it true. Wanting to believe something doesn't make it worthy of belief. But though this desire is not a sufficient condition for belief, it is a necessary condition.

This desire to believe is a moral and spiritual event. It is part of redemption, in which the Spirit takes away the veil Satan has laid over our eyes.

The confession says that the Spirit's testimony works by his "bearing witness by and with the Word in our hearts." It is significant that although the Spirit's testimony is different from the testimony of the church and of the evidences, it does not abandon the Word itself. It is, first, "by" the Word. That is, the Spirit draws upon the Word's inherent power (Heb. 4:12) and glorious truth (see above) to break through the unbelieving heart. Second, it is "with" the Word in our hearts. Since the Spirit's work is subjective and not merely objective, the Spirit adds something to the content of Scripture. But in this subjective work, he is *with the Word*; the Word is never out of the picture. It is this Word that enters our heart, that we can no longer resist.

How to Find God's Will

This discussion brings us to paragraph 6, which tells us how to find "the whole counsel of God" (Acts 20:27). I take it that here "the whole counsel of God" refers to everything God wants us to know, everything we have come to call "divine revelation." Paragraph 6 subdivides this content into "all things necessary for His own glory, man's salvation, faith and life." We should note that these categories are very broad. Theologians have sometimes tried to limit the scope of divine revelation to "man's salvation," so as to justify human autonomous reasoning outside the sphere of salvation. (So theologians have claimed that Scripture contains errors in areas supposedly outside this sphere.) But the confession clearly will not allow this limitation. Some have also appealed to "faith and life" as a way to limit the scope of revelation. But there is no reason to think the confession should be read in this way. Faith is what we believe, and life is what we do.

And even if it were possible to limit "man's salvation" and/or "faith and life" to some narrow sphere of human knowledge, certainly there cannot be any such limit on the phrase "all things necessary for His own glory." For absolutely everything has the purpose of glorifying God. Question and answer 1 of the Westminster Shorter Catechism describe glorifying God as "the chief end of man," the very purpose for which God made human beings. Indeed, we saw in paragraph 5 that one of the significant evidences for Scripture's truth is precisely this breadth, "the scope of the whole (which is, to give all glory to God)." Clearly, paragraph 5 is saying that the scope (the subject matter) of Scripture is the glory of God in everything. *Everything* has that purpose, and Scripture shows us how everything brings him glory and how we should seek his glory in everything we do.

From paragraphs 4 and 5, we might be led to suppose that divine revelation is a combination of Scripture itself and something in addition to Scripture brought to us by the Holy Spirit. But perhaps to our surprise, the confession again stresses that Scripture itself is all we need. According to paragraph 6, the whole counsel of God either is "expressly set down in Scripture, or by good and necessary consequence may be deduced from Scripture." This is the familiar distinction between what Scripture explicitly teaches and what it implicitly teaches. The implicit teachings of Scripture are derived from the explicit teachings by logical deduction. For example, "All men are sinners; David is a man; therefore David is a sinner." Scripture does not say in so many words "David is (was) a sinner," but that statement follows from "All men are sinners" (see Rom. 3:23) by good and necessary consequence.[6]

---

6. "Good" here refers to logical validity and "necessary" to the certainty of the conclusion generated by the argument.

So according to paragraph 6, the whole counsel of God is limited to the explicit and implicit content of Scripture. The paragraph adds two violations of this limitation: "new revelations" and "traditions of men." I mentioned earlier that the confession was written in the context of Reformation controversy. Often the confession opposes the attempt by Roman Catholics to place tradition over the Bible, and it does that again here. The other regular opponent of the Protestant Reformers was the "sectarian" or "Anabaptist" theology, which sometimes argued that the Spirit gives the church "new revelations" beyond the biblical canon. So paragraph 6 rules out both of these proposed additions to the canonical source of the whole counsel of God.

But as we saw earlier, the confession never minimizes the work of the Holy Spirit, despite the sectarians' distortions of his role. We saw earlier that it is the Spirit who opens our sinful eyes to receive the truth of Scripture. Now, in paragraph 6, we see that the Spirit, having opened our eyes, gives us an "inward illumination" so that we can understand what is revealed in the Word.

The whole counsel of God, of course, does not include our mistakes and misinterpretations. It is an objective reality, the content of Scripture we are responsible to see but sometimes fail to see, because of our finitude and remaining sin. So the inward illumination of the Spirit is revelatory in that it uncovers the true meaning of Scripture underneath our distortions of its content. Illumination does not add content to the biblical canon, but it enables us to see that canon as it is.

Have we then completely identified the revelation of God's will? So far, we would have to describe that revelation as (1) Scripture's explicit teaching, (2) Scripture's implicit teaching, and (3) the Spirit's influence to properly understand 1 and 2. And yet this list of factors would seem to be incomplete. There are many things God evidently wants us to know that cannot be found either explicitly or implicitly in Scripture. That would include, for example, the scientific knowledge we need to "be fruitful and multiply and fill the earth and subdue it, and have dominion over the fish of the sea and over the birds of the heavens and over every living thing that moves on the earth" (Gen. 1:28). Scripture itself does not contain directions for catching fish, except for Jesus's command before the disciples' miraculous catch (Luke 5:4), and there does not seem to be a way for us to obtain such directions by logical deduction from the biblical text.

So it would seem that God does reveal to us some facts beyond the explicit and implicit content of Scripture. Not only Scripture but also the created world reveals God. This is the common theological doctrine of "general revelation," set forth in passages like Psalm 19:1 and Romans 1:19–21. Through the world God has made, and apart from Scripture, human beings know God in an important sense, even apart from the internal testimony of the Holy Spirit.

It is obvious that we must resort to general revelation often in daily life. Through general revelation we learn what time it is, whether it is raining, how far we must drive to our next destination, and billions of other facts. But paragraph 6 of the confession tells us that the knowledge of general revelation is also important in the church. It indicates "some circumstances concerning the worship of God, and government of the church, common to human actions and societies, which are to be ordered by the light of nature." I presume that these circumstances include the time of worship, the arrangement of seats, the number of songs and hymns to be sung, and so forth.[7] These "are to be ordered by the light of nature, and Christian prudence."

But even these are not to be ordered without the Scriptures. These circumstances must be arranged "according to the general rules of the Word, which are always to be observed." That is, when, for example, we decide how to arrange the seats in the worship area, our decision must be consistent with biblical principles of worship. For example, it would not be best to put the seats on top of one another.

A problem arises here. If the precepts of Scripture, even in worship, must be supplemented by precepts from outside of Scripture (that is, from general revelation), how is Scripture sufficient? The answer, I think, is that Scripture itself authorizes us to make such use of general revelation. Scripture teaches us what general revelation is (Ps. 19:1; Rom. 1:19–21), and it regularly authorizes us to make use of it. It tells us, for example, to count the cost before we build a tower (Luke 14:28). Counting the cost will mean assessing our financial situation,

---

7. I have elsewhere explored more fully the scope of these circumstances, as distinguished from "elements," "expressions," "forms," and so on. See my "A Fresh Look at the Regulative Principle," in Frame, *Selected Shorter Writings*, vol. 3 (Phillipsburg, NJ: P&R, 2016).

which we will not be able to find in the Bible alone. And it will mean researching the cost of tower-building materials in the current economy.

Scripture tells us not only to obey God's explicit commandments but also to employ "wisdom" (as in Proverbs, Ecclesiastes, 1 Corinthians 1–3), the "prudence" prescribed in paragraph 6.

So the right use of general revelation is not a violation of *sola Scriptura*. It is simply an application of Scripture, in effect an implicit content of Scripture. When we act wisely based on general revelation, we are doing what Scripture tells us to.

In this sense, biblical revelation is the only revelation there is, for it encompasses and includes general revelation. All general revelation is defined and directed by Scripture. So the Word of God that directs our decisions consists entirely of Scripture, *sola Scriptura*.

Conclusions on Self-Attestation

I began this chapter by asking questions about the concept of self-attesting Scripture. Initially, that concept raises the question How can any piece of writing attest itself? To deal with this question, I explored the concept of self-attestation in chapter 1, paragraphs 4–6 of the Westminster Confession of Faith. The answer to our question, from paragraph 4, is that Scripture is the Word of God, and only God can attest the Word of God. There is no higher authority sufficient to attest God's own authority. But if Scripture is his Word, the same may be said of Scripture: there is no other authority high enough to attest Scripture, to prove that it has authority.

Paragraph 5 indicates that Scripture's self-attestation does not rule out evidence from the history of the church, from Scripture itself, and from the inner testimony of the Holy Spirit. Indeed, when they are rightly understood, each of these is part of Scripture's own self-witness. For these evidences do nothing more than to set forth the glory that is inherent in the Word itself. The same is true from the doctrine of general revelation in paragraph 6: properly used, general revelation is itself a form of Scripture's self-witness. As such, when God reveals himself, he attests himself.

3

Multiple Patterns Reflecting the Trinity and Coinherence in Verbal Communication

Vern S. Poythress

ABSTRACT: The Son who is the image of the Father is the starting point for a series of reflections: Adam is made in the image of God, and Adam fathers a son, Seth, after his image (Gen. 5:3).[1] The series of reflections leads to coinherent perspectives, which can be applied to divine verbal communication as a reflection of the Trinity.

This chapter develops three perspectives on reflections focusing respectively on the original, the image, and the harmonious relation between the two. These three perspectives are coinherent in a manner reflecting the original coinherence in persons of the Trinity. Using this pattern of reflections of coinherence, we can see multiple patterns of coinherence in verbal communication: eternal communication within the Trinity (John 1:1), communication creating the world (Gen. 1:3; Ps. 33:6), covenantal communication to mankind (John 17:8; 2 Tim. 3:16; 2 Pet. 1:21), and communication between

---

1. An earlier version of this chapter was presented as a paper for the annual meeting of the Evangelical Theological Society, San Antonio, Texas, November 15–17, 2016.

human beings (Col. 3:16). The original pattern or archetype lies in God the Father speaking the Word in the context of the Holy Spirit as akin to the breath of God (Job 33:4) and as a recipient of divine speech (John 16:13). This pattern is reflected with other levels of communication. The unity of meaning, the distinctiveness of persons, and their coinherent fellowship are reflected in communication.

By understanding the Trinitarian foundation reflected in human communication, we may grow in praising God for the reflections of his character in the world and the profundity of the gift of wisdom given to us through the Word of Christ, the Son of the Father in the communion of the Holy Spirit.

———

Since my friend Wayne Grudem has been a long-time defender of the integrity and truthfulness of divine communication in Scripture, I would like to offer for his Festschrift a further reflection about divine verbal communication.

Stages in Communication

How do we understand divine communication to us? This communication has more than one stage. Revelation 1:1–3 describes several stages:

> The revelation of Jesus Christ, which *God* gave *him* to show to *his servants* the things that must soon take place. He made it known by sending *his angel* to *his servant John*, who bore witness to the word of God and to the testimony of Jesus Christ, even to all that he saw. Blessed is *the one who reads aloud* the words of this prophecy, and blessed are *those who hear*, and who keep what is written in it, for the time is near.

The message originates in "God" (1:1), that is, God the Father. The Father gives it to Jesus Christ, who sends "his angel" to "his servant John" (1:1). John writes the message (Rev. 1:11; 22:10). It then gets read aloud and heard (1:3). Other passages in Revelation indicate that the words are also communicated through the Spirit (1:10) and are "what the Spirit says to the churches" (2:7, 11, 17, 29; 3:6, 13, 22).

The communication has still another layer, because the servants of Christ are described as witnesses in 2:13; 6:9; 11:3. They imitate the fundamental witness of Jesus Christ, "the faithful and true witness" (3:14).

The stages mentioned in Revelation are unusually many. But the idea of stages is broader. In divine communication, the word of God is normally mediated through prophets, apostles, and other messengers, whether divine, angelic, or human. The Bible itself is the Word of God, written with human hands. Jesus Christ has a central mediating role, as he indicates in John 17:8: "For I [Jesus] have given them the words that you gave me, and they have received them and have come to know in truth that I came from you; and they have believed that you sent me."

"The words" originate with God the Father ("you"). Christ receives them and gives them to the disciples. The context shows that, in this early part of John 17, Christ is focusing on those who are physically present before him, primarily the twelve apostles. They pass on the word to a larger group: "I do not ask for these only, but also for those who will believe in me through *their word*" (17:20). The Holy Spirit as "another Helper" (John 14:16) has a role in conveying the word as well.

> When the Spirit of truth comes, he will guide you into all the truth, for he will not speak on his own authority, but whatever he *hears* he will *speak*, and he will *declare* to you the things that are to come. He will glorify me, for he will take what is mine and *declare it* to you. All that the Father has is mine; therefore I said that he will take what is mine and *declare it* to you. (John 16:13–15)

Trinitarian Revelation

This passage shows us the work of all three persons of the Trinity. Since this revelatory work is central to redemption, it suggests that all the revelation from God to man will have a Trinitarian basis. Most of the time in the Bible, this Trinitarian basis is implicit, but it becomes explicit in this key passage, John 16:13–15. And indeed, once we observe the Trinitarian pattern, we can observe aspects of it elsewhere.

John 1:1 describes the second person of the Trinity as "the Word." The allusion to Genesis 1 in John 1:1–3 shows that the eternal Word lies in the background of the specific utterances in Genesis 1 through which God creates light (1:3), the expanse (1:6), and other elements in the created world. John 1:1 also serves as part of the prologue introducing the earthly ministry of the Word, a ministry in which he speaks what the Father gives him: "For I have not spoken on my own authority, but the Father who sent me has himself given me a commandment—what to *say* and what to *speak*. And I know that his commandment is eternal life. What I *say*, therefore, I *say* as the Father has *told* me" (John 12:49–50). The Scripture is described as spoken by the Spirit (e.g., Acts 1:16; 4:25; Heb. 3:7; 2 Pet. 1:21), and 1 Peter 1:11 even describes him as "the Spirit of Christ" in the prophets.

A Pattern of Likeness and Reflections

How then do we understand the passing on of divine messages? The key passages involving the persons of the Trinity show that the message passed on to us has first been communicated between persons of the Trinity. In John 17:8 Christ indicates that he has "given them the words that you [the Father] gave me," showing that communication comes from the Father to the Son. John 16:13 shows that what belongs to the Father and the Son is *heard* by the Spirit, who then speaks. We must have in mind the relations between persons of the Trinity and ask what implications these relations have for communication. Because we are dealing with a level involving *divine* communication, we must also ask about the relation of the communication between divine persons and the communication to human persons. What is the significance of the transition from divine to human?

To answer this question, we have to take some space to reckon with the meaning of humanity. After this reflection, we will return to consider divine messages. Asking about humanity leads naturally to considering the creation of man in the image of God. Scholarship has seen much debate about the meaning of the image of God. But for our purposes it is not necessary to settle these debates. It suffices to observe that human beings are like God in a cluster of ways. These similarities can be observed and affirmed even if we do not immediately associate them with the phrase "the image of God." In fact, when the Bible describes God as speaking, this speaking is analogous to human speaking. Without an analogy between God and man, the language of speaking would make no sense.

The language concerning image also has an analogy in God himself, because Christ is called the image of God in 2 Corinthians 4:4: "In their [unbelievers'] case the god of this world has blinded the minds of the unbelievers, to keep them from seeing the light of the gospel of the glory of Christ, who is *the image of God.*" The mention of "light" and "glory" offers an indirect allusion to passages in the Old Testament where God appears in light and glory. Moreover, in Ezekiel 1 God appears in glory in the "likeness" of a human form: "seated above the likeness of a throne was a *likeness* with a human appearance" (1:26). Ezekiel summarizes in a way that indicates that the glory of the Lord appeared: "Such was the appearance of the *likeness* of the *glory* of the Lord" (1:28). Immediately after this vision, Ezekiel hears the voice of the Lord (1:28–2:1). In Ezekiel 1–2, revelation comes from God to man. This revelation includes a visual component, which reveals glory and the "likeness" with a human appearance. It also includes a verbal component, in the form of divine speech. The two components are two sides to the same overall experience.

The connection between Old Testament theophanies of glory and Christ is confirmed two verses after 2 Corinthians 4:4, where Paul says that God "has shone in our hearts to give the light of the knowledge of the *glory* of God in the face of Jesus Christ" (4:6). The glory of God (4:6) is also the glory of Christ (4:4). And this glory is seen "in the face of Jesus Christ," an expression that alludes to Old Testament passages concerning the face of God and the presence of God. Christ as "the image of God" reflects the glory of God, that is, the glory of the Father. The idea of reflection is built into what Christ is as *image.*

Second Corinthians 4:4 occurs in the context of communicating the *gospel,* "the gospel of the glory of Christ." We might suppose that the language of image or reflection is appropriate only for Christ in his incarnation. But Colossians 1:15–16 goes further: "He [the Son] is the *image* of the invisible God, the firstborn of all creation. For by him all things were created, in heaven and on earth." The divine Son is the "image," now in the context of the fact that he is the divine Mediator of *creation.* So there is an original relation of reflection between the Father and the Son, even apart from redemption and the incarnation. The deepest and most ultimate instance of reflection is found not in man, who is made in the image of God, but in the Son, who is eternally the image of God.

Hebrews 1:3, without using exactly the same terminology, has a similar idea: "He [the Son] is the radiance of the glory of God and the *exact imprint* of his nature, and he upholds the universe by the word of his power." Like Colossians 1:15, the last clause, about upholding the universe, shows once again that the concept of reflecting God belongs to the Son as a divine person, not merely to his human nature. The expression "the radiance of the glory of God" alludes again to Old Testament theophanies in which God's glory appears.

It is interesting that the previous verses in Hebrews 1, namely verses 1–2, have focused on the Son's role as the final Prophet, by whom God "has spoken" (1:2). Communication from God (1:1–2) and the appearing of God in glory that reflects him (1:3) go hand in hand.

Perspectives on Reflections

To understand more thoroughly the nature of reflections, it is convenient to employ three different perspectives. We can illustrate using the particular case where God creates man in his image (Gen. 1:26–27). The first perspective starts with a focus on the original pattern that is going to be reflected. We focus on God as the origin and then see how the reflection derives from him. Let us call this perspective the *originary* perspective.[2] The second perspective starts with the reflection itself, in this case Adam. It then considers how this reflection derives from a previous pattern. Let us call this perspective the *manifestational* perspective, because the reflection "manifests" the pattern that it reflects. This theme of manifestation is particularly evident in the case of theophanies. A theophany manifests the presence of God. The third perspective starts with a focus on the relation between the original pattern and its reflection. It then considers how the relation connects the original and the reflection. Various features are shared by way of analogy between the original and the reflection. In the case of the creation of man in the image of God, we consider ways in which man is like God, and the ways in which the act of creation and the created product (man) show similarities that tell us both about God and about man. Let us call this third perspective the *concurrent* perspective, because the shared features are "concurrently" in the original and in the reflection.

---

2. The labels come from Vern S. Poythress, *God-Centered Biblical Interpretation* (Phillipsburg, NJ: P&R, 1999), 36–42.

The same three perspectives can easily be applied to the theophany in Ezekiel 1. This theophany contains a "likeness with a human appearance" (1:26). The originary perspective starts with the original pattern, which is clearly God himself. It is God who always exists who has manifested himself to Ezekiel. The manifestation derives from God the original. The manifestational perspective begins with the manifestation, namely, the likeness with a human appearance. This manifestation is at the center of Ezekiel's vision. From the manifestation we understand that it is a manifestation of something—a reflection of God the original. Finally, the concurrent perspective focuses on the relation between the original and the manifestation, that is, between God and the likeness. The throne on which the likeness sits expresses and reflects God's power and authority. The likeness with human appearance expresses God's human-like abilities, which are displayed in God's speech and his rule. The brightness (1:27) displays God's purity and glory. The passage concludes in a summary that speaks of "the likeness of the glory of the LORD" (1:28). The glory is clearly the glory of the Lord, a glory displayed visibly in the brightness of the manifestation. Glory is then a concurrent feature, both of the Lord and of the manifestation, because the manifestation reflects the glory that belongs innately to the Lord. It should be noted that the actual effect of the vision on Ezekiel is to convey to him the experience of the glory of the Lord. Ezekiel does not *become* the manifestation that he sees. But he does receive an impact, and that impact lies in the reception of the glory of the Lord.

The creation of man in the image of God in Genesis 1 has an organic relation to Ezekiel 1. It is because man is made in the image of God that it is appropriate that God appears in human form in Ezekiel 1.

Both Genesis 1 and Ezekiel 1 have an organic relation to 2 Corinthians 4:4. The language of "image of God" in 2 Corinthians 4:4 is a clear allusion to Genesis 1:26–27. The language concerning "glory" in 2 Corinthians 4:4 (and 4:6) has a relation to many Old Testament theophanies, but certainly also to Ezekiel 1. The relation to Ezekiel 1 is confirmed in Revelation 1:12–16, where Christ appears in glory. Revelation 1:12–16 combines features from Daniel 7:9–10, 13; 10:5–6; and Ezekiel 1:26–28. The fire, the brightness, the gleaming metal, and the overall human appearance all feature in Revelation 1:12–16.

These relations between Ezekiel 1:26–28 and the New Testament show that Ezekiel 1:26–28 is an adumbration of the revelation of God in Christ. God, who stands behind the manifestation in Ezekiel 1, corresponds with God the Father in the New Testament. The human likeness corresponds to Christ the Son. Is there a role corresponding to the Holy Spirit? First Peter 4:14 associates the Spirit closely with glory: "The Spirit of *glory* and of God rests upon you." This verse is one of a number of verses that associate the Spirit with the glory of Old Testament theophanies (see, e.g., Isa. 63:10–12).[3]

Reflecting the Trinity

The three perspectives on reflections in theophany correspond to the ways that the three persons of the Trinity participate in theophany. The originary perspective begins with a focus on God the Father as the origin of theophanic manifestations. The manifestational perspective begins with a focus on the manifestation that the theophany brings about. The Old Testament manifestations foreshadow the coming of Christ as the climactic manifestation of God, in his incarnation. The concurrent perspective focuses on glory that is shared, which antici-pates the Holy Spirit. Just as the glory comes to Ezekiel and impacts him, the Holy Spirit in the New Testament brings the glory of Christ to us so that we see it. This glory is the glory of the Father in the Son, as 2 Corinthians 4:4, 6 indicates. The expression "the glory of Christ" in verse 4 is linked to the expression "the glory of *God* in the face of Jesus Christ" in verse 6. In verse 6, the work of the Holy Spirit is implicit in the fact that this shining of glory brings about inward "knowledge" "in our hearts," which requires the illumination of the Holy Spirit applying the message of the gospel to our hearts (1 Thess. 1:5).

The three perspectives on reflections are possible because of the prior differentiation in the way reflections unfold. The perspectives are, if you will, epistemic reflections of the nature of theophany. And, as we have seen, theophany in its structure of reflection reflects God's Trinitarian character.

The triad of perspectives can in fact be applied to God himself, in the mystery of the Trinity. The Son is the image of the Father, according

---

3. Meredith M. Kline, "The Holy Spirit as Covenant Witness" (ThM thesis, Westminster Theo-logical Seminary, 1972); Kline, *Images of the Spirit* (Grand Rapids, MI: Baker, 1980).

to Colossians 1:15. This relation of image is an eternal relation. Let us consider this relation as a relation involving reflection. The originary perspective begins with God the Father as the original pattern. The manifestational perspective begins with God the Son as the manifestation and reflection of the Father ("the exact imprint of his nature," Heb. 1:3). And what of the concurrent perspective? It begins with the relation. And what is the relation between the Father and the Son? It is a relation in the fellowship of the Holy Spirit, who expresses the eternal love between the Father and the Son (John 3:34–35). We might expect this result on the basis of the fact that God expresses himself in revelation in harmony with who he always is. Thus, theophanies and their fulfillment in the incarnation reveal the same God who always is, in the fellowship of the persons of the Trinity.

Coinherence

This eternal fellowship in the Trinity involves mutual indwelling of the persons, as expressed in John 17:21: "that they may all be one, just as you, Father, are *in* me, and I *in* you, that they also may be in us, so that the world may believe that you have sent me." The next verses in John 17 speak about the glory shared by the Father and the Son: "The *glory* that you have given me I have given to them, that they may be one even as we are one, I in them and you *in* me" (17:22). The language of glory hints at the presence of the Holy Spirit, and so does the language of indwelling, since it is through the Holy Spirit that the Father and the Son dwell in believers (John 14:17; Rom. 8:9–11).

Several terms have been used to designate the mutual indwelling of the persons of the Trinity—*circumcessio, perichoresis,* and the term I will use, *coinherence.* Coinherence is a unique property belonging to the persons of the Trinity. But we can see a kind of derivative reflection of the original coinherence when we come to theophany. God is present *in* the manifestation in human appearance in Ezekiel 1:26. And he is present *in* the glory of this manifestation. In addition, the glory and the manifestation in human appearance lie within the cloud of glory that comes to Ezekiel, which represents the presence of God. This presence of God in his manifestation foreshadows the presence of God the Father in Christ during his earthly life. Jesus points to the indwelling of the Father: "Do you not believe that I am *in* the Father and the Father is *in* me? The words that I say to you I do not speak on my own authority, but the Father who *dwells in* me does his works" (John 14:10).

Derivative Coinherence

The three perspectives on reflections show in themselves a derivative coinherence. Each perspective presupposes the others and in a sense has the others "within" it. If we start with the originary perspective, to look on something *as an original* already implies that the original has generated a copy, a reflection. The originary perspective *begins* with the original but also moves out from there to consider the relation of the original to its reflection. When we use the perspective to contemplate the reflection, we are exercising the ability to have the equivalent of the manifestational perspective within the originary perspective with which we started. And, of course, when we contemplate the relation between the original and its reflection, we are exercising a form of the concurrent perspective, which is defined as focusing on the relation between the original and its reflection.

Similarly, from the manifestational perspective, we start with the manifestation or reflection. But this starting point already implies that there is an original pattern that the reflection reflects. Hence we end up focusing also on the original, and then we have the equivalent of the originary perspective.

If we start with the concurrent perspective, this perspective presupposes an original and a reflection, between which a relation exists. So, implicit in the concurrent perspective is the originary perspective, focusing on the original, and the manifestational perspective, focusing on the reflection.

In sum, the originary perspective, the manifestational perspective, and the concurrent perspective form a natural triad. Each presupposes the others and each is "in" the others. All these perspectives are used by us with our finite minds. Our minds are not identical with God's. But we can know God. Our minds reflect, on the level of the creature, the knowledge that God himself has as the infinite God with infinite knowledge. Our knowledge reflects the knowledge of God. Likewise, the coinherence of the three perspectives, a coinherence we experience within our finite minds, reflects the original coinherence among the persons of the Trinity.

The pattern of reflection manifested in coinherence is a pattern that itself comes from God. The original for the pattern is found in the Son, who is the image of the Father. The relation of the Father to the Son is the original or archetypal instance of a pattern of reflection. This relation of reflection is itself reflected in the relation between God and man when God creates man in his image. The relation of reflection is also reflected in the pattern of triadic perspectives. The triad consisting in the originary perspective, the manifestational perspective, and the concurrent perspective reflects the triad of the persons of the Trinity. Moreover, the coinherence among the three perspectives reflects the original coinherence among the persons of the Trinity.

Application to Speech

Now we can return to consider the speech and messages of God. The pattern of reflections has relevance for understanding the speech of God. As John 14:10 indicates, the speech of the Son takes place through the indwelling of the Father. When taken alone, John 17:8 might lead us to think that there are two completely distinct speeches with two sets of words and two speakers. On the one hand, the Father "gave" to the Son "words." That constitutes the first speech. On the other hand, the Son has given words to the disciples. That constitutes the second speech. The only thing in common would then be the fact that it happens to be the same words that make up the content of the two speeches. But a picture in which the two speeches are separated is not really correct. When the Son gives words to the disciples, the Father is present *in* the Son. The Father is speaking in the Son. The Son's words reflect the Father's words, so that we can use the three perspectives on reflections. But it is also true that the words coinhere, and the persons who speak the words coinhere. So when the disciples receive the Son's words, the Father is not in the distant background, in such a way that the Son alone is the speaker. Rather, both are present, and both are speaking. But they speak in differentiated ways. The Father is still the origin for the words, and the Father speaks in the Son, who does the works of the Father on earth.

All of this communication takes place in the power of the Holy Spirit. The Spirit is in the Father and in the Son, and vice versa. So we can more thoroughly appreciate the implications of John 16:13–15, where the Spirit speaks what he has heard. The words that the Spirit is passing on are not words that we should think of as having been given by the Father and the Son after which the Father and the Son have walked away. The Father and the Son are present in the words of the Spirit. This presence is to be understood as analogous to the way in which the Father and the Son "make [their] home" with a believer, in the language of John 14:23. The Father and the Son indwell believers. They do this through the indwelling of the Holy Spirit, in whom and through whom the Father and the Son dwell in human beings.

The Original for Speech

Since we are applying the principles for reflections to divine speech, it is natural to ask what is the original divine speech. The original is the Word, as John 1:1 says. The original speech is the speech where the Father is the speaker and the Son is the speech. The Spirit is present in the divine communion of persons. A human speaker expresses himself in speech, and so "indwells" his speech by expressing *himself*. By analogy, the Father is *in* the Word that he speaks. He is in the Word in the fellowship of the Holy Spirit. Elsewhere, in John 16:13, the Bible represents the Holy Spirit as the hearer of divine speech (and, in 1 Cor. 2:10–11, the searcher of divine knowledge). The Holy Spirit is also likened to the breath of God that carries his speech in power to its destination (Ezek. 37:9, 14). Either way, the Holy Spirit is associated with the movement of the Word to its destination.

As we observed, John 1:1–3 contains allusions to Genesis 1. It thereby indicates that the eternal Word mentioned in John 1:1 is the original for the specific divine utterances in Genesis 1, such as "Let there be light" (1:3). We can now construe this reality as an instance involving reflection. The original is the eternal divine Word of John 1:1. The reflection or manifestation is found in the specific utterance of Genesis 1:3. The reflection *manifests* the original. The divine Son is present in the specific speeches. There is a coinherent relation between the original eternal Word and the specific words.

We can extend this pattern to the cases where God addresses human beings. As we have seen from John 17:8, Christ gives to human beings "the words that you gave me." These words reflect the words that the Father has given to the Son. And these words, in turn, reflect an even deeper original, namely, that the Son *is* the Word. Through the coinherence of indwelling, the original fellowship between the Father and the Word in the Spirit is also genuinely and profoundly present in the very words that the disciples receive from the Son.

The Presence of God in Our Words

The message in words from the apostles is infallible. When we receive the words and digest them, our digestion is fallible. But, for those whom the Spirit illumines, the digestion is nevertheless real. We have the Word written on the heart (Heb. 8:10; 10:16). When "the word of Christ" dwells in us richly, we may teach and admonish "one another in all wisdom," a wisdom that is from Christ (Col. 3:16). The Father, the Son, and the Spirit, by dwelling in us, enable us to speak "the word of Christ" to others; this speech is not ours *in isolation* from the reality of indwelling. God speaks through us and is present in his Word that goes forth from us. Fallibility implies that truthfulness must ultimately be checked by conformity to the written Word of Scripture. But divine presence extends also to our speech when we are filled with the Holy Spirit.

Meaning, Power, and Presence

God's Trinitarian dwelling in his Word has implications for how we think about the meaning, power, and presence of God in his Word.[4] God is present in the truth of his meanings and in the power of his omnipotence. Meaning, power, and presence in God are not separable but, we may say, coinherent. Each is "in" the other two. Each presupposes the other two. Just as the attributes of God coinhere in the one God, so the attributes coinhere in the eternal Word, and then they coinhere derivatively (by reflection!) in the particular words of particular utterances. That is true when God creates the world. The utterance "Let there be light" has meaning and power, and manifests the presence of God in the created world. Its meaning, power, and presence are coinherent. Likewise, when God speaks to human beings at Mount Sinai, he speaks meanings in power and in presence.

---

4. For a discussion of the triad of meaning, power, and presence, as a variation on John Frame's triad for lordship (*authority*, power, and presence), see Vern S. Poythress, *In the Beginning Was the Word: Language—A God-Centered Approach* (Wheaton, IL: Crossway, 2009), chap. 3.

This coinherence of meaning, power, and presence has implications for interpreting the Bible. Interpreters can fall into major methodological errors if they try to have one of the three without the others. If they try to have presence without meaning, it is mysticism. They try to surpass the word of the Bible in favor of some wordless union with God, rather than dwelling *in* the words (and the words dwelling in them, John 15:7) to have communion. Or consider another problem. Seeking to control meaning "scientifically" usually means falling into the error of trying—at least temporarily—to have meaning without power and presence. By ignoring the presence of God himself, they falsify the purpose of Scripture and refuse to honor God. Or interpreters may try to have power without meaning or presence. The power is the power of transformation, which an interpreter may seek by importing special meanings that move him and excite him inwardly. But ignoring the real meanings also means missing the real power. The power of God is found not in whatever we may choose to make the Word of God mean but in what God does in fact say, which is filled with power and presence.

Climax in Christ

This communication in meaning, power, and presence comes to a climax in Christ. Christ provides the climax of the meanings of revelation as the final Prophet (Heb. 1:1–2). Christ brings the power of the kingdom of God for salvation. And Christ is "God with us" (Matt. 1:23), the climactic manifestation of the presence of God. The words that Christ gives to the disciples reflect and therefore convey, by the indwelling of the Trinitarian God, the meaning and power and presence of Christ. Through Christ we receive the words of the Father to the Son (John 17:8), through which we have communion with the eternal God, who created and sustains the whole world "by the word of his power" (Heb. 1:3).

4

Revelatory Gifts of the Spirit and the Sufficiency of Scripture

Are They Compatible?

Sam Storms

There was a time when charismatic renewal, at least in North America, was referred to somewhat pejoratively as "the tongues movement."[1] But no longer. Although the spiritual gift of tongues remains controversial, we've entered a season in the life of the church where the gift of prophecy has emerged as the touchpoint for debate and concern.

Among the countless books that have been published on prophecy, none has exerted a degree of influence comparable to that of Wayne Grudem's *The Gift of Prophecy in the New Testament and Today* (Wheaton, IL: Crossway).[2] First released in 1988, it was initially designed

---

1. One example of this is seen in Robert Gromacki, *The Modern Tongues Movement* (Grand Rapids, MI: Baker, 1967).
2. Among the more scholarly works on the gift of prophecy, one thinks immediately of David Hill, *New Testament Prophecy* (Atlanta: John Knox, 1979); David E. Aune, *Prophecy in Early Christianity and the Ancient Mediterranean World* (Grand Rapids, MI: Eerdmans, 1983); Christopher Forbes, *Prophecy and Inspired Speech: In Early Christianity and Its Hellenistic Environment* (Peabody, MA: Hendrickson, 1997); Thomas W. Gillespie, *The First Theologians: A Study in Early Christian Prophecy* (Grand Rapids, MI: Eerdmans, 1994); and Cecil M. Robeck Jr., *Prophecy in Carthage: Perpetua, Tertullian, and Cyprian* (Cleveland, OH: Pilgrim, 1992). There are countless

to be a popularization of his doctoral dissertation, which was first published as *The Gift of Prophecy in 1 Corinthians* (Washington, DC: University Press of America, 1982). It has since been released in a second edition in 1997, and again in 2000 with no revisions other than seven new appendixes. The appeal and impact of Grudem's work are that, unlike so many other popular treatments of the topic, he provides a solid, biblically rooted and theological basis for the nature and exercise of this spiritual gift. Grudem's primary focus was on the biblical text rather than anecdotal evidence for the existence of the gift in the life of the church. This isn't to suggest that scholarly treatments of prophecy were previously nonexistent, but Grudem's reputation as an evangelical, Reformed theologian who champions the doctrines of both the Bible's inerrancy and its functional authority served to win his work a hearing among fellow evangelicals who largely had dismissed the charismatic movement as excessively emotional and theologically shallow.

This isn't to suggest that Grudem's book has been spared criticism. Indeed, numerous attempts to counter his arguments have been published.[3] Among the principal objections to his thesis is that his view of the contemporary validity of so-called "revelatory" gifts, such as prophecy, word of knowledge, and word of wisdom, poses a direct threat to the truth of the Bible's sufficiency. Grudem himself acknowledged as much in his preface to the 1997 edition of his book, noting that "one or two critics have claimed that I deny the authority or sufficiency of Scripture (doctrines that I have in fact defended in writing at some length!). They have not understood my position or represented it accurately."[4]

---

popular works on prophecy, the more helpful of which are Jack Deere, *Surprised by the Voice of God: How God Speaks Today through Prophecies, Dreams, and Visions* (Grand Rapids, MI: Zondervan, 1996), and *The Beginner's Guide to the Gift of Prophecy* (Grand Rapids, MI: Chosen Books, 2008); Bruce Yocum, *Prophecy: Exercising the Prophetic Gifts of the Spirit in the Church Today* (Ann Arbor, MI: Servant, 1976); Graham Houston, *Prophecy: A Gift for Today?* (Downers Grove, IL: InterVarsity Press, 1989); David Pytches, *Prophecy in the Local Church: A Practical Handbook and Historical Overview* (London: Hodder and Stoughton, 1993); and Clifford Hill, *Prophecy Past and Present: An Exploration of the Prophetic Ministry in the Bible and the Church Today* (Ann Arbor, MI: Servant, 1991).

3. Numerous journal articles have interacted critically with Grudem's thesis, but three books in particular are devoted to responding to his arguments: O. Palmer Robertson, *The Final Word: A Biblical Response to the Case for Tongues and Prophecy Today* (Edinburgh, UK: Banner of Truth, 1993); Kenneth L. Gentry Jr., *The Charismatic Gift of Prophecy: A Reformed Response to Wayne Grudem* (Memphis: Footstool, 1989); and Michael John Beasley, *The Fallible Prophets of New Calvinism: An Analysis, Critique, and Exhortation concerning the Contemporary Doctrine of "Fallible Prophecy"* (Pfafftown, NC: Armoury Ministries, 2013).

4. Wayne Grudem, *The Gift of Prophecy in the New Testament and Today*, rev. ed. (Wheaton, IL: Crossway, 2000), 13.

This brings us to the question posed in the title of this chapter. Does Grudem's understanding of the spiritual gift of prophecy undermine or threaten the sufficiency of Holy Scripture? If we are to answer this question, we need to understand what is meant and entailed by the doctrine of biblical sufficiency.

The Sufficiency of the Christian Scriptures

Grudem argues:

> The sufficiency of Scripture guarantees that God will not give any new revelation in this age that adds to *the moral standards that he requires for all Christians to obey* during the church age. However, the sufficiency of Scripture does not mean that God will not give *additional specific directions to individual persons* for them to obey (such as a calling to serve in a certain church, or a calling to the mission field, etc.).[5]

When Grudem turns to an actual definition of the sufficiency of Scripture, he writes, "The sufficiency of Scripture means that Scripture contains all the words of God which he intends his people to have at each stage of redemptive history, and that it contains everything we need God to tell us for salvation, for trusting him perfectly, and for obeying him perfectly."[6]

In view of Paul's reference to "every good work" in 2 Timothy 3:16–17, Grudem insists that we can rest assured "there is *no* 'good work' that God wants us to do other than those that are taught somewhere in Scripture. Scripture can equip us for *every* good work."[7] Again, "The sufficiency of Scripture shows us that no modern revelations from God are to be placed on a level equal to Scripture in authority."[8] Grudem does not say that no such "revelations" exist, but only that they are always subordinate to the final authority of Scripture itself.

More recently, in his excellent treatment of *sola Scriptura*, Matthew Barrett defines the sufficiency of Scripture in these terms:

---

5. Grudem, *Gift of Prophecy*, 257.
6. Grudem, *Gift of Prophecy*, 258.
7. Grudem, *Gift of Prophecy*, 258.
8. Grudem, *Gift of Prophecy*, 263–64.

The sufficiency of Scripture means that all things necessary for salvation and for living the Christian life in obedience to God and for his glory are given to us in the Scriptures. Not only is the Bible our supreme authority, it is the authority that provides believers with all the truth they need for reconciliation with God and for following after Christ.[9]

Barrett also reminds us that "while Scripture is sufficient, this does not mean that all things will be explicitly spelled out on the pages of Scripture."[10] Some matters "are not addressed *directly* by God's Word"[11] but come to us indirectly. This means "that the Bible does not demand the exclusion of extrabiblical data. . . . Human knowledge and thought in all disciplines always involves and requires extrabiblical data."[12] No one on either side of the charismatic debate would suggest that nuclear physicists should derive all their knowledge of the sub-atomic world by reading Scripture. Whereas God is both Creator and providential Lord over every molecule, atom, and quark, knowledge of these specific elements and their properties is not addressed in the Bible. The same may be said about the disciplines of mathematics, sociology, library science, and automotive mechanics, just to mention a few.

Those who believe in the cessation of the spiritual gift of prophecy, such as Richard Gaffin,[13] believe that to admit the possibility of revelation beyond Scripture, primarily through the spiritual gift of prophecy, unavoidably implies a certain "insufficiency" in Scripture that needs to be compensated for. But it is altogether insufficient to affirm the Bible's sufficiency without then asking, What is Scripture sufficient *for*? As noted above, no one believes that the Bible is sufficient to provide us with exhaustive information on every conceivable subject. Rather, we affirm that when it comes to essential "teaching" on the nature of God and the content of the gospel or the ethical principles that reprove and correct and train us in righteous living (2 Tim. 3:16) or, as Peter says, whatever is required for "life and godliness" (2 Pet. 1:3), the Bible contains everything we need. It suffers from no deficiency. It stands in

---

9. Matthew Barrett, *God's Word Alone: The Authority of Scripture* (Grand Rapids, MI: Zondervan, 2016), 334.

10. Barrett, *God's Word Alone*, 336.

11. Barrett, *God's Word Alone*, 336.

12. Barrett, *God's Word Alone*, 339.

13. See his contribution (as well as my own) in *Are Miraculous Gifts for Today? Four Views*, ed. Wayne Grudem (Grand Rapids, MI: Zondervan, 1996).

no need of supplement from human insight or research. But it is no threat to biblical sufficiency to argue that God may still communicate with his people in highly personal and intimate ways and grant them guidance on matters where the Bible is noticeably silent.

So, for example, when a young man recently approached me, having discerned a "call" to devote his life to reaching the unreached with the gospel, there was no specific guidance in the Bible that might suggest he should consider moving to a remote village in northern India instead of inner-city Hong Kong. And when Paul defines for us the purpose of prophecy (1 Cor. 14:3), we need not fear that the Bible's sufficiency has been compromised should the Spirit speak words that bring to an individual encouragement, consolation, and spiritual strength. As I have written elsewhere:

> The close of the biblical canon marks the point at which the general principles of God's universal will are complete. All the doctrines, as well as all ethical principles, essential for the life of God's people have been revealed. Nothing further will be said by God to extend or expand or contradict them. The Bible establishes the theological and ethical boundaries of what God will ever say.
>
> But guidance and revelation and wisdom by which we gain the knowledge of how to apply these principles and truths in the practical details and decisions of life are ongoing. When we listen to God we do not expect him to say anything doctrinally or ethically new. But we do expect him to speak to the situation in which we find ourselves with wisdom and direction and insight and encouragement in *living out* the truths he has *written in.*[14]

What Is the Spiritual Gift of Prophecy?

If we are going to determine whether a conflict exists between this understanding of biblical sufficiency and the contemporary validity of revelatory gifts of the Spirit, we need a working definition of prophecy itself. Grudem defines prophecy as "a very human—and sometimes partially mistaken—report of something the Holy Spirit brought to someone's mind."[15] Again, it is "the spontaneous, powerful working

14. Sam Storms, *Convergence: Spiritual Journeys of a Charismatic Calvinist* (Kansas City, MO: Enjoying God Ministries, 2005), 182–83.
15. Grudem, *Gift of Prophecy*, 18.

of the Holy Spirit, bringing things to mind when the church is gathered for worship, giving 'edification, encouragement, and comfort' which speaks directly to the needs of the moment and causes people to realize that 'truly God is among you' (1 Cor. 14:25)."[16]

You will notice that Grudem uses the language of the Holy Spirit "bringing things to mind" in a spontaneous fashion, "things" not explicitly set forth in Scripture. Would it not be more helpful if we simply said that the Spirit oftentimes "reveals" things otherwise unknown to the recipient of such a "revelation"? This is typically where evangelical cessationists get nervous. The idea that God might still be providing his people with "revelation" of any sort is thought to suggest, if not require, a repudiation of the notion that what we have already received in canonical and inspired form in the Bible is sufficient. If God has supplied us in Scripture itself with everything necessary for life and godliness, what need would there be for him to reveal anything beyond what we already possess?

Part of the problem is in the way we employ the terms "revelation" and "reveal." The verb "reveal" (*apokaluptō*) occurs twenty-six times in the New Testament, and the noun "revelation" occurs eighteen times. In every instance the reference is to divine activity, never to human communication. However, not every act of divine revelation is equal in authority. The tendency among many evangelicals is to improperly assume that any time a "revelation" is granted, it bears the same universally binding authority, sufficient to warrant its inclusion in the biblical canon. But divine "revelation" comes in a variety of different forms. For example, consider Paul's statement in Philippians 3:15. There were present in Philippi some who took issue with certain elements in Paul's teaching. He appeals to all who are "mature" to "think" as he does. If some do not, Paul is confident that "God will reveal" to them the error of their way and bring them into conformity with apostolic truth. We see from a text like this that God can "reveal" to a Christian, or in some manner disclose to a believer's mind, truths that no one would ever regard as canonical or bearing the authoritative weight of inspired biblical texts. The Spirit, instead, would do much as Grudem has said: bring to mind spontaneously some insight or truth designed exclusively for some

---

16. Grudem, *Gift of Prophecy*, 18–19.

individual or group and never intended by God to be taken as universally authoritative or binding on the conscience of other believers. As Grudem himself has noted:

> Once more, it would not be possible to think that every time a believer gained new insight into his privileges as a Christian and reported it to a friend, the actual words of that speech would have been thought to be God's very words. It would be the *report* of something God had "revealed" to the Christian, but the report would only come in merely human words.[17]

Jesus employed the verb "reveal" to describe his own gracious activity in making known the Father to those who previously had no saving knowledge of him. But surely no one would insist that the insight given to such folk should be written down and preserved as canonical for subsequent generations of Christians. Paul again used the language of "revelation" to describe the activity of God in making known the reality of divine wrath against those "who by their unrighteousness suppress the truth" (Rom. 1:18). Thus, God's act of divine disclosure is again unrelated to the inspiration of texts that carry an intrinsic authority.

In view of this, D. A. Carson has rightly pointed out that not all "revelatory" activity of God comes to us as Scripture-quality, divinely authoritative, canonical truth. Thus, says Carson:

> when Paul presupposes in 1 Corinthians 14:30 that the gift of prophecy depends on a revelation, we are not limited to a form of authoritative revelation that threatens the finality of the canon. To argue in such a way is to confuse the terminology of Protestant systematic theology with the terminology of the Scripture writers.[18]

This brings us to the crux of my argument. Cessationists argue that New Testament prophecy invariably yields Scripture-quality words from God that are equal in authority to the canonical text itself. In other words, most (if not all) cessationists believe that all "revelatory" words from God must be treated as equal to and as universally binding

---

17. Grudem, *Gift of Prophecy*, 65.
18. D. A. Carson, *Showing the Spirit: A Theological Exposition of 1 Corinthians 12–14* (Grand Rapids, MI: Baker, 1987), 163.

on the conscience of God's people as the "words" that ultimately were canonized in the sixty-six books of the Bible. If the cessationist is correct, then the postcanonical or contemporary validity of certain revelatory gifts, like prophecy and word of knowledge, would indeed compromise the finality and authority of the Bible.

But does the New Testament actually portray the "revelation" that comes via prophecy and word of knowledge as infallible, universally authoritative, and potentially canonical? Do the numerous descriptions of revelatory gifts in actual practice require us to conclude that the authors of the Bible regard them as providing us with Scripture-quality words? My answer to both questions is no.

The Gift of Prophecy in Practice

In addition to the texts we've already noted, several others lead me to conclude that not all "revelatory" activity was designed by God to be received as universally authoritative or canonical. Principal among them are several statements in 1 Corinthians 14. In this chapter we find the closest thing in Scripture to a description of a corporate worship celebration. Paul gives explicit instruction on the preparation of individual Christians as they come to a corporate gathering. He writes: "When you come together, each one has a hymn, a lesson, a revelation, a tongue, or an interpretation. Let all things be done for building up" (1 Cor. 14:26). Evidently a "revelation" would have been given to one or several individuals prior to the meeting (although a person could also be the recipient of a spontaneous revelation during the meeting, as we'll see in 14:30). The content of such revelation is not specified, nor are the means by which it was dispensed. But if all "revelation" carries the authoritative weight of Scripture itself, one cannot help but wonder what happened to these many revelatory words that were spoken in the corporate gatherings at Corinth and at other churches throughout the ancient world. Paul certainly was not in the least concerned that steps be taken to preserve these "revelations." In fact, it is entirely probable that he anticipated some of them, perhaps even all, would be lost or discarded and thus inaccessible to subsequent generations of the body of Christ. We see this in his instruction concerning what should happen when one believer is the recipient of a "revelation" while another is speaking:

Let two or three prophets speak, and let the others weigh what is said. If a revelation is made to another sitting there, let the first be silent. For you can all prophesy one by one, so that all may learn and all be encouraged, and the spirits of prophets are subject to prophets. (1 Cor. 14:29–32)[19]

Paul's seeming indifference to the prophetic word being spoken by the first prophet catches many by surprise. Some insist that his instruction does not necessarily entail the loss of the first prophetic speech. Could not that person simply remain silent until the second had finished and then resume where he or she left off? But as Grudem has pointed out:

> If the first prophet was *expected* to resume speaking, why then would Paul command this *first* prophet to be silent at all? If the first prophet could retain his revelation and speak later, then so could the second prophet. And in that case it would make much more sense for the second prophet to wait, instead of rudely interrupting the first prophet and making him give his speech in two parts.[20]

Again, Paul's apparent lack of concern for the loss of such prophetic words seems incompatible with a belief that they were equal in authority with Scripture itself.

There is yet another statement by Paul in 1 Corinthians 14 that would lead us to believe that the "revelation" behind a prophetic utterance did not carry authoritative weight equal to apostolic teaching. It would appear that some in the Corinthian church were insisting that because they had "heard" from God in some "revelatory" manner, others should always submit to or heed their instruction. But Paul has a different perspective. He writes:

> Or was it from you that the word of God came? Or are you the only ones it has reached? If anyone thinks that he is a prophet, or spiritual, he should acknowledge that the things I am writing to you are a command of the Lord. If anyone does not recognize this, he is not recognized. (1 Cor. 14:36–38)

---

19. I agree with Roy E. Ciampa and Brian S. Rosner that "Paul could mean the evaluation of the prophets themselves, but more likely he has in mind the evaluation of the messages given by them" (*The First Letter to the Corinthians*, PNTC [Grand Rapids, MI: Eerdmans, 2010], 715).

20. Grudem, *Gift of Prophecy*, 63.

Paul isn't denying that such "prophets" existed in Corinth (and in other local churches). He has clearly affirmed that this is one of many spiritual gifts, indeed, the one gift that serves far better than uninterpreted tongues to edify or build up the body of Christ (1 Cor. 14:3–5). He has stated clearly in verse 29 that "prophets" were present in Corinth, and he encouraged their revelatory ministry. He even appears to envision the possibility that any or all Corinthian believers might at some time exercise this gift. In verse 24 he speaks of the spiritual benefits that accrue to unbelievers "if *all* prophesy," and in verse 31 he endorses the possibility that "you can *all* prophesy one by one."[21]

Thus, when Paul comes to verses 36–38, he isn't denying or withdrawing his earlier affirmation of the validity of "prophets" in the church or their potential for building up other believers. He is simply making it clear that whatever "revelation" may come to them, it is always subject to the more ultimate and binding authoritative utterances of himself as an apostle. In fact, immediately following this warning to all prophets in Corinth that they must yield to his superior apostolic authority, he encourages believers in Corinth to "earnestly desire to prophesy" (14:39)! I find it remarkably instructive that Paul would subordinate prophetic "revelation" to his own apostolic authority and then encourage the congregation in Corinth to be earnest in their pursuit of that very gift!

I take all this to mean that Paul's statement is designed to prevent them from making up guidelines for public worship, based on an alleged prophetic word, contrary to what he has just stated. His point is that a Scripture-quality, authoritative "word of God" has not, in fact, been forthcoming from the Corinthian prophets. Paul does not deny that they have truly prophesied, but he denies that their "words" were equal in authority to his own. Such words were in fact of a lesser authority.

This is clearly reinforced in 1 Corinthians 14:37–38, where Paul writes: "If anyone thinks that he is a prophet, or spiritual, he should acknowledge that the things I am writing to you are a command of the Lord. If anyone does not recognize this, he is not recognized." Paul is claiming a divine authority for his words that he is just as obviously

---

21. The force of "all" here has been disputed. Interpretations range from "all" the prophets, to "all" without distinction as to gender or social standing (rather than a universal "all" without exception), to "all" potentially but not in actual practice. The last view strikes me as the most likely.

denying to the Corinthians. "According to Paul," notes Grudem, "the words of the prophets at Corinth were not and could not have been sufficiently authoritative to show Paul to be wrong."[22] Once again, then, my question for the cessationist is how Paul could have said this if in fact the "revelation" on which prophecy was based was itself Scripture-quality and as authoritative for the lives of all people everywhere as were the words of Paul, Peter, Luke, and John.

Still, though, Paul believed the prophecy at Corinth to be a good and helpful gift of God, for he immediately thereafter exhorted the Corinthians once again to "earnestly desire to prophesy" (14:39)! He obviously believed that the spiritual gift of congregational prophecy that operated at a lower level of authority than did the apostolic, canonical expression of it was still extremely valuable to the church. One must also wonder about this exhortation if Paul actually viewed the revelation on which prophecy was based as infallible, morally authoritative, and essential to establishing the foundation of the universal church. *Are we really prepared to say that the apostle urged every Christian in every local congregation to earnestly desire that he or she might be the recipient of inspired and authoritative revelation that would serve to lay the foundation for the body of Christ throughout all ages?* I'm not.

To these texts we must also add those in which Christians are urged to exercise discernment and judgment in weighing or assessing the validity of any purported claim to divine revelation. One must ask whether this responsibility, as described in these passages, is consistent with the cessationist notion that all prophetic revelation comes in the form of Scripture-quality information. The two texts I have in mind are 1 Thessalonians 5:19–22 and 1 Corinthians 14:29.

The former of these texts is addressed to a congregation that highly esteemed the Word of God and that Paul regarded as remarkably mature. The apostle said of the Thessalonians, "When you received the word of God, which you heard from us, you accepted it not as the word of men but as what it really is, the word of God, which is at work in you believers" (1 Thess. 2:13). Cessationists would have us believe that these Christians were instructed by Paul (and others) that all prophetic utterances were equal in authority to Scripture itself, indeed equal in authority to the very words that Paul is in the process of writing to

---

22. Grudem, *Gift of Prophecy*, 68.

them in his first epistle (as well as his second). But if that were the case, how does one account for the fact that they had come to "despise" such revelatory disclosures rather than highly esteem them? Yet this is precisely what the Thessalonians had done. Thus, Paul's exhortation that they not "quench the Spirit" by "despis[ing] prophecies" (1 Thess. 5:19–20) but instead "test [or weigh, assess, judge, and evaluate] everything" and then "hold fast what is good" and "abstain from every form of evil" (5:21–22).

To what does the noun *prophēteia* ("prophecies") refer? Is it the gift of prophecy itself, the person who claims to be speaking prophetically, or the verbal utterances of the person who prophesies? The strong likelihood is the third option, as the use of the plural and the absence of the definite article suggest. This is confirmed in verse 21a, where the alternative to despising "prophecies" is that "everything" should be tested. Again, the plural "everything" (or "all things") that must be tested has for its antecedent the "prophecies" in the immediately preceding verse. Much to our dismay, Paul "does not specify what criteria should be used in determining whether something is good or evil, but presumably he expected his readers to weigh supposed Spirit-inspired words and deeds against the doctrinal and ethical norms they had received from him."[23] Gordon Fee believes the answer is found in two additional Pauline texts. We know that many in the church in Thessalonica were disturbed by a false report regarding the arrival of the "day of the Lord" (2 Thess. 2:2). In response Paul urged them, "Stand firm and hold to the traditions that you were taught by us, either by our spoken word or by our letter" (2 Thess. 2:15). Perhaps, then, "the first test is the apostolic proclamation of/teaching about Christ. This is a test that has to do with the theological or doctrinal content of the utterance."[24] The second test derives from Paul's teaching in 1 Corinthians 14:3, where he says that prophecy has for its purpose "upbuilding and encouragement and consolation." "This," says Fee, "is the test of purpose, as well as content, and has to do with its helpfulness to the believing community."[25]

---

23. Charles A. Wanamaker, *The Epistles to the Thessalonians: A Commentary on the Greek Text* (Grand Rapids, MI: Eerdmans, 1990), 203.

24. Gordon D. Fee, *The First and Second Letters to the Thessalonians* (Grand Rapids, MI: Eerdmans, 2009), 222.

25. Fee, *First and Second Thessalonians*, 222.

Now let's set this exhortation in 1 Thessalonians 5 alongside Paul's own personal experience as recorded in Acts 21. We are told that when he arrived in Tyre, "through the Spirit [*dia tou pneumatos*[26]] they [the disciples at Tyre] were telling Paul not to go on to Jerusalem" (21:4). Upon arriving in Caesarea several days later, he was the recipient of a prophetic word from a man named Agabus to the effect that, if he were to go to Jerusalem, he would be bound by the Jews and delivered over to the Gentiles. It is entirely likely that Agabus was joined in this word to Paul by the "four unmarried daughters" of Philip, each of whom "prophesied" (21:9). In any case, Agabus prefaced his word with the statement, "Thus says the Holy Spirit" (21:11a). The specific way in which the Spirit "spoke" through the disciples at Tyre and revealed this scenario to Agabus is not made known. Agabus, unlike those in Tyre, did not himself tell Paul not to continue his journey to Jerusalem, but upon hearing his revelatory vision concerning Paul, Luke and the people in Caesarea "urged him not to go up to Jerusalem" (21:12b).

Here is where the connection with 1 Thessalonians 5 comes into play. Paul chose *not* to heed the advice given to him (Acts 21:13). In the final analysis, following what must have been highly emotional dialogue (see 21:13–14) in which no agreement could be reached (21:14a), the apostle kept his prior commitment to finish the journey. The conclusion of all concerned was mutual: "Let the will of the Lord be done" (21:14b).

At no time did Paul push back against either the Christians in Tyre or Agabus and insist that the Spirit did *not* reveal that his arrival in Jerusalem would bring harsh persecution. He did not suggest that the revelatory vision or word that Agabus claimed came from the Spirit was in fact fabricated or misguided. Why, then, did Paul choose to act contrary to what the disciples in Tyre had said? The answer is found earlier in Acts 19:21. There we read that "Paul resolved in the Spirit to pass through Macedonia and Achaia and go to Jerusalem, saying, 'After I have been there, I must also see Rome.'" Paul's decision to go to Jerusalem was as much a product of the Spirit's revelatory ministry as was that of the Christians in Tyre and of Agabus, who warned him of persecution should he go there. Paul resolved "in the [Holy] Spirit" to

---

26. This same Greek phrase appears in Acts 11:28 to describe the means, manner, or perhaps better still the source and power through which Agabus delivered his prophetic word concerning an impending famine.

make the journey. This understanding is confirmed in Acts 20:22–23, where the apostle declares, "And now, behold, I am going to Jerusalem, constrained by the Spirit, not knowing what will happen to me there, except that the Holy Spirit testifies to me in every city that imprisonment and afflictions await me."

How do we account for Paul's decision to resist the urging of his friends that he not go to Jerusalem?[27] Clearly the Spirit who spoke to believers in Tyre and to Agabus and the four daughters of Philip had also revealed to Paul that he *should* go, notwithstanding what others might say. Indeed, he was "constrained" by the Spirit to finish this journey to Jerusalem.

I believe the best way to account for this is by recognizing that in any particular "prophetic utterance" there are at least three elements. There is (1) the *revelation* from the Spirit, which in all instances is inspired and infallible. There is also (2) the *interpretation* of what that revelation means. Finally, there is an attempt to make (3) *application* to the person(s) involved. Here is how I explained this elsewhere:

> Through some supernatural means that is not specified, the Holy Spirit communicated to the believers at Tyre that if Paul went to Jerusalem he would be persecuted, perhaps even killed. On the basis or on the grounds of this revelation, they in turn *interpreted* this to be God's warning for him not to go. They then *applied* this to Paul by issuing a stringent warning and urged him to change his plans. . . . On this scenario, the disciples at Tyre, and later at Caesarea, all received the same revelation. They either had a distinct impression in their hearts or heard the Spirit speak audibly or more likely had a vision of Paul being threatened and beaten and perhaps in prison as a result. This *revelation* was unmistakable. Because this revelation was from God, it was infallible and altogether true. But they then *interpreted* the revelation as meaning that extremely perilous times awaited Paul. He was subject to severe persecution, perhaps even martyrdom. This in turn led to the *application*. They concluded that *it was not God's will* for Paul to go to Jerusalem. It simply didn't register with them that going to Jerusalem could be a good thing. Why would anyone venture into a territory where he knew perse-

---

27. I have addressed several possible explanations in my book, *Practicing the Power: Welcoming the Gifts of the Holy Spirit in Your Life* (Grand Rapids, MI: Zondervan, 2017), 113–14, and won't rehearse them here.

cution was certain to occur? And why would God lead him there? Combined with their love for him and their desire for his safety, they told and even urged him not to go. In other words, they got the revelation right, as well as the interpretation, but misapplied it in terms of how Paul should react.[28]

And what was Paul's response? He did precisely what he instructed the Thessalonians to do whenever a prophetic utterance is delivered. He *tested* it. He weighed and analyzed it against the standard of his own experience with the Spirit. Based on earlier, repeated guidance from the Spirit, Paul knew that the Christians in Tyre and Agabus and the others were correct that should he go to Jerusalem, he would be sorely persecuted. But he obviously concluded that they had either misinterpreted or, more likely, out of understandable concern for his welfare, misapplied the revelation by insisting that he not continue his trip.

Thus, we see that Paul's own personal practice as a recipient of a prophetic utterance indicates that he did not regard the revelatory word as bearing Scripture-quality authority. Whereas the revelation itself was altogether true, it was communicated by fallible human men and women. It strikes me as most plausible to conclude that Paul believed all prophetic utterances to be a mixture of sorts in which the infallible divine revelation is processed through the fallible interpretive grid of Christian men and women who, in turn, on occasion, make applications that are inconsistent with either what Scripture might already have made clear or what one's own experience under the guidance of the Spirit had previously established.

There is another, quite similar passage. Although I realize that cessationists have a different understanding of 1 Corinthians 14:29, I believe Paul is saying here much the same thing as he says in 1 Thessalonians 5:19–22: "Weigh" (*diakrinō*) what is said by the prophets. That is, sift the word and identify what is of God and what is the human and thus fallible admixture. Thiselton provides this helpful explanation:

> The others are to distinguish between (i) prophetic speech which is God-given and coheres with the gospel of Christ and the pastoral situation and (ii) speech which is merely self-generated rhetoric reflecting the speaker's disguised self-interests, self-deceptions, or

---

28. Storms, *Practicing the Power*, 114.

errors, albeit under the guise of supposed "prophecy." We have argued . . . that this includes a claim to communicate gospel preaching pastorally contextualized. The authentic is to be sifted from
the inauthentic or spurious, in the light of the OT scriptures, the
gospel of Christ, the traditions of all the churches, and critical
reflections. Nowhere does Paul hint that preaching or "prophecy"
achieves a privileged status which places them above critical reflection in the light of the gospel, the Spirit, and the scriptures. It is
never infallible.[29]

I find it difficult to believe that Paul would have commanded this
sort of assessment if all prophetic words were by definition inerrant,
Scripture-quality revelation from God. Thus David Garland is likely
correct in his assessment of what Paul means:

The assumption is that the prophets do not speak with unquestion-
able divine authority. The congregation is not to accept everything
that is said just because a person claims to speak under the influence
of the Spirit. The prophet's words invite appraisal and discussion.
. . . This is quite different from ascertaining whether the individual
is a true or a false prophet. Presumably, the speakers reside in
their midst, and the congregation would not need to examine them
week after week, but they do need to evaluate what they say. . . .
Prophets must allow the content of their revelation to be tested in
the community and may need reminding that their "prophecy" is
only partial and temporary ([1 Cor.] 13:9–10).[30]

Where Are All the Inspired Revelatory Words?

Yet another forceful argument against the proposal by cessationists
that all revelatory speech was equivalent to canonical Scripture is the
actual manner in which we would expect such prophetic revelation
to have been treated. To say the same thing, if the "revelation" that
is the basis of all prophetic ministry was, as the cessationist claims,
always and without exception equal in authority to the very words of
Scripture, we should expect to see certain things in Scripture that are
decidedly absent.

---

29. Anthony C. Thiselton, *The First Epistle to the Corinthians: A Commentary on the Greek Text* (Grand Rapids, MI: Eerdmans, 2000), 1140, emphasis original.
30. David E. Garland, *1 Corinthians* (Grand Rapids, MI: Baker Academic, 2003), 662.

Paul's instruction to the churches throughout the first-century world would undoubtedly have been identical to his instruction to the Corinthians. The apostle did not embrace one perspective on revelatory gifts that would apply to the Corinthians and yet another, different perspective for the churches in Macedonia and Italy and elsewhere. Likewise, the same set of practical guidelines imposed on the Corinthians would have been required of all Christians in every other city and church.

This means that if the cessationist is correct regarding the nature and authority of prophetic revelation, we would be more than justified in our expectation of a certain scenario throughout the Mediterranean world. But, in fact, such a scenario is conspicuous by its absence. Let me explain.

A good place to begin is with the day of Pentecost as described in Acts 2. There Peter described what life and ministry would be like during the age of the new covenant:

And in the last days it shall be, God declares,
    that I will pour out my Spirit on all flesh,
and your sons and daughters shall prophesy,
    and your young men shall see visions,
    and your old men shall dream dreams;
even on my male servants and female servants
    in those days I will pour out my Spirit, and they shall
        prophesy. (Acts 2:17–18)

According to the cessationist understanding of such revelatory gifts, as well as the "revelation" that forms the basis of the "dreams" and "visions" that Peter said would be the experience of young and old and male and female, God would everywhere provide inerrant, universally authoritative truths to those who were neither apostles nor elders in the local church. These, quite clearly, are average Christian men and women, young and old.

Cessationists have often been heard to ask, "If the Spirit were still giving divine revelation, why wouldn't we gather up and include those words in our Bibles?" Clearly, the cessationist believes that all such revelatory disclosures that Peter declared would be forthcoming were spiritually and morally equivalent to Scripture and thus warrant inclusion in our Bibles. He would necessarily say the same thing about the prophetic revelation being granted to Christians in Rome (Rom. 12:6), in Ephesus (Acts 19:5–7; Eph. 4:11; 1 Tim. 1:18), in Caesarea (Acts 21:8–9), in Thessalonica (1 Thess. 5:19–22), and of course in Corinth (1 Corinthians 12–14), as well as in countless other cities throughout the Mediterranean world of the first century.

This raises two crucial questions. First, what happened to all the content of these revelatory words, images, visions, dreams, impressions, and other expressions through which God made himself known? If, as most cessationists contend, all such "revelation" should be regarded as equally authoritative as Scripture itself and essential to the establishment of the foundation of the universal body of Christ (Eph. 2:19–21), where is it? In an unpublished paper Wayne Grudem similarly asks:

> Were thousands of "prophets" actually speaking the very words of God? Were God's people to be expected to go around to the many hundreds or even thousands of churches in the first century world and collect the prophecies given week after week, and write them down, and produce hundreds of volumes of "words of the Lord" which they were to obey as they obeyed Scripture? In fact, we have no record of anything like this happening, nor do we have any record anywhere in the New Testament of churches recording or preserving these prophecies as if they were "words of the Lord." Rather they preserve and obey the writings and teachings of the apostles, not of the prophets.[31]

As best I can tell, the only two recorded prophecies that were preserved and included in the canonical text of Scripture were both from Agabus (Acts 11:27–30 and 21:10–12). Does it not seem odd that no effort was made to retain and impose on the consciences of all Christians everywhere so much as a single syllable from all those alleged Scripture-quality and divinely inspired words?

My second question grows out of the exhortation of Paul that Christians should "earnestly desire the higher gifts" (1 Cor. 12:31), among which are (perhaps even most of all) the gift of prophecy. Again, in 1 Corinthians 14:1, he writes, "Pursue love, and earnestly desire

---

31. This paper was written in response to one of his most vocal critics. Grudem has chosen not to publish it yet, but shared its contents with me.

the spiritual gifts, especially that you may prophesy." And as much as Paul wanted all his readers to speak in tongues, he desired "even more" that they should "prophesy" (1 Cor. 14:5). Finally, he closes 1 Corinthians 14 with the exhortation "So, my brothers, earnestly desire to prophesy, and do not forbid speaking in tongues" (14:39).

Now, let's pair this series of exhortations with what cessationists say about the nature of prophetic revelation. The latter, not to be repetitive, is allegedly equivalent in authority and importance to Scripture itself. Prophets, so they contend, served to provide those foundational theological truths and ethical principles on which the universal body of Christ (the church) would be built. This would require us to believe that Paul urged every Christian man and woman, young or old, to earnestly desire and pray that God would grant them those inspired and infallible theological concepts, moral values, and practical guidelines to which all Christians in every subsequent age of the church would be bound to believe and follow. I find this highly unlikely, if not impossible.

Conclusion

One can readily discern from this chapter that I share Wayne Grudem's perspective on the nature of New Testament prophecy. Both of us embrace the contemporary validity of certain revelatory spiritual gifts simultaneously with our unwavering affirmation of the complete sufficiency and authority of Holy Scripture. This isn't because Wayne has been a longtime close friend of mine or because we share a number of other theological convictions (such as our views on complementarianism and Reformed soteriology). I share Wayne's view because I believe it is what the Bible teaches. And I am extraordinarily honored to have been given the opportunity to contribute to this volume, which acknowledges and expresses deep appreciation for both Wayne's godly life in the service of the Lord and his faithful work in evangelical biblical and theological studies.

5

Developing Doctrine
from Scripture

A Case Study in the Doctrine of the Trinity

Bruce A. Ware

I have had the distinct privilege of knowing Wayne Grudem for over twenty-five years. I've known *of* him longer. The first time I ever saw Wayne "in action" was at an annual meeting of the Evangelical Theological Society, held at Moody Bible Institute in 1984. I was new on the faculty of Bethel Theological Seminary, and a van load of us had driven to Chicago to attend the sessions. I will never forget witnessing Dr. Grudem's presentation of mountains of biblical and lexical evidence supporting a complementarian understanding of the roles of men and women in ministry and in the home. His argumentation was thorough, exact, and simply overwhelming as he supported his claims with scores of passages coupled with mounds of technical lexical data, all of which appeared on overhead projection sheets. Here I saw first-hand what I have since witnessed many times—Grudem's vigorous, detailed, comprehensive, and unrelenting defense of truth, yet delivered with warmth, generosity, graciousness, and winsomeness (including his engaging smile), as disarming as it was compelling. Little did I know then that Wayne would one day become both an esteemed colleague (I joined him on the faculty of Trinity Evangelical Divinity School in 1991) and a dear friend.

One hallmark of Grudem's writing and teaching over the whole of his ministry has been his commitment to follow the teaching of Scripture to the best of his understanding and to the best of his ability. This is not to say that he disregards the previous development of doctrines through the history of the church or insights from philosophy or the social sciences, for he surely does not. But it is to say that he is truly committed to *sola Scriptura*, that Scripture alone is the only final and only ultimately authoritative source for faith and practice. I have enjoyed a delicious irony about Wayne for as long as I've known him— that while he vigorously supports the ongoing gift of prophecy in the church, he likewise is one of the strongest, most capable, and fully uncompromising defenders of the absolute and exclusive authority of the Bible that evangelicalism has to offer. For Grudem, whatever the Bible teaches as true is true, and this alone has the final word, even if we are helped along the way from other guides, be they historical or contemporary.

While the biblical fortitude of Grudem's theological development is evident in all his work, one area where this is especially important is in his development of the doctrine of the Trinity. Here, as elsewhere, while Grudem is conversant with the historical development of the doctrine—indeed, he appeals to it at important points along the way— his endeavor is to uncover the vast array of biblical teachings that call for understanding the triune persons as (1) absolutely coequal in their deity as fully and eternally God and (2) distinct in their persons as eternal Father, Son, and Spirit, evidencing distinct roles marked, among other things, by an eternal relation of authority and submission within the Godhead.

In what follows, there simply is not sufficient space to depict all of the biblical support Grudem puts forth for the full Trinitarian doctrine that he upholds. For example, in his *Systematic Theology* he devotes extended attention to the biblical evidence for the deity of the Father, and of the Son, and of the Spirit. He holds that all three persons are coequal and coeternal as fully God, and he rightly understands this view as fully in keeping with the long-cherished Nicene and orthodox tradition he seeks to advance.[1] He also argues at length against the early heresies of Arianism and modalism, showing biblically where these fail.[2]

As important as these matters are, I will not here elaborate on these and several other areas of Grudem's Trinitarian commitments. I will instead consider the claim Grudem makes that the Scriptures reveal the Father, Son, and Holy Spirit in a relation to one another that depicts an eternal authority and submission structure, where the Father always has authority over his Son and the Spirit, the Son—while always submitting to the Father—also exerts authority over the Spirit, and the Spirit always serves the interests and facilitates the work of the Son, to the glory of God the Father.

Even here, I must narrow the focus to examining some of the main evidence Grudem puts forward for the Son's submission to the Father in eternity past. Why focus on the claim of eternal relations of authority and submission? Two reasons: (1) Many readers will know that this particular area of Grudem's Trinitarian formulation is the subject of significant discussion and even severe criticism. Some evangelical egalitarians have taken issue with this proposal for nearly three decades,[3] and more recently some Reformed complementarian theologians (along with some others) have also expressed their disagreement with this view.[4] The controversy surrounding this position, then, warrants

1. Wayne Grudem, *Systematic Theology: An Introduction to Biblical Doctrine* (Leicester, UK: Inter-Varsity Press; Grand Rapids, MI: Zondervan, 1994), 231–39.

2. Grudem, *Systematic Theology*, 241–46.

3. See, e.g., Royce G. Gruenler, *The Trinity in the Gospel of John: A Thematic Commentary on the Fourth Gospel* (Grand Rapids, MI: Baker, 1986); Gilbert Bilezikian, "Hermeneutical Bungee-Jumping: Subordination in the Godhead," *JETS* 40, no. 1 (March 1997): 57–68; Stanley J. Grenz, "Theological Foundations for Male-Female Relationships," *JETS* 41, no. 4 (December 1998): 615–30; Millard Erickson, *God in Three Persons: A Contemporary Interpretation of the Trinity* (Grand Rapids, MI: Baker, 1995); Kevin Giles, *The Trinity and Subordination: The Doctrine of God and the Contemporary Gender Debate* (Downers Grove, IL: InterVarsity Press, 2002); Kevin Giles, *Jesus and the Father: Modern Evangelicals Reinvent the Doctrine of the Trinity* (Grand Rapids, MI: Zondervan, 2006); Millard J. Erickson, *Who's Tampering with the Trinity? An Assessment of the Subordination Debate* (Grand Rapids, MI: Kregel, 2009); and Thomas H. McCall, *Which Trinity? Whose Monotheism? Philosophical and Systematic Theologians on the Metaphysics of Trinitarian Theology* (Grand Rapids, MI: Eerdmans, 2010).

4. A vibrant internet discussion began with the posting of an essay by Liam Goligher, "Is It Okay to Teach a Complementarianism Based on Eternal Subordination?," Mortification of Spin, June 3, 2016, http://www.alliancenet.org/mos/housewife-theologian/is-it-okay-to-teach-a-complementarianism-based-on-eternal-subordination#.V2glDvkrKUl. A helpful listing of blogs contributing to the online debate can be found at http://www.booksataglance.com/blog/thirtieth-updated-edition-trinity-debate-bibliography/.

particular attention to Grudem's biblical case at this point.[5] (2) Fewer readers may be aware, however, that very little response has been given to the actual biblical support that Grudem has offered. Most (not all) of the objections to Grudem's view are historical and philosophical in nature, while much of the biblical case Grudem has presented is often ignored. It seems appropriate, then, in this volume particularly, to put on display some of the biblical case Grudem has made for his position.

Grudem's Biblical Argument for Authority and Submission among the Trinitarian Persons in Eternity Past

The main published descriptions and defenses of the Trinity in Grudem's writings are the following:

- chapter 14 of his *Systematic Theology*[6]
- sections 2–4 in chapter 10 of his *Evangelical Feminism and Biblical Truth*[7]
- chapter 10, providing biblical evidence for the eternal submission of the Son to the Father, in *The New Evangelical Subordinationism?*, edited by Dennis Jowers and Wayne House[8]
- chapter 1, assessing evangelical feminists' arguments on the Trinity, in *One God in Three Persons*, edited by Bruce Ware and John Starke[9]

A careful reading of these sections of Grudem's writings devoted to the Trinity shows how deeply he is committed to unpacking and following exactly what he sees Scripture to teach regarding the

---

5. I was also named in this debate as holding essentially the same position as the one held by Wayne Grudem, viz., the eternal relations of authority and submission among the Trinitarian persons. Both of us offered some limited response in blog posts following the initial posting by Liam Goligher, which one can access through the Books at a Glance website cited above. I also have provided expanded answers to these objections as part of a chapter I've written in a three-views book, *Trinitarian Theology: Theological Models and Doctrinal Application*, ed. Keith S. Whitfield (Nashville: B&H Academic, forthcoming).

6. Wayne Grudem, "God in Three Persons: The Trinity," in Grudem, *Systematic Theology*, 226–61.

7. Wayne Grudem, "Evangelical Feminist Claims from Theology and from Ideas of Fairness and Justice," in *Evangelical Feminism and Biblical Truth: An Analysis of More Than One Hundred Disputed Questions* (Sisters, OR: Multnomah, 2004), 405–37.

8. Wayne Grudem, "Biblical Evidence for the Eternal Submission of the Son to the Father," in *The New Evangelical Subordinationism? Perspectives on the Equality of God the Father and God the Son*, ed. Dennis W. Jowers and H. Wayne House (Eugene, OR: Pickwick, 2012), 223–61.

9. Wayne Grudem, "Doctrinal Deviations in Evangelical-Feminist Arguments about the Trinity," in *One God in Three Persons: Unity of Essence, Distinctions of Persons, Implications for Life*, ed. Bruce A. Ware and John Starke (Wheaton, IL: Crossway, 2015), 17–45.

self-revelation of God as both one and three. Anyone conversant with literature on the doctrine of the Trinity can attest to how uncommon it is to see sustained biblical defenses of the doctrine. Historical and philosophical developments abound, with brief mentions of texts of Scripture. While many of these treatments are helpful and instructive, if we truly live out our evangelical (not to mention Protestant) commitment to *sola Scriptura*, we must devote careful attention to specific teachings of Scripture that help us formulate the doctrine of the Trinity, as we would in any other area of theology. Grudem has done just this, and he is to be commended for his attention to the details of the text of Scripture, even if not all will agree with his conclusions at every point.

Among the most important of his contributions on this doctrine is his sustained biblical defense of the relations of authority and submission among the Trinitarian persons. A reading of his argumentation from his work broadly yields some important categories in which he understands the self-revelation of God in Scripture to depict just this eternal authority-submission structure. As a summary of these, consider the following:

The Trinitarian Names: Father, Son, and Holy Spirit

The Father, the Son, and the Holy Spirit are coequal and coeternal, since each person possesses fully and eternally the one and undivided divine nature. As Grudem asserts, "Each member of the Trinity is fully God," and "each person fully shares in all the attributes of God."[10] But their identities as persons involve more than their full equality in nature. It is essential that we affirm also that each person is distinguishable from the other persons, lest we depart from Trinitarian monotheism to Unitarianism or modalism. To say this differently, God is both one and three—he is one in nature but three in persons, and the threeness is just as necessary to Trinitarian doctrine as is the oneness.

At the most basic level, Scripture indicates that what signifies the distinction of persons is their respective names. Of course, there is more than this, but not less. As Grudem states, the persons of the Trinity are not "Person A, Person A, Person A,"[11] nor are they friends of

---

10. Grudem, *Systematic Theology*, 248; cf. 233–39.
11. Grudem, *Evangelical Feminism and Biblical Truth*, 433.

one another, or brothers, or triplets.[12] Rather, God's self-revelation in Scripture names the three persons of the Godhead as the Father, and the Son, and the Holy Spirit. Notice two things about the names Father and Son, in particular. First, they indicate a relationship where the Father is Father only because he is Father of the Son, and the Son is Son only insofar as he is Son of the Father. In other words, this specifies a particular kind of relationship that eternally exists between these two persons. Again, they are not, by name, eternally friends or eternally brothers; rather, one is eternally Father of his Son, and the other is eternally Son of his Father.[13] Second, not only do the very names Father and Son signify intimacy of relationship and mutual sharing of vision and purpose, but throughout the Bible (e.g., Mal. 1:6) they signify that one has authority and the other submits.[14]

Grudem engages an objection sometimes made at this point that whereas authority and submission do rightly mark the relationship of fathers with young children, this is not the case in adult father-son relationships. But as Grudem notes, Scripture indicates several instances of fatherly authority in relation to adult children. He points to the Joseph account, for example, where Jacob exerts authority over his adult sons (Gen. 42:2–4, 38; 43:2, 11–13; 45:28; 46:28; 49:1–27, 29, 33), and the brothers appeal to their father's authority (even if deceptively) to try

---

12. Grudem, "Doctrinal Deviations," 19.

13. Some egalitarians have denied the assertion that Father and Son are eternal names, as claimed here. See Grudem, "Doctrinal Deviations," 28–32, for responses to this denial. Among the passages Grudem discusses in his response are Heb. 1:1–3, where the Son both creates the universe and holds it together by the word of his power, and John 3:16–17, where God (the Father) sent into the world his Son. The Son, then, refers to the second person of the Trinity's identity in eternity past, long before the incarnation.

14. It is fair to say that in Grudem's published writings to date, he has argued for the distinction between Father and Son to be seen biblically only through the authority of the Father and submission of the Son. He writes in his *Systematic Theology*, for example, "If the Son is not eternally subordinate to the Father in role, then the Father is not eternally 'Father' and the Son is not eternally 'Son'" (251). This reflects his view, until recently, that the classic doctrine of the eternal begetting of the Son is merely another way of saying that the Son is eternally Son of the Father without adopting the notion of eternal generation per se. So, what constitutes the sonship of the Son? Answer: he submits to his Father. But in this past year, both Grudem and I have now adopted as our own convictions the classic doctrine of the eternal generation of the Son. The Son is eternal Son precisely because he is eternally begotten of the Father, and the Father is eternal Father precisely because he eternally begets his own Son. Part of what contributed to our change of mind on this is a study on *monogenēs* demonstrating that it is best understood as "only begotten" and not merely as "one of a kind" or "unique" (see Charles Lee Irons, "A Lexical Defense of the Johannine 'Only-Begotten,'" in *Retrieving Eternal Generation*, ed. Fred Sanders and Scott R. Swain [Grand Rapids, MI: Zondervan, 2017], 98–116; originally "A Lexical Defense of the Eternal Generation of the 'Only-Begotten' Son" [paper delivered at the Far West Regional meeting of the Evangelical Theological Society, April 11, 2014]). Even though Grudem had argued strongly for years for the "unique" view of *monogenēs* (see app. 6 to his *Systematic Theology*, 1233–34), I know through personal conversation and he announced publicly at ETS, November 2016, that he now affirms that *monogenēs* is best understood as "only begotten."

to prevent Joseph from taking revenge (Gen. 50:16–17). Grudem also points out that adult sons who do not respect the authority of their fathers are seen as sinful—for example, the sons of Eli (1 Sam. 2:12–25) and Absalom (2 Samuel 15–17).[15] So, even though the names Father and Son refer to these Trinitarian persons analogically, it is artificial to remove from them what is everywhere in the Bible, namely, that the father leads, directs, and exerts rightful authority, whereas the son is to follow the lead of his father.

The Roles of the Father, Son, and Holy Spirit

The Father, Son, and Holy Spirit have different primary functions as revealed in Scripture. This second point flows naturally from the first. Because the Father is eternal Father, he always acts in ways that give expression to his paternal hypostatic identity as Father. And because the Son and Holy Spirit are who they are, they likewise act in ways reflecting their distinctive hypostatic identities. As Grudem states, while there is no difference at all in attributes between the Father, Son, and Spirit, since each possesses all of the attributes of the divine nature equally and fully, the Father's uniqueness is seen "in the way he *relates as Father* to the Son and Holy Spirit," and the same can be said of the other Trinitarian persons.[16]

Grudem argues this point fully aware of the appeal sometimes made to the inseparability of operations *ad extra* of the Trinitarian persons. Millard Erickson, for example, summarizes his understanding as follows: "The various works attributed to the different persons of the Trinity are in fact works of the Triune God. One member of the Godhead may in fact do this work on behalf of the three and be mentioned as the one who does that work, but all participate in what is done."[17] In his response, Grudem sees a significant measure of truth in Erickson's claim, but he also warns that seeing each Trinitarian person as participating in what each other person does can lead to a view that contradicts what we see in Scripture. Grudem writes:

> There are two senses in which I would partially agree with what Erickson says: (1) First, each person of the Trinity is fully God, and

15. Grudem, "Biblical Evidence for Eternal Submission," 230–31.
16. Grudem, *Systematic Theology*, 254.
17. Erickson, *Who's Tampering with the Trinity?*, 135.

part of the deep mystery of the Trinity is that the very being (or substance) of each person of the Trinity is equal to the whole being of God. So when one person of the Trinity is acting, it is also true, in some sense that we only understand very faintly, that the entire being of God is acting. This is because of what is sometimes called perichoresis, that each of the persons of the Trinity is somehow present "in" the other two persons. Jesus said, "the Father is in me and I am in the Father" (John 10:38).

(2) In another sense, each of the members of the Trinity fully agrees with the actions of any member of the Trinity. Thus, when the Father sent the Son into the world, both the Father and Son wholly agreed with that action, and so did the Holy Spirit.

However, Erickson seems to be saying something different. He seems to be saying that the actions of any one person of the Trinity are the actions, *not just of the whole being of God*, but *of every person in the Trinity*. And to say this comes carelessly close to denying what is taught by literally hundreds of passages of Scripture that speak of *different* actions carried out by different members of the Trinity.[18]

So Grudem argues at length that the roles of the Father, the Son, and the Spirit differ from each other in significant ways, while they are the unified works of the one God. Nonetheless, these functions or activities carried out by the three Trinitarian persons do tell us much about the identity of each, and these functions also reveal the eternal relations of authority and submission expressed in the ways in which the Triune persons relate and carry out their roles.

While nearly all would agree that the Son submits to the Father in his incarnate life and ministry on earth, some dispute that this submission stretches back to eternity past and forward to eternity future. Grudem amasses a significant display of biblical teachings and passages which show, however, that this submission of the Son to the Father is ever present. Furthermore, one never encounters anywhere in Scripture a reversal of this order. Whereas the Father commands and the Son obeys, the Father sends and the Son goes, the Father wills and the Son carries out the will of the Father, never do we see the reverse. Where does the Son send and the Father go? Where does the Son will

---

18. Grudem, "Biblical Evidence for Eternal Submission," 256, emphasis original.

and the Father carry out the will of the Son? Interestingly, we do see the Son send, and the Son will, but the one whom he sends and the one who carries out his will is never the Father, but is the Holy Spirit (e.g., John 15:26; 16:12–15). Here are some of the ways in which we see the authority of the Father and submission of the Son exhibited in eternity past:

1. *The plan of salvation is designed by the Father, to be carried out through the obedience of the Son and the Spirit.* At a basic level, all agree that there are distinct Trinitarian roles in the execution of the plan of salvation. The most obvious examples are these: the Son is the Trinitarian person who becomes incarnate, and the Spirit is the Trinitarian person who descends on the church at Pentecost. But what is not always acknowledged is that the differences in roles involve not only the execution of the plan of salvation but also its very design. Grudem quotes Ephesians 1:3–5 and then comments:

> This passage speaks of acts of God "before the foundation of the world." Long before the Son's Incarnation, the Father is the one who *chooses* and *predestines*, and the Son is already designated as the one who would come in obedience to the Father in order to be our Savior and earn our adoption as God's children.
>
> It does not say "the Father and Son chose us." It says the Father chose us in the Son. It does not say, "The Father suggested some people for salvation and the Son agreed on some and disagreed on others." It says the Father chose us in the Son. This happened before the foundation of the world and it indicates a unique authority for the Father—an authority to determine the entire history of salvation for all time, for the whole world.[19]

The plan of salvation is sometimes spoken of as if it were the collective decision of the three Trinitarian persons in eternity past, designing together what would take place. But is this what the Bible teaches? Everywhere one looks, one sees the plan of the Father before the foundation of the world, a plan implemented through the sending of the Son and the Spirit. Consider other texts to which Grudem appeals:

---

19. Grudem, "Biblical Evidence for Eternal Submission," 232, emphasis original.

- Ephesians 1:9–11, in which the role of planning, purposing, willing, and intending all of history that results in the summing of all things in Christ belongs to the Father
- Ephesians 3:9–11, where the eternal purpose of the Father has been to bring about a union of Jew and Gentile in one body in Christ
- Romans 8:29–30, where the Father predestines us to be conformed to the likeness of his Son
- 2 Timothy 1:9, where before the ages had begun, the Father's own purpose and grace were given to those he would call, that they might be "in Christ" in the end
- 1 Peter 1:20, where the Father fore-favored ("foreknew") his Son before the foundation of the world to be the One who would come to bring about our salvation.[20]

Now, to say that the plan of salvation was the design of the Father is not to suggest that the Son or Spirit differed with or objected to this plan. On the contrary, it always is the heart of the Son to embrace the will of the Father, and the heart of the Spirit to embrace the will of the Son as the Son receives and carries out this plan from the Father. Though there is full and heartfelt agreement among the Trinitarian persons on the plan of salvation—and in this sense one can rightly say that the plan of salvation is the one plan of all three—Scripture nonetheless indicates an order or initiation or design attributed to the Father's plan for all of history, one involving the Son's carrying out the will of his Father. Hear these helpful words from Grudem:

> Of course, the Son was in full agreement with the Father regarding this eternal plan of salvation. We should never confuse the idea of the Father's authority with any thought that the Son disagreed with the Father's plan or reluctantly submitted to the Father's plan. Jesus said, "My food is to do the will of him who sent me and to accomplish his work" (John 4:34). He was the true fulfillment of the words of the Psalmist who said, "I delight to do your will, O my God; your law is within my heart" (Ps 40:8). The Son and the Spirit fully agreed with the plans of the Father. But if we are to be faithful to the meaning of . . . Eph 1:3–5, we still must say that in the eternal councils

---

20. See especially Grudem's discussion in "Doctrinal Deviations," 37–41.

of the Trinity, there was a role of planning, directing, initiating, and choosing, that belonged specifically to the Father.[21]

2. *Creation is accomplished by the Father, through the Son and Spirit.* Although Christ is spoken of several times as Creator of all that is, these very contexts indicate that the Son created as directed by the Father. The language of "from the Father, through the Son," applies extensively to the work of the Father and Son, and this certainly is the case in regard to creation. Grudem writes, "God the Father spoke the creative words to bring the universe into being. But it was God the Son, the eternal Word of God, who carried out these creative decrees."[22] Examining the distinct yet unified roles of the Trinitarian persons in creation, Grudem cites and discusses John 1:1–3; 1 Corinthians 8:6; Colossians 1:16–17; Hebrews 1:1–2; and Psalm 33:6. His most developed discussion appears in his chapter "Biblical Evidence for the Eternal Submission of the Son to the Father." After considering the passages listed above, he comments:

> In the process of creating the universe, the role of initiating, of leading, belongs not to all three members of the Trinity equally, but to the Father. The Father created through the Son. This cannot be a submission limited to the Incarnation . . . , for it was in place *at the first moment of creation.* The Son did not create through the Father, nor would that have been appropriate to the personal differences signified by the names Father and Son. . . . All things (that is, the entire universe) come "from" the Father (who directs and initiates) and "through" the Son (who carries out the will of the Father). This was the pattern in planning salvation prior to creation, and this is also the pattern in the process of creating the world.[23]

I think it is worth asking, Is Grudem reading too much into the statements of 1 Corinthians 8:6 (that creation comes "from" the Father and "through" the Son) and Hebrews 1:1–2 (that the Father has spoken now through his Son "through whom" he, the Father, also made the world)? Do these passages really convey an authority of the Father and a submission of the Son? This is a valid question and one important

---

21. Grudem, "Biblical Evidence for Eternal Submission," 232–33.
22. Grudem, *Systematic Theology,* 249.
23. Grudem, "Biblical Evidence for Eternal Submission," 243, emphasis original.

to consider. In response, I would ask, Why would the biblical authors state creation in precisely these terms if they did *not* mean to convey an ultimate authority of the Father in creation?

Obviously, they could have spoken of creation coming from the one God without specifying an order of divine agency relating to the persons. Clearly, Genesis 1:1 was understood this way for centuries until Trinitarian ways of thinking were developed, due to the coming of the Son from the Father. The fact that the New Testament authors do not speak of creation simply from the one God with no hypostatic distinctions is due, in my judgment, to two things. First, the high Christology of the New Testament authors led them to focus primary attention on Christ as the Creator, that is, as the one who directly brought into existence all that is created. Clearly John 1:3 and Colossians 1:16 do just this, and both are in contexts in which the deity of the Son has been declared and now is defended through the doctrine of divine creation through the Son. Second—and remarkably, given their high Christology—the New Testament authors do not also assert Christ as the sole agent, or as the ultimate agent, standing behind creation. In all these texts, ultimacy goes to the Father, who stands behind creation in some unique fashion as the one who planned and designed all that would come to be; and yet the Father executes his plan through the Son, who is given the role of bringing into existence the whole of this created order. So, although biblical writers could have spoken of creation as coming simply from the one God, or they could have indicated a symmetry in creation coming from the Father and the Son (with, presumably, the Spirit included) in which no order of agency was specified, they did not do this. Instead they uniformly indicate a primacy of the Father in creation, from whom creation comes ultimately. And yet the Father grants to the Son the role of activating that divine creation design in bringing into existence all that is.

I would argue that Grudem is correct, then, in seeing authority and submission exhibited in the way creation happens, according to the writers of the New Testament. For creation to come about "from" the Father and "through" the Son says more, in my judgment, than merely that both Father and Son were involved together and in unity in bringing creation about. Certainly this is true, but it misses the point of the wording found particularly in 1 Corinthians 8:6 and Hebrews 1:2. We are not told that creation is "from the Father and the Son," or that the "Father and Son" created the world. No, creation occurs as "from the Father" and "through the Son," or by the agency of the Son "through whom" the Father created the world. So any attempt at symmetry here fails; these texts do not say merely that creation comes "from the Father and the Son." Another evidence of this failure is that one simply cannot rightly reverse the order given in these texts. That is, one cannot rightly assert that creation occurs "from the Son" and "through the Father" or by the agency of the Father "through whom" the Son created the world. Absolutely not. These texts require the primacy of the Father in which the Son carries out the work of creation as given him from the Father. Therefore, it seems inescapable that the Father stands as ultimate (i.e., the one "from" whom creation has come), as the one who plans and ordains the whole of the created order, and the Son does in eternity past what we see over and again in the incarnation: he does the work the Father gives him to do. Authority and submission are involved, then, in the manner by which the one triune God creates.

3. *The Father's sending the Son into the world and the Spirit's being sent by the Father and the Son both indicate an authority attached to the "sending" and a submission required of the ones "sent."* In Trinitarian discussions, some have sought to explain the Father's sending of the Son into the world entirely as the outworking *ad extra* of the eternal modes of subsistence *ad intra*. That is, because the Father begets the Son eternally (*ad intra*), so the Father is also the one who sends his Son in history (*ad extra*). And while the Spirit proceeds from the Father and the Son eternally (*ad intra*), so the Father and Son send the Spirit at Pentecost in history (*ad extra*).

While I agree with this connection between the eternal modes of subsistence and the economic modes of operation, I think this explanation, though true, fails to give a full accounting of what the Scriptures point to in the Father's sending of the Son into the world. After all, it is the Father's deep love for sinners that moves him to send his Son. Both John 3:16 and 1 John 4:10 indicate just this. And it is the Father's purpose, in sending his Son, that people be saved, not condemned (John 3:17). A deeply personal and passionate motive of love stands behind the Father's sending of his Son, and a specific purpose that can only be accomplished through the work of his Son likewise accounts for why the Father sent his dearly beloved Son to die for sinners. Because the Father's motive of love and purpose to save are what stand behind his choice to send his Son, it surely follows that he thereby exerts authority in so doing.

After commenting on John 3:16–17 as a sample passage for the many Johannine and other New Testament texts speaking of the Father's sending of his Son, Grudem adds:

> The Father *sending* the Son into the world implies an authority that the Father had prior to the Son's humbling himself and becoming a man. This is because to have the authority to send someone means to have a *greater authority* than the one who is sent. He was first "sent" as Son, and then he obeyed and humbled himself and came. By that action he showed that he was subject to the authority of the Father before he came to earth.[24]

Some have objected to this understanding, arguing that the Father's sending of the Son does not indicate a greater authority of the Father over the Son; it rather signifies only that the Son came as the messenger of the Father, heralding his Word. Grudem cites Kevin Giles at this point, who has sought to interpret the Father's sending of the Son merely through the lens of "messenger" (Heb. *shaliah*) with no particular authority of the sender or submission/obedience of the one sent.[25] Grudem replies:

> Giles simply misunderstands the Jewish *shaliach* concept: (a) It refers to the authority of the messenger *with respect to the recipients of the message*: the messenger carries the authority of the sender (such as the king). The concept is never used to argue that the messenger has the same authority as the king who sent him! (b) The concept is heavily rooted in many Old Testament verses that speak of God "sending" the prophets to the people (Exod. 3:14 God said to Moses, "I AM WHO I AM." And he said, "Say this to the people of Israel, 'I AM has sent [Heb. *shaliah*] me to you.'"). Surely this does not mean that Moses is claiming to be equal in authority to the great I AM, to God himself! Nor would any of the prophets claim this. When rightly understood, the Jewish "messenger" concept

---

24. Grudem, "Biblical Evidence for Eternal Submission," 244, emphasis original.
25. Giles, *Jesus and the Father*, 119–20.

only strengthens the idea of greater authority for the sender than the one who is sent.[26]

The Father's authority in sending the Son provides more evidence that the Father's authority stretches back as far as Scripture allows us to see—to the very decision of the Father, before the foundation of the world, that he would save sinners through the life, death, and resurrection of his Son. That the Father had this authority and that the Son willingly and joyfully embraced this will of the Father indicate an authority-and-submission relationship within the Trinity in eternity past.[27]

Conclusion

In the preceding discussion, we've seen a distinction in roles among the Trinitarian persons that could be summarized as follows: the Father uniformly takes the role of initiating, planning, designing, directing; whereas the Son embraces, follows, submits, obeys, assents; and the Spirit supports, empowers, assists, and carries forward. But it is exactly here that a very important question arises, one that helps bring clarity to the issue of whether the Trinitarian relations of authority and submission are indeed eternal. As Grudem states it, the question is this: "But why do the persons of the Trinity take these different roles in relating to creation?" He continues:

Was it accidental or arbitrary? Could God the Father have come instead of God the Son to die for our sins? Could the Holy Spirit have sent God the Father to die for our sins, and then sent God the Son to apply redemption to us?

No, it does not seem that these things could have happened, for the role of commanding, directing, and sending is appropriate to the position of the Father after whom all human fatherhood is patterned (Eph 3:14–15). And the role of obeying, going as the Father sends, and revealing God to us is appropriate to the role of the Son, who is also called the Word of God (cf. John 1:1–5, 14, 18; 17:4; Phil. 2:5–11). These roles could not have been reversed or the

26. Grudem, "Biblical Evidence for Eternal Submission," 245.
27. For further discussion on the sending of the Son by the Father, see also Christopher W. Cowan, "'I Always Do What Pleases Him': The Father and Son in the Gospel of John," in Ware and Starke, *One God in Three Persons*, 47–64.

Father would have ceased to be the Father and the Son would have ceased to be the Son. And by analogy from that relationship, we may conclude that the role of the Holy Spirit is similarly one that was appropriate to the relationship he had with the Father and the Son before the world was created.[28]

If the Scriptures do indeed present to us the self-revelation of God, and if everything in the Scriptures depicts the Father, and the Son, and the Spirit in a way that distinguishes their roles in the manner we have seen above, then it follows that the Father, Son, and Spirit relate eternally to one another in a relation of authority and submission within the Godhead. Abundant biblical testimony has led Grudem to this conclusion. And while all that is argued on this issue is consistent with the historic position of the church, what drives Grudem more than anything else to adopt this view is simple: the Bible tells him so.

---

28. Grudem, *Systematic Theology*, 250.

PART 2

*BIBLICAL
STUDIES*

6

Across the Kidron

Reading the Psalms with David and Jesus

John DelHousaye

At the Bible's center, the Psalms express a unique relationship between God and a people who identify with King David (r. 1010–970 BC) and, later, Jesus Christ. The American archeologist James Pritchard collected "Hymns and Prayers" from around the Ancient Near East.[1] They have similar themes and language, but an important difference: David's neighbors speak to gods, but their gods never respond. In the Psalms, the king often expresses fear of abandonment, yet God is not silent. The king's words come from a broken heart on fire for God's presence.

Jesus cited the Psalms more than any other book in the Bible. After his suffering and resurrection, Jesus returned to his disciples and "opened their minds to understand" them before ascending to the Father (Luke 24:44–45). Throughout the New Testament we find this unique way of reading the Psalms: David prays for God's people, who experience life's joys and sufferings, and he is allowed by the Holy Spirit to see their common salvation in Christ, the Messiah, who

1. James B. Pritchard, ed., *Ancient Near Eastern Texts Relating to the Old Testament*, 3rd ed. (Princeton: Princeton University Press, 1969), 365–401.

appropriates the prayers to show their fulfillment in his suffering and glory. As we are united to Christ and led by the Spirit, the prayers of David and Jesus become our own through their faithfulness on the way to glory. The Psalms are the words of David, Jesus, and God's people.

David

David is the most fully developed, complex personality in the Old Testament.[2] At least seventy-three of the 150 psalms are attributed to the king.[3] Except for Moses (Psalm 90) and some anonymous psalmists, the other contributors are part of his entourage.[4] We also have something like an ancient biography in three books (1 Sam. 16:1–31; 2 Sam.; 1 Kings 1:1–2:12) that is retold in a fourth (1 Chron. 11:1–29:30).[5] The literary critic Robert Alter (b. 1935) notes, "The story of David is probably the greatest single narrative representation in antiquity of a human life evolving by slow stages through time, shaped and altered by the pressures of political life, public institutions, family, the impulses of body and spirit, [and] the eventual sad decay of the flesh."[6] The Scottish minister Andrew Bonar (1810–1892) draws out a theological implication: "It was for this end that God led David the round of all human conditions, that he might catch the spirit proper to every one, and utter it according to the truth."[7]

God's people may come to the Psalms with any emotion or life situation and see a mirror of their soul.[8] Those returning to God often

---

2. So also David Wolpe, *David: The Divided Heart* (New Haven, CT: Yale University Press, 2014), x.

3. See Psalms 3–9; 11–32; 34–41; 51–65; 68–70; 86; 91*; 101; 103; 104*; 108–10; 122; 124; 131; 133; 138–45. The asterisks mark where the Old Greek translation attributed Davidic authorship.

4. The other named contributors are Solomon (Psalms 72; 127); the priests Jeduthun (Psalms 39; 62; 77), Heman (Psalm 88), Ethan (Psalm 89), Asaph (Psalms 50; 73–83); and the sons of Korah (Psalms 42; 44–49; 84–85; 87–88).

5. See the contributions in *The Fate of King David: The Past and Present of a Biblical Icon*, ed. Tod Linafelt, Timothy Beal, and Claudia V. Camp (New York: T&T Clark, 2010).

6. Robert Alter, *The David Story: A Translation with Commentary of 1 and 2 Samuel* (New York: Norton, 1999), ix.

7. Andrew Bonar, *Christ and His Church in the Book of Psalms* (Grand Rapids, MI: Kregel, 1978), vii.

8. Athanasius (ca. 295–d. 373), bishop of Alexandria, wrote a letter to Marcellinus that established the Christian approach to the Psalms. The text can be read in *Athanasius: The Life of Antony and the Letter to Marcellinus* (New York: Paulist, 1980), 101–30. Marcellinus, a deacon, had become ill and was taking the down time for Bible study. He wanted to learn "the meaning contained in each psalm." Athanasius shows how the Psalms mirror "the emotions of each soul" (chaps. 2, 10). They are like a garden with fruit for every season. Most of the letter pairs each psalm to a specific life experience (chaps. 14–26). John Calvin (1509–1564) similarly emphasizes the range of emotion in the Psalms. Reading is cathartic, a release from "all the distracting emotions with which the minds of men are wont to be agitated" (*Commentary on the Book of the Psalms*, trans. James Anderson [Grand Rapids, MI: Eerdmans, 1963], xxxvii).

struggle in their prayer because they do not understand their emotional state—"Why are you cast down, O my soul, / and why are you in turmoil within me?" (Ps. 42:5, 11; 43:5)—or they presume that one has to feel a certain way before one may talk with God.[9] David provides the language of the heart and models honest worship.

Several psalms have inscriptions that relate the prayers to David's life.[10] They usually indicate times of crisis:

- when he fled from Absalom his son (3:1)
- concerning the words of Cush, a Benjamite (7:1)
- on the day when the Lord rescued David from the hand of all his enemies, and from the hand of Saul (18:1)
- at the dedication of the temple (30:1)
- when David changed his judgment before Abimelech, so that he drove him out, and he went away (34:1)
- when Nathan the prophet went to David, after the king had gone in to Bathsheba (51:1)
- when Doeg, the Edomite, came and told Saul, "David has come to the house of Ahimelech" (52:1)
- when the Ziphites went and asked Saul, "Is not David hiding among us?" (54:1)
- when the Philistines seized David in Gath (56:1)
- when David fled from Saul, in the cave (57:1)
- when Saul sent men to watch David's house in order to kill him (59:1)
- when David strove with Aram-naharaim and Aram-zobah, and when Joab on his return struck down twelve thousand of Edom in the Valley of Salt (60:1)
- when he was in the wilderness of Judah (63:1)
- when he was in the cave (142:1)

The king was not spared the consequences of living in a fallen world. He was hounded by King Saul and betrayed by his son Absalom.

---

9. Pss. 42:5, 11; 43:5.
10. Pss. 3:1; 7:1; 18:1; 30:1; 34:1; 51:1; 52:1; 54:1; 56:1; 57:1; 59:1; 60:1; 63:1; 142:1. The historical relationship of these inscriptions to the psalms is debated, but the matter is irrelevant to my argument. We find inscriptions in the Old Greek and Dead Sea Scrolls, and this means that at least some of them were common before Christ.

The inscription for Psalm 51, "When Nathan the prophet went to him, after he had gone in to Bathsheba," memorializes David's own greatest season of failure. He confesses,

> Against you, you only, have I sinned
>   and done what is evil in your sight,
> so that you may be justified in your words
>   and blameless in your judgment. (51:4)

David sinned against God, failed to offer a godly example to the next generation, and brought great suffering to his community. The Bible presents sin, a willful defiance of God's will, as the fundamental problem in the God-human relationship. The apostle Paul cites this confession in Romans:

> Then what advantage has the Jew? Or what is the value of circumcision? Much in every way. To begin with, the Jews were entrusted with the oracles of God. What if some were unfaithful? Does their faithlessness nullify the faithfulness of God? By no means! Let God be true though every one were a liar, as it is written,
>
> > "*That you may be justified in your words,*
> >   *and prevail when you are judged.*" (3:1–4)[11]

David speaks for his people (in the same letter, he is quoted as chiding Israel for their unbelief[12]), but the confession is part of the apostle's larger argument that everyone is a sinner before God. After introducing the solution—Jesus Christ, a Messiah who dies in the place of God's people and then shares his resurrection and justification before God—Paul cites David's gratitude for receiving mercy:

> Blessed are those whose lawless deeds are forgiven,
>   and whose sins are covered;
> blessed is the man against whom the Lord will not count his sin.
>   (Rom. 4:7–8, citing Ps. 32:1–2)

The king now represents any sinner overwhelmed by God's grace.

---

11. Occasional italics within Scripture quotations in this chapter have been added to alert readers to embedded citations of psalms in the New Testament.
12. Rom. 11:9–10, citing Ps. 68:23.

Two moments actualized David's special relationship with God. When Saul fell out of favor with God, "Samuel took the horn of oil and anointed him in the midst of his brothers. And the Spirit of the Lord rushed upon David from that day forward" (1 Sam. 16:13). This allowed God to speak through him, like an oracle, and for David to see part of God's plan. God also made a covenant with the king—namely, that one from his family would represent God's people forever (2 Sam. 7:4–16; Ps. 89:3). But after several evil descendants, David's house fell to the Babylonians (586/587 BC). Instead of losing faith in God, many looked forward to a messiah.[13]

Messiah

The Hebrew word for "messiah" (*mashiah*), often translated in Greek as *christos*, which in turn is transliterated in the Bible as "Christ," occurs ten times in the Psalms.[14] Some claim *messiah* refers only to God's people as anointed collectively,[15] but we should avoid a false dichotomy. "Anointed one," the meaning of the epithet, was applied to Israel's kings and most naturally refers to a descendant who represents his people before God. Before Jesus, we find a fairly consistent messianic expectation: God "is king; he has appointed an earthly vice-regent who represents his heavenly rule on earth; the earthly vice-regent and his people travail against the rebellious of the earth."[16] Psalms of Solomon, a Jewish work that was probably completed during the reign of Herod the Great (40–4 BC), looks forward to the "Lord Christ" (*christos kyrios*, 17.32), a son of David, who fulfills God's promises to his ancestor (17.21, 24).[17] After ousting the Romans

---

13. Brevard S. Childs, *Introduction to the Old Testament as Scripture* (Philadelphia: Fortress, 1979), 516. See also William C. Pohl IV, "A Messianic Reading of Psalm 89: A Canonical and Intertextual Study," *JETS* 58, no. 3 (September 2015): 507–25.

14. See Pss. 2:2; 18:51; 20:7; 28:8; 84:10; 89:39, 52; 105:15; 132:10, 17. Jesus alludes to the final occurrence (John 5:32–35).

15. See Marko Marttila, *Collective Reinterpretation in the Psalms* (Tübingen: Mohr Siebeck, 2006), 178.

16. Michael K. Snearly, *The Return of the King: Messianic Expectation in Book V of the Psalter* (London: Bloomsbury, 2016), 1.

17. The Greek text for the citations in this paragraph is from Robert B. Wright, *The Psalms of Solomon: A Critical Edition of the Greek Text* (New York: T&T Clark, 2007), 176–201. James Charlesworth describes the seventeenth psalm in this collection as "the *locus classicus* for belief in a Davidic Messiah" (foreword to Wright, *Psalms of Solomon*, vii). The reading χριστὸς κυρίου in the Rahlfs edition is an unjustified emendation. The Greek and Syriac manuscripts read as nominatives (Wright, *Psalms of Solomon*, 194). See also J. Schaper, *Eschatology in the Greek Psalter*, WUNT 2/76 (Tübingen: Mohr Siebeck, 1995), 72–76.

(17.22, 24–25) and the corrupt Jewish leadership (17.36), retrieving the *diaspora*, and restoring tribal divisions (17.28), the Messiah will establish God's kingdom as an independent state. Like David, he is a shepherd (17.40) imbued with "the spirit of holiness" (17.37). But, unlike the king, he is sinless (17.36). The peoples (Gentiles) will also come (17.31, 34), although the Messiah's relationship to these outsiders is ambiguous. He will judge them—purging "Jerusalem from Gentiles" (17.22)—but they will also come to Jerusalem to worship (see Isa. 2:1–5). He "will have Gentile peoples serving him under his yoke" (17.30). Yet the psalmist claims he "will be merciful to all the Gentiles" (17.34).

Head

The New Testament opens with the claim that Jesus Christ (Messiah) is "son of David" (Matt. 1:1), although the relationship is complex.[18] On the one hand, Jesus challenges the messianism of his day by distancing himself from the title (Mark 12:35–37). He avoids violence in his ministry and pursues the unrighteous outsider. As the parables teach, the kingdom of God will not conform to human expectation. Jesus anticipates the inclusion of the Gentiles (Matt. 8:5–13; John 12:20–26).

On the other hand, Jesus appropriates King David's words and actions. The Psalms are repeated and completed in Christ.[19] The opening threat of accountability for the wicked (Ps. 1:5) becomes the finale of the parable of the net: "So it will be at the end of the age. The angels will come out and separate the evil from the righteous" (Matt. 13:49).[20] They will stand before Jesus, who will use David's words against them: "Depart from me, you workers of lawlessness" (Matt. 7:23, citing Ps. 6:8). But in the parable of the tenants, the first psalm's description of "fruit in its season" is promised to God's people: "He will put those wretches to a miserable death and let out the vineyard to other tenants who will give him the fruits in their seasons" (Matt. 21:41, alluding to Ps. 1:3).[21] We find a similar promise through allusion in the Beatitudes:

---

18. Matthew intends the messianic sense ("who is called Christ," Matt. 1:16).

19. "David's story . . . helped shape, in no small way, the gospel conceptions of Jesus, who is presented as his messianic descendent" (Linafelt, Beal, and Camp, *Fate of King David*, xiii).

20. The allusion is recognized by the *Loci Citati Vel Allegati* in the Nestle-Aland *Novum Testamentum Graece*.

21. This is noted in *Loci Citati Vel Allegati*.

"Blessed are the meek, for they shall inherit the earth" (Matt. 5:5). Earlier, David promised:

In just a little while, the wicked will be no more;
    though you look carefully at his place, he will not be there.
But the meek shall inherit the land
    and delight themselves in abundant peace. (Ps. 37:10–11)

The king suffered betrayal, and Jesus applies the relevant psalm to Judas Iscariot (Ps. 41:9; John 13:18). Facing an unjust death, Jesus cries, "Now is my soul troubled" (John 12:27, citing Ps. 6:3).[22] In Gethsemane, he echoes a refrain that runs through the forty-second and forty-third psalms: "My soul is very sorrowful" (Mark 14:34; see Ps. 42:5, 11; 43:5). On the cross, he utters two psalms: "My God, my God, why have you forsaken me?" (Mark 15:34, citing Ps. 22:1); "Father, into your hands I commit my spirit!" (Luke 23:46, citing Ps. 31:5). David's words are actualized in two ways. The king prayed in fear of death; Jesus actually dies with the psalms on his lips. The Father does not merely respond in word but actually raises Jesus from the dead.

The Psalms are to the Gospels as they are to the story of David: they disclose the mind of the king "in the process of becoming the mind of Christ."[23] David and his distant Son are united in their love for God the Father. We see this in the Lord's Prayer ("Our Father"), which echoes David's final prayer: "Blessed are you, O LORD, the God of Israel *our father*, forever and ever" (1 Chron. 29:10).

Body

In our earliest witnesses, Jesus ends the prayer he gave the disciples with "deliver us from evil" (Matt. 6:13). Later tradition probably added "For yours is the kingdom and the power and the glory forever. Amen,"[24] in homage to David's prayer:

---

22. The wording is very similar to the Old Greek: ἡ ψυχή μου τετάρακται // ἡ ψυχή μου ἐταράχθη σφόδρα (Ps. 6:4).
23. Donald Sheehan, *The Psalms of David* (Eugene, OR: Wipf & Stock, 2013), xxv.
24. Ὅτι σοῦ ἐστιν ἡ βασιλεία καὶ ἡ δύναμις καὶ ἡ δόξα εἰς τοὺς αἰῶνας. Ἀμήν. A few manuscripts simply add "Amen." The most elaborate is from the miniscule 1253: "For yours is the Kingdom of the Father and of the Son and of the Holy Spirit forever. Amen."

> Yours, O LORD, is the greatness and *the power* and *the glory* and the victory and the majesty, for all that is in the heavens and in the earth is yours. Yours is *the kingdom*, O LORD, and you are exalted as head above all. Both riches and honor come from you, and you rule over all. In your hand are power and might, and in your hand it is to make great and to give strength to all. And now we thank you, our God, and praise your glorious name. (1 Chron. 29:11–13)[25]

Apparently, later disciples heard the cue and strengthened the link between the two prayers. A form of the addition occurs in the Didache: "For yours is the power and the glory forever" (8.2); a prayer for the Eucharist (Communion) immediately follows: "We give you thanks, our Father, for the holy vine of David your servant" (9.1).[26]

Identifying Jesus with David, the man who felt all things, complements the incarnation, as the author of Hebrews makes explicit:

> When Christ came into the world, he said,
>
>> "Sacrifices and offerings you have not desired,
>>> but a body have you prepared for me;
>> in burnt offerings and sin offerings
>>> you have taken no pleasure.
>> Then I said, 'Behold, I have come to do your will, O God,
>>> as it is written of me in the scroll of the book.'"
>
> When he said above, "You have neither desired nor taken pleasure in sacrifices and offerings and burnt offerings and sin offerings" (these are offered according to the law), then he added, "Behold, I have come to do your will." (Heb. 10:5–9, citing Ps. 40:6–8)

This bond helps explain how "in every respect" Jesus "has been tempted as we are, yet without sin," a messianic expectation (Heb. 4:15). Christ did not rebel against God but identified with a sinful king who represented God's people.

---

25. This is noted in the textual apparatus of the 28th edition of the Nestle-Aland text. See also Graham N. Stanton, *Jesus and Gospel* (Cambridge: Cambridge University Press, 2004), 8–9.

26. *Acts of Paul* notes that "psalms of David" were recited alongside the Eucharist (9) (Edgar Hennecke, *New Testament Apocrypha*, ed. Wilhelm Schneemelcher and R. McL. Wilson, trans. Ernest Best, David Hill, George Ogg, G. C. Stead, and R. McL. Wilson, 2 vols. [Philadelphia: Westminster, 1964], 2:380).

For this reason, Jesus brings his disciples into the repetition of the David story:

> One Sabbath he was going through the grainfields, and as they made their way, his disciples began to pluck heads of grain. And the Pharisees were saying to him, "Look, why are they doing what is not lawful on the Sabbath?" And he said to them, "Have you never read what David did, when he was in need and was hungry, he and those who were with him: how he entered the house of God, in the time of Abiathar the high priest, and ate the bread of the Presence, which it is not lawful for any but the priests to eat, and also gave it to those who were with him?" (Mark 2:23–26, alluding to 1 Sam. 21:1–6)

Jesus compared them to David's "young men" (1 Sam. 21:4), a retinue of soldiers who shared in the crises of the king but also in his victory and blessing. The anecdote anticipates the Lord's Supper: "And as they were eating, he took bread, and after blessing it broke it and *gave it to them*, and said, 'Take; this is my body'" (Mark 14:22, echoing 2:26). This action inaugurated the "new covenant," which completed the promise God made to David (Luke 22:20).

Augustine and Martin Luther

The close relationship between David, Jesus, and God's people has been recognized throughout church history. Augustine and Martin Luther serve as examples.

Augustine (354–430) provides the longest Patristic commentary on the Psalms, *Enarrationes in Psalmos* ("Conversations in the Psalms"). The work began as sermons in Carthage before large audiences. Augustine initially labored to isolate the voices in the Psalms but came to see their unity. The "I" of the Psalter is what he called the "whole Christ" (*totus Christus*): "The voice of Christ and His Church was well-nigh the only voice to be heard in the Psalms."[27] To express this union, he appropriated Paul's description of Jesus as the Head and the church as his body: "Everywhere diffused throughout is that man whose Head is above, and whose members are below. We ought to recognize his voice

---

27. "Vix est ut in Psalmis inveniamus vocem nisi Christi et Ecclesiae" (Augustine, *Exposition of Psalm 58*). See Joseph Carola, *Augustine of Hippo: The Role of the Laity in Ecclesial Reconciliation* (Rome: Pontificia Università Gregoriana, 2005), 157–217.

in all the Psalms."[28] During the siege of Hippo, the dying Augustine asked for the seven penitential psalms to be copied and hung beside his bed, so that he could read, weep, and repent.[29]

The Seven Penitential Psalms (1517, rev. 1525) was the first book Martin Luther (1483–1546) prepared for publication.[30] Lecturing on them at the University of Wittenberg contributed to his understanding of justification through faith alone. An Augustinian monk, Luther presumed *totus Christus*: "In the Book of Psalms," he claimed, "we have not the life of one of the saints only, but we have the experience of Christ himself, the head of all the saints."[31] Since Christ enters us in faith, we feel his "sighs and groans" in the face of temptation.[32]

Psalm 2

This Davidic, Head-and-body reading can be shown in how the New Testament writers appropriate the second psalm:

Why do the nations rage
  and the peoples plot in vain?
The kings of the earth set themselves,
  and the rulers take counsel together,
    against the LORD and against his Anointed [*Messiah*], saying,
"Let us burst their bonds apart
  and cast away their cords from us."

He who sits in the heavens laughs;
  the Lord holds them in derision.
Then he will speak to them in his wrath,
  and terrify them in his fury, saying,

28. Augustine, *Exposition of Psalm 43*. This does not seem to be an idiosyncratic reading in Africa. Tertullian writes, "Almost all the Psalms are spoken in the person of Christ, being addressed by the Son to the Father—by Christ to God" (*omnes poene [pené] Psalmi Christi personam sustinent.—Filium ad Patrem, id est Christum ad Deum verba facientem repraesentant*). This was an especially popular quote in the nineteenth century. See, for example, George Horne, *A Commentary on the Book of Psalms* (James Anderson, 1822), xxv.

29. Brian Stock, *Augustine the Reader: Meditation, Self-Knowledge, and the Ethics of Interpretation* (Cambridge: Harvard University Press, 1996), 11, citing Possidius, Vita S. Augustini 31 (Patrologia Latina 32.63).

30. Jaroslav Pelikan and Daniel E. Poellot, eds., *Luther's Works* (St. Louis, MO: Concordia, 1958), xiv.

31. Martin Luther, *A Manual of the Book of Psalms*, trans. Henry Cole (London: Seeley and Burnside, 1837), 5.

32. Luther, *Manual*, 6. Luther emphasized a union of faith over ontology (Brian Brock, *Singing the Ethos of God: On the Place of Christian Ethics in Scripture* [Grand Rapids, MI: Eerdmans, 2007], 202).

"As for me, I have set my King
on Zion, my holy hill."

I will tell of the decree:
The LORD said to me, "You are my Son;
today I have begotten you.
Ask of me, and I will make the nations your heritage,
and the ends of the earth your possession.
You shall break them with a rod of iron
and dash them in pieces like a potter's vessel."

Now therefore, O kings, be wise;
be warned, O rulers of the earth.
Serve the LORD with fear,
and rejoice with trembling.
Kiss the Son,
lest he be angry, and you perish in the way,
for his wrath is quickly kindled.
Blessed are all who take refuge in him.

The Words of King David

The psalm lacks an inscription in our Hebrew and Greek manuscripts, but Luke presumes that David, led by the Holy Spirit, is the speaker (Acts 4:25).[33] This identification is perhaps not surprising because of the king's influence throughout the Psalms. But in the context of Luke's presentation, Davidic authorship was the understanding of the first believers, who were taught by the apostles (Acts 2:42), who had been guided into this way of reading by Jesus after his resurrection. In the psalm, God echoes the promise he made to the king: "I will be to him a father, and he shall be to me a son" (2 Sam. 7:14).[34]

But the content of Psalm 2 does not describe any historical moment when Israel ruled the nations.[35] David is not writing about himself or any of his sons before the Babylonian captivity, unless the language is not intended to be taken literally. By the time of Jesus, the second

---

33. Luke is also aware of its order (Acts 13:33).
34. Tremper Longman, "The Messiah: Explorations in the Law and Writings," in *The Messiah in the New and Old Testaments*, ed. Stanley Porter (Grand Rapids, MI: Eerdmans, 2007), 13–34, especially 17.
35. Longman, "The Messiah," 18.

psalm was read messianically.[36] Indeed, for the first time in the Psalms, the king speaks of a "messiah," although this is somewhat obscured by the translation "Anointed" (Ps. 2:2). The Greek translation used by the early church reads "Christ" (*christos*). So the Holy Spirit allowed David to see the salvation of God's people in Christ, which fomented human rebellion.

When the king grew old, he nevertheless foresaw the body of Christ overcome corruption. Preaching the gospel to Gentiles at Antioch in Pisidia, Paul cites the second psalm, "You are my Son, / today I have begotten you" (Acts 13:33) and applies it to the resurrection with a link to a psalm that Peter cited to Jews at Pentecost: "You will not let your Holy One see corruption" (Acts 13:35, echoing 2:27, a citation of Ps. 16:10). Peter expresses the special reading that has occupied our study:

> Brothers, I may say to you with confidence about the patriarch David that he both died and was buried, and his tomb is with us to this day. Being therefore a prophet, and knowing that God had sworn with an oath to him that he would set one of his descendants on his throne, he foresaw and spoke about the resurrection of the Christ, that he was not abandoned to Hades, nor did his flesh see corruption. This Jesus God raised up, and of that we all are witnesses. (Act 2:29–32)

The Words of Jesus, Our Head

Psalm 2 is echoed in the Father's response to Jesus's anointing by the Holy Spirit at his baptism:[37]

> In those days Jesus came from Nazareth of Galilee and was baptized by John in the Jordan. And when he came up out of the water, immediately he saw the heavens being torn open and the Spirit de-

---

36. Longman, "The Messiah," 20. Rabbinic literature does the same (b. Sukkah 52a; Genesis Rabbah 44:8).

37. W. Davies and D. Allison conclude, "The first line of our text is from or has been influenced by Ps. 2:7 (LXX?) while the next two lines are derived from a non-LXX version of Isa. 42:1" (*The Gospel according to Saint Matthew*, vol. 1 [London: T&T Clark, 1988], 338). See also Stanton, *Jesus and Gospel*, 43; Rick Watts, "The Psalms in Mark's Gospel," in *The Psalms in the New Testament*, ed. Steve Moyise and Maarten J. S. Menken (New York: T&T Clark, 2004), 25–46, especially 25; Everett Ferguson, *Baptism in the Early Church: History, Theology, and Liturgy in the First Five Centuries* (Grand Rapids, MI: Eerdmans, 2009), 123; Stephen P. Ahearne-Kroll, "Psalms in the New Testament," in *The Oxford Handbook of the Psalms*, ed. William P. Brown (Oxford: Oxford University Press, 2014), 269–80, especially 274; Justin Martyr, *Dialogue with Trypho* 38.3; 56.14; 63.4–6; 86.3.

scending on him like a dove. And a voice came from heaven, "*You are my beloved Son*; with you I am well pleased." (Mark 1:9–11)

So Jesus begins to repeat and complete the Davidic story. The king's words "The LORD said to me, 'You are my Son,'" (Ps. 2:7) become his own.

However, it is important, because of the heresy of adoptionism, to point out that Jesus also uses the Psalms to distance himself from David (Mark 12:35–37). He is not bound by that designation. If we allow Jesus to hold a complex self-understanding, he is the promised Messiah, the Son of David, but more than that. The Psalms feature God speaking to God, a mystery that Jesus appropriates: "The Lord said to my Lord" (Mark 12:36). A merely human king, like David, would have to be adopted to become God's son. But adoption language is reserved for disciples in the New Testament. Instead, throughout the Gospels, Jesus presents himself as God.

In Mark, the Father's announcement at the Son's baptism is immediately challenged by Satan. But immediately after calling four disciples, Jesus begins to cast out Satan's forces.[38] Luke applies the second psalm to opposition from Herod Antipas, a son of Herod the Great, and Pilate, the prefect of Rome:

> When they were released, they went to their friends and reported what the chief priests and the elders had said to them. And when they heard it, they lifted their voices together to God and said, "Sovereign Lord, who made the heaven and the earth and the sea and everything in them, who through the mouth of our father David, your servant, said by the Holy Spirit,
>
> > "'*Why did the Gentiles rage,*
> >   *and the peoples plot in vain?*
> > *The kings of the earth set themselves,*
> >   *and the rulers were gathered together,*
> >   *against the Lord and against his Anointed*'—
>
> for truly in this city there were gathered together against your holy servant Jesus, whom you anointed, both Herod and Pontius Pilate, along with the Gentiles and the peoples of Israel, to do whatever

---

38. Mark 1:12–28.

your hand and your plan had predestined to take place. And now, Lord, look upon their threats and grant to your servants to continue to speak your word with all boldness, while you stretch out your hand to heal, and signs and wonders are performed through the name of your holy servant Jesus." (Act 4:23–30)

The first part of the psalm (2:1–3) describes the rebellion of the Gentiles, which the Jerusalem church interprets as being fulfilled at the cross. However, their antipathy toward the Messiah continues by their persecuting God's people. The fullness of God's response, the second part (2:4–12), will take place at the parousia. In the meantime, the church prays for refuge to complete her mission (Acts 4:29–30). The Father's response is remarkable: "And when they had prayed, the place in which they were gathered together was shaken, and they were all filled with the Holy Spirit and continued to speak the word of God with boldness" (Act 4:31).

Like the Gospels, Revelation brings Satan into the conflict: "And the dragon stood before the woman who was about to give birth, so that when she bore her child he might devour it. She gave birth to a male child, one who is *to rule all the nations with a rod of iron*, but her child was caught up to God and to his throne" (Rev. 12:4–5). The vision rehearses the incarnation and ascension of Christ. In fulfillment of the second psalm, he "is to rule all the nations with a rod of iron." The woman plays the role of Mary, who also represents God's people. When Satan can no longer harm Christ, he turns on her (Rev. 12:13).

The Words of God's People, His Body

To the prophet John the resurrected Lord Jesus says: "The one who conquers and who keeps my works until the end, to him I will give authority over *the nations*, and *he will rule them with a rod of iron*, as when earthen pots are broken in pieces, even as I myself have received authority from my Father" (Rev. 2:26–27). The focus has shifted from the Head to the body of Christ, although a union between Jesus and the disciples has been intimated in the other passages. This too is a natural interpretation of the second psalm, which moves from an individual to the community.[39] Jesus promises a shared destiny: if we are willing to suffer with him, the glory of his resurrection and ascension will be ours as well. "Kiss the Son" is our exhortation to the world.

Jesus's baptism has traditionally been understood as the formal introduction of the triune God to humanity.[40] Disciples are similarly baptized "in the name of the Father and of the Son and of the Holy Spirit" (Matt. 28:19). Baptism embodies or represents our union with Christ, which brings us into God's family. We too are "beloved" by the Father and filled with the Spirit.

The complete fulfillment of the psalm is depicted in the seventh-trumpet judgment:

> Then the seventh angel blew his trumpet, and there were loud voices in heaven, saying, "The kingdom of the world has become the kingdom of our *Lord and of his Christ*, and he shall reign forever and ever." And the twenty-four elders who sit on their thrones before God fell on their faces and worshiped God, saying.

> "We give thanks to you, Lord God Almighty,
>   who is and who was,
> for you have taken your great power
>   and begun to reign.
> *The nations raged,*
>   but your *wrath* came,
>   and the time for the dead to be judged,
> and for rewarding your servants, the prophets and saints,
>   and those who fear your name,
>   both small and great,
> and for destroying the destroyers of the earth."
>   (Rev. 11:15–18)

There are no longer two kingdoms, and justice is realized. The great voice and elders mark the moment.

---

39. David L. Peterson and Kent Harold Richards, *Interpreting Hebrew Poetry* (Minneapolis: Fortress, 1992), 92.

40. The Eastern church celebrates this revelation on January 6, the Feast of Epiphany, as Jacob of Serugh (ca. 451–521) notes: "At the time of the Epiphany of Christ, the Trinity appeared at the Jordan" (*On the Baptism of Christ*, cited in Robert Wilken, *The Spirit of Early Christian Thought: Seeking the Face of God* [New Haven, CT: Yale University Press, 2003], 326).

Conclusions

Disciples have read the Psalms in three overlapping yet distinct contexts: as the prayers of David, Christ (the Head), and the church (his body). Reading the Psalms with David connects the disciple to a very ancient tradition—one that predates the Greek philosophers, Buddha (ca. 563–483 BC), and Confucius (551–479 BC). (David is not a mythological hero, but a flesh-and-blood person. A stele from Tel Dan, which can be dated a little less than two centuries from the biblical account, reads "The house of David.")[41] Reading with the king encourages transparency before God.

The Psalms are fulfilled in Jesus Christ, the Messiah. His resurrection and ascension are God's ultimate answer to David's prayers. Since we, the people of God, share Christ's destiny, God has already answered all our prayers for salvation.

Reading the Psalms with Christ fosters intimacy like that of a bride and groom making a new life together for better, for worse, for richer, for poorer, in sickness, and in health. As the Gospels narrate what Jesus did, we can read the Psalms to know how he felt. We can weep with David after Absalom's betrayal as he crossed the Kidron—"And all the land wept aloud as all the people passed by, and the king crossed the brook Kidron, and all the people passed on toward the wilderness" (2 Sam. 15:23)—and with Christ, who, betrayed by Judas, took the same path on the way to the cross—"When Jesus had spoken these words, he went out with his disciples across the brook Kidron, where there was a garden, which he and his disciples entered" (John 18:1).[42] David and Jesus are *with* God's people, and we are with them in our prayers. Our sorrow will turn to joy, and we will be together forever.

---

41. George Athas, "Setting the Record Straight: What Are We Making of the Tel Dan Inscription?," *Journal of Semitic Studies* 51 (2006): 241–56. Scholars debate the relationship between the "historical David" and Scripture, as they do with Christ, and the debate will continue.
42. Raymond E. Brown, *The Gospel according to John (xiii–xxi)* (London: Chapman, 1966), 806.

7

The Transforming Power of Christ's Love

Ephesians 1:16–19; 3:14–21

John J. Hughes

Ephesians is unique among Paul's epistles[1] because of its lengthy, two-part prayer[2] (Eph. 1:16–19; 3:14–21) with its lofty theological themes that are challenging to understand. At the end of the epistle, Paul exhorts us to pray "at all times in the Spirit, with all prayer and supplication. To that end, keep alert with all perseverance, making supplication for all the saints" (Eph. 6:18). Having given us a long, theologically rich prayer, and having concluded his epistle with a strong exhortation to pray, Paul would have expected us to appropriate for our prayers the themes and

---

1. I understand this letter to be Pauline. For detailed discussions regarding its authorship and provenance, see the commentaries referenced below.
2. Technically, Eph. 1:16–19 and 3:14–21 are reports of Paul's prayers—"prayer reports"—but since Paul prayed for what he reported on, I will refer to them as "prayers." What appears to be two separate prayers in Ephesians (1:16–19 and 3:14–21) are essentially one prayer in two parts. "For this reason" in 3:14 harkens back to the "For this reason" in 3:1, which harkens back to Paul's intercessory prayer in 1:16–19. In other words, Paul twice broke off his initial prayer, only to resume it and carry it to its conclusion in 3:14–21 (F. F. Bruce, *The Epistles to the Colossians, to Philemon, and the Ephesians*, NICNT [Grand Rapids, MI: Eerdmans, 1984], 324, hereafter abbreviated Bruce, *CPE*).

petitions in his prayer. But the major themes that Paul's prayer touches on are difficult for most Christians to understand. These include

- "in the heavenly places," touched on in 1:19–23[3] and 3:14–15;
- "the powers"[4] and their presence in the heavenly places, touched on in 1:19–23 and 3:14–15;
- the ideas of "fullness" and "filling," touched on in 1:23 and 3:19; and
- the epistle's pervasive portrayal of the church as the focal point of the Father's cosmic plan and corresponding redemptive activity "to unite all things" in heaven and on earth in Christ (1:10),[5] touched on in 1:16–18.

Paul's closing exhortation to pray "at all times in the Spirit . . . for all the saints" (Eph. 6:18)[6] introduces the final section of his extended teaching (6:10–20) on "spiritual warfare," which includes two of the themes listed above: "in the heavenly places" and "the powers."

This chapter is my attempt to open up Paul's prayer as a way of honoring my dear friend of over forty years, Wayne Grudem—a godly man, a consummate scholar, a strong leader, and one who is steeped in fervent, believing prayer—so that we can better heed Paul's admonition to pray regularly and frequently for ourselves and our fellow Christians, and to do so with greater understanding, increased specificity, and expanded expectations.

Our exploration of Paul's prayer will benefit from an initial examination of "in the heavenly places" and "the powers."[7] These terms

---

3. Although technically the first part of Paul's prayer breaks off after Eph. 1:19, verses 20–23 explain the idea of "the immeasurable greatness of [the Father's] power toward us" (1:19a) by showing that "according to the working of his great might" (1:19b) refers to the Father's raising Christ from the dead and exalting him to his right hand as the victorious cosmic Lord over "the powers" (who have been subjected under his feet) for the sake of the church.

4. A phrase I will use to refer collectively to the "rulers," "authorities," and "cosmic powers over this present darkness"—to "the spiritual forces of evil in the heavenly places" (Eph. 6:12; cf. 1:21; 3:10), as well as to the Devil (4:27; 6:11), who also is called "the prince of the power of the air" (2:2). For a thorough survey of the various ways "the powers" have been understood, see P. T. O'Brien, "Principalities and Powers: Opponents of the Church," in *Biblical Interpretation and the Church: Text and Context*, ed. D. A. Carson (Exeter, UK: Paternoster, 1984), 110–50.

5. E.g., Eph. 1:9–10, 20–23; 2:6–7; 3:9–11; 6:10–20.

6. Bruce, *CPE*: "So far as the construction goes, 'praying' (with the following 'keep awake') seems to belong to the series of participles dependent on the imperative 'stand' at the beginning of 6:14 ('having girt,' 'having shod,' 'having taken up')."

7. "In the heavenly places" defines the "sphere" in which we enjoy our blessings in Christ (Eph. 1:3); "the powers" refers to the evil inhabitants of this sphere, who seek to harm Christians but over whom Christ rules (6:12; 3:10 with 1:20–23).

merit discussion for three reasons. Theologically, the terms are interrelated, they pervade the epistle's teaching, and they are among the most difficult to understand. Culturally, for Western Christians the ideas represented by these terms play little, if any, role in our understanding of our redemption, and they have a correspondingly insignificant role in our prayer lives. Exegetically, we cannot understand specific petitions in Paul's prayer without understanding these terms.

"In the Heavenlies"

"In the heavenly places" (lit. "in the heavenlies"—ἐν τοῖς ἐπουρανίοις) occurs five times in Ephesians—1:3, 20; 2:6; 3:10; 6:12—and nowhere else in the New Testament or in pre-first-century Greek literature.[8] It is used in a local[9] and formulaic[10] sense to refer to the realm, sphere, or dimension that is God's abode (1:3, 20; 2:6)—the heavenly realm—as well as the abode of the "principalities and powers" (ESV: "rulers and authorities")—evil angels (3:10; 6:12).[11]

Paul also employs the usual word for heaven, οὐρανός, in Ephesians 1:10; 3:15; 4:10; and 6:9.[12] "In the heavenlies" and "heaven" denote the same reality, but with different connotations. The term οὐρανός is commonly used when contrasted, expressly or by implication, with "earth" (γῆ),[13] while ἐν τοῖς ἐπουρανίοις may have

---

8. A search of the full Thesaurus Linguae Graecae corpus for ἐν τοῖς ἐπουρανίοις in all Greek literature before the first century AD returns no hits. See Andrew T. Lincoln, "A Re-Examination of 'The Heavenlies' in Ephesians," *NTS* 19 (1973): 468–83, and his *Paradise Now and Not Yet: Studies in the Role of the Heavenly Dimension in Paul's Thought with Special Reference to His Eschatology*, SNTSMS 43 (Cambridge: Cambridge University Press, 1981), for a detailed and seminal treatment of the role that "heaven" (and related concepts, e.g., "heavenlies") plays in Paul's theology in general and in his eschatology in particular. The adjective ἐπουράνιος is used nineteen times in the New Testament, twelve times in Paul's writings: the five references in Ephesians and 1 Cor. 15:40 (2x), 48 (2x), 49; Phil. 2:10; 2 Tim. 4:18.

9. Lincoln, *Paradise*, 140 and 140n25, lists many other concurring authorities. M. Jeff Brannon, *The Heavenlies in Ephesians: A Lexical, Exegetical, and Conceptual Analysis*, Library of New Testament Studies (London: T&T Clark, 2013), notes that although ἐπουράνιος may have different nuances, it "is spatially distinct from the earth," and it is synonymous with other terms for "heaven," such as οὐρανός (101).

10. Lincoln, "Re-Examination," 469, 476.

11. Gordon D. Fee, *God's Empowering Presence: The Holy Spirit in the Letters of Paul* (Peabody, MA: Hendrickson, 1994), 735 and 735n202 (hereafter abbreviated Fee, *GEP*), shows that because "the powers" are uniformly evil in Eph. 6:12, "the powers" in 3:10 should be understood accordingly, and so throughout the epistle. In Rom. 8:38, Paul pairs "angels" with "rulers"—οὔτε ἄγγελοι οὔτε ἀρχαί—and includes οὔτε δυνάμεις a bit further along in the verse. This is the only place in the Pauline corpus where "angel(s)" occurs with one of the "power" terms.

12. Eph. 1:10: τὰ ἐπὶ τοῖς οὐρανοῖς καὶ τὰ ἐπὶ τῆς γῆς; 3:15: πᾶσα πατριὰ ἐν οὐρανοῖς καὶ ἐπὶ γῆς; 4:10: ὁ καταβὰς αὐτός ἐστιν καὶ ὁ ἀναβὰς ὑπεράνω πάντων τῶν οὐρανῶν; and 6:9: ὁ Κύριός ἐστιν ἐν οὐρανοῖς.

13. Brannon, *Heavenlies*, 210–11.

been a religious term, used by the epistle's initial recipients, that Paul adopts and adapts to help them understand that "Christ himself is now seated 'in the heavenlies' as 'head over' all the spirit powers for the sake of the church (1:20–23), and God in the richness of his mercy has seated us all (Jew and Gentile together) with Christ 'in the heavenlies' (2:6)."[14]

"In the heavenlies" denotes heaven as the sphere that is God's abode, the abode of "the powers," the place from which Christ rules the cosmos, and the arena in which the church on earth is involved.

"The Heavenlies" and Paul's Eschatology

In order to understand how the heavenly realm can be the abode of good *and* evil "principalities and powers" (Eph. 3:10; 6:12), we need to briefly examine the role of "the heavenlies" in Paul's eschatology.

As an educated Jew, Paul would have understood creation to consist of two spheres: heaven and earth (Gen. 1:1). The heavenly and earthly spheres originally were unified under God's uncontested lordship.[15] There was peace within and between both spheres. Both angels and humans loved and obeyed God and enjoyed rich, personal fellowship with him. God communed in the garden with the man and the woman, his special creations to whom he had given dominion over all the earth (Gen. 1:26–28) and whom he created "a little lower than the heavenly beings" (Ps. 8:5).[16] For example, when angels observed the creation of earth (Job 38:4–7), we are told that

> the morning stars sang together
> and all the sons of God shouted for joy. (Job 38:7)[17]

God addressed his heavenly council when he created man (Gen. 1:26),[18] and he fellowshipped with Adam and Eve in the garden before the fall (Gen. 2:15ff.; cf. 3:8–10).

---

14. Fee, *GEP*, 668.

15. The way in which the Father's purpose "to unite all things" in Christ, "things in heaven and things on earth" (Eph. 1:10), is fleshed out in Ephesians can help us to understand how the heavenly and earthly realms were unified prior to the fall.

16. The LXX reads "angels," as does Heb. 2:7: "You made him for a little while lower than the angels."

17. Notice the word *all* in "all the sons of God shouted for joy"—כָּל־בְּנֵי אֱלֹהִים—suggesting the pre-fall state of angels.

18. The "us" in Gen. 1:26 is best interpreted as a reference to the divine council, as is the "us" in Gen. 3:22: "Behold, the man has become like one of us in knowing good and evil" (see Bruce K.

Genesis 1:31 says, "And God saw everything that he had made, and behold, it was very good." Genesis 2:1 reads, "The heavens and the earth were finished, and all the host of them" (cf. Ex. 20:11). The "everything" (Gen. 1:31) includes all the angels, and "all the host" (Gen. 2:1) is a specific reference to them.[19] Sometime between the "very good" of Genesis 2:1 and the temptation scene in Genesis 3, Satan and many angels rebelled and fell.[20] The fall of mankind, preceded by the fall of many angels, created disunity within and between the heavenly and earthly spheres. Fallen angels and fallen humankind were now in rebellion against God. When God drove Adam and Eve from the garden (Gen. 3:22), he placed the cherubim there to prevent mankind from accessing the tree of life (Gen. 3:24), a tree now located "in the paradise of God" (Rev. 2:7)—heaven (Rev. 22:2, 14, 19).[21]

After the fall of the human race, angels have continued to be active in both spheres. Fallen angels—"the powers"—who are active in heaven are also active on earth, as texts like Job 1:6; 2:1; Zechariah 3:1ff.; Ephesians 3:10; 6:10–20; and many, many others show. "The powers" are at war with good angels (see, e.g., Dan. 10:13; Rev. 12:7–9), with mankind (Eph. 2:1–3; Rev. 12:9, 12b), and with the church (Eph. 6:10–20; Rev. 12:13–17).[22] They are at war with God. No one is immune to their attacks.[23] Three times their leader, the Devil, tempted Jesus (Matt. 4:1–11), and he was instrumental in Jesus's death.[24]

Waltke and Cathi J. Fredericks, *Genesis: A Commentary* [Grand Rapids, MI: Zondervan, 2001], 64–65; Meredith G. Kline, *Images of the Spirit* [Eugene, OR: Wipf & Stock, 1999], 22–23).

19. 1 Kings 22:19; Neh. 9:6; Isa. 24:21; cf. Deut. 4:19; 17:3.

20. Although the Bible does not explicitly state when angels were created or when they fell, we know the following: that angels were created before the seventh day of creation, when "the heavens and the earth were finished, and all the host of them" (Gen. 2:1; cf. Ex. 20:11); that there are fallen and unfallen angels (1 Tim. 5:21; 2 Pet. 2:4; Jude 6; Rev. 12:4, with 7–9; cf. Matt. 25:41); that the speaking serpent in Genesis 3 was Satan (Rev. 12:9; cf. Rom. 16:20); and that angels ("cherubim") appear with God in the judgment scene in the garden of Eden (Gen. 3:22–24).

21. Robert H. Mounce, *The Book of Revelation*, rev. ed., NICNT (Grand Rapids, MI: Eerdmans, 1998), 72, notes: "Paradise was originally a Persian word for pleasure garden. In later Judaism, it was used to portray the abode of the righteous dead. The paradise of God in Revelation symbolizes the eschatological state in which God and people are restored to that perfect fellowship which existed before the entrance of sin into the world."

22. See Timothy G. Gombis, "The Triumph of God in Christ: Divine Warfare in the Argument of Ephesians" (PhD diss., University of St. Andrews, 2005), and his *The Drama of Ephesians: Participating in the Triumph of God* (Downers Grove, IL: IVP Academic, 2010), for a thorough treatment of the divine-warfare theme in Ephesians. Also Lincoln, "Re-Examination," 475–76.

23. Even Peter could be influenced by Satan; Matt. 16:16–17 with 22–23 is instructive. Also see Luke 22:31–34, where Jesus tells Peter that "Satan demanded to have you [plural—all the disciples], that he might sift you [singular—Peter] like wheat" (22:31). "Behind" or "within" the earthly drama is the heavenly.

24. Luke 4:13; 22:3, 53; John 13:27.

Although "the Lord has established his throne in the heavens, / and his kingdom rules over all" (Ps. 103:19; cf. Pss. 11:4; 115:3),[25] Jesus could still call the Devil "the ruler of this world" (John 12:31; 14:30; cf. 2 Cor. 4:4; Eph. 2:2) and teach us to pray for the coming of God's kingdom,

> Our Father in heaven,
> hallowed be your name.
> Your kingdom come,
> your will be done,
>   on earth as it is in heaven. (Matt. 6:9–10)

And we are to ask the Father to "deliver us from the evil one" (Matt. 6:13, ESV mg. for τοῦ πονηροῦ;[26] cf. Matt. 16:19). God is absolutely sovereign. Christ's crucifixion, resurrection, and exaltation sealed Satan's fate (1 Cor. 15:24–28; Eph. 1:19–23; Col. 2:13–15); his days are numbered, and he knows it (Rev. 12:12).[27] But within God's redemptive plan, and for his own purposes, he has allowed the Devil room to operate (e.g., 1 John 5:19) until Christ returns in judgment (e.g., 1 Cor. 15:24–28).[28] Similarly, in Ephesians there is an already/not-yet aspect

---

25. Cf. Ps. 2:1–6; Isa. 66:1; Matt. 5:34; 23:22; Acts 7:49.

26. In Matt. 6:13, the ESV reads "deliver us from evil" and offers "the evil one" as an alternative reading. D. A. Carson, "Matthew," in *Matthew, Mark, Luke*, ed. Frank E. Gaebelein, EBC 8 (Grand Rapids, MI: Zondervan, 1984), 174, notes:

> The words *tou ponērou* ("the evil one") could be either neuter ("evil"; cf. Luke 6:45; Rom 12:9; 1 Thess 5:22) or masculine ("the evil one," referring to Satan: [Matt.] 13:19, 38; Eph 6:16; 1 John 2:13–14; 3:12; 5:19). In some cases the Greek does not distinguish the gender (see on [Matt.] 5:37). However, a reference to Satan is far more likely here for two reasons: (1) "deliver us" can take either the preposition *ek* ("from") or *apo* ("from"), the former always introducing things from which to be delivered, the latter being used predominantly of persons (cf. J. B. Bauer, "Liberanos a malo," *Verbum Domini* 34 [1965]: 12–15 Zerwick par. 89); and (2) Matthew's first mention of temptation (4:1–11) is unambiguously connected with the Devil. Thus the Lord's model prayer ends with a petition that, while implicitly recognizing our own helplessness before the Devil whom Jesus alone could vanquish (4:1–11), delights to trust the heavenly Father for deliverance from the Devil's strength and wiles.

27. Eph. 3:9–11, especially 10, makes a similar point, as we will see below. In his *Christ and Time: The Primitive Christian Conception of Time and History*, rev. ed. (Philadelphia: Westminster, 1964), 84, Oscar Cullmann illustrates how the center of redemptive history has been reached, although the end is still to come. Using a World War II analogy, Cullmann says that "the decisive battle in a war" (D-Day) can be reached in its early stages and "yet the war still continues" until "Victory Day" (V-E Day). D-Day is analogous to the decisive victory of Christ's crucifixion-resurrection-exaltation over the Devil and "the powers." V-E Day is analogous to his triumphal return (parousia).

28. See, e.g., Acts 3:19–21 (esp. 21 regarding Jesus: "whom heaven must receive until the time for restoring all the things about which God spoke by the mouth of his holy prophets long ago") and Rom. 11:25–26 (esp. 25b: "a partial hardening has come upon Israel, until the fullness of the Gentiles has come in"); cf. Luke 21:24; 2 Pet. 3:9.

to Christ's rule over "the powers," for example, Ephesians 1:21–22 (the "already") with 2:2 and 6:12 (the "not-yet").[29]

Paul understands history to consist of two ages—this age and the age to come (Eph. 1:21)[30]—with both encompassing heaven and earth. This age is fallen. Paul calls it "this present darkness" (6:12). The "course of this world" follows "the prince of the power of the air" (2:2)—the Devil (4:27; 6:11)—and is under his evil influence and God's wrath (2:2b–3). The age to come (cf. 2:7) will be one of perfect righteousness, peace, and joy (Rom. 14:17).[31] Christ will have destroyed "every rule and every authority and power"; all his enemies, heavenly and earthly, will be under his feet (1 Cor. 15:24–25). God the Father will be "all in all" (1 Cor. 15:28).

Paul teaches that God's redemptive plan encompasses heaven and earth. Its penultimate goal is to restore cosmic wholeness by unifying heaven and earth in the Messiah (Eph. 1:9–10);[32] its ultimate goal is that once again, God would be "all in all" (1 Cor. 15:28).[33] Christ is the focus of this plan. His crucifixion marks the disarming of "the powers" and God's triumph over them (Col. 2:13–15). His resurrection and exaltation to reign in power[34] as cosmic Lord, at the Father's "right hand in the heavenly places" (Eph. 1:20–23), until all his enemies (heavenly and earthly) have been destroyed (1 Cor. 15:24–25), mark the beginning of the age to come (cf. Eph. 4:8–10). Thus in Ephesians, "in the heavenlies" refers to heaven as it "takes its place in the cosmic

---

29. Andrew T. Lincoln, *Ephesians*, WBC (Dallas: Word, 1990), 35.

30. Paul used various terms to denote the two ages: "this world" (Rom. 12:2; 1 Cor. 7:31; 2 Cor. 4:4; Eph. 2:2), "this age" (1 Cor. 1:20; 2:6–8; 3:18), "present evil age" (Gal. 1:4), "end of the ages" (1 Cor. 10:11), "coming ages" (Eph. 2:7), "new creation" (2 Cor. 5:17; Gal. 6:15), "the domain of darkness" (Col. 1:13), and "this present darkness" (Eph. 6:12).

31. See my article "Perspectives on the Kingdom of God in Romans 14:17," in *Redeeming the Life of the Mind: Essays in Honor of Vern Poythress*, ed. John M. Frame, Wayne Grudem, and John J. Hughes (Wheaton, IL: Crossway, 2017), 360–86.

32. Eph. 1:10 reads ἀνακεφαλαιώσασθαι τὰ πάντα ἐν τῷ Χριστῷ. Lincoln, *Ephesians*, 33, notes that this clause "refers to the summing up and bringing together of the diverse elements of the cosmos in Christ as the focal point." Cf. Rom. 13:9, the only other use of ἀνακεφαλαιόω in the New Testament.

33. The phrase "that God may be all in all"—[τὰ] πάντα ἐν πᾶσιν—in 1 Cor. 15:28 refers to the sole, supreme, complete, uncontested, perfect, universal, cosmic rule of God the Father in heaven and earth—the perfect exercise of his lordship throughout both spheres of creation. Gordon D. Fee, *The First Epistle to the Corinthians*, NICNT (Grand Rapids, MI: Eerdmans, 1987), 760, says: "God will be supreme in every quarter and in every way. In Paul's view the consummation of redemption includes the whole sphere of creation as well (cf. Rom. 8:19–22; Col. 1:15–20). Nothing lies outside God's redemptive purposes in Christ, in whom all things finally will be 'united' (Eph. 1:9–10)."

34. Hughes, "Perspectives on the Kingdom," 363–64, 372.

drama of redemption, that is, in that act of the drama which Christ has inaugurated by his resurrection and exaltation."[35]

Having been raised from the dead as "the last Adam," Christ "became life-giving Spirit" (πνεῦμα ζωοποιοῦν, 1 Cor. 15:45b, a verse to which we will return later). Henceforth, the Spirit acts on behalf of Christ, who is present with us, among us, and in us by means of and as the Spirit. The new age—the world to come—that has arrived in Christ and in which we participate is fundamentally one of the Spirit, which is why Paul speaks of our having been sealed with "the *promised* Holy Spirit" (Eph. 1:13). By virtue of our union with Christ, through the Spirit we already experience the life of this new age, but not yet in its eschatological fullness (e.g., Eph. 2:7). The two ages coexist and overlap, and as those who are "in Christ," we experience both ages and both spheres (the heavenly and the earthly) concurrently.[36] God has "made us alive together with Christ" and "raised us up with him and seated us with him in the heavenly places" (Eph. 2:6). "Our citizenship is in heaven, and from it we await a Savior, the Lord Jesus Christ, who will transform our lowly body to be like his glorious body, by the power that enables him even to subject all things to himself" (Phil. 3:20–21; cf. Col. 3:1–4; 1 Thess. 1:10). But until the arrival of "the day of redemption" (Eph. 4:30; cf. 1 Cor. 15:20–28), for which believers have been sealed by the promised Spirit (Eph. 1:13–14; cf. Rom. 8:23; 2 Cor. 1:22), when we inherit "the kingdom of Christ and God" (Eph. 5:5), "the powers" will continue to be active "in the heavenly places" (6:10–20) and on earth (2:1–3). This already/not-yet nature of our current existence as believers surfaces in both parts of Paul's prayer and informs its petitions.

"The Heavenlies" and "the Powers"

Ephesians depicts the heavenly realm as the spiritual, or metaphysical, environment in which earthly life transpires. Although the heavenly realm is "higher" than (authoritative over) the earthly, it surrounds and interpenetrates it. The heavenly realm is neither spatially distant nor chronologically future; nor is it a sphere that is walled off from earthly existence. It is coterminous and coextensive with our everyday

---

35. Lincoln, *Paradise*, 141.
36. Lincoln, "Re-Examination," 481.

lives; it is here and now, and it suffuses earthly existence. Human life is lived simultaneously in both realms—the earthly and the heavenly—where Christians and non-Christian alike are exposed to "the powers." Because Christians are seated with Christ in the heavenlies (Eph. 2:6) and under *his* dominion,[37] they are protected from the *dominion* of the powers, though not from their attacks (6:10–20).[38] Non-Christians, on the other hand, are not under Christ's protection; they are under the powers' dominion (2:1–3).[39]

Paul's unambiguous teaching that "the powers" are real, evil metaphysical beings (fallen angels) who help to promote disobedience—rebellion against God—among non-Christians (Eph. 2:1–3), who seek to destroy the church (Eph. 6:10–20), and who are enemies of Christ is a disturbing teaching for many Christians that can result in one of two extremes: denying the existence of the Devil and his cohorts or becoming overly fascinated with them. We need to guard against demythologizing the teaching of Ephesians 6:10–20 (and the other references to "the powers"), that is, denying the existence of evil angels and of the Devil's schemes; or, having recognized their existence, we must not "attribute to them a prominence all out of proportion to that which Paul here affords them."[40] To do the former is the equivalent of taking a stroll through a minefield, oblivious to what lies buried beneath the soil. To the extent that we do the latter, we diminish the victory that Christ has won over "the powers." We are to take them with "dead seriousness," while recognizing "that they are a tethered foe, restrained by Christ's victory over them in the cross and resurrection (Col. 2:15; Eph. 2:6–7)."[41] No matter how oblivious we may be to "the powers," they are our very real and very active enemies—facts that helped to shape Paul's prayer.

---

37. The verbs ἐνήργηκεν and καθίσας, which are used in Eph. 1:20 to refer to the Father's having raised Christ and seated him at his right hand in the heavenly places, are used in their compound forms (συνήγειρεν and συνεκάθισεν) in 2:6 to refer to God's having "raised us up with him and seated us with him in the heavenly places in Christ Jesus" (but not at the Father's right hand).

38. Col. 1:13: "He has delivered us from the domain of darkness and transferred us to the kingdom of his beloved Son."

39. Heb. 12:22ff. illustrates this "interpenetration" of the earthly and heavenly realms. The "already" of verses 22–24 is balanced by the "not yet" of verses 12:26b–27, and both are brought together in verse 28.

40. Fee, *GEP*, 726.

41. Fee, *GEP*, 726. For more detail on "the powers" in Ephesians, see Clinton E. Arnold, *Power and Magic: The Concept of Power in Ephesians* (Grand Rapids, MI: Baker, 1997).

The *Berakah*

The first part of Paul's prayer is his natural response to the extended blessings (*berakah*) that he outlines in Ephesians 1:3–14.[42] The opening words of the *berakah*—"Blessed be the God and Father of our Lord Jesus Christ, who has blessed us in Christ with every spiritual blessing in the heavenly places" (1:3), the epistle's subtitle or topical sentence[43]—encapsulate and forecast the main themes of the epistle as a whole, including those in Paul's prayer.

In the *berakah*, Paul enumerates seven soteriological blessings. They begin with God's eternal redemptive plan (Eph. 1:4–5), continue into its accomplishment and application (1:7–10), and anticipate its consummation (1:11–14). As Christians, we have

- been elected to holiness in Christ (1:4),
- been predestined in love[44] for adoption through Christ (1:5),
- been redeemed and forgiven our trespasses through Christ's blood (1:7),
- been granted knowledge of the mystery of God's will (eternal redemptive plan) to unite all things in heaven and on earth in Christ (1:9–10),
- obtained an inheritance in Christ (1:11) that is guaranteed by our having
- been sealed with the promised Holy Spirit (1:11, 13–14), with the result that we have
- hope that results from that sealing (1:12).

Each of these redemptive blessings is ours by virtue of our union with Christ.[45] All of these blessings flow from the Father through the Son and are appropriated by the Holy Spirit. Every blessing is Christocentric. The blessings are squarely placed within Paul's already/not-yet,

---

42. Peter T. O'Brien, *The Letter to the Ephesians*, PNTC (Grand Rapids, MI: Eerdmans, 1999), 127.

43. Fee, *GEP*, 666.

44. The commentaries by Bruce, Lincoln, and O'Brien, as well as J. Armitage Robinson, *St. Paul's Epistle to the Ephesians*, 2nd ed. (London: Macmillan, 1904), 34, 146, and Harold W. Hoehner, *Ephesians: An Exegetical Commentary* (Grand Rapids, MI: Baker Academic, 2002), understand "in love" to belong to the preceding "holy and blameless before him." S. M. Baugh, *Ephesians*, Evangelical Exegetical Commentary (Bellingham, WA: Lexham, 2016), 82–83, makes a strong case for understanding "in love" to go with the following "he predestined us," as represented by the ESV, NASB, and NIV.

45. Notice the use of "in Christ" (1:3), "in him" (1:4, 7, 11, 13), "in the Beloved" (1:6), "through Jesus Christ" (1:5), and "through his blood" (1:7).

two-age eschatological scheme (Eph. 1:9–10, 13–14, 21; 2:7; cf. 6:12), and the sphere in which we experience them is "the heavenly places" (1:3). God's redemptive plan to unite all things in heaven and on earth in Christ (1:10) is cosmic in scope. The phrase "things in heaven" encompasses "the powers," while "things on earth" embraces Jews and Gentiles—the entire fallen creation is in view. "This cosmic summing up has a proleptic realization in the Church which unites Jews and Gentiles,"[46] and this knowledge assures us of God's power in Christ over "the powers."

The First Part of Paul's Prayer (Eph. 1:16–19)

As we saw above, "for this reason" in Ephesians 1:15 links Paul's prayer to the majestic spiritual blessings that are ours in Christ in the heavenly realm (1:3–14).[47] These blessings are so stupendous, profound, and fundamental to our knowing the Father and what he has done for us in Christ that Paul prays that the "Father of glory" would "give you the Spirit of wisdom and of revelation in the knowledge of him" (1:17) so that we may gain Spirit-given insight into the Father and his redemptive plans, purposes, and actions in Christ (esp. 1:8–10).[48] Although many English translations render πνεῦμα as "a spirit," the majority of commentators translate it as "the Spirit" (so the ESV).[49] Paul's emphasis in his prayer is on the Spirit's role as revealer. "The Spirit who grants wisdom is also (especially) the one who grants the revelation of God and his ways."[50]

Paul is not praying for an initial impartation of the Spirit, or for an additional impartation of the Spirit, or that God would give us new special revelation through the Spirit. He is asking that the Spirit whom we already possess as Christians would open the eyes of our understanding to who God is and to what he has done for us in Christ, specifically to the meaning and significance for us of three of God's blessings found in the *berakah*: the *hope* to which he has called us (Eph. 1:12), the *inheritance* that he has in us (1:11, 14), and his *power* that is at work for us (implied by the phrase "to unite all things in him," 1:10). The content of "hope"

46. Lincoln, *Ephesians*, 35.
47. O'Brien, *Ephesians*, 124–25.
48. O'Brien, *Ephesians*, 132.
49. See the discussion and evidence in Fee, *GEP*, 674–76 and notes 50–52.
50. Fee, *GEP*, 675.

and "inheritance" is part of the "not yet" of our redemptive experience in Christ. "The immeasurable greatness of [the Father's] power toward us [εἰς ἡμᾶς] who believe" (1:19)—the "already" of our experience—assures us of the certainty and security of that hope and inheritance.[51]

The intertwined concepts of hope and inheritance in Ephesians 1:18 point back to Paul's statements about these same topics in 1:11–14, the concluding verses of the *berakah*—comments that are bracketed by the conception of inheritance in the opening and closing verses (11 and 14). It's instructive to view the beginning and end of this pericope in isolation from the intervening clauses: "In him [Christ] we have obtained an inheritance . . . [and] were sealed with the promised Holy Spirit, who is the guarantee [or "down payment"] of our inheritance until we acquire possession of it" (1:11a, 13b–14). Paul's main interest in the closing verses of the *berakah* is the inheritance, which is ours in Christ and whose future realization is now guaranteed by our having been sealed with the promised Holy Spirit. As in Ephesians 1:18, the inheritance belongs to the "not yet."

According to Paul, the inheritance is a result of our having been predestined according to the eternal purposes of God, "who works all things according to the counsel of his will" (Eph. 1:11), and this takes us back to predestination "according to the purpose [lit. "good pleasure"—κατὰ τὴν εὐδοκίαν] of his will" in verse 5. In that verse, the purpose of predestination is "for adoption as sons" (εἰς υἱοθεσίαν). Thus there is a relation between predestination unto sonship in 1:5 and the inheritance that results from predestination in 1:11. The inheritance is related to sonship, but not in the way that we are accustomed to thinking.

What is the inheritance, and what should we anticipate experiencing when the "not yet" becomes the "right now" (Eph. 1:14)? How one understands the passive ἐκληρώθημεν in 1:11 is determinative for both questions.[52] Bruce translates this as "we were claimed by God as his portion."[53] He says:

51. See Fee's discussion of this in *GEP*, 677–78. The three objects of Paul's prayer—hope, inheritance, and power—are placed in parallel as three noun clauses: τίς ἐστιν . . . τίς . . . καὶ τί. The first two clauses (Eph. 1:18) are an appositional pair. The second interprets the first.

52. ESV, "we have obtained an inheritance"; so KJV, NASB, NKJV, and NRSV. The HCSB has "received an inheritance."

53. Bruce, *CPE*, 262. So Robinson, *Ephesians*, 34, 146; Hoehner, *Ephesians*, 227 ("we are God's possession"); O'Brien, *Ephesians*, 115–16, 121–22; Lincoln, *Ephesians*, 36 (tentatively).

The reason for the rendering "we were claimed by God as his portion" (rather than "we were assigned our portion") is that it is in keeping with OT precedent. In the Song of Moses (Deut. 32:8–9) the nations of the world are assigned to various angelic beings ("the sons of God"),[54] but Yahweh retains Israel as his personal possession:

> "For the LORD's possession is his people,
> Jacob his allotted heritage."[55]

So here, believers in Christ are God's chosen people, claimed by him as his portion or heritage. That this is the sense is confirmed by the reference in v. 18 to "the glorious wealth of his inheritance in the saints."[56]

Our hope is not so much that we possess an inheritance as it is that we are God's *sons*, whom he has chosen to be *his inheritance*[57]— a mind-expanding and soul-stirring idea, to say the least! In Ephesians 1:14, the ESV's "until we acquire possession of it" (for the underlying τῆς περιποιήσεως) is better translated by the ESV's marginal reading: "until God redeems his possession."[58] O'Brien says, "Redemption, which is a present 'spiritual blessing' at 1:7, here signifies the final deliverance (cf. 4:30), when God takes full and complete possession of those who are already his."[59]

According to Ephesians, what should believers expect to experience when God redeems his possession? Everything included in our having been sealed with the promised Holy Spirit (Eph. 1:13),[60] the complete and final realization of all the blessings outlined in the *berakah*

Baugh, *Ephesians*, 93–94, translates the passive ἐκληρώθημεν as "were appointed," "we have been apportioned." ASV: "also we were made a heritage"; CSB: "we were also made His inheritance."

54. Bruce, *CPE*, 263n87.

55. Cf. Deut. 4:20; 1 Kings 8:51; Pss. 33:12; 106:40.

56. Bruce, *CPE*, 263.

57. Cf. 1 Pet. 2:9: "But you are a chosen race, a royal priesthood, a holy nation, a people for his own possession, that you may proclaim the excellencies of him who called you out of darkness into his marvelous light."

58. O'Brien, *Ephesians*, 121–23, presents a strong argument for taking the expression to refer to Christians as God's possession/inheritance, rather than to Christians possessing the promised inheritance. Also Bruce, *CPE*, 266–67.

59. O'Brien, *Ephesians*, 122.

60. In his comments on Ephesians 1:14, Lightfoot says, "The present gift of the Spirit is only a *small fraction* of the future endowment" (J. B. Lightfoot, *Notes on Epistles of St Paul from Unpublished Commentaries* [London: Macmillan, 1895], 324, emphasis original).

(1:3–14),[61] answers to the petitions in Paul's prayer that surpass our imaginations—in short, nothing less than the fullness of the age to come. In addition to our being resurrected (1 Cor. 15:12–58), this includes (1) face-to-face knowledge of God,[62] (2) knowledge of God that is as intimate and perfect as is possible for creatures to have,[63] (3) the completion of our transformation into the likeness of Christ,[64] (4) having a place in the perfected kingdom of God,[65] (5) experiencing the unity of heaven and earth (Eph. 1:10),[66] (6) a society characterized by godly love,[67] and (7) an immeasurable experience of God's love for us in Christ Jesus.[68]

Paul concludes the first part of the prayer[69] by turning from a contemplation of God promises regarding the future to an affirmation of his mighty work in the present; he argues, in effect, that our current experience of God's power guarantees the future realization of his promises.[70] Paul prays that we would understand "what is the immeasurable greatness of his power toward us[71] who believe" (Eph. 1:19). The future that the Father has promised is made certain by "the immeasurable greatness of his power" exercised on our behalf over "the powers" in the present.[72]

God's power at work on our behalf is *immeasurably* great.[73] In order to give us maximal assurance and confidence in God and his

---

61. Bruce, *CPE*, 269: "Prayer is offered that the ideal set forth in the *eulogia* may be realized in their experience—perfectly in the resurrection age but in measure at present through the ministry of the Spirit."

62. Eph. 1:4: "that we should be holy and blameless *before him*," emphasis added. Cf. 1 Cor. 13:12; Eph. 4:13; 5:27; Col. 1:22; 1 John 3:2.

63. 1 Cor. 13:12; Eph. 4:13; 5:31–32; cf. 1 John 3:2.

64. Eph. 1:4; 4:13, 24; 5:27; 1 John 3:2; cf. 2 Cor. 3:17–18.

65. Eph. 5:5; cf. Isa. 65:17; 1 Cor. 15:20–28; 2 Pet. 3:13; Rev. 21:1. See Hughes, "Perspectives on the Kingdom," 360–86.

66. Cf. Eph. 4:13; Col. 1:20.

67. Eph. 1:15; 4:2, 15–16; 5:2; 6:24.

68. Eph. 2:7 with 1:4; 2:4; 3:14–21; 5:2, 25; 6:23.

69. Eph. 1:19 officially concludes Paul's prayer. So Bruce, *CPE*, 271.

70. As Paul wrote to the Philippians, "I am sure of this, that he who began a good work in you will bring it to completion at the day of Jesus Christ" (1:6).

71. Bruce, *CPE*, 268n115, notes, "The context suggests that εἰς ἡμᾶς means not merely 'toward us' but 'in us' (cf. ἐν ἡμῖν, Eph. 3:20)."

72. Although Paul does not explicitly equate the working of God's power with the work of the Spirit in this passage, he does make this connection in Rom. 15:13 and later in Eph. 3:16. Cf. Eph. 3:7, 20.

73. "Immeasurable," from ὑπερβάλλω, is used five times in the New Testament, all in Paul's writings, and always as a present active participle. Three of these uses are Eph. 1:19 ("the immeasurable greatness of his power"); 2:7 ("immeasurable riches of his grace"); 3:19 ("the love of Christ that surpasses knowledge"). The other two uses are 2 Cor. 3:10 ("the glory that surpasses it") and 9:14 ("the surpassing grace of God").

promises, Paul underscores and amplifies *immeasurable* (in "the immeasurable greatness of his power") in verses 20–23, where he identifies this divine power with the power that raised Christ "from the dead and seated him at his right hand[74] in the heavenly places far above all rule and authority and power and dominion, and above every name that is named, not only in this age but also in the one to come" (1:20–21).[75] Christ is not merely above the powers; he is *far above* (ὑπεράνω) them. He's not only far above the four named powers;[76] he is far above "*every name* that is named."[77] And this is true not only for "this age"; it's true for *all eternity*, for "the [age] to come."[78]

Furthermore, not only is Christ far above every name that is named; God has put all things (including the powers) "under his feet" (1:22).[79] "The powers are not simply inferior to Christ; they are also subject to him.[80] Ephesians 1:20–22 paints an unmistakable portrait of Jesus Christ as the victorious *Lord* (cf. 1:3, 17). Christ is the supreme Lord of creation[81]—Lord of the cosmos, the cosmic Lord. In this role, the Father "gave him as head over all things to the church" (1:22). As Lord of creation, Christ is also its Head (κεφαλὴν), its supreme authority,[82]

---

74. A direct allusion to Ps. 110:1; the position of supreme power. See David M. Hay, *Glory at the Right Hand: Psalm 110 in Early Christianity* (Atlanta: Society of Biblical Literature, 1973); Bruce, *CPE*, 272; and O'Brien, *Ephesians*, 140–41, and his excellent summary on pp. 272–73 of the use of Ps. 110:1 in the New Testament. See Acts 2:33–34; 7:55–56; Rom. 8:34; Eph. 1:20; Col. 3:1; Heb. 1:3, 13; 8:1; 10:12; 12:2; 1 Pet. 3:22.

75. Cf. Col. 1:16.

76. Three of the four powers enumerated in Eph. 1:21 are used in Col. 1:16, but in a different order, and Colossians omits "power" and adds "thrones." Paul is not concerned to present a taxonomy of angelic relationships, which is why he adds "and above every name that is named" in Eph. 1:21, as if to say, "No matter which 'deity' may be in question, Christ is above that deity as his Lord." So O'Brien, *Ephesians*, 142–43.

77. Cf. Phil. 1:9–11. The name above every name that will be universally acknowledged is *Lord* (O'Brien, *Ephesians*, 142).

78. Eph. 1:21 is the only place in Paul's writings where the two ages are explicitly contrasted.

79. A direct allusion to Ps. 8:6, which in the New Testament is applied to Christ as the last Adam in 1 Cor. 15:27 and Heb. 2:6–9. See the discussion of this verse in Bruce, *CPE*, 274, who notes, "In 1 Cor. 15:24–28 the words of Ps. 8:6 are linked with those of Ps. 110:1, 'Sit at my right hand, till I make your enemies your footstool,' the 'enemies' being identified as 'every principality and every power and might.'"

80. O'Brien, *Ephesians*, 145.

81. Bruce, *CPE*, says that Christ "exercises universal lordship." Cf. Matt. 28:18; Acts 2:36; 10:36; Rom. 10:12; Rev. 17:14; 19:16; cf. Col. 1:15–20.

82. As Col. 2:10 makes clear; Christ is "the head of all rule and authority." Eph. 1:22 says, "head over all things," which, given the context, certainly includes "the powers." See O'Brien, *Ephesians*, 145–46, for a good defense of this position. He notes, "The term 'head' expresses his ruling authority" (146). After a detailed discussion of κεφαλή, Hoehner, *Ephesians*, 285–87, concludes: "Certainly, when this word is used in relationship to Christ, it refers to his authority over the church (Eph. 5:23; Col. 1:18), although in Col. 2:10 it speaks of him being head of all rule and authority. In the present context . . . God gave him (as head over all things) to the church" (286–87).

and the Father's gift[83] to the church.[84] Thus Christ is Lord of creation
and Lord of the church.[85] Christ has been invested with the Father's
full authority to rule over all things; he has been endowed with God's
power to control all things; and the Spirit works on his behalf to carry
out his will throughout the cosmos and in the church,[86] including the
future realization of God's promises for the church (e.g., inheritance,
redemption). Because Christ is Lord of all, the Father will "unite all
things in him, things in heaven and things on earth" (1:10).[87]

Paul concludes his affirmation and explanation of the Father's
mighty work in the present through Christ on behalf of Christians
by stating that the church "is his body, the fullness of him who fills
all in all" (Eph. 1:23; cf. 4:10). The last clause is one of the most
difficult to understand in the whole epistle.[88] Bruce's explanation
makes the most sense to me: The use of τὸ πλήρωμα "is a finish-
ing touch or summary (epiphōnēma) of what has been said from
verse 20 onwards."[89] It is "in apposition to the whole idea of the

---

83. "Gave" should be given its usual sense here as elsewhere in Ephesians; so O'Brien, *Ephesians*, 145, and Hoehner, *Ephesians*, 285.

84. O'Brien, *Ephesians*, 145n212, the emphasis is on "the church."

85. Bruce, *CPE*, 274: "With the insistence on his universal lordship goes the implication that he is also the church's lord."

86. See John M. Frame, *Systematic Theology: An Introduction to Christian Belief* (Phillipsburg, NJ: P&R, 2013), 14–35, for a discussion of the three lordship attributes: control, authority, and presence.

87. Paul describes this as "the mystery" of God's will that reveals the ultimate goal of his re-demptive purposes in Christ (Eph. 1:9, the completion of which will result in God's being "all in all," as discussed above): to unite in him all things in heaven and all things on earth (1:10). Paul mentions "the mystery" six times in Ephesians (1:9; 3:3, 4, 9; 5:32; 6:19; cf. Rom. 16:25–26; Col. 1:26, 27; 2:2; 4:3). The term refers to a fundamental aspect of God's redemptive plan that was hidden but whose meaning has now been revealed in Christ (Eph. 3:1–6). The mystery is related to the concept of "unification" and therefore to "wholeness" and "peace." Paul portrays three pairs of entities that will be unified: "things in heaven and things on earth" (1:10), Gentiles and Jews (3:3–4, 6, 9; 6:19), and Christ and the church (5:32). The Christ-church marriage analogy (5:22–33) may help to explain how the unification of heaven and earth progresses in the present. Jesus is the church's Lord and Savior. As the church, his body, his Lord, his self-sacrificial, salvific love works in her to make her holy—the goal of our election (5:27 with 1:4)—effecting a union with him that is as intimate as the one-flesh union in marriage (5:31–32), as well as a union among the members of the body. To the extent that people from all nationalities are united under Christ's lordship in the church, "the powers" lose "territory" (influence), and the unification of heaven and earth progresses—a process that can only be completed by Christ's return. Thus Paul saw the church in eschatological terms as the vanguard and arena of the Father's activity to unify heaven and earth under Christ's lordship—to effect cosmic redemption. This, I believe, was the major motivation for Paul's ministry to the Gentiles, and this may be why he asked in the closing verses of Ephesians for the readers to pray "that words may be given to me in opening my mouth boldly to proclaim the mystery of the gospel" (6:19), a request made at the close of Paul's extended teaching about the church's involvement in spiritual warfare with "the powers" and their leader, the Devil.

88. Space prohibits a discussion of the issues here. I refer interested readers to the commentaries by Bruce, Hoehner, Lincoln, and O'Brien.

89. Bruce, *CPE*, 276, citing J. A. Bengel, *Gnomon Novi Testamenti*, 3rd ed. (London: Williams and Norgate, 1862), 699.

preceding phrase, i.e., as Christ transcendent over and immanent within the church."[90]

If we follow current usage and treat the participle as a passive in sense as well as in form, it is not necessary to take the subject as being either Christ or God, but rather as being the church.[91] If *plērōma* is in apposition to the general sense of what precedes, the sense may well be that Christ, who is transcendent over the church, his body, is also immanent within it and fills it "as it attains to the maximum of its perfect plenitude"—that is, as it is being totally filled. The fullness of deity resides in him, and out of that fullness his church is being constantly supplied.[92]

Understood that way, "fullness" in this context refers to the presence of the risen and exalted Lord in the church, and "fills all in all" refers to his transcendence over the cosmos on behalf of the church.[93] This understanding fits well with the idea developed above that Ephesians 1:20–23 functions to give Christians maximal assurance and confidence in the Father and his promises. Christ as *Lord* is transcendent over the church, and as *Lord* he is immanent within it, filling it with the fullness of his presence.[94] His powerful, sovereign presence as Lord guarantees the future realization of our hope—the fulfillment of God's plan to unite heaven and earth in Christ (1:9–10). Thus the filling is not physical or spatial; it refers to Christ's *sovereign rule* "over all things" on behalf of the church,[95] to his lordship. So important is this

---

90. Bruce, *CPE*, 276, citing H. Chadwick, "Ephesians," in *Peake's Commentary on the Bible*, ed., Matthew Black and H. H. Rowley (London, 1962), 983.

91. So Lincoln, *Ephesians*, 73: "Taking πλήρωμα as a reference to the Church is in line with Eph. 3:19, where the prayer is that believers might be filled with all the fullness of God."

92. Bruce, *CPE*, 277; cf. John 1:16. Hoehner, *Ephesians*, 298, also understands πλήρωμα and πληρουμένου as passives and τὰ πάντα ἐν πᾶσιν adverbially, saying, "This would indicate that the church is filled by Christ who is being filled (by God) entirely or in every way (JB, NEB, NJB)." As Hoehner points out (299), "By accepting the participle (πληρουμένου) as passive, it makes reference to Christ being filled with God's πλήρωμα, as Paul taught in Col. 1:19 and 2:9." Cf. Eph. 1:23; 4:10, 13.

93. Lincoln, *Ephesians*, 77, notes: "Although Christ is in the process of filling the cosmos, at present it is only the Church which can actually be called his fullness. The church appears, then, to be the focus for and medium of Christ's presence and rule in the cosmos. This entails neither that the Church is the exclusive medium of Christ's presence and rule nor that it will eventually fill the world."

94. Lincoln, *Ephesians*, 75: "In the OT God's glorious presence could be seen as permeating not only the creation but also the temple (cf. Isa. 6:1; Ezek. 43:5; 44:4; Hag. 2:7), so it should not be surprising that in an epistle which calls the Church 'a holy temple in the Lord . . . a dwelling place of God in the Spirit' ([Eph.] 2:21, 22) it should also be seen as the place of the dynamic fullness of God in Christ."

95. Cf. O'Brien, *Ephesians*, 151. Lincoln, *Ephesians*, 77, says:

Christ pervades all things with his sovereign rule as he directs them to their divinely appointed goal, the restoration of their meaning and harmony (cf. [Eph.] 4:10; 1:10). It could well be

idea of "filling" for Paul that he returns to it at the end of his prayer in Ephesians 3:19.

This first part of Paul's prayer focuses on three things: the hope that the Father has given us, the inheritance that he has in us, and the "immeasurable greatness of his power toward us." It is a prayer addressed to the Father that begins by asking him for Spirit-given knowledge of him and, by implication, what he has done for us in Christ—the hope, inheritance, and power that are the prayer's three main petitions. It is a prayer that teaches us as adopted sons of God to ask our heavenly Father to help us know him better. It is a future-oriented prayer; it focuses on the "glorious inheritance" that the Father has in us, and it encourages us to contemplate the specific "riches" of that inheritance. As such, it is a "heavenly oriented" prayer, a prayer with a huge eschatological dimension. It also is an existentially oriented prayer; it encourages us to have an unshakable hope in that multifaceted inheritance and, by implication, in the triune God who guarantees it. Finally, it is a prayer that takes into account our need for assurance, which it provides by reminding us of "the immeasurable greatness" of the Father's "power toward us," which he has demonstrated by raising and exalting Christ to his right hand as the Lord over all "the powers," as the one who also fills the church with his presence.

The Second Part of Paul's Prayer (Eph. 3:14–21)

First and foremost in Ephesians 3:14–21, Paul is interested in amplifying and expanding the notion of Christ's power at work on behalf of the church (Eph. 1:19–23). In both parts of the prayer (1:16–19 and 3:14–21), Paul prays to the Father, requesting that the Spirit may grant his readers greater knowledge of what the Father has done for us in Christ, and in both parts of the prayer (as well as throughout the epistle), Paul explains this. Paul realizes that only by the Spirit working with the Word (e.g., teaching, instruction, doctrine) can we have personal knowledge of God that is life-changing.

The third element of Paul's earlier prayer—"what is the immeasurable greatness of his power toward us who believe" (Eph. 1:19)—is taken up in the initial element of his prayer in chapter 3: "to be strengthened

---

that just as 1:20, 22 draw on 1 Cor. 15:24–28 but place Paul's thoughts in a context of realized eschatology, so this phrase in [Eph.] 1:23 recalls the notion of 1 Cor. 15:28 that God will be all in all, πάντα ἐν πᾶσιν, but transfers it to Christ and makes it a present reality.

with power through his Spirit in your inner being" (3:16). The words δυνάμεως and κράτους from 1:19 are picked up in 3:16 in the phrase δυνάμει κραταιωθῆναι. O'Brien notes, "The buildup of power terms in v. 19 anticipates both the latter prayer and the doxology of 3:20–21."[96] Additionally, this second part of the prayer is connected to the *berakah*. "Every family in heaven" (3:15) echoes the "all things in heaven" (1:10), which earlier we saw includes "the powers" in the heavenly places. The prayer's interest in "filling" and "fullness" (3:19) harkens back to 1:23. The first part of the prayer is more closely tied to the *berakah*, while the second part is closely tied to the third petition of the first part.

Laying aside for the moment the introductory verses (3:14–15) and the prayer's concluding doxology (3:20–21), Paul's prayer in Ephesians 3:16–19 consists of three main requests, each introduced by ἵνα plus a subjunctive verb: (1) verses 16–17, (2) verses 18–19a, and (3) verse 19b. The first request is followed by a pair of parallel infinitive clauses, as is the second request. Both the first and second requests ask for divine empowerment to be like Christ, while the third request asks for divine filling, which is another way of requesting divine empowerment to be like Christ. In both infinitive pairs, the second infinitive explains/ advances the first. There is an upward progression from the first request to the second and the third: from power for Christ to dwell in our hearts, to strength to comprehend his incomprehensible love for us, to being filled with God's fullness. As Lincoln notes, "By the time the third ἵνα clause has been reached, the prayer has gathered rhetorical momentum, and the final request becomes the climactic one—'that you might be filled up to all the fullness of God.'"[97]

Outlined, and with the English word order mostly following that of the Greek, the structure of the prayer in Ephesians 3:16–19 looks like this:

1. That he may grant you, according to the riches of his grace, *power*
   a. to be strengthened through his Spirit in the inner man
   b. [that is, for] Christ to dwell[98] through faith in your hearts—in love being rooted and grounded—

---

96. O'Brien, *Ephesians*, 138.
97. Lincoln, *Ephesians*, 197.
98. See Hoehner, *Ephesians*, 480–81, for a discussion of the three main views of the syntactical relationship of κατοικῆσαι ("dwell," 3:17) to 3:16b–19. I am following the second view—as represented by Fee, *GEP*, 694, 696, and O'Brien, *Ephesians*, 258, especially note 151—that κατοικῆσαι

2. That you may have *strength*
   a. to comprehend with all the saints what is the breadth and length and height and depth
   b. [that is] to know the love of Christ that surpasses knowledge
3. That you may *be filled* with [or "into"] all the fullness of God

Since through Christ we "have access in one Spirit to the Father" (Eph. 2:18), whom we can approach with "boldness and access with confidence" (3:12; cf. Heb. 4:16), Paul's prayer in Ephesians 3 begins with a reference to "the Father" (3:14), just as he began the first part of the prayer in chapter 1 by addressing "the Father of glory" (1:17), and just as the *berakah* begins: "Blessed be the God and Father of our Lord Jesus Christ" (1:3). Paul's kneeling posture (3:14) is an act of worship or homage before the sovereign Father,[99] "from whom every family in heaven and on earth is named" (3:15)—a phrase that emphasizes the Father's sovereignty over every human and angelic family (including "the powers" in 3:10), just as in 4:6 Paul refers to "one God and Father of all, who is over all and through all and in all."[100] This affirmation of God's universal dominion is mirrored in the first line of the prayer's closing doxology—"to him [the Father] who is able to do far more abundantly than all that we ask or think" (3:20). The Father's sovereignty guarantees that he will answer Paul's prayer (3:16–19); "the riches of his glory" (3:16) indicates that he will do so "far more abundantly" than we can ask or imagine (3:20).

Paul can affirm the Father's universal sovereignty *and* Christ's universal sovereignty, because in terms of his redemptive-historical role as Messiah, Christ's rule as cosmic Lord is derivative; it has been granted to him by the Father (Eph. 1:20–23) until all God's enemies are de-

---

explains/clarifies κραταιωθῆναι, rather than the third view, which sees κατοικῆσαι as the result of κραταιωθῆναι, or the first view, which sees a strict parallelism between κατοικῆσαι and κραταιωθῆναι.

99. Lincoln, *Ephesians*, 201–2. Hoehner, *Ephesians*, 473, notes that κάμπτω is used four times in the New Testament, all in Paul (Rom. 11:4; 14:11; Eph. 3:14; Phil. 2:10). Rom. 11:14 and Phil. 2:10 are quoting Isa. 45:23; Rom. 11:4 is quoting 1 Kings 19:18. According to Robinson, *Ephesians*, 83, κάμπτω τὰ γόνατά μου in Eph. 3:14 is derived from Isa. 45:23.

100. See Hoehner, *Ephesians*, 474–76. Naming in the Bible expresses sovereignty over those named. Here the term "Father" (Πατέρα) is used to refer to God as the sovereign creator of "every family" (πᾶσα πατριὰ)—heavenly as well as earthly. As such, he is the "cosmic Father" (Lincoln, *Ephesians*, 203). The reference to "the rulers and authorities in the heavenly places" in Eph. 3:10 suggests that in 3:15 Paul is referring to angels. Regarding heavenly families, see Heb. 12:9 and James 1:17. "Heaven" (οὐρανός) and "earth" (γῆ) are paired in Ephesians only here and in 1:10.

feated (1 Cor. 15:24–26), at which time "the Son himself will also be subjected to him who put all things in subjection under him, that God may be all in all" (1 Cor. 15:28).[101]

Paul's prayer that Christians would know "the immeasurable greatness" of God's power (Eph. 1:19) focused in a formal manner on the Father's sovereign power exercised on behalf of the church through Christ, and Ephesians 3:14–15 likewise affirms his universal sovereignty. Building on this concept, Paul prays boldly and with confidence in Ephesians 3:16–17 that the Father, by means of "his Spirit," would strengthen Christians in our "inner being," that is, that Christ may dwell in our hearts by faith.[102] Paul's prayer for power in 3:16–17 is for Christians' inner transformation by means of the Spirit of Christ.[103]

The Spirit is called "his [the Father's] Spirit" (Eph. 3:16)—"the promised Holy Spirit" (1:13; cf. Acts 1:4–5) sent by the Father.[104] As such, the Spirit is both the source and the means by which Christians are strengthened,[105] and this strengthening consists in nothing less than *Christ* dwelling in our hearts in a vivifying, vitalizing manner. The Spirit's strengthening activity does not temporally precede Christ's indwelling; the empowering and the indwelling are *concurrent*; they are two ways of talking about the same experience.[106]

This raises the question Why, and on what basis, does Paul equate the Spirit's strengthening action with Christ's indwelling presence—the Spirit with Christ? According to 1 Corinthians 15:45b—which is set in the context of Paul's extended discussion of the already of Christ's resurrection, the "not yet" of ours, and the nature of Christ's resurrected and exalted existence—"the last Adam became life-giving Spirit" (πνεῦμα ζῳοποιοῦν). In his discussion of this verse, Richard Gaffin shows that

---

101. See my earlier discussion of the phrase "that God may be all in all" in 1 Corinthians 15:28 and Fee's remarks there. Cf. 1 Cor. 15:27b: "But when it says, 'all things are put in subjection,' it is plain that he [the Father] is excepted who put all things in subjection under him [the Son]."

102. Paul was praying not for an initial indwelling of Christ but for a continual indwelling. Cf. Eph. 5:18.

103. The prayer is overtly Trinitarian.

104. The Spirit is also sent by the Son, e.g., John 14:16; 15:26; 16:7, 13–15. Cf. Acts 16:7; Rom. 8:9; Gal. 4:6; Phil. 1:19; 1 Pet. 1:11. Acts 2:33: "Being therefore exalted at the right hand of God, and having received from the Father the promise of the Holy Spirit, he has poured out this that you yourselves are seeing and hearing."

105. Fee, *GEP*, 695, emphasizes source; O'Brien, *Ephesians*, 257, emphasizes agency/means. Fee (695) lists these verses as other "collocations" of *Spirit* and *power*: Rom. 15:13, 19; 1 Cor. 2:4; 2 Cor. 6:6–7; 1 Thess. 1:5; 2 Tim. 1:7. Also see Rom. 1:4.

106. "His indwelling is not something additional to the strengthening, but a further definition of it" (O'Brien, *Ephesians*, 258n151).

πνεῦμα refers to the Holy Spirit (and so should be Πνεῦμα),[107] that Christ *became* (not "is") the Spirit, that this "becoming" took place at his resurrection, that the becoming invested Christ with the same life-giving power that was at work in *his* resurrection, that henceforth the Spirit operates in a life-giving role on Christ's behalf, that Paul is making a functional (not an ontological) identification between Christ and the Spirit, that this identification is the central aspect of Christ's redemptive-historical role as the last Adam (Head of the new creation order), that Paul is portraying Christ as resurrected *and* exalted, and that this verse is fundamental to understanding Paul's Christology, pneumatology, and soteriology.[108] Gaffin says: "Only by virtue of the functional identity of the Spirit and Christ, effected redemptively-historically in his resurrection, is Christ the communicator of life. No principle in Paul's soteriology is more fundamental."[109] In a similar vein (commenting on Rom. 8:2), John Murray said, "The Holy Spirit is the Spirit of Christ . . . and it is only in Christ Jesus that the Spirit's power is operative unto life."[110]

Christ is so intimately, thoroughly, and powerfully present with and in Christians by means of the Spirit that to be strengthened in our inner being by the Spirit is the same as Christ dwelling in our hearts. Bruce puts it succinctly: "The ministry of the Spirit is devoted to making the presence and power of the risen Christ real to those whom he indwells: hence the experience of the indwelling Spirit and of the indwelling Christ is the same experience."[111] Lincoln carries this idea further: "Believers do not experience Christ except as Spirit and do not experience the Spirit except as Christ. The implication, as far as this prayer is concerned, is that greater experience of the Spirit's power will mean the character of Christ increasingly becoming the hallmark of believ-

---

107. So John Murray, *The Epistle to the Romans*, 2 vols. (Grand Rapids, MI: Eerdmans, 1984), 1:276.

108. Richard B. Gaffin Jr., *Resurrection and Redemption: A Study in Paul's Soteriology*, 2nd ed. (Phillipsburg, NJ: Presbyterian and Reformed, 1987), 78–91. Also see his "'Life-Giving Spirit': Probing the Center of Paul's Pneumatology," *JETS* 41, no. 4 (December 1998): 573–89, especially 582: "From the viewpoint of an overall theology of the NT, 1 Cor. 15:45b is fairly and helpfully seen as a one-sentence commentary on the significance of Pentecost, along with the resurrection and ascension. Paul here telescopes what Peter delineates in his Pentecost sermon in Acts 2:32–33ff . . . As 'the life-giving Spirit,' (the resurrected and ascended) Christ is the one who baptizes with the Spirit."

109. Gaffin, *Resurrection*, 89. Also see Gaffin's remarks on 2 Cor. 3:17, "Now the Lord is the Spirit, and where the Spirit of the Lord is, there is freedom" (92–97).

110. Murray, *Romans*, 1:276. Cf. John 6:63; Rom. 8:2, 6, 11; 1 Cor. 15:45; 2 Cor. 3:6; Gal. 6:8.

111. Bruce, *CPE*, 326. Cf. John 16:13–15; Rom. 8:9–11.

ers' lives."[112] The experience of the Spirit, of the indwelling Christ, is nothing less than an experience, in principle, of the life of the age to come—of the "not yet" side of Paul's eschatology.

Paul prays that by means of the Spirit, on the one hand, and their faith, on the other, his readers would experience the powerful, constant presence of Christ in their "hearts" (Eph. 3:17a)—the center of their beings,[113] which Bruce wonderfully refers to as "the immortal personality which constitutes here and now the seed of that fuller immortality to be manifested in the resurrection age."[114]

"That you, being rooted and grounded in love" (3:17b; cf. Col. 2:7), is best understood as joined to the following "[that you] may have strength to comprehend with all the saints" (Eph. 3:18a), with the rootedness and groundedness understood as already existing by virtue of Christ's indwelling.[115] Since Ephesians 3:19 speaks of "the love of Christ," that is, the love that Christ has for us, it makes sense to understand "love" in verse 17 as a reference to Christ's love or the Father's love revealed in and expressed by Christ.[116] "Rooted" is a botanical metaphor, and "grounded" is an architectural one. Together they express the same idea: being firmly and decisively established in God's love for us in Christ[117]—a love expressed in all the blessings bestowed on us by the Father in the *berakah*; in our having been sealed with the promised Holy Spirit; in our having been made alive, raised, and seated with Christ in the heavenly realms, and so on. "This love is the love of God revealed in Christ and poured into his people's hearts by the Spirit, so that they in turn may show it to one another and to all."[118]

---

112. Lincoln, *Ephesians*, 206.
113. The verb κατοικέω, "may dwell" (Eph. 3:17), "connotes a settled dwelling, as opposed to παροικέω, a temporary sojourn (Luke 24:18; Heb. 11:9)" (Hoehner, *Ephesians*, 480). Bruce, *CPE*, 327, translates Eph. 3:17a, "that Christ may take up residence in your hearts." In Col. 1:19 and 2:9, Paul used κατοικῆσαι to refer to the fullness of God dwelling bodily in Christ. "May dwell" explains "be strengthened," as we have seen, indicating that Paul prayed for a *powerful* indwelling. "In your inner being" (Eph. 3:16) and "in your hearts" (3:17) are correlative. Both refer to the seat of our personality, to our knowing-willing-feeling moral self.
114. Bruce, *CPE*, 326.
115. So Hoehner, *Ephesians*, 483, and O'Brien, *Ephesians*, 360, who understands the two participles "being rooted and grounded in love" as expressing "the contemplated result of the two previous infinitives ["strengthened," "dwell"], which in turn provides the condition for the next request."
116. So Bruce, *CPE*, 327. Cf. "God's love has been poured into our hearts through the Holy Spirit who has been given to us" (Rom. 5:5).
117. Hoehner, *Ephesians*, 484. O'Brien, *Ephesians*, 260, observes, "The word order of the original stresses love, while the two perfect passive participles depict the notions of progress and resulting state."
118. Bruce, *CPE*, 327.

Ephesians 3:18 and 19 are correlative petitions—"to comprehend," "to know"—that together form the object of the strengthening and indwelling of 3:16b–17a. Although the phrase "may have
strength to comprehend with all the saints what is the breadth and
length and height and depth" (3:18) lacks a referent for its dimen-
sional language, it seems best to understand that to be the love of
Christ.[119] The four dimensions refer to a single entity, a totality that
"evokes the immensity of a particular object, and that object is not
made explicit until the next and parallel clause, namely, the love of
Christ."[120]

"To comprehend" (καταλαβέσθαι) in verse 18 is paralleled by
"to know" (γνῶναι) in verse 19, the latter advancing on the former
idea by suggesting "not just intellectual apprehension but personal
knowledge."[121] Paul is not merely speaking in these verses of an intellectual or doctrinal grasp of what it means for Christ to love us.[122] He
is also speaking about *experiencing* Christ's love in a personal (existential and subjective), transforming manner in our hearts, the seat of
our being where Christ dwells. Regarding this, D. A. Carson writes:

> This cannot be merely an intellectual exercise. Paul is not asking
> that his readers might become more able to articulate the greatness
> of God's love in Christ Jesus or to grasp with the intellect alone how
> significant God's love is in the plan of redemption. He is asking God
> that they might have the power to grasp the dimensions of that love
> in their experience. Doubtless that includes intellectual reflection,
> but it cannot be reduced to that alone.[123]

Paul's petition in Ephesians 3:18–19 is for his readers, along "with
all the saints," "to comprehend" and "to know" "the love of Christ
that surpasses knowledge" (the incomprehensible)—an enchanting
oxymoron that beckons us to plumb the depths of the immense love

119. This the most popular interpretative option. See the list of supporting commentators in
O'Brien, *Ephesians*, 263.
120. Lincoln, *Ephesians*, 212, after surveying all the interpretative options (207–13). He notes
that the "climactically parallel clause" (3:19a) not only explains but also advances the meaning of
the vaguer clause (3:18b).
121. Lincoln, *Ephesians*, 212.
122. Though he certainly believed in the necessity of sound teaching (Eph. 4:11–16) for growing
into "the fullness of Christ" (4:13).
123. D. A. Carson, *Praying with Paul: A Call to Spiritual Reformation*, 2nd ed. (Grand Rapids,
MI: Baker Academic, 2014), 168.

that Christ has for us[124] through worship, study, prayer, fellowship, and meditation.[125] Christ's love for us is so immeasurable (3:18) that no matter how much of it we fathom, we can never know it exhaustively. Knowing Christ's love intellectually and experientially requires participation in the body of Christ, as "with all the saints" in verse 18 suggests. And as Ephesians 2:22 says, in Christ we "are *being built together* into a dwelling place for God by the Spirit."[126]

To sum up Ephesians 3:16–19a, Christ dwells in our hearts through the Spirit to empower us to know his boundless love. Verse 19 explains why. The final petition and the ultimate goal of Paul's prayer is "that you may be filled with all the fullness of God" (3:19b). In short, Paul prays for the Father to empower us (3:16) to be filled with his fullness (3:19). More specifically, Paul prays that Christ's dwelling in our hearts would strengthen us (3:16a, 18a) to experience his immense love, with the result that we would be filled with all of God's fullness. "By knowing the love of Christ, and only so, is it possible to be filled up to the measure of God's own fullness."[127]

What, then, does Paul mean by "that you may be filled with all the fullness [τὸ πλήρωμα] of God" (Eph. 3:19b), the prayer's final and climactic petition? Earlier, we saw that "the fullness" in Ephesians 1:23 refers to the powerful presence of the risen and exalted Lord on behalf of the church that assures us of his control. The idea in Ephesians 3:19b is similar but more existential.[128] In 3:19b "the fullness" refers to the empowering, loving presence of Christ, ruling in the hearts of Christians, that conforms us to his likeness, enabling us to grow in holiness and purity (Eph. 1:4; 5:27; cf. Col. 1:22; 1 Thess. 3:13).[129] In both verses, Christ's lordship is in view. He is Lord over the church

---

124. Lincoln, *Ephesians*, 214, notes that God's love and Christ's love "are two sides of the same coin." Cf. Rom. 8:35 ("the love of Christ)" with Rom. 8:39 ("the love of God in Christ Jesus our Lord"); 2 Cor. 5:14; Gal. 2:20.

125. E.g., Pss. 49:3; 63:6; 77:3, 6, 12; 119:15, 23, 27, 48, 78, 97, 99, 148; 143:5; 145:5.

126. Yet another Trinitarian formulation.

127. Bruce, *CPE*, 329.

128. By "more existential" I do not mean "more individualistic." There is a tension of the eschatological already/not-yet between Eph. 1:13 and 3:19. The former pictures the church as already filled with Christ's presence, and the latter as needing to be filled. Lincoln, *Ephesians*, 214: "What the church already is in principle, it is increasingly to realize in its experience."

129. Lincoln, *Ephesians*, 214: "The fullness of God, which is best explained as his presence and power, his life and rule, immanent in his creation, has been mediated to believers through Christ, in whom the fullness was present bodily."

(1:22–23), and "through faith" (3:17) we are to welcome him daily as Lord within our lives (3:19).

The result of the Spirit's strengthening, of Christ's indwelling, and of our growing in knowledge of Christ's love is transformation into the likeness of the One whose love we experience—into the likeness of Christ.[130] Knowing the love of Christ in our hearts is transformative. The more we know his love personally, the more "filled" with him we are, the more conformed to his likeness we become—increasingly filled with his life and power.[131] We need the character of Christ to be formed *in* us so that his redemptive purposes may be fulfilled *through* us. We must be transformed *by* Christ's love before we can transform others *with* his love. Thus the ultimate goal of Paul's prayer—that we "may be filled with all the fullness of God"—has to do with personal and corporate transformation into conformity with Christ in thought, word, and deed. Both ideas—personal and corporate conformity to Christ—occupy Paul in chapters 4 and 5, and both ideas are as much eschatological as they are ethical.[132]

The way that we become truly Christlike is to be transformed by knowing Christ's love for us, a knowing that involves (1) biblical teaching—doctrine (e.g., the *berakah*)—in the context of the church (Eph. 4:11–16), (2) our personal and communal experience of Christ's love (3:16–19), and (3) the Spirit's work in and among us (1:17; 3:16).

---

130. See 2 Cor. 3:16–18 for a similar idea.

131. Lincoln, *Ephesians*, 214–15. Eph. 5:18—"And do not get drunk with wine, for that is debauchery, but be filled with the Spirit"—is a parallel thought, expressed as an imperative. Rather than being filled with wine and coming under its power, we are to be filled with the Spirit and come under his rule (a thought that governs Paul's exhortations through 6:9), which is the same as being filled with Christ and being under his rule. Being filled with the Spirit results in Christlike behavior in word, thought, and deed, rather than in wine-induced, inebriated behavior. The present tense "be filled" indicates that Christians are to continue to be filled, that the filling is not a once-and-for-all experience but is meant to be a continuing one. The Spirit mediates God's fullness to Christians (cf. 3:19; 4:13; also Gal. 5:25: "If we live by the Spirit, let us also keep in step with the Spirit").

132. Paul begins Ephesians 4 by saying: "I therefore, a prisoner for the Lord, urge you to walk in a manner worthy of the calling to which you have been called" (4:1). This requires being equipped and built up through sound teaching (4:11–15) "until we all attain to . . . the measure of the stature of the fullness of Christ" (4:13). We are to put off our old selves (4:22) and "put on the new self, created after the likeness of God in true righteousness and holiness" (4:24). We are to "be imitators of God, as beloved children. And walk in love, as Christ loved us and gave himself up for us, a fragrant offering and sacrifice to God" (5:1–2). Paul says, "Look carefully then how you walk, not as unwise but as wise, making the best use of the time, because the days are evil" (5:15–16). We are to "be filled with the Spirit" (5:18) and to submit "to one another out of reverence for Christ" (5:21). We are to "be strong in the Lord and in the strength of his might" (6:10). We are to "put on the whole armor of God" that we "may be able to stand against the schemes of the devil" (6:11). Transformation into Christ's image requires the Spirit's work in our lives and our serious, deliberate, disciplined, Scripture-guided response to that work.

These can be respectively thought of as normative, existential, and situational perspectives.[133]

Paul concludes his prayer in Ephesians 3 with a doxology. In verse 20, he refers to the Father as the one "who is able to do far more abundantly than all that we ask or think, according to the power at work within us." The "power" (δυνάμει) that Paul prayed for in verse 16 is the "power" (δύναμιν) that is now "at work within us" (3:20). This power that is now "at work" (ἐνεργουμένην) in us (3:20) is the same power that God "worked" (ἐνήργηκεν) in Christ when he raised him from the dead (1:20). It is the power of the Spirit.[134] Having asked the Father to fill believers with the very fullness of his presence, Paul assures his readers that as big a prayer as that is, nothing is too big for the Father, who can raise the dead— that in fact not only is the Father able to answer the prayer for filling, but he can do so "far more abundantly" than all we can ask or think. The Father's "capacity for giving far exceeds his people's capacity for asking—or even imagining."[135]

The doxology concludes in Ephesians 3:21: "to him be glory in the church and in Christ Jesus throughout all generations, forever and ever. Amen."[136] Paul ascribes glory to the Father, the riches of whose glory he appealed to in 3:16, to whose glory he referred in 1:17, and whose glory he thrice praises in the *berakah* (1:6, 12, 14).[137] It is fitting that the church, as the sphere where the Father rules through Christ (1:22b, 23; 2:22; 3:10), who is immanent by means of the Spirit (2:18, 22; 3:16–17), is the sphere where the Father's glory is acknowledged,[138] where the "manifold wisdom" of his plan to unite heaven and earth in Christ (3:11 with 1:9–10) is "made known to the rulers and authorities in the heavenly places" (3:10) as a divine proclamation of his victory

---

133. This triad cuts across three common and unhealthy dichotomies often associated with sanctification: legalism versus antinomianism, doctrine versus experience, and individualism versus collectivism.

134. See, Fee, *GEP*, 695. Bruce, *CPE*, 331: "By the Spirit who imparts this power to believers the full realization of God's gracious purpose for them and in them becomes possible."

135. Bruce, *CPE*, 330.

136. See O'Brien, *Ephesians*, 268–69, and Lincoln, *Ephesians*, 216–18, for discussions of the doxology's unusual features.

137. Interestingly, in Eph. 1:6 the praise is related to our predestination to adoption as sons; in 1:12 it is related to hope; and in 1:14 it is related to inheritance. Earlier, I briefly noted that sonship, inheritance, and hope are closely related, and that the *berakah* ends with a focus on inheritance.

138. Lincoln, *Ephesians*, 217.

in Christ and of their impending doom.[139] "In the church" is parallel to "in Christ Jesus." Because Christians are "in Christ," he is "the sphere in which their glorification of God takes place."[140]

Paul's prayer in Ephesians 1:16–19, which ended with a request for his readers to know "the immeasurable greatness" of the Father's power "toward us who believe," resumes in 3:16 with a request that the Father would strengthen us "with power through his Spirit" in our inner beings, that Christ would dwell in our hearts through faith. This is followed by a petition for strength to know the incomprehensible love that Christ has for his people, so that (the third petition) we may be filled with God's fullness. This filling is progressive and transformational; it transforms us into Christ's likeness. Thus the church grows to maturity in proportion to her understanding and experience of the Father's love for us in Christ, as that love results in a growing fullness of the presence, rule, and character of Christ in our lives by means of the Holy Spirit.

Like the first part of the prayer, the concluding part is addressed to the Father, and also like the first part of the prayer, it begins by asking for a work of the Spirit in our lives, in this case for him to strengthen us in our inner beings. If the first part of the prayer may be characterized as one of *apprehending* God and what he has done for us, this closing part may be characterized as one of *appropriating* what God has done for us. The first part of the prayer focuses more on the accomplishment of redemption, the second more on its application. Because of the focus on application, this second part is more existential in orientation than the first, but like the first, the eschatological dimension is present throughout.

Paul's prayer teaches us to ask the Father for the Spirit to strengthen us and for Christ to dwell in our hearts; and it teaches us to keep asking for these things, not as if they were not already ours but because having them in increasing measure is essential for growing to maturity. This prayer also teaches us to ask the Father for strength to know and experience Christ's immeasurable love for us.

---

139. Lincoln, "Re-Examination," 474–75. R. P. Martin, "Ephesians," in *New Bible Commentary Revised* (London: Inter-Varsity Press, 1970), 1113: "The hostile angelic powers are not only held in wonder, but their death-knell is sounded with the proclamation that God in Christ has decisively acted for cosmic salvation and so brought their malign régime over human life to an end" (cited in Lincoln, "Re-Examination," 474).

140. Lincoln, "Re-Examination," 474.

An intellectual grasp of this love is insufficient for God's purposes for our lives because it does not transform our inner beings, our hearts. God wants us to experience Christ's love for us personally *in* our hearts, that we may be transformed by it into loving Christ *with* our hearts, not just intellectually. Our love for Christ grows in proportion to our understanding who he is and what he has done for us, on the one hand, and to experiencing that love in our hearts, on the other. Ultimately, this prayer teaches us to pray for transformation into the likeness of Christ, which is God's goal for us individually and corporately.[141] As Ephesians 1:4 says, God "chose us in him before the foundation of the world, that we should be holy and blameless before him" (cf. Eph. 5:25–27; Col. 1:22; Heb. 12:14; 1 Pet. 1:15–16).[142]

But this is not merely a prayer for sanctification. Seen in the broader context of Ephesians's eschatological themes and their Christological focus, it is also a prayer for the advancement of the Father's goal to "unite all things in him [Christ], things in heaven and things on earth" (Eph. 1:10). The process of being transformed into Christ's likeness, of growing in holiness and righteousness—individually and corporately—is a process of progressively coming under Christ's *lordship*. The more we as individuals and as the church come under his lordship, the more we help facilitate the reunification of heaven and earth because we will[143]

- no longer follow "the prince of the power of the air, the spirit that is now at work in the sons of disobedience" (Eph. 2:2b; cf. 4:17–19);
- "walk in a manner worthy of the calling to which [we] have been called" (Eph. 4:1);[144]

---

141. As Paul wrote in Rom. 8:29, God has predestined us "to be conformed to the image of his Son, in order that he might be the firstborn among many brothers." Cf. 1 Cor. 15:49; 2 Cor. 3:18.

142. Bruce, *CPE*, 255: "The purpose of God's choosing his people in Christ is that they should be 'holy and blameless' in his presence, both here and now in earthly life and ultimately when they appear before him."

143. The following is a sampling of Paul's teaching in Ephesians 4–6. It is fascinating to see how the particulars of the parenesis in these chapters build on and are derived from chaps. 1–3 (Bruce, *CPE*, 333n1, observes that Eph. 4:1, like Rom. 12:1, opens with παρακαλῶ οὖν ὑμᾶς; cf. 1 Cor. 4:16). It is also illuminating to see how the parenesis includes a number of references to the Devil and to his deceitful ways. Every encouraged behavior in chaps. 4–6 plays a role in furthering Christ's lordship and, therefore, the reunification of heaven and earth.

144. Bruce, *CPE*, 333, commenting on the transition from chaps. 1–3 to 4–6 says, "As members of the new humanity, the readers have already been reminded of the purpose to which God has

- be "eager to maintain the unity of the Spirit in the bond of peace" (Eph. 4:3);
- resist false doctrine, human cunning, and crafty, deceitful schemes (Eph. 4:14) and instead speak "the truth in love" and so "grow up in every way into him who is the head, into Christ" (Eph. 4:15);
- "no longer walk as the Gentiles do, in the futility of their minds" (Eph. 4:17);
- "put off" the "old self" (Eph. 4:22a) and "put on the new self, created after the likeness of God in true righteousness and holiness" (Eph. 4:24);
- "put away falsehood" and "speak the truth" with our neighbors (Eph. 4:25);
- "give no opportunity to the devil" (Eph. 4:27);
- not "grieve the Holy Spirit of God, by whom [we] were sealed for the day of redemption" (Eph. 4:30);
- "be imitators of God, as beloved children. And walk in love, as Christ loved us and gave himself up for us, a fragrant offering and sacrifice to God" (Eph. 5:1–2);
- "take no part in the unfruitful works of darkness, but instead expose them" (Eph. 5:11);
- "look carefully" how we "walk, not as unwise but as wise, making the best use of the time, because the days are evil" (Eph. 5:15–16);
- "understand what the will of the Lord is" (Eph. 5:17) and "be filled with the Spirit" (Eph. 5:18);
- "be strong in the Lord and in the strength of his might" (Eph. 6:10);
- "put on the whole armor of God, that [we] may be able to stand against the schemes of the devil" (Eph. 6:11);
- pray "at all times in the Spirit, with all prayer and supplication" (Eph. 6:18); and
- boldly proclaim "the mystery of the gospel" (Eph. 6:19).

Paul's prayer is a big prayer. He prayed for big things because he knew God is a big God who can answer our biggest prayers in ways that surpass our biggest expectations. Many years ago, J. Armitage

---

called them: the hope of their calling (Eph. 1:18) requires lives which are in keeping with their high destiny."

Robinson,[145] when reflecting on the bigness and boldness of the astounding final petition in Paul's prayer—"that you may be filled with all the fullness of God" (Eph. 3:19)—wrote these famous words:

> No prayer that has ever been framed has uttered a bolder request. It is a noble example of παρρησία, of freedom of speech, of that "boldness and access in confidence" [Eph. 3:12] of which he has spoken above. Unabashed by the greatness of his petition, he triumphantly invokes a power which can do far more than he asks, far more that even his lofty imagination conceives. His prayer has risen into praise. *"Now unto Him that is able to do exceeding abundantly above all that we ask or think, according to the power that worketh in us, to Him be the glory in the church and in Christ Jesus, throughout all ages, world without end. Amen."*[146]

May the Lord teach us to pray boldly, with greater understanding, increased specificity, and expanded expectations, knowing that our heavenly Father's capacity for answering our prayers far exceeds our capacity for framing them.[147] May we ask the Father to strengthen us so that Christ dwells in our hearts and we experience the transforming power of his incomprehensible love, that we "may be filled with all the fullness of God."

---

145. At various times fellow of Christ's College (Cambridge), vicar of All Saints' Church (Cambridge), dean of Westminster, and dean of Wells.
146. Robinson, *Ephesians*, 89.
147. To paraphrase Bruce, *CPE*, 330.

8

The Spirit and the Church

Priorities from 1 Corinthians 12–14

Jeff T. Purswell

It is a great privilege to contribute to this Festschrift in honor of Wayne Grudem. Wayne's life has been a blessing to my own in more ways than I can enumerate here. As my first systematic theology professor at Trinity Evangelical Divinity School in 1994, Wayne modeled for me a relentlessly biblical and deeply doxological approach to the discipline of theology. Throughout my time at Trinity I was in Wayne's student fellowship group, where I observed the intimacy of his prayer life and experienced his personal care. As Wayne's teaching assistant from 1995–1997, I saw up close the hallmarks of his scholarship: meticulous, persistent, and unswervingly aimed at Christ's honor. I experienced Wayne's generosity in his invitation to distill his *Systematic Theology* into a much shorter and more accessible book.[1] Most significantly, as Wayne's friend for twenty-three years, I have been enriched and inspired by his encouragement, wisdom, loyalty, and example of integrity, childlike faith, and deep devotion to Jesus Christ.

---

1. Wayne Grudem, *Bible Doctrine: Essential Teachings of the Christian Faith*, ed. Jeff Purswell (Grand Rapids, MI: Zondervan, 1999).

As the subtitle of this book suggests, an animating burden of Wayne's academic life has been the nexus between God's Word and God's people. As Wayne reminded us in the preface to *Systematic Theology*: "Theology is meant to be *lived* and *prayed* and *sung*! All of the great doctrinal writings of the Bible . . . are full of praise of God and personal application to life."[2] In addition, a prominent focus of much of Wayne's writing has been the person of the Holy Spirit and his activity among Christians and the church.[3] As a tribute to this burden and focus, this chapter will explore a central text in the New Testament's teaching on the Holy Spirit, 1 Corinthians 12–14, with the goal of identifying some key priorities that should guide the thinking and practice of believers, and especially pastors, concerning the work of the Holy Spirit.

Scope and Relevance

Space prohibits detailed exegesis of 1 Corinthians 12–14, much less a thorough treatment of the work of the Holy Spirit.[4] However, certain aspects of these chapters make them particularly relevant for thinking biblically about the Spirit's work among his people.

First of all, *this text has the church in view.* Far from a theoretical treatise on the Holy Spirit, 1 Corinthians 12–14 deals with the Spirit's role among the people of God as he manifests God's presence, endues the church with gifts, and empowers and builds up the church as God's people. For pastors in particular, these chapters equip us with pneumatology that is aimed at the church.

In addition, *these chapters have the gathered assembly in view.* So many of the questions we face concerning the Spirit's work—and especially many of the controversies—involve the role the Holy Spirit plays as the church gathers. Although this text does not answer all our questions, it provides critical insights for how our pneumatology is to inform our gatherings as churches.

---

2. Wayne Grudem, *Systematic Theology: An Introduction to Biblical Doctrine* (Leicester, UK: Inter-Varsity Press; Grand Rapids, MI: Zondervan, 1994), 16–17, emphasis original.

3. E.g., Wayne Grudem, *The Gift of Prophecy in 1 Corinthians* (Washington, DC: University Press of America, 1982); *The Gift of Prophecy in the New Testament and Today* (Wheaton, IL: Crossway, 1988); *Are Miraculous Gifts for Today? Four Views*, ed. Wayne Grudem (Grand Rapids, MI: Zondervan, 1996).

4. What follows has the more modest goal of exposition. At points, some of the more important exegetical details will be included in the footnotes.

Finally, because this text is to a large extent corrective, *it illumi-nates certain tendencies we can have in this area of our doctrine and practice.* In many ways (and I say this as one who believes in the con-tinuity of spiritual gifts), the charismatic movement suffered because it paid insufficient attention to Paul's priorities in these chapters and the discernment they provide. Just as importantly, the teaching of these chapters should promote not only a greater awareness of the Spirit's work among his people but also a greater desire for that work.

Context and Structure

The Corinthian correspondence gives us a fascinating window into the rollicking relationship that existed between the apostle Paul and the church in Corinth. In 1 Corinthians, Paul is essentially responding to cir-cumstances that had developed between the time he founded the church (ca. mid–AD 50) and the writing of the letter about three to four years later (spring 54 or 55). One factor that prompted Paul's letter is a letter the Corinthians themselves wrote to Paul (cf. 7:1: "Now concerning the matters about which you wrote . . ."), and much of our letter consists of Paul's responses to concerns raised by this church (cf. 7:25; 8:1; 12:1; 16:1). Chapters 12–14 constitute another such response, this time on the matter of "spiritual gifts."[5]

The ensuing discussion follows an A-B-A' chiastic arrangement that is typical of Paul's style of argumentation in this letter as he ad-dresses various situations among the church at Corinth.[6] Paul's argu-ment begins with a general discussion of the subject of spiritual gifts (A = chap. 12), which provides an overall framework for understand-ing the gifts. This is followed by what appears to be a digression but, upon reflection, proves to be a critical theological foundation for the immediate argument: love transcends all the gifts and is to govern their exercise (B = chap. 13). Paul's discussion culminates with a direct

5. Despite recent modifications of the understanding of the "now concerning" (*peri de*) con-struction, most commentators identify this instance as introducing a topic drawn from the Corin-thians' letter to Paul. For the use of *peri de* as marking Paul's responses to the Corinthian letter, see John C. Hurd, *The Origin of I Corinthians* (New York: Seabury, 1965), 63–74. For its more general use as merely a topic marker, see M. Mitchell, "Concerning Περὶ δέ in 1 Corinthians," *NovT* 31, no. 3 (1989): 229–56.

6. For a description of Paul's A-B-A' pattern of argumentation, see Gordon D. Fee, *The First Epistle to the Corinthians*, NICNT (Grand Rapids, MI: Eerdmans, 1987), 15–16. See also Ray-mond F. Collins, *First Corinthians*, Sacra Pagina (Collegeville, MN: Liturgical, 1999), 306, who notes that this triadic form was characteristic of many classical letters, as opposed to the more personal letters found among Hellenistic papyri.

response to the primary issue at hand: the nature, function, and relative utility of prophecy and tongues in the public worship of the church (A' = chap. 14). However much he may be responding to a question, Paul is more directly addressing and bringing pastoral correction to a problem in the Corinthian church: the improper assessment and practice of the gift of tongues and its effect on the worshiping community.[7]

The emphases and proportions revealed by this structure are of more than mere historical interest. For the pastor grappling with congregational issues or the Christian confused by conflicting opinions on spiritual gifts, Paul's combination of theological instruction, ethical exhortation, and practical guidance provides clarity and wisdom in an area so often void of both. Moreover, given the remedial nature of these chapters, they are ideal for establishing important priorities in how the church relates to the Spirit's work. The balance of this chapter will outline six such priorities.

The Priority of the Gospel (1 Cor. 12:1–3)

It is all too easy to skip over the opening verses of chapter 12 in anticipation of the discussion of the gifts, but verses 1–3 set an important trajectory for Paul's argument. As noted above, Paul transitions by introducing the topic at hand: "Now concerning spiritual gifts . . ." The word "gifts" is actually absent from the sentence; the phrase translated "spiritual gifts" is more literally "spiritual things," that is, phenomena inspired by the Holy Spirit.[8] Paul's opening response is a bit unexpected. After recalling their former life in paganism (12:2), he contrasts two confessions in verse 3: "Jesus is accursed!" and "Jesus is Lord." What is the point of this contrast?

It is unlikely that anyone in the church is saying "Jesus is accursed," which no doubt would have brought a much stronger rebuke by Paul! Nor does it appear Paul is providing criteria for discerning

---

7. So also Fee, *First Corinthians*, 571; David E. Garland, *1 Corinthians*, BECNT (Grand Rapids, MI: Baker, 2003), 558–59. Cf. M. Mitchell, *Paul and the Rhetoric of Reconciliation* (Tübingen: Mohr, 1991), 279–80. *Pace* D. L. Baker, "The Interpretation of 1 Corinthians 12–14," *Evangelical Quarterly* 46 (1974): 231, who sees Paul as merely responding to Corinthian questions with instruction and guidance.

8. The term is *pneumatikōn*, from the adjective meaning "spiritual," and in this form could be either masculine or neuter: "spiritual people" or "spiritual things." Given that it introduces a discussion on gifts, along with the clearly neuter use in 14:1, the latter seems most likely. So most commentators, e.g., Joseph A. Fitzmyer, *First Corinthians*, Anchor Bible (New Haven, CT: Yale University Press, 2008), 457.

authentic spiritual utterances; there is nothing in chapter 12 about true or false messages or discerning such things.[9] Rather, Paul is pointing out something fundamental about the Corinthian Christians, and indeed anyone else who confesses Jesus as Lord. This saving confession can only be produced by the work of the Holy Spirit (12:3). With this affirmation, Paul lays the foundation for his entire response by making it clear just who has the Holy Spirit. Certainly in their former pagan days the Corinthians did not (12:2), nor do those who pronounce Jesus cursed (most likely, unbelieving Jews—cf. Deut. 21:23; 1 Cor. 1:23).[10] Only those who make a saving confession of Christ have the Holy Spirit—and, by implication, all those who do confess Christ have the Spirit.

Here, then, is the definitive mark of the Holy Spirit's work in the life of a believer. Paul had made a similar point in 1 Corinthians 2 when addressing factions in the Corinthian church. It is the Christian—the person who has grasped God's wisdom in Christ (1:18–24; 2:6–7), who was chosen by God to be "in Christ Jesus" (1:26–31), whose faith is in the power of God through Christ (2:1–5), and to whom God has revealed all that is given to him in Christ (2:9–13)—who has the Spirit of God, and who is therefore "spiritual" in the most fundamental sense. Paul now applies the same reality in dealing with spiritual gifts. To the vaunted Corinthians who exalted spiritual utterances—or to *any* Christian enamored with spiritual gifts or phenomena or experiences—Paul extols the saving knowledge of Jesus Christ as the pinnacle of spiritual experience in this age.

The implications of this claim are far-reaching. The reality that every authentic Christian possesses the Spirit demolishes any artificial distinctions or hierarchies among believers. This also informs the whole category of "spiritual experiences": the most powerful spiritual experience one can have in this age is the miracle of regeneration. The eye-opening, heart-transforming work of the Spirit through the gospel of Christ is the greatest miracle we will ever experience (cf. Luke 10:20). Paul also provides important theological guidance here. One's

---

9. Grudem, *Gift of Prophecy*, 167, notes the inadequacy of the confession "Jesus is Lord" in verse 3 if it were a test of prophetic inspiration.

10. Although dismissed by some interpreters, Garland, *1 Corinthians*, 570–71, makes a strong case for seeing unbelieving Jews behind this anathema. J. M. Bassler, "1 Cor 12:3—Curse and Confession in Context," *Journal of Biblical Literature* 101 (1982): 415–18, plausibly suggests that Paul may be recalling his former life in Judaism when he himself might have pronounced such a curse.

pneumatology must never be isolated from one's Christology. Our consideration of the Spirit's work and our application of the Spirit's work in our lives and churches must never be untethered from Christ and his saving work, for it is precisely Christ and his work to which the Spirit bears witness (John 14:17–21; 16:12–15; cf. 2 Cor. 3:3, 16–18; 4:5–6), and it is the benefits of Christ's work that the Spirit applies to the believer's life (e.g., 2 Cor. 1:21–22; Gal. 4:6; Eph. 1:13–14).[11]

No priority in our pneumatology is superior to the gospel and its effects in the lives of God's people.

The Priority of Diversity (1 Cor. 12:4–11)

Having established the fundamental criterion for what it means to be "spiritual," Paul next establishes a framework for understanding spiritual gifts. Through a series of three parallel clauses in 12:4–6, Paul broadens the category of *pneumatika* ("spiritual things"—12:1) beyond the narrow bounds of certain gifts and, presumably, gifted people, to embrace all dimensions of the church's life.

First, the rhetorically powerful, threefold repetition of "varieties" (*diaireseis*) immediately points to a plurality of spiritual expressions. Although the idea of variety is no doubt implied, the term is probably better rendered "distributions," stressing that such expressions are not individual accomplishments but sovereign bestowals of the Spirit.[12] In addition, Paul uses three different terms to express different aspects of the Spirit's work. The first term, "gifts," stresses the free, undeserved nature of these expressions. With this word Paul appears to transform the terminology and the terms of the discussion; the Corinthians ask about "spiritual phenomena" (12:1), but Paul refers to "gracious

---

11. As we will see, this is not to minimize the empowering work of the Spirit through spiritual gifts, nor to imply that after salvation Christians need a second experience of the Spirit for empowerment, much less to suggest any conflict between Paul's perspective and, say, Luke's in the book of Acts. As Max Turner observes, "The one gift of the Spirit to the Christian at conversion is God's empowering presence which brings not only sonship and new creation life but also the different charismata of the Spirit of prophecy such as those outlined in 1 Corinthians 12–14 and Romans 12" (Max Turner, *The Holy Spirit and Spiritual Gifts* [Peabody, MA: Hendrickson, 1998], 154). Again, "For Paul it is precisely the wisdom-granting revelatory Spirit—that is, the Spirit *as the 'Spirit of prophecy'*—who enables the understanding of the cross that leads to conversion and continuing authentic faith (Gal. 3:1–5; 1 Cor. 2:10–14; 2 Cor. 3:16–18; 4:13; Eph. 3:16–19)" (156).

12. The cognate verb *diaireō* in 12:11 clearly means "apportions" or "distributes," which supports this sense of the noun in 12:4 (BDAG, 229. So C. K. Barrett, *The First Epistle to the Corinthians*, Black's New Testament Commentary [repr., Peabody, MA: Hendrickson, 1996], 283). This understanding is strengthened by the inclusion formed by verses 4 and 11, both of which contain a *diaire-* cognate and *to auto pneuma*—"the same Spirit."

gifts."[13] Paul then speaks of "service" (*diakoniōn*, 12:5), applying the Spirit's work beyond the sphere of more evidently "supernatural" phenomena to normal acts of service and ministry in the church. The final term, "activities" (*energēmatōn*), underlines the power of God that is at work in all of these expressions among believers, however spectacular or commonplace.[14] All of this is placed within a Trinitarian formulation which, with the threefold repetition of "same" (*autos*—"the same Spirit . . . the same Lord . . . the same God"), stresses that all the gifts, however prominent or humble, come from the same divine source.

Paul summarizes these observations in verse 7, which is perhaps the theme verse of the entire chapter: "To each is given the manifestation of the Spirit for the common good." In a final switch of terms, Paul employs "manifestation" (*phanerōsis*) as an umbrella term for all that the Spirit does in believers, thus demolishing any fundamental distinction between them. The word "each" is emphatic, emphasizing the diversity of the Spirit's work: there is no spiritual elite among God's people, but each person is gifted by the Spirit.[15] A balancing emphasis falls at the end of the verse, which provides the purpose for the gifts: "for the common good." The Spirit's work thus strikes a beautiful symmetry among the people of God: "To each . . . for the good of all."

The foundational instruction in these verses not only lays a critical foundation for Paul's directives in chapter 14 but also is immediately and broadly relevant for any consideration of spiritual gifts in the church. Fundamentally, spiritual gifts are gracious endowments of a generous God, not personal accomplishments or badges of spirituality. As such, they are to be neither gloried in nor viewed suspiciously, but rather gratefully received. More specific in these verses is Paul's emphasis on diversity and its many implications. First, *all Christians are gifted by the Holy Spirit*. There are no ungifted Christians, and therefore no ungifted small groups or churches—which should be encouraging news to so many who consider themselves deficient in gifting and unquali-

---

13. D. A. Carson, *Showing the Spirit: A Theological Exposition of 1 Corinthians 12–14* (Grand Rapids, MI: Baker, 1987), 23. Collins, *First Corinthians*, 452, judges the switch in terms "jarring." Turner, *Holy Spirit*, 264, notes that the noun *charisma* ("gift") derives from the verb *charizomai* ("give graciously") rather than *charis* ("grace"), thus stressing the free and gracious nature of the thing given.

14. Fee, *First Corinthians*, 588.

15. *Pace* Fee, *First Corinthians*, who makes too much of the absence of Paul's more usual *eis hekastos*. As Fitzmyer, *First Corinthians*, 465–66, remarks, "Paul thinks indeed that 'every last person in the community' is so endowed."

fied to serve in the church. Second, the diversity of the gifts and their common source in God means that *all the gifts are supernatural.* Our man-centered tendency to rank gifts by their impressiveness is completely foreign to Scripture, which makes no distinction between "natural" and "supernatural" gifts.[16] Scripture neither denigrates any gift as inferior nor exalts any gift as indicating a greater level of spirituality. In short, there *are* no "unspectacular" gifts, only unappreciated gifts.

Recognizing the divine source and nature of spiritual gifts frees us to value all the gifts and to see God at work through each of them. For pastors in particular, this implies both a responsibility and a privilege: to draw people's attention to the fact that the Spirit is powerfully at work in them, whether they recognize it or not (and most people typically do *not*). Not only does this honor the work of the Spirit, but there is no way to provide more biblical encouragement than to say to another believer, "I see God at work in your life, and this is how . . ."[17]

The Priority of Unity (1 Cor. 12:12–31)

After stressing the Corinthians' diversity in the previous paragraph, in 12:12 Paul begins to stress the complementary priority that, amid their diversity, they are in reality unified in Christ at the deepest level. He provides the theological basis for their unity in verses 12–13, employing the familiar analogy of the body. Just as various members are unified in the human body, so also are diverse Christians unified in the body of Christ. The language is both striking and sobering. We might have expected Paul to complete the analogy in verse 12 by saying, "so it is with the church." He instead writes, "so it is with Christ," and by so doing he identifies

---

16. Herman Ridderbos, *Paul: An Outline of His Theology* (Grand Rapids, MI: Eerdmans, 1975), 442, observes the following:

> The . . . charismatic is not only that which is spectacular and unusual. . . . *Charisma* is everything that the Spirit wishes to use and presses into service for equipping and upbuilding the church, what can serve for instruction and admonition and for ministering to one another, or even the effective direction and government of the church. The whole distinction between charismatic and non-charismatic ministries in the church therefore cannot be reconciled with the Pauline conception of *charisma.*

Pace James D. G. Dunn, *Jesus and the Spirit* (London: SCM, 1975), 253–56, who views spiritual gifts as specific, observable *events* of God's activity that manifest his power and should not be confused with "a human capacity heightened, developed or transformed" (255).

17. Paul himself provides such an example in this very letter. To a church rife with problems, which he is about to correct, Paul nevertheless begins in 1 Cor. 1:4–9 with sincere (not merely rhetorical) encouragement—even celebrating the presence of spiritual gifts that some in the church are abusing!

the members of the church directly with Christ himself.[18] This places our relationships within Christ's body on a completely different plane. Far from being merely horizontal sins, our proud individualism and factionalism are offenses against Christ, violating the very union with him that believers share together. Perhaps at this point the Corinthians recalled Paul's starkly freighted question when addressing factions in the church in 1:13: "Is Christ divided?"

The basis for this in 12:13 (*gar*—"for") is particularly important in a context where spiritual gifts are a source of controversy: it is precisely "in one Spirit" that "all" are baptized into the one body of Christ, and it is "one Spirit" of which "all" are made to drink.[19] In verses 4–11, Paul has shown how the Spirit's work in each Christian produces diversity within the church; in verse 13 he now declares that the Spirit's work in every Christian produces an inviolable unity among them.

Paul goes on to apply the analogy of the body by vividly personifying various parts of the human body in verses 15–26 and, in so doing, makes two primary applications. Imagine some body parts (here, the foot and ear) pronouncing that, because they are not more prominent parts (hand, eye), they do not belong to the body. Paul's rhetorical questions highlight the absurdity of this to stress the divine design inherent in the body's diversity (12:18). As a result, no member can say, "I don't belong. I'm not gifted. I'm not needed." In Christ's body, every member fulfills a specific role and is necessary to the whole. Verses 21–26 come from the opposite angle, with prominent parts (eye, head) saying to less prominent parts (hand, feet), "I have no need of you." Paul dispenses with rhetorical questions and straightforwardly asserts, "On the contrary, the parts of the body that seem to be weaker are indispensable" (12:22).[20] Paul's words

---

18. Richard B. Hays, *First Corinthians*, Interpretation (Louisville: John Knox, 1997), 213. See also Fitzmyer, *First Corinthians*, 477; Carson, *Showing the Spirit*, 42–43.

19. The ESV's "in one Spirit" renders *en heni pneumati*. Many English versions translate the phrase as "by one Spirit," from which some imply that the Spirit is the agent doing the baptizing. This in turn underlies the common Pentecostal interpretation that 12:13 speaks of something *different* from the "baptism in the Holy Spirit" understood as an experience distinct from conversion and spoken of by John the Baptist and Jesus (Matt. 3:11; Acts 1:5). See, e.g., Harold D. Hunter, *Spirit Baptism: A Pentecostal Alternative* (Eugene, OR: Wipf & Stock, 2009), 56–60. It is possible that *en* has instrumental force, i.e., Jesus baptizes believers *by means of* the Holy Spirit (so Daniel B. Wallace, *Greek Grammar beyond the Basics* [Grand Rapids, MI: Zondervan, 1996], 374), although a locative sense seems most likely: the Spirit is the sphere in which believers are immersed (see Murray J. Harris, *Prepositions and Theology in the Greek New Testament* [Grand Rapids, MI: Zondervan, 2012], 230–31). For a thorough treatment of 12:13 and its theological implications, see Grudem, *Systematic Theology*, 766–73.

20. The use of "weaker" in 12:22 appears aimed directly at the Corinthian situation, since Paul addressed the strains between the "strong" and the "weak" in 8:7–13. So also Hays, *First*

leave no room for attitudes of superiority, independence, or condescension. Even the most seemingly insignificant Christian is in fact "indispensable" (12:22) and invested by God with "greater honor" (12:24), which suggests an irresistible conclusion: it falls to more prominent members to shower honor upon those who appear to human eyes inconsequential.[21]

The teaching in this section, while commonplace when addressing ecclesiology, is perhaps less so in addressing pneumatology. When discussing spiritual gifts, our eyes almost reflexively turn inward either to fixate upon ourselves or to compare ourselves with others (favorably or unfavorably). This text—and indeed, the thrust of the entire New Testament—radically reorients our individualized thinking to a Christ-centered, corporate focus. Every member of Christ's body has been immersed in the Spirit's life-giving power—that's what a Christian *is* (12:12–13). Every member of the church has been vitally united with Christ, and thereby vitally united with all other believers. Their interests are our interests; their joys are our joys; their suffering, our suffering (12:21–26). Every member of the church has been gifted by the Spirit, and *in such a way* that the members are interdependent (12:18). There is a divine configuration to the body of Christ such that all the members need each other, and therefore they should appreciate each other, depend upon each other, and honor each other. Spiritual gifts, then—and indeed all our thinking about the Spirit—should function to draw our eyes not inward but upward and outward, to the God who graciously gives us his Spirit and to others in whom the Spirit is at work for our good.

The Priority of Love (1 Cor. 13:1–13)

Chapter 13 is rightly beloved for its beauty and enduring resonance, but far too often it is lifted from its context in 1 Corinthians 12–14.[22] As noted above, this chapter forms the second of three segments of Paul's argument in these chapters, a seeming digression from the topic at hand but in reality the theological foundation for the entire section. Commentators label it with such terms as "an encomium in praise of love" (which it is), rich with rhetorical flourishes, balanced pairs,

---

Corinthians, 215. Garland, *1 Corinthians*, 596, suggests an echo of God's choice of the weak in the world (1:27).

21. Mitchell, *Rhetoric*, 269.

22. Even a commentator of Conzelmann's stature insists that "the passage must be expounded in the first instance on its own" (Hans Conzelmann, *1 Corinthians*, trans. James W. Leitch, Hermeneia [Philadelphia: Fortress, 1975], 218).

chiasmus, and hyperbole.[23] Functionally, however, the chapter serves as an exhortation aimed directly at the Corinthian situation. Here Paul lays out a vision of life that sets forth love as the quintessence of the Christian life and, therefore, the governing factor for the use of all spiritual gifts. Once again, Paul is transforming the Corinthians' categories and, as a result, reshaping their pneumatology.

This idea emerges in the transition between chapters 12 and 13. After exhorting the Corinthians to desire "higher gifts," Paul pauses to show them "a still more excellent way" (12:31b).[24] The situation requires more than direction on which gifts are most profitable; the church needs a paradigm shift on the very nature of its life together. His argument, though sublime, is simple: without love, spiritual gifts, and even heroic displays of sacrifice, are worthless. They do nothing to contribute to the church's well-being, and they say nothing about one's spiritual condition. There is only one conclusive mark of the Spirit's presence, and that is love.

Space prevents a thorough treatment of chapter 13, but its force and importance in Paul's argument must not be overlooked. If we are to hold our pneumatology not simply with the right content but also with the proper proportions, then love must be placed at center stage. No virtue or gift exceeds it in importance, and no priority should displace it in the life of the church. And we must avoid the false dichotomy that sets love over against the Spirit's work; to do so is to misconstrue the Spirit's work, the definable mark of which is not spiritual gifts but love. Drawing from Paul's description, *the* greatest mark of the Spirit's work is a life that displays selfless service in concrete actions for the good of others. Finally, love—the kind of love described in verses 4–8, embodied most fully in Jesus Christ, whose character is meant to shine through the lives of members of his body—must govern the exercise of spiritual gifts in the church. As we will see, Paul will encourage even the Corinthians to desire spiritual gifts (14:1), but our zeal for any gift is to be enveloped in the garment of love.

---

23. Fitzmyer, *First Corinthians*, 487, notes the chapter's rhetorical dimensions, while questioning its designation as a "hymn," lacking as it does meter, liturgical traces, or any mention of Christ or God.

24. It would be a mistake to understand Paul as saying that love renders spiritual gifts unimportant. He does not so much *compare* gifts with love as show how the former are worthless without the latter. "Thus it is not 'love versus gifts' that Paul has in mind, but 'love as the only context for gifts'" (Fee, *First Corinthians*, 625).

The Priority of Pursuit (1 Cor. 12:31; 14:1, 39)

Pursuing gifts is admittedly not a primary emphasis in 1 Corinthians 12–14. However, it seems important to include, given how often it is overlooked and how striking some of Paul's commands are in this text. In a context where Paul corrects a church for misunderstanding or misusing spiritual gifts, he nevertheless commands—*twice*—that spiritual gifts be "eagerly desired"!

Paul's positive attitude toward these gifts was expressed in the opening chapter of this letter. Within his customary opening thanksgiving, Paul gives thanks for the Corinthians' rich endowment "in all speech and all knowledge" (1:5), and he affirms that they "are not lacking in any gift" (1:7). It is, of course, true that Paul will soon correct the Corinthians on these very matters, and the introduction of these themes is preparatory for that.[25] Nonetheless, Paul's thanksgiving is sincere, as it draws attention to the divine source of the Corinthians' speech, knowledge, and gifts, however they may be misunderstood or misused.[26]

The first of the two commands noted above comes in 12:31, just prior to the chapter on love: "But earnestly desire the higher gifts."[27] The verb (*zēloute*) is a strong one, and when used positively carries the sense of a devoted posture toward something or someone, for example, "strive," "desire earnestly," "seek with zeal or enthusiasm."[28] Garland well captures the sense here: "to devote oneself to something with fervor."[29] At this point, "higher [or "greater"—*ta meizona*] gifts" is left undefined, but Paul will define them in chapter 14 as gifts that most edify others. To be sure, Paul goes on in 12:31b to point to "a

---

25. See P. T. O'Brien, *Introductory Thanksgivings in the Letters of Paul*, Supplements to Novum Testamentum 49 (Leiden: Brill, 1977), 107–37.

26. So also Anthony C. Thiselton, *The First Epistle to the Corinthians*, NIGTC (Grand Rapids, MI: Eerdmans, 2000), 93.

27. Verse 31 reads *zēloute de ta charismata ta meizona*. The verb *zēloute* could be either indicative or imperative; those who opt for the indicative suggest various senses for the verse and Paul's intentions. Most commentators take the verb as an imperative, since the same verb occurs in 14:1 and 14:39, both of which are clearly imperatives, and the former of which appears to resume the thought of 12:31a. However, even here interpretations vary: is this a Corinthian slogan Paul counters (or adjusts), or is it a command Paul issues? For a thorough treatment of the issues and a defense of this as a Pauline command, see Carson, *Showing the Spirit*, 53–58. David E. Aune, *Prophecy in Early Christianity and the Ancient Mediterranean World* (Grand Rapids, MI: Eerdmans, 1983), 199, sees these commands as evidence for "congregational prophecy" over against the office of prophet.

28. BDAG, 427; Franco Montanari, *The Brill Dictionary of Ancient Greek*, ed. Madeleine Goh and Chad Schroeder (Boston: Brill, 2015), 892.

29. Garland, *1 Corinthians*, 600. Thiselton, *First Corinthians*, 1025, suggests "being busy at what is of deep concern."

still more excellent way" of love as the ground for all the gifts.[30] This serves, however, not to marginalize the command in verse 31a but to put it in its necessary context.

The second command to "earnestly desire" gifts appears in 14:1, which resumes the idea in 12:31a. The verb is the same (*zēloute*), but the object is different: "Pursue love, and earnestly desire the spiritual gifts [*ta pneumatika*], especially that you may prophesy." Paul returns here to the term that opened this section in 12:1, probably reflecting the Corinthians' own question. There is, no doubt, some overlap in the meaning of *pneumatika* and *charismata* (12:31a), but it appears that here Paul has especially in mind gifts that involve inspired speech in the public assembly.[31] Regardless of the precise referent (which includes at least prophecy—14:1b), Paul's command that this church fervently devote itself to spiritual gifts, especially in light of the abuses of some gifts at Corinth, is stunning.

What is true in so many areas of the Christian life also applies to spiritual gifts: Scripture commands not merely a belief or practice but also an *attitude*. Paul's instruction in these chapters implies that it is not enough simply to affirm spiritual gifts, but they are to be eagerly desired.[32] Of course, these chapters provide plentiful protection against an undue fascination with spiritual gifts.[33] Moreover, in view of the overwhelming emphasis in the New Testament on the Spirit's role in producing Christlike character (e.g., 2 Cor. 3:17–18; Gal. 5:16–18, 22–25; Eph. 5:18–21), spiritual gifts are *not* the pinnacle of spiritual experience, much less the most important aspect of the Christian life. That does not, however, render them *unimportant*. They are, after all, *gifts* from God to his people, expressions of the Holy Spirit's enabling

---

30. In 12:31b Paul conceives of love not as a *charisma* that trumps all other gifts but as the criterion for all the gifts (Carson, *Showing the Spirit*, 57).

31. In light of the Corinthians' apparent question about *pneumatika* in 12:1, Paul's use of terminology in chap. 12, and the focus on prophecy and tongues in chap. 14, it seems likely the term in 14:1 reflects (at least some of) the Corinthians' narrowly circumscribed understanding of the Spirit's activity regarding inspired speech (cf. Baker, "1 Corinthians 12–14," 229). Although I do not accept many elements of Ellis's view of pneumatic leadership in Corinth (E. E. Ellis, *Prophecy and Hermeneutic in Early Christianity* [Grand Rapids, MI: Eerdmans, 1978], his definition of *ta pneumatika* is helpful: "gifts of inspired perception, verbal proclamation and/or its interpretation" (24).

32. While discernment and biblical proportion are vital, these commands at least raise the question as to whether an "open but cautious" posture toward spiritual gifts does justice to Paul's exhortations.

33. For example, God is sovereign in the distribution of the gifts (12:11, 18); not everyone will have certain gifts (12:29–30); we must avoid exalting one gift over another as more significant or "supernatural" or indicative of God's power or blessing (12:4–11); the most apparently insignificant gifts are worthy of great honor (12:21–25); gifts are worthless apart from love (13:1–3); and all gifts are given for the good of others (12:7).

power for life and ministry. As such, they are to be "earnestly" desired. Indeed, gifts can even be prayed for, as Paul directs in 1 Corinthians 14:13.[34] If these commands are embraced with biblical proportion and with a desire to honor Christ and serve others, Scripture gives us every hope that through spiritual gifts we may experience more of the Spirit's power working in and through our lives.

The Priority of Edification (1 Cor. 14:1–26)

The fascination and speculation that surround chapter 14 should not blind us to its principal thrust. Here Paul comes to the third segment of his teaching in this section and directly addresses the particular situation in Corinth. To a church where some were exalting the gift of tongues and misusing them in the congregation, Paul establishes this timeless principle: *Whatever gifts a Christian may experience, the priority and goal of their expression within the church is the building up of others.*[35]

The priority of edification rings throughout this chapter. The term in its various forms ("edification"—*oikodomē*; "edify"—*oikodomeō*) appeared eight times earlier in the letter, but in 14:1–26 alone it occurs seven times (14:3, 4 [2x], 5, 12, 17, 26). Here is the chief intention of the gifts and the criterion by which they are to be measured. In fact, in the context of Paul's argument that begins with the command "Pursue love" (14:1), edification really becomes an expression of love.[36]

This explains why Paul redirects the church to the gift of prophecy over (uninterpreted) tongues. The idea of prophecy first appeared in this letter in 11:4–5 (in its verbal form) and has been assumed since then (six uses—five nominal—in chaps. 12–13). Its basic idea involves speech on

---

34. See Grudem, *Gift of Prophecy*, 259–61. The objection that, since God is sovereign in the giving of gifts, Paul could not really be instructing the Corinthians to pursue them, reveals a rather wooden understanding of the relationship between divine sovereignty and human responsibility. One might just as well say that we should not pursue holiness because, after all, it is God who sanctifies us!

35. The structure of this section illuminates Paul's concern and this governing theme:

- 14:1–5: Comparison of tongues and prophecy, with prophecy being superior for edification
- 14:6–12: The reason for (and illustrations of) the unprofitability of tongues: unintelligibility
- 14:13–19: Practical instruction for speaking in tongues: aim for intelligibility
- 14:20–25: Comparison of tongues with prophecy, with prophecy being superior

In this loose chiasmic framework, Paul directly compares prophecy and tongues in paragraphs 1 and 4. Between this comparison is a specific focus on the Corinthians' use of tongues, which is the exclusive focus of paragraphs 2 and 3. Neither of these two paragraphs mentions prophecy, and both end by reaffirming the priority of edification.

36. Cf. 8:1, where Paul explicitly links love with edification. See Fee, *First Corinthians*, 652.

behalf of God; the prophet functions as "God's spokesperson."[37] As
it appears in the New Testament, prophecy can be more specifically
described as a verbal proclamation based upon a divine revelation.[38]
This distinguishes New Testament prophecy from teaching, as well as
preaching, focused on the exposition of texts; Paul, for example, never
uses the words *prophesy* or *prophecy* in reference to his own preaching;
his gift lists distinguish between prophecy and other forms of speech
(such as teaching, the "word of wisdom/knowledge," and exhortation);
and his close equation of prophecy with interpreted tongues suggests
the more spontaneous nature of this gift.[39]

In this context, Paul commends prophecy because of its potential
to edify the gathered church through encouragement and consolation,
while tongues, at least without interpretation, edify only the individual
(14:1–5).[40] Paul's argument reveals yet another priority for the gathered
church, which in fact is the prerequisite for edification: *intelligibility*.

---

37. Collins, *First Corinthians*, 491. Cf., e.g., 2 Sam. 12:25; Jer. 1:9.

38. Grudem, *Gift of Prophecy*, 139–44, persuasively argues that prophecy in 1 Corinthians and the New Testament as a whole exhibits two distinctive features: (1) it is based on an *apokalypsis* (14:30; cf. 14:25; Acts 11:18; 21:10), and (2) there is a public proclamation. For similar definitions of prophecy (though from different angles and with different emphases), cf. Aune, *Prophecy*, 339; Christopher Forbes, *Prophecy and Inspired Speech in Early Christianity and Its Hellenistic Environment*, WUNT 2/75 (Tübingen: Mohr Siebeck, 1995), 219; Dunn, *Jesus and the Spirit*, 228–29; Turner, *Holy Spirit*, 187.

39. *Pace* David Hill, *New Testament Prophecy* (Atlanta: John Knox, 1979), who defines prophecy as "pastoral preaching which . . . offers guidance and instruction" (127); see esp. 110–40. For a critique of this equation of gifts, see Turner, *Holy Spirit*, 210–12. Cf. also Dunn, *Jesus and the Spirit*, 228–29.

40. Space prohibits a detailed treatment of the gift of tongues. For a survey of this phenomenon in the New Testament, see Turner, *Holy Spirit*, 221–39. The relative paucity of New Testament references has yielded a vast body of literature seeking to identify similar phenomena or terminology in extrabiblical or pre-Christian sources. The scholarly consensus that locates similar speech in Hellenistic antiquity has been persuasively countered by Forbes, *Prophecy*, 103–62. Against views of tongues as ecstatic speech akin to that in pre-Christian Judaism, see E. A. Engelbrecht, "'To Speak in a Tongue': The Old Testament and Early Rabbinic Background of a Pauline Expression," *Concordia Journal* 22 (1996): 295–302, although Engelbrecht's own thesis that "to speak in a tongue" is a common Semitic idiom adopted by Paul forces too strict a conclusion upon too little evidence. At the risk of oversimplification, we might summarize this gift in Paul as Spirit-inspired speech addressed to God that is unintelligible to the speaker and to others (unless it is interpreted). Commentators differ as to whether these are unlearned human languages (e.g., Robert H. Gundry, "'Ecstatic Utterance' [N.E.B.]?," *JTS* 17 [1966]: 299–307) or angelic languages—"tongues of angels" (13:1), (e.g., Barrett, *First Corinthians*, 299–300; Fee, *First Corinthians*, 598; Dunn, *Jesus and the Spirit*, 244). Paul's emphasis, however, is not on the nature of the language but on the fact that it is unintelligible, and at any rate he mentions in 12:10 "[various] kinds of tongues" (*genē glōssōn*). It is perhaps best to hold that Paul envisions various kinds of Spirit-inspired, unintelligible speech (so also Turner, *Holy Spirit*, 229). Gordon Fee, *God's Empowering Presence: The Holy Spirit in the Letters of Paul* (Peabody, MA: Hendrickson, 1994), 890, slightly modifying the view in his commentary, allows for both human and angelic languages, although he suggests that the Corinthians understood their tongues to be the latter. For tongues as a "sign for unbelievers" (14:22), see Wayne Grudem, "1 Corinthians 14:20–25: Prophecy and Tongues as Signs of God's Attitude," *WTJ* 41, no. 2 (Spring 1979): 381–96.

Prophecy's superiority to (uninterpreted) tongues lies in the fact that it is understandable. And it is not alone in this, for Paul lists *four* gifts in verse 6 that possess this characteristic (which prevents us from prioritizing prophecy above any and all other gifts). Only when the content and effect of spiritual gifts are understood can there be edification, whether it be a believer who is encouraged and comforted (14:3) or a nonbeliever who encounters God's presence and is convicted (14:25).

It now becomes clear what Paul means by "higher gifts" in 12:31. In the context of the gathered assembly, certain gifts are "greater" to the extent that they build up the gathering as a whole.[41] As bestowals from a gracious God, all gifts bring blessing and are to be desired (14:1b), but it is those having the greatest potential for building up the church as a whole that are to be particularly desired and pursued (14:1c). It is no surprise that Paul includes "knowledge" and "teaching" in this context (14:6), which harks back to the prominence given earlier to the "utterance of wisdom/knowledge" (12:8) and the role of "apostles" and "teachers" (12:28).[42] Even though the once-for-all delivered gospel (15:1–5) and authoritative Scripture (cf. 2:9; 4:6; also 14:37, which claims authority for Paul's apostolic teaching) do not preclude revelatory gifts in Paul's mind, they nonetheless function as the church's sole authority and stand at the center of its worship (cf. 2:2; 4:6; 14:36).[43]

Paul's guidance in this section is equally important for the pastor planning his Sunday meeting and the Christian entering congregational worship. Broadly speaking, God's glory is our uppermost consideration in worship (cf. 10:31), but penultimate to that (and as a means to that)

---

41. Although Paul is bringing correction to the Corinthians, we should not mistake his comment that (uninterpreted) tongues edify only the individual (14:4) as derogatory. However much speaking in tongues might have been misused in Corinth, it is nonetheless a divine gift, it is Godward speech identified as prayer and praise (14:14–17), and Paul gives thanks to God for his own abundant experience of this gift (14:18). Moreover, when accompanied by interpretation, this gift also has potential to edify the congregation (14:5, 13, 27). Those who criticize the self-edifying nature of tongues fail to recognize that the use of *any* gift brings blessing to the one exercising it. One might add that private prayer, which greatly edifies the one praying, is not for that reason to be shunned.

42. Despite the link of the "word of wisdom" and "word of knowledge" with revelatory gifts in many charismatic circles, Paul's use of "wisdom," "knowledge," and "word" throughout this letter suggests much more naturally that these gifts fall within the realm of teaching and doctrine.

43. In Grudem, *Gift of Prophecy* and other publications, the honoree of this Festschrift has played a central role in advancing the position that the gift of prophecy in view in 1 Corinthians is of a different nature from the authoritative prophecy of Old Testament canonical prophets and the authoritative writings of New Testament apostles. In the present volume, Sam Storms, "Revelatory Gifts of the Spirit and the Sufficiency of Scripture: Are They Compatible?" explores the less-authoritative nature of this gift and its compatibility with authoritative Scripture.

is the building up of believers in their faith. Edification is a concrete expression of love (cf. 8:1) and the goal to which all our energies and gifts should be directed. As important as an individual's gifts are, when they are not used for the building up of others, they fail to fulfill the very purpose for which God gave them.

Conclusion

Like all of Paul's instruction in his letters, 1 Corinthians 12–14 is occasional in nature and does not tell us everything we would like to know either about Christian worship in general or about spiritual gifts in particular. However, it is their very occasional nature that renders these chapters so helpful, both in imparting discernment to understand the work of the Holy Spirit and in suggesting priorities as we apply the Spirit's work in our lives and churches. Moreover, although Paul brings much correction to the Corinthians, these chapters should not dampen our zeal for the Spirit's work, but instead kindle it.

As we have seen, it is the Spirit who opens our eyes and hearts to the glory of the gospel of Christ. The Spirit distributes a diversity of gifts, revealing his powerful presence in the life of every believer. This very diversity is designed to effect a rich interdependence among believers, unifying us as members of Christ's own body. The conclusive mark of the Spirit's work is the love he engenders in the hearts of believers, which in turn provides the key criterion for applying our pneumatology. Armed with love, we are then positioned to pursue spiritual gifts, which are gracious bestowals of God's enabling power for life and ministry. Finally, the purpose and goal of these gifts is not mere experience, much less self-indulgence or self-aggrandizement, but building up other believers for the glory of Christ.

In sum, these chapters bear eloquent testimony to the reality that the Holy Spirit is at work among God's people in a thousand different ways, many of which we can take for granted, some of which we may have ignored. They also remind us that the God who is omnipresent delights to be *actively* present among his people, often in quiet ways and at times in discernibly dynamic ways through gifts the Holy Spirit imparts to believers. In recent decades, few evangelical scholars have more faithfully reminded the church of this reality than has Wayne Grudem, in whose honor this chapter is gratefully offered.

9

Translating God's Words

Why Literary Criteria Matter

Leland Ryken

Because we know Martin Luther primarily as a theologian, church reformer, and Bible translator, we can hardly avoid being surprised by the strong endorsement he gives to literary expertise as a prerequisite to proper understanding and teaching of the Bible. Luther begins his endorsement with the statement, "I am persuaded that without knowledge of literature pure theology cannot at all endure." He then proceeds to make the claim that "there has never been a great revelation of the Word of God unless He has first prepared the way by the rise and prosperity of languages and letters [the old term for literature], as though they were John the Baptists." Luther ends with the following striking declaration: "Certainly it is my desire that there shall be as many poets and rhetoricians as possible, because I see that by these studies, as by no other means, people are wonderfully fitted for the grasping of sacred truth and for handling it skillfully and happily."[1]

1. Martin Luther, Letter to Eoban Hess, in *Luther's Correspondence and Other Contemporary Letters*, trans. Preserved Smith and Charles M. Jacobs, vol. 2 (Philadelphia: Lutheran Publication Society, 1918), 176–77.

These statements by Luther can stand as an epigraph for the essay that follows. My title encompasses the three topics that I will cover. I have construed the concept of translating God's words in a dual sense—the translation of the Bible from the original languages into English, and the interpretation and application of the Bible in such a way that Christians absorb its truth and beauty into their daily lives, along the lines of Luther's "grasping" and "handling" of the Bible. The literary criteria that I reference are principles that flow from the literary nature of the Bible, a topic that will lead me to explore what it means that the Bible is literature.

The Literary Nature of the Bible

The literary study of the Bible has been a major part of my career for nearly half a century. Its origin was my teaching Psalm 23 to an adult Sunday school class during my last term in graduate school in Eugene, Oregon. As I have plied my trade in this corner of the vineyard, I have not hesitated to serve as an apologist for the idea of the Bible as literature in addition to being a practitioner of literary analysis of the Bible. I have not found it burdensome to make the case for viewing the Bible as literature for conservative evangelicals who find the concept new and potentially suspect. I have wanted to make an impact on people who actually read the Bible, not academicians pursuing their scholarly careers. And who are these people who read the Bible?

C. S. Lewis answers that question in a famous essay entitled *The Literary Impact of the Authorised Bible*. In this essay Lewis pays his disrespects to secular scholars who read the Bible *only* as literature by saying that "those who read the Bible [only] as literature do not read the Bible." Then he makes a prediction that has surely been confirmed many times over: the Bible "will not continue to give literary delight very long except to those who go to it for something quite different. I predict that it will in the future be read, as it always has been read, almost exclusively by Christians."[2]

As a spokesman for the idea of the Bible as literature, I have learned to follow a twofold process. First, people need to be relieved of possible misgivings about a literary approach to the Bible, and this has required

---

2. C. S. Lewis, "The Literary Impact of the Authorised Version," in *Selected Literary Essays*, ed. Walter Hooper (Cambridge: Cambridge University Press, 1969), 142, 145.

me to outline what it does *not* mean that the Bible is literature. With the field cleared of misconceptions, people are open to receive what it *does* mean that the Bible is literature. I will follow this time-tested procedure below.

Dispelling Misconceptions: What "the Bible as Literature" Does Not Mean

Although the segment of my audience that is initially resistant to the idea of the Bible as literature has usually been conservative evangelicals, I will also record that some of my most enthusiastic supporters have come from those ranks. When my original book on the subject was released, the first review to appear in print was a ringing endorsement from someone who taught at Prairie Bible Institute in Canada. My first invitation to speak on the subject came from Philadelphia College of the Bible. By contrast, some (not all) members of my own English Department at Wheaton College disparaged my claims regarding the Bible as literature. In my role of apologist for a literary approach to the Bible, I have dealt primarily with four potential objections.

Potential objection 1: To speak of the Bible as literature seems like a liberal idea and the product of modern unbelief. Several misconceptions converge here. First, the idea of the Bible as literature is not a modern idea. It began with the writers of the Bible, as I will show. Such towering theological stalwarts from the past as Augustine, Luther, and Calvin did not doubt that the Bible possesses literary qualities. Today the literary approach is widely acknowledged and often practiced in evangelical schools, colleges, and seminaries. When I read literary analysis of the Bible by scholars at large, I find the same range of attitudes, from conservative to liberal, that I find in other types of biblical analysis.

I make a practice of beginning my course in the literature of the Bible by reading two pages of quotations from the Bible in which the writers make claims about Scripture—its inspiration, its reliability, its status as being not the word of people but of God, and its unique powers. Then I assert that for me the literary study of the Bible begins where any other study of the Bible begins—by accepting as true all that the Bible says about itself. I find no discord between what I believe theologically about the Bible and my literary study of it. In fact, the two reinforce each other.

Potential objection 2: To say that the Bible is literature is to imply that it is fictional rather than factual. Although fictionality is common in literature, it is not an essential ingredient of it. The properties that make a text literary are unaffected by whether the material is historically accurate or fictional. A text is literary whenever it displays ordinary literary qualities. In my expository writing courses I assign students to write a paper that asserts a thesis about a story narrated by scientist Loren Eiseley in his autobiography. The narrative of Eiseley's first childhood encounter with evil is so dense with literary technique that the story would be right at home in my literature courses. Yet I have no reason to believe that the account is anything other than factual.

To cite a parallel example, the genre of the television sports report is filled with convention and artifice without thereby becoming a fiction. The reporter is filmed with a stadium or arena in the background. At some point the reporter either interviews an athlete or is momentarily replaced by a clip of sports action. The report and interview consist almost entirely of sports clichés, and it is a virtual requirement that the athlete speak of just wanting to "go out there and do my best." At the end, the reporter stares into the camera and signs off with a catchy one-liner or a handoff to the newscasters in the studio. The conventional nature of all this is obvious. Every report follows the same format. But this does not make the report fictional. There is an unwarranted assumption in some quarters that the presence of literary conventions and artifice in the Bible signals that the content is fictional rather than factual.

Potential objection 3: To approach the Bible as literature means approaching it only as literature, without attention to the Bible's unique spiritual qualities. C. S. Lewis and T. S. Eliot are among those who have expressed this fear, but the danger is greatly exaggerated. We do not urge people to avoid reading the Bible as history for fear that they will read it only as a history book. The very nature of the Bible makes it impossible to read it only as literature or history. Three types of writing converge in the Bible—the literary, the historical, and the theological. Most passages combine them. To neglect any one of the three is to distort the nature of the Bible. More often than not, the history and theology are packaged in a literary format, and this means that there is no theology and history without the literary form in which they are expressed.

Potential objection 4: To speak of the Bible as literature is to reduce it to the level of ordinary literature. To say that the Bible is literature is simply an objective description of the form in which the Bible comes to us. There is no intention either to elevate or to demote the Bible. I will record my agreement with a viewpoint expressed by nineteenth-century English poet Samuel Taylor Coleridge, who asserted that his *methodology* was to read the Bible "as I should read any other work." But the *effect* of his encounter with the Bible was that "in the Bible there is more that *finds* me than I have experienced in all other books put together; . . . the words of the Bible find me at greater depths of my being."[3] In other words, if we read the Bible as literature, it elevates itself and reveals its unique spiritual quality and power.

To summarize, it would be tragic if we allowed ourselves to be deterred from the literary study and enjoyment of the Bible by objections that turn out to be fallacies. We do not need to abandon the special status that we accord the Bible in order to read it in keeping with its literary nature.

What It Means That the Bible Is Literature

The idea of the Bible as literature began with the writers of the Bible. One evidence of this is the way in which they refer with technical precision to various literary genres or types of writing: proverb, saying, chronicle, complaint (lament psalm), oracle, parable, song, epistle, and many more. This shows that the authors wrote in an awareness of established literary conventions, something that is reinforced by the ways in which many biblical genres and techniques are parallel to the literature of surrounding cultures. The importance of this is that one of the ways in which the human race through the ages has defined literature is by its genres. Everyday discourse consists of expository or

---

3. Samuel Taylor Coleridge, *Confessions of an Inquiring Spirit* (Stanford, CA: Stanford University Press, 1967), 41, 43.

informational writing or speech; literature consists of distinctly literary genres such as story, poem, and vision, and these are plentiful in the Bible.

Of course, we are not limited to the genres named by the writers of the Bible. Nor are we limited simply to the terms by which biblical authors refer to their genres and other literary forms. The most important evidence is the degree to which literary forms permeate the Bible on every page. If we construe the concept of literary form broadly to cover anything having to do with *how* the writers have expressed their content, the total number of literary forms in the Bible runs to more than 250.[4] Any book comprising this many literary genres and techniques is a work of literature. In fact, the overall genre of the Bible is the literary anthology, similar to familiar anthologies of English and American literature. A literary anthology is a book composed by many authors writing in numerous genres, and that is exactly what the Bible is.

The first thing that "the Bible as literature" means, then, is that the Bible is a literary anthology in which we find distinctly literary genres, forms, and techniques on virtually every page. A second distinguishing literary feature of the Bible is an extension of this. Biblical authors make abundant use of special techniques of language and rhetoric (arrangement of material). Metaphors, similes, symbols, and other figures of speech are examples of special uses of language. Examples of rhetorical patterning are the parallel lines of biblical poetry, patterns of repetition in the famous beatitudes of Jesus, and the encomium to love in 1 Corinthians 13.

The two traits covered above (literary genres and special resources of language and rhetoric) belong to the *form* of literary discourse, but literature is also known by its *content*. Whereas expository discourse consists of propositions, abstract vocabulary, accumulation of factual data, and logical arrangement by thesis and topic sentences, a work of literature is an embodiment of human experience concretely rendered. The immediate goal of a literary text is to make us share an experience, not grasp an idea. Literature is incarnational, embodying ideas or meaning in concrete form. What a Bible scholar says about the parables of Jesus is true of all literature: a parable "is not a delivery system for

---

4. Leland Ryken, *A Complete Handbook of Literary Forms in the Bible* (Wheaton, IL: Crossway, 2014).

an idea. It is not a shell casing that can be discarded once the idea (the shell) is fired. Rather a parable is a house in which the reader or listener is invited to take up residence . . . and look out on the world."[5]

None of this is to deny that literature embodies themes and ideas. But if this were the most important thing, all the writer would need to do is list the ideas. Literature enacts human experiences, giving us the example that enshrines the precept. The seventh commandment states God's prohibition against adultery as a precept; the story of David and Bathsheba gives us the example in the form of a literary narrative that leads us to vicariously experience the sequence of events that the text places before us. Literature is *truthful to life and human experience*, and this is a category of truth separate from ideational truth. As literature holds life before us, we come to see it clearly. Literature gives us knowledge in the form of right seeing. A related trait that distinguishes literature is that it embodies universal, timeless human experience in such a way that we can see ourselves and life around us in the concrete particulars of the story. The customary way of stating this is that history and the daily news tell us what *happened*, while literature tells us what *happens*. Of course the Bible does both.

A final trait that characterizes literature is that it is an art form in which beauty of expression is important. This artistry starts at the minute level of the very words, so that we can accurately speak of the creation of verbal beauty as one of the tasks that literary authors perform for us. Beginning at this micro level, literary artistry then reaches out to such broader elements of artistic form as unity of composition, theme-and-variation as an organizational principle, balance, contrast, and such like. American poet Robert Frost famously said that a poem is "a performance in words," alerting us that a literary author intends to entertain us with the exploitation of the resources of literary technique.[6] The author of the book of Ecclesiastes tells us that he arranged his material "with great care," and additionally that he "sought to find words of delight" (Eccles. 12:9–10). Literature is an art form in which beauty of expression is important and rewarding.

---

5. Kenneth E. Bailey, *The Cross and the Prodigal*, 2nd ed. (Downers Grove, IL: InterVarsity Press, 1973), 87.

6. Robert Frost, quoted in Elizabeth Drew, *Poetry: A Modern Guide to Its Understanding and Enjoyment* (New York: Dell, 1959), 19. Frost had similarly said in a lecture, "In writing . . . you must have form—performance" ("The Poet's Next of Kin in College" [lecture delivered at Princeton University, October 26, 1937]).

Approaching the Bible as Literature

Most evangelicals give lip service to what I have said about the literary nature of the Bible. The problem is that when they interact with the biblical text, they ignore what they endorse as a theory. Overwhelmingly they revert to traditional methods of biblical scholarship, reducing the text to a series of propositions and escaping from the text into context. Unwittingly they proceed as if the Bible were a theological outline with proof texts attached. I myself consult and refer to theology books regularly, and every week I have occasion to engage in enlightened proof texting, so I should not be understood as opposing these things. But any piece of writing needs to be analyzed in keeping with the kind of discourse that it is. If the text is a story, we need to talk about plot, setting, and character. Commentary that does not talk about these things has missed the mark.

Our first task as readers is to relive a text as fully as possible. This can happen only if we read a text in terms of its genre and literary technique. We cannot relive a poem, for example, without assimilating the images, metaphors, and other figures of speech. The starting point for reading literarily is to acquaint ourselves with how literature works. Teachers of literature are rarely invited to the table of biblical interpretation, but they need to be invited, as Martin Luther recognized. Pastor R. Kent Hughes hit the nail on the head when he said to me one day that "all genuine biblical exposition is literary commentary."

English Bible Translation and Literary Criteria

The foregoing section has explained what the idea of literary criteria means. Briefly stated, literary criteria are methods of dealing with the Bible in keeping with its literary nature. With that as a foundation, I am ready to explore why and how literary criteria are important to translating God's Word, in the dual sense of translation from the original languages into English and interpreting and applying the Bible as we translate it into our lives.

A Brief History of English Bible Translation

There are two ways in which Bible translation is of practical importance.[7] One is the actual practice of producing an English Bible trans-

---

7. The material that I cover in this unit of my essay receives more expansive treatment in three books that I have published with Crossway: *The Word of God in English: Criteria for Excellence*

lation. After the appearance of multiple new translations in the past two decades, surely the era of producing new English Bibles is over for the foreseeable future. The issue has more urgency, therefore, for readers who face the need to choose an English Bible translation for personal or communal use, and I have therefore written with them chiefly in mind.

Since I will be discussing English Bible translations in terms of their adherence to or deviation from literary criteria, I will begin by reviewing what those criteria are. An English Bible measures up to literary criteria if it reproduces in English the following qualities of the original Hebrew or Greek text:

- variety of style
- verbal beauty
- the imagery and figurative language of poetic passages
- rhetorical patterning
- multiplicity of meaning where words and phrases possess it
- distinctive features of various genres
- concreteness of vocabulary (the criterion of literature as incarnation)
- affective power

In addition to retaining these literary qualities of the original text, an English Bible translation is literary if it meets certain criteria of English language and style, especially smoothness of rhythm, aphoristic spark and memorability, and appropriate tone (including exaltation and dignity of expression).

The King James Version can be taken as representative of the dominant tradition of English Bible translation from the beginning through the middle of the twentieth century. The KJV built upon and summed up an entire century of English Bible translation that preceded it, and it was then the almost universally used English Bible for three and a half centuries. The King James Bible is nothing less than a touchstone for all of the literary criteria that I mentioned in the preceding paragraph.[8] This, in turn, was enabled by the translation philosophy of the KJV,

---

in Bible Translation (2002); *Understanding English Bible Translation* (2009); *The ESV and the English Bible Legacy* (2011).

8. This is the main thesis of my book *The Legacy of the King James Bible* (Wheaton, IL: Crossway, 2011).

which today goes by the name of "essentially literal translation." The goal of an essentially literal translation is to retain the very words of the original text to the degree allowed by modern English. That philosophy was never in serious doubt until the middle of the twentieth century.

That is when a rival translation theory took root and came to dominate English Bible translation. It is known as dynamic equivalence, based on the premise that translators are free to depart from the English word or phrase that *corresponds* to what the biblical authors wrote (the goal of essentially literal translation) and instead *substitute* other words (finding something equivalent rather than correspondent). The words *correspondence* and *equivalence* signal the difference between the two philosophies. In actual practice, the concept of *equivalence* covered only a small part of what the new translators did. The new philosophy sanctioned such broad activities as changing syntax and word order, simplifying the content of the original to match a target audience, adding interpretive commentary to the text, and removing figurative language.

An additional component was part of the seismic shift in translation theory and practice, and its importance has been underestimated because it was not singled out as part of the new mood. This additional development was a deliberate move to use colloquial diction and the speech patterns of contemporary everyday conversation, as distinct from the exaltation and dignity of the King James tradition. The result of this colloquializing was to reinforce the license of dynamic equivalent translators to depart from what the authors of the Bible wrote. A leading goal of translations in the new tradition was to make the English Bible sound as different from the King James Bible as possible, and to produce the effect of the daily newspaper and the chatter at the corner coffee shop.

Why and How Literary Criteria Matter in English Bible Translation

I cannot cover the whole subject as I have done in my books on English Bible translation, so I will choose three representative situations where, as suggested by the title of this essay, literary criteria make a huge difference in English Bible translation. The difference that literary criteria make can be shown in two ways—by seeing what is gained when literary criteria are respected in translation and by seeing what is lost when literary criteria are ignored and disparaged. While the KJV is the gold standard for incorporating literary criteria into an English translation, I will quote from the English Standard Version as the translation that carries on that tradition in modern English. For comparison, I will also quote from several dynamic equivalent translations but will not identified them specifically because it is the principle of dynamic equivalence and colloquializing that is important, not a specific translation.

Verbal beauty and dignity of expression. I will start at the level of words. While the stylistic range of the Bible is large, it is nonetheless a book that possesses dignity. It is what scholars call a sacred book. A sacred book should sound like a sacred book. Even works of modern realistic fiction that have as a goal to reproduce the speech patterns of everyday conversation do not sound exactly like everyday conversation. But that is a nonissue here, because the Bible is a work of ancient literature, not a work of modern realism.

The effect of verbal beauty as a literary quality is to heighten the impact of a statement, to make it stick in the memory, and to elevate its importance. For example, in the midnight encounter of Ruth and Boaz on the threshing floor, Boaz expresses his admiration of Ruth with the statement, "All my fellow townsmen know that you are a worthy woman" (Ruth 3:11; the RSV's "woman of worth" is even more evocative). This stately epithet elevates Ruth above the commonplace to the heroic status that the story as a whole accords to her. As we move down the following series of translations, we lose the literary effect, and the stature of Ruth progressively shrinks: "fine woman," "capable woman," "wonderful person," "a real prize."

My heart soars when I read in 1 Samuel 10:26 that King Saul initially surrounded himself with "men of valor whose hearts God had touched." That description possesses the literary quality of verbal beauty, which in turn dignifies the content of the statement. Colloquial translations in the modern mode deliberately depart from the literary quality of being other than ordinary, and the power of the statement evaporates: "warriors," "powerful men," "strong men," "young men," "fighting men," "band of men"—not "men of valor."

Greek dramatist Aristophanes famously said that "high thoughts must have high language."[9] Bible translations that accept this literary

---

9. Aristophanes, *The Frogs*, trans. Dudley Fitts (New York: Harcourt, Brace, 1955), 108.

dictum elevate their readers, stir their spirits, and make them remember what they read. Translations that abandon literary criteria for the idiom of the bus stop are flat and eminently forgettable. It pains me to stand before a class of thirty-five students and discover that no one can identify an allusion to Jesus's statement about the broad and narrow ways in the Sermon on the Mount, but I can hardly blame the students when it is their colloquial modern translations that have conditioned them to experience the Bible as nothing special.

Poetry. At least a third of the Bible comes to us as poetry, and that percentage rises if we include the incidence of imagery, metaphor, and other figures of speech in the prose sections. I feel almost foolish to assert that retaining the poetry of the biblical text is a literary quality that makes a difference in English Bible translations. The truth is that poetry was one of the first things to go in modernizing translations. I have space to explore just one example, but it represents a principle that cuts a broad swath through the Bible.

Psalm 1:1 uses an evocative metaphor and archetype to describe the behavior that the godly person avoids:

> Blessed is the man
> who walks not in the counsel of the wicked.

Walking down a path embodies multiple meanings, as most images and metaphors do. It encompasses such qualities as deliberate choice, long-term progression in the same direction, and arrival at a destination based on what path a person has followed. Do these meanings *matter* in the statement? Of course they do, and they depend on translators' retaining the imagery of the original text.

This very text has entered the debate between rival translation philosophies. The chief founder of dynamic equivalence and colloquial style, Eugene Nida, declared that the metaphor in Psalm 1:1 seems "strange" to "many modern readers," and that removing the metaphor makes the verse "so much clearer."[10] Translators who agree with Nida produce translations such as the following, all of which remove the metaphor or add interpretive commentary beyond what the biblical poet wrote:

---

10. Eugene A. Nida, *Good News for Everyone* (Waco, TX: Word, 1977), 9–10.

Happy is the one
who does not take the counsel of the wicked as a guide.

God blesses those people
who refuse evil advice.

Oh, the joys of those
who do not follow the advice of the wicked.

What is lost when we ignore the literary criterion of retaining the poetry of the Bible? The first thing we lose is called verbal or plenary inspiration of Scripture. This doctrine asserts that God inspired the very words of the Bible, and that they are the exact words that God wanted us to have. This offense is usually not linked to eliminating the poetry of the Bible, and in fact it is not limited to that. But I want to call attention to the seriousness of the matter when we treat literary criteria as optional frosting on the cake.

Abandoning the poetry of Psalm 1:1 also dissipates the affective and imaginative power of the statement. Poetry is concrete and achieves its effects with a certain indirection and subtlety. It activates us to picture things, and to engage in interpretation to figure out the meanings. A translation that "spells it out" lacks these qualities. Additionally, biblical scholar Raymond Van Leewen asks the very appropriate question of who gave us biblical metaphors in the first place. His answer (and mine): the Holy Spirit who inspired the authors of the Bible.[11]

Excellence of rhythm. For a final example of how literary criteria make a difference in Bible translation I have chosen a quality that does not reside in the Hebrew or Greek of the original text but is instead related to the English language. Smoothness of rhythm is an extremely important quality in any text, and preeminently with the biblical text that is read and heard in oral performance. Good rhythm is not primarily the domain of a handful of literary scholars; instead I have repeatedly found that ordinary people who lack the technical language to analyze rhythm are nonetheless quick to pick up on bad rhythm when they hear it. I regard good rhythm in an English Bible as a qualifying

---

11. Raymond C. Van Leewen, "We Really Do Need Another Translation," *Christianity Today*, October 22, 2001, 31.

exam. If a translation cannot measure up in this area, it is not in the running to be regarded as a superior Bible.

Rhythm is the regular recurrence of a pattern of sound. When the medium is language instead of music, rhythm refers to the flow of words and phrases. The goal of rhythm is smoothness—not a monotonously regular flow but a flow that is predominantly regular. The very word *rhythm* implies a back-and-forth recurrence, the rise and fall of language. Anything that impedes the smoothness of the flow and produces a staccato effect is detrimental to good rhythm.

The best test of rhythm is simply to read a passage aloud. If in oral reading a passage ebbs and flows smoothly, avoids abrupt stops between words and phrases where possible, and provides a sense of continuity, the translation is metrically excellent. If a translation bumps along, impedes the flow of language, and is consistently staccato in effect, it is rhythmically inferior. Poetic rhythm is more concentrated than prose rhythm, but the basic principles are the same in both cases. The main difference is that poetry is composed of metrical feet (the arrangement of accented and unaccented syllables), while prose uses larger syntactic units like phrases. In both poetry and prose, good rhythm consists of wavelike recurrence, a rise and fall in the movement of language. The technical term for this is *cadence*.

For purposes of illustration, I will compare how three translations render verses 4 and 7 of the encomium to love in 1 Corinthians 13. The first translation, the ESV, makes the grade; the other two typify the abruptness and lack of grace that are a hallmark of translations that turn their back on the King James tradition:

> Love is patient and kind; love does not envy or boast. . . . Love bears all things, believes all things, hopes all things, endures all things.

> Love is patient, love is kind. It does not envy, it does not boast, it is not proud. . . . It always protects, always trusts, always hopes, always perseveres.

> Love is kind and patient, never jealous, boastful, proud, or rude. . . . Love is always supportive, loyal, hopeful, and trusting.

The first rendition is graceful and winsome; the latter two are abrupt and jarring.

Why does the literary criterion of smooth rhythm matter in an English Bible translation? For three reasons.

One reason is aesthetic: good rhythm is beautiful to hear. Actually, good and bad rhythm are discernible even in silent reading. Beauty matters to God, who is its source. If beauty matters to God, it should matter to those who produce and read Bible translations. T. S. Eliot coined the phrase "auditory texture" to name the aural quality of literature that sounds beautiful to the ear, and he correctly said that literature that possesses such beauty penetrates "far below the conscious levels of thought and feeling, invigorating every word."[12]

Additionally, good rhythm is essential to any text that is uttered and heard orally. The Bible is preeminently an oral book, read aloud in public worship, on ceremonial occasions, and around the table. Exaltation of spirit and beauty of holiness in public worship took a huge hit when dynamic equivalent translations entered the scene. I lived through the revolution and was shocked by the diminishment that set in.

Thirdly, good rhythm is an aid to memory as well as to oral performance. A line that flows smoothly and sets up a regular cadence is easier to memorize than a line that bumps along and impedes the flow of thought. Good rhythm is aphoristic in effect. Literary critic F. L. Lucas, after lamenting what modernizing translations have done to the King James rendition "Come unto me, all ye that labour and are heavy laden, and I will give you rest," comments that modernization "ruins the beauty of rhythm which has helped the memories of generations, and kept the Bible running in their heads."[13] Someone else has written that a modernizing translation aimed at a sixth-grade level "does slip more easily into the modern ear, but it also slides out more easily."[14]

What I have said here should be regarded as exposing only the tip of the iceberg. I have asserted and illustrated how verbal beauty, concrete language, and effective rhythm make a difference in English Bible translation. Those three literary criteria are part of a longer list of literary qualities that are either present or absent in any English Bible. English Bible translation took a wrong turn when it abandoned

---

12. T. S. Eliot, *The Use of Poetry and the Use of Criticism* (London: Faber and Faber, 1933), 118–19.

13. F. L. Lucas, "The Greek 'Word' Was Difference," in *Literary Style of the Old Bible and the New*, ed. D. G. Kehl (Indianapolis: Bobbs-Merrill, 1970), 51.

14. Dwight Macdonald, "The Bible in Modern Undress," in Kehl, *Literary Style*, 38.

literary standards as a guideline. I will note as a parting thought that in all of my debates with advocates of dynamic equivalent and colloquial translations, the latter have never attempted to make a case for the literary excellence of their translations.

Literary Interpretation of the Bible

In addition to literal translation of the original Hebrew and Greek texts into English, there is also a figurative translation that we perform. The words on the page require us to comprehend and interpret them. This is a form of translation from the verbal level to the level of meaning. But that does not complete the process. Once we have comprehended what the text says by interpreting it accurately, we need to transfer that knowledge into daily living—a translation of truth into action. In this concluding section I will explain how literary criteria make a difference in comprehending and interpreting the Bible. I will leave it to my readers to ponder how what I say in this essay extends to the application of Scripture to their daily lives.

Literary Hermeneutics

The foundation of what I am about to say is the literary nature of the Bible itself, as discussed in my opening section. Considered in terms of its format, the Bible is a literary anthology, comprising many literary genres and forms. For most evangelicals, that is head knowledge only; it does not govern how they interact with the Bible. To approach the Bible as literature means *to do justice to* the literary qualities of the Bible—to literary genres and techniques, special resources of language and rhetoric, concrete embodiment of human experience, and artistic beauty. Why should we do justice to the literary nature of the Bible? To answer that question takes us into the realm of hermeneutics, or the principles of interpretation.

Authorial intention. The claim that we must read and interpret a text in keeping with the author's intention is a mainstay and even cornerstone of evangelical hermeneutics. The problem is that we do not rigorously apply that principle to the literary intention of the biblical authors. It stands to reason that if biblical authors embody their discourse in literary genres and forms, they *intend* that we read and interpret the text in keeping with ordinary literary methods of analysis. If a biblical author wrote a narrative, for example, he *intended* us to analyze the story in terms of plot, setting, and character. A biblical poet *intends* that we unpack the meanings of the images and figures of speech. If a biblical author infuses his writing with artistry and verbal beauty, surely he *intends* that we pay attention to these aesthetic qualities and not ignore them.

The whole text. This is not a customary label in hermeneutics, but it will serve my purpose. What I have in mind is that everything that an author put into a biblical text should be regarded as important. If the author, writing under the inspiration of the Holy Spirit, put something into the text, it is important, having been put there for a purpose. As I have intimated throughout this essay, much of what exists in the Bible is of a literary nature. There is far too much interpretive selectivity practiced in evangelical circles, as only certain theological aspects of a biblical text are considered worthy of attention. The antidote is simple: if an author put something into the text, it should interest us.

Specificity of the text. I have been implying this principle, but it needs to be stated as a separate point. Our handling of a text must do justice to the specificity of what is before us. This extends, for example, to the genre in which a work comes to us. We need to read and interpret a biblical text in terms of its specific genre. Often multiple genres converge, and each one is important. Paying attention to genre yields insights and enjoyment, and can spare us from misinterpretation. Because the customary use to which we put the Bible is theological and devotional, it is understandable that we come to view everything in the Bible as being theological and devotional in nature. We end up with a one-dimensional Bible.

Avoiding reductionism. This leads naturally to the related point that good interpretation avoids reductionism. The form that this reductionism typically takes is reducing a text to a series of theological or moral ideas. But a literary text embodies human experience first. From these embodied experiences we can infer or deduce themes and ideas, but those ideas are not an adequate substitute for the embodied experiences. Fiction writer Flannery O'Connor repudiated "the notion that you read the story and then climb out of it into the meaning," insisting rather that "the whole story is the meaning, because it is an experience, not an abstraction."[15] Reliving the text needs to be the first item on our agenda as readers and interpreters.

Meaning through form. Because the Bible is God's Word to us, and because its message is what governs our lives, we slip into thinking of the literary forms of the Bible as *only* the forms or vehicle by which God's truth is communicated. But we have the word order wrong: literature is not *only the forms* in which the Bible comes to us but *the only forms* in which the content of the Bible exists. Meaning is embodied in specific forms. Without the form, there is no meaning. There is thus a sense in which literary form is precedent, or comes first—not in terms of importance, but in terms of what we need to pay attention to first. Form is meaning. Content is communicated through form. If the form is literary in nature, we at once face the need to engage in literary analysis.

Concluding Thoughts

Because literary terminology is unfamiliar to many readers of the Bible, the impression might arise that viewing the Bible as literature involves adding something to the Bible. But this is a false impression. When we engage in literary analysis of the Bible, we are not reading into Scripture; we are merely reading Scripture. We are paying attention to something that is already present in the text.

It should not surprise us that the Bible comes to us in literary format. A look at the history of the human race shows that people are "wired" to express and understand their experiences in the form of stories, poems, and visions. That is how people are created. It should seem natural rather than strange to us that God's Word would adhere to how people are inclined to express truth and feeling.

As for the unfamiliarity that we might initially experience in approaching the Bible as literature, that is actually a mark in its favor. Adding literary considerations lends an element of freshness to our reading of the Bible. That is not the reason we do it, but it is a beneficial side effect. Not every fresh approach to the Bible is valid, but the

---

15. Flannery O'Connor, *Mystery and Manners* (New York: Farrar, Straus & Giroux, 1957), 73.

literary approach has the advantage of being the right way to read and interpret the Bible, for reasons noted above. Additionally, literature has enjoyment as a goal, and my students and readers have regularly recorded that an element of enjoying Scripture accompanied their newly found literary awareness. The writer of Ecclesiastes, we should remember, "sought to find words of delight" (Eccles. 12:10).

Did God inspire the forms of the Bible or only the content? It is a logical inference from what we believe about the inspiration of the Bible that God did inspire the forms. According to 2 Peter 1:21, the authors of the Bible "spoke from God as they were carried along by the Holy Spirit." If God superintended the writers of the Bible to write as they did, we can infer that the forms in which the authors expressed themselves were part of divine oversight. The literary forms of the Bible deserve an attention commensurate with their inspiration by God.

I began with an epigraph by Martin Luther, and I will end with an even more frequently quoted statement by C. S. Lewis: "There is a . . . sense in which the Bible, since it is after all literature, cannot properly be read except as literature; and the different parts of it as the different sorts of literature they are."[16]

---

16. C. S. Lewis, *Reflections on the Psalms* (New York: Macmillan, 1958), 3.

10

Much Ado about Headship

Rethinking 1 Corinthians 11:3

Thomas R. Schreiner

ABSTRACT: In this chapter three questions in 1 Corinthians 11:3 will be investigated. First, does Paul address husbands and wives or men and women? The matter is sharply debated in scholarship today, and I will argue that the answer should be nuanced. In other words, Paul addresses all men and women, but husbands and wives are especially in view. Second, what does the word "head" mean here? Does it mean "source," "preeminent" or "foremost," or "authority"? Here I want to suggest, despite some strong arguments to the contrary, that authority captures the sense. Third, what are the Trinitarian implications of God being the head of Christ? Does the wording suggest that the Father has attributes *ad intra* not shared by the Son? I will argue that such a conclusion doesn't follow and consider the role of 1 Corinthians 15:28 in presenting my answer. My study is not comprehensive, but the purpose of this chapter is to reflect on options discussed in scholarship and to give some reasons for the exegetical and theological decisions proposed.

———

It is a privilege to write this brief essay in honor of Wayne Grudem. The Lord has used Wayne's books and articles to encourage and strengthen the church of Jesus Christ in this generation. His writing is marked by unusual clarity, and thus those who are young believers or those who have not engaged in technical studies can understand him. At the same time, he has the ability to write on technical issues, which is evidenced by his work on the word *kephalē* (κεφαλή, "head").[1] Wayne is bold and courageous and willing to take a stand on controversial issues. I have known Wayne personally for many years and have been challenged by his love for the Lord Jesus Christ and his keen desire to live in a godly way. I offer this essay to Wayne with thankfulness for his writings and friendship.

In this chapter I want to examine afresh the meaning of 1 Corinthians 11:3. I wrote an essay on 1 Corinthians 11:2–16 around twenty-five years ago.[2] Space is lacking to treat the entire passage here, or even to explore fully the issues arising in this verse. Still, a fresh discussion of 1 Corinthians 11:3 might prove helpful since the text addresses both the relationship between men and women and our understanding of the Trinity. Readers will see the influence of Wayne Grudem on my thought, though I frame some things differently than he does.

Setting the Scene

Before embarking on a more detailed discussion of the verse, we need to introduce the passage in its context. Perhaps it is best to begin by citing 1 Corinthians 11:3. Two translations reveal immediately at least one interpretive difference. The ESV reads, "But I want you to understand that the head of every man is Christ, the head of a wife is her husband, and the head of Christ is God." An alternative rendering is found in the CSB, "But I want you to know that Christ is the head of every man, and the man is the head of the woman, and God is the head of Christ." I will return shortly to whether the verse refers to men and women or husbands and wives.

In looking at the passage as a whole, we see that Paul discusses in 1 Corinthians 11:2–16 whether women (or wives) should wear some

---

1. See note 9 for references.
2. Thomas R. Schreiner, "1 Corinthians 11:2–16: Head Coverings, Prophecies, and the Trinity," in *Recovering Biblical Manhood and Womanhood*, ed. Wayne Grudem and John Piper (Westchester, IL: Crossway, 1991), 124–39, 485–87.

kind of head covering in church.[3] Paul has just finished discussing food offered to idols (1 Cor. 8:1–11:1), and in 11:2–14:40 he addresses the adornment of women (11:2–16),[4] behavior at the Lord's Supper (11:17–34), and spiritual gifts (12:1–14:40). In each of these cases what is suitable in public worship is considered. Paul's advice in 11:2–16, then, doesn't have to do with private meetings but concerns proper conduct when the church is gathered. We could say that practical ecclesiological issues are worked out in these chapters. When we turn to the one verse before us, 1 Corinthians 11:3, we learn quite quickly that it is littered with controversies. In this short essay three questions in 11:3 will be investigated. First, does Paul address husbands and wives or men and women? Second, what does the word "head" mean here? Does it mean source, preeminent or foremost, or authority? Third and finally, what are the Trinitarian implications of God being the head of Christ? Does the wording suggest that the Father has an *ad intra* authority not shared by the Son? Let me immediately add a caveat. All of these issues are addressed in detail in other studies, and I can scarcely claim that enough argumentation is given to resolve these matters definitively here. My purpose is to reflect on options discussed in scholarship and to give some reasons for the exegetical and theological decisions proposed here.

---

3. It is keenly debated whether the referent is head coverings or hairstyle. For the latter, see, e.g., James B. Hurley, "Did Paul Require Veils or the Silence of Women? A Consideration of 1 Cor. 11:2–16 and 1 Cor. 14:33b–36," *WTJ* 35, no. 2 (Winter 1973): 193–200; Hurley, *Man and Woman in Biblical Perspective* (Grand Rapids, MI: Zondervan, 1981), 254–71; J. Murphy-O'Conner, "Sex and Logic in 1 Corinthians 11:2–16," *CBQ* 42 (1980): 488–89; Murphy-O'Conner, "1 Corinthians 11:2–16 Once Again," *CBQ* 50 (1988): 268; David E. Blattenberger, *Rethinking 1 Corinthians 11.2–16 through Archaeological and Moral-Rhetorical Analysis* (Lewiston, NY: Mellon, 1997); Philip B. Payne, *Man and Woman, One in Christ: An Exegetical and Theological Study of Paul's Letters* (Grand Rapids, MI: Zondervan, 2009), 204–10. A reference to a head covering of some kind is more probable. See, e.g., David Gill, "The Importance of Roman Portraiture for Head Coverings in 1 Corinthians 11:2–16," *TynBul* 41 (1990): 245–60; David E. Garland, *1 Corinthians*, BECNT (Grand Rapids, MI: Baker, 2003), 516–21; Eckhard J. Schnabel, *Der erste Brief des Paulus an die Korinther*, 3rd ed., Historisch Theologische Auslegung (Witten: SCM R. Brockhaus, 2014), 599–604.

4. Cynthia Long Westfall, *Paul and Gender: Reclaiming the Apostle's Vision for Men and Women in Christ* (Grand Rapids: MI, Baker Academic, 2016), 31–37, argues that the women wanted to wear veils and were being prevented from doing so by men for a variety of reasons. Such a reading of the cultural context is interesting, but clear evidence that the men were suggesting thus is lacking in the text. Nor does it account well for the logic in the text, which links man being the head with women wearing a veil (1 Cor. 11:3–6). If men were preventing women from wearing veils, Paul would speak to the issue more directly and criticize the men, especially since not wearing veils indicated sexual availability according to Westfall. Westfall limits this sexual availability to lower-class women, female slaves, and freedwomen. Against Westfall, there is no indication in the text that only these women were dispensing with veils. The claim that the men were compelling women to remove their veils fails to convince. The admonition is quite general, and we should beware of the many attempts to establish the meaning of the text from an alleged background, for such alleged backgrounds are legion.

Husbands and Wives or Men and Women?

We saw in the two translations cited above that the ESV refers to husbands and wives in 1 Corinthians 11:3, whereas the CSB uses the language of men and women. Perhaps the most influential argument for seeing a reference to wives comes from Bruce Winter. He argues that the very subject addressed, the wearing of veils, indicates that wives are the referent.[5] Other arguments in favor of this reading can also be adduced. It seems to make more sense to say that the husband is the head of his wife instead of saying that men are the head of women (11:3), for we don't read elsewhere that men in general are the head of women, but a husband does function as the head of his wife (Eph. 5:22–24). Furthermore, it is difficult to see how a woman being uncovered dishonors every man in the congregation (1 Cor. 11:5), but we can see how it would dishonor her husband as her head. Also, claiming that women in general are "the glory of" men (11:7) introduces a thought that isn't found elsewhere in Paul or Scripture.

Good arguments, however, can also be presented for seeing a reference to women in general. Winter's argument from veiling isn't decisive. As David Garland points out, women who weren't married could also pray and prophesy, and thus we shouldn't restrict what Paul says to married women.[6] In other words, do the instructions about veiling apply exclusively to those who are married? It seems odd to envision single women or widows praying or prophesying in the assembly without wearing head coverings (11:5), while those who are married are required to wear veils of some kind. The comment about wearing veils "because of the angels" (11:10) also applies more convincingly to women in general and not just wives. We don't have to try to untie the knot here about what Paul means when he says "because of the angels" (11:10), but we should notice that it seems askew to say that only married women should have "authority" on their heads because of angels. Why would the angels be concerned that only married women wear veils while praying or prophesying, especially when the issue is behavior at public worship?

---

5. Bruce W. Winter, *After Paul Left Corinth: The Influence of Secular Ethics and Social Change* (Grand Rapids, MI: Eerdmans, 2001), 127; Winter, *Roman Wives, Roman Widows: The Appearance of New Women and the Pauline Communities* (Grand Rapids, MI: Eerdmans, 2003), 77–96. See also Westfall, *Paul and Gender*, 26–28.
6. Garland, *1 Corinthians*, 514.

Paul's comments in verses 11–12 also suggest that he casts the net more widely than marriage, for he reflects on the creation account where Eve came from Adam. Paul probably alludes to marriage in verse 11, but he also strays outside the orbit of marriage in his discussion (11:12). The argument from nature (11:13–15) also supports the notion that Paul doesn't confine himself to marriage. If nature teaches women to wear long hair, it seems that this instruction isn't limited to married women.

It should also be noted that when Paul addresses husbands and wives exclusively, there are clear indications in the text of a married relationship (see 1 Cor. 7:2–5, 8–16; Eph. 5:22–23; Col. 3:18–19; cf. 1 Pet. 3:1–7).[7] Still, some of the evidence for seeing wives in 1 Corinthians 11:2–16 is quite strong. I suggest, therefore, a mediating solution. Paul's instructions in this text are for both married and unmarried women in the congregation. Nevertheless, there is a fluidity and a looseness in his discussion; and thus, even though Paul refers to women in general, he glides over to the relationship between husbands and wives, especially in 11:4–5. Such a move isn't surprising since most of the women were probably married. Indeed, the corresponding discussion in 1 Corinthians 14:33b–36 may suggest that wives in particular were the offenders with respect to veiling. When we think about 11:3 in particular, Paul doesn't restrict himself exclusively to husbands and wives. It doesn't follow from this that every man is the head of every woman in the congregation. Instead Paul thinks more generally and cosmically—we could say ecclesiologically—in the passage, and thus in verse 3 he reflects on the creational differences between men and women. Paul's instructions, then, naturally apply in a specific way to the marriage relationship, but his main concern in this text is not marriage but the adornment of women in the corporate assembly. Hence, he naturally thinks of the relationship between men and women in general, not just wives and husbands.

"Head" as Source, Preeminent, or Authority?

It is well known that an intense controversy has been going on for years over the meaning of the word *kephalē* ("head") in Paul, especially in

---

7. See my discussion of this matter in Thomas R. Schreiner, "1 Timothy 2:9–15: A Dialogue with Scholarship," in *Women in the Church: An Analysis and Application of 1 Timothy 2:9–15*, ed. Andreas Köstenberger and Thomas R. Schreiner, 3rd ed. (Wheaton, IL: Crossway, 2016), 177–80.

verses that address the relationship between men and women and husbands and wives. Such a discussion is crucial for 1 Corinthians 11:3, since the term appears three times in the verse. Many have argued that the word "head" means "source."[8]

Wayne Grudem's careful work on the meaning of *kephalē*, however, is convincing, and he has established clearly in my judgment that the word regularly means "authority over" in metaphorical contexts.[9] In terms of men and women, we see this especially in Ephesians 5:22–24, where husbands are identified as heads of their wives. Wives are called upon to submit to their husbands since the husband is the head. Semantically and contextually it makes excellent sense for wives to submit to their husbands inasmuch as husbands function as the authority over their wives. Glossing the word *kephalē* with the translation "source" doesn't fit in Ephesians since a husband isn't the source of his wife. Wives don't derive their physical life from husbands, and so husbands aren't the source biologically. Nor do wives obtain spiritual life from their husbands (they get that from Christ), and so husbands aren't the source spiritually. There is no meaningful sense in which husbands function as the source of their wives. It does make sense, though, to say that husbands function as the authority over their wives, and thus wives should submit to them.

This is not to say that the word *kephalē* never means "source" in Paul. It is quite possible that *kephalē* means "source" in two Pauline passages. Context is decisive in assigning meaning to a word. Perhaps in Ephesians 4:15 the term means "source" since Paul speaks of the body growing, and the Head of the body, who is Christ, could be conceived of as the source of that growth. Colossians 2:19 may be

---

8. E.g., Gilbert Bilezikian, *Beyond Sex Roles: What the Bible Says about a Woman's Place in Church and Family*, rev. ed. (Grand Rapids, MI: Baker, 1985), 215–52; Berkeley Mickelsen and Alvera Mickelsen, "What Does *Kephalē* Mean in the New Testament?," in *Women, Authority and the Bible*, ed. Alvera Mickelsen (Downers Grove, IL: InterVarsity Press, 1986), 97–110; Catherine Clark Kroeger, "The Classical Concept of Head as 'Source,'" in *Equal to Serve: Women and Men in the Church and Home*, ed. Gretchen Gaebelein Hull (Old Tappan, NJ: Revell, 1987), 267–83; Gordon D. Fee, *The First Epistle to the Corinthians*, rev. ed., NICNT (Grand Rapids, MI: Eerdmans, 2014), 555–57; Westfall, *Paul and Gender*, 38–40, 79–105.

9. Wayne Grudem, "Does Κεφαλή ('Head') Mean 'Source' or 'Authority Over' in Greek Literature? A Survey of 2,336 Examples," *TJ* 6, no. 1 (Spring 1985): 38–59; Grudem, "The Meaning of Κεφαλή ('Head'): A Response to Recent Studies," *TJ* 11, no. 1 (Spring 1990): 3–72; Grudem, "The Meaning of Κεφαλή ('Head'): An Examination of New Evidence, Real and Alleged," *JETS* 44, no. 1 (March 2001): 25–65. See also Joseph A. Fitzmyer, "Another Look at "ΚΕΦΑΛΗ in 1 Corinthians 11.3," *NTS* 35 (1989): 503–11; Fitzmyer, "*Kephalē* in 1 Corinthians 11:3," *Interpretation* 47 (1993): 52–59.

construed in a similar way. Here Paul contemplates the growth of the body of Christ, and the word "head" may designate the source from which the body receives nourishment and growth.[10]

It follows, then, that the translation "source" for *kephalē* is also possible in 1 Corinthians 11:3. Some might object on Trinitarian grounds, for how could God be the source of Christ? Those who defend the rendering "source" understand that Paul speaks here of the economic Trinity. God sent Christ in the incarnation. If one were to read this in terms of eternal relations, the verse could be understood as referring to the eternal generation of the Son without implying the intrinsic inferiority of the Son. Furthermore, one could defend the translation "source" in verse 3 from verse 8, where Paul says that "woman [came] from man." Paul repeats the same thought in verse 12, and then turns it around and says that all men come from women.

The rendering "source," then, is possible but is unconvincing for lexical, theological, and contextual reasons. First, the lexical reason. I think Grudem has shown that reading *kephalē* as designating authority is the most common meaning of the word. The second reason is theological. In Ephesians 5:22–24 Paul clearly uses *kephalē* to refer to the husband as the authority over his wife. It is most natural to conclude that he uses *kephalē* with the same meaning here, even though the discussion goes beyond husbands and wives. In any case, Paul still refers to men and women. Third, we see a contextual reason. Paul requires women to adorn themselves a certain way in the congregation because of their relationship to men. The adornment of the women signals submission to male leadership in the church, and such submission is Paul's concern in the other text about men and women in 1 Corinthians, namely, 14:33b–36.[11]

Richard Cervin and Andrew Perriman, however, suggest still another interpretation. They think the word *kephalē* means something

---

10. See Clinton E. Arnold, "Jesus Christ: 'Head' of the Church (Colossians and Ephesians)," in *Jesus of Nazareth: Lord and Christ: Essays on the Historical Jesus and New Testament Christology*, ed. Joel B. Green and Max Turner (Grand Rapids, MI: Eerdmans, 1994), 346–66.

11. Some scholars understand this text to be an interpolation. Against this, see D. A. Carson, "'Silent in the Churches': On the Role of Women in 1 Corinthians 14:33b–36," in Grudem and Piper, *Recovering Biblical Manhood and Womanhood*, 141–45; Curt Niccum, "The Voice of the Manuscripts on the Silence of Women: The External Evidence for 1 Corinthians 14.34–35," *NTS* 43 (1997): 242–55.

like "preeminent" or "foremost."[12] Others concur with this reading. For instance, David Garland reads the word this way and claims that the point is how the woman represents the man.[13] Wayne Grudem has effectively responded to Cervin and others of like mind,[14] and thus my objections focus on whether such an interpretation squares with 1 Corinthians 11:2–16.

As noted previously, Garland understands the word "head" in terms of representation. Such an idea makes sense, but it is harder to see how the idea of representation is derived from words like "preeminent" and "foremost." We can all understand that man might represent woman, but words like "preeminent" and "foremost" don't bring the idea of representation to our minds. Clearer evidence is needed to support the idea that one can move from preeminence to representation. Even if representation were a satisfactory gloss for "head" (though the evidence for such is lacking), we need to see more clearly how man represents woman and what it means in the context of 11:2–16 to say that the man represents the woman. To elaborate, we need an explanation as to why women need to wear veils if men represent them.

Let's return to the notion that "head" here means "preeminent" or "foremost." We still have to discern the significance of such a rendering. We have to unpack the sense in which the man is preeminent or foremost. Certainly, the words "preeminent" and "foremost" are metaphorical. The question is what do they signify? It is doubtful that Paul thinks of men as preeminent physically, intellectually, or emotionally. Others say that it means preeminent socially, but such a reading fails to persuade. Roy Ciampa and Brian Rosner rightly remark, "Even if by 'head' Paul means 'more prominent/preeminent partner' or (less likely) 'one through whom the other exists,' his language and the flow of the argument seem to reflect an assumed hierarchy. . . . In this context the word almost certainly refers to one with authority over the other."[15]

Others claim that there is no notion of authority here but that Paul focuses on social relations. Admittedly, this is a difficult passage, and

---

12. Richard S. Cervin, "Does Κεφαλή Mean 'Source' or 'Authority' in Greek Literature? A Rebuttal," *TJ* 10, no. 1 (Spring 1989): 85–112; Andrew C. Perriman, "The Head of a Woman: The Meaning of Κεφαλή in 1 Cor. 11:3," *JTS* 45 (1994): 602–22.
13. Garland, *1 Corinthians*, 516.
14. Grudem, "Meaning of Κεφαλή: A Response," 3–72.
15. Roy E. Ciampa and Brian S. Rosner, *The First Letter to the Corinthians*, PNTC (Grand Rapids, MI: Eerdmans, 2010), 509.

there are certainly social and cultural dimensions of the text that we need to attend to. For instance, honor and shame play a significant role in this text, and Paul is concerned that women don't bring shame on men. Still, the attempt to limit the text to social realities may blind us to its theological dimension. We could fall into the trap of separating the social and theological dimensions of the discussion too sharply from one another. Actually, social and theological realities converge on one another here in remarkable ways.

The fundamental problem with an exclusively sociological reading is that it doesn't account well for the flow of thought in 1 Corinthians 11:3. The social reading of the text shuts out the theological dimension of the text, but the light of theology isn't so easily extinguished. Verse 3 concludes with the claim that God is the head of Christ. I will discuss in more detail below what Paul means by such a statement. What is crucial to observe here is that such a statement doesn't merely designate social relations between God and Christ. Some might see a reference to the ontological Trinity, while others think it refers to the economic Trinity, but in either case the assertion is deeply theological. What Paul says about God's relationship to Christ in verse 3 shows that the cultural and social dimensions of the passage can't be sundered from theology. God's relationship to Christ isn't merely social, nor is it cultural. And Paul wants his readers to see the relationship between men and women as analogous in some sense to God's relationship to Christ.

We have further evidence that Paul reflects on the relationship of men and women theologically. Men aren't to cover their heads since they are "the image and glory of God," while women are "the glory" of men (11:7). This verse is fascinating in its own right, and it isn't my intention to explicate it here. What Paul says here is deeply theological, and its significance can't be limited to the social circumstances of the Corinthian church. Similarly, Paul takes us back in verse 8 to the creation account, to the story in Genesis 2:18–25, where the woman is taken from the man. When Paul says in verse 9 that man "was not created for woman but woman for man," he almost certainly reflects on the same narrative in Genesis 2. More particularly, he alludes to the notion that Eve was made as a "helper" (Gen. 2:18, 20). Every step we take, of course, in this discussion is freighted with controversy, but it is sufficient to note the theological accent in the text.

An appeal to the creation narrative indicates that Paul's discussion isn't merely social or cultural but is also theological. Paul spies in the creation account a difference between men and women that must manifest itself in the cultural situation in Corinth. A woman dishonors her head if she prophesies without proper adornment (1 Cor. 11:4–6). Women who aren't properly adorned flout the leadership of the church. Such a reading coheres with 1 Corinthians 14:33b–36, where the behavior of women in the assembly is indicted because their actions betray a lack of submission to their husbands. What Paul says in 1 Corinthians 11:3 can't be limited to social realities. Instead, the theological, social, and cultural merge in this text, and Paul's social and cultural instructions flow from his theology.

To sum up, even if *kephalē* means "preeminent" or "foremost," the word still has the meaning "authority over." Paul isn't only saying that men are preeminent over women in cultural or social terms, just as he isn't saying that God is merely the social head of Christ. Paul reflects on culture and theology in this passage. We shouldn't be surprised that he applies his theology to a particular cultural situation.

What Are the Trinitarian Implications?

The meaning of 1 Corinthians 11:3 is also bound up with our understanding of the Trinity. Indeed, we have a recipe for controversy, since the Trinity and the relationship between men and women come together in the same verse. We begin by noting the order of the propositions in the verse. First, Paul says that Christ is "the head of every man," which means that Christ is the authority over every man. Certainly this doesn't mean that Christ is not the authority over women. Paul emphasizes here the particular authority Christ exercises over men. He then says that man is head over woman, which means in this context that male leadership expresses itself in a particular way in public worship. When women prayed or prophesied in Paul's day, they were to adorn themselves with a veil or covering of some kind to signify their submission to male leadership in the church. The cultural and the theological dimensions coalesce here so that the authority of men is reflected by whether women adorn themselves properly when praying and prophesying.

Paul concludes by saying that God is the head of Christ. It is this statement, of course, that has precipitated recent controversy on the Trinity, especially as it relates to complementarianism. Complementarians have often pointed to what is said here as a defense of their position, and I have done so myself, defending this view in my earlier article on 1 Corinthians 11, written twenty-five years ago. Matters have gotten very interesting in the last few years. Egalitarians have been charging for some time that some complementarians are promoting a view of the Trinity that is deficient or even unorthodox.[16] Then in June of 2016 additional observers made the charge that the view of the Trinity being promoted by some complementarians is unorthodox.[17]

It may be helpful to note that cultural and theological fashions change, and evangelicals are not free from such changes, since we too are affected by the climate in which we live. Evangelicals who came to theological maturity in the 1960s through perhaps the 1980s or even the early 1990s found themselves in a situation where their theology needed to be substantiated by careful exegesis. The historical-critical method reigned supreme in biblical studies, and evangelicals desired to show exegetically and biblically that their doctrinal conceptions were based not on tradition but on sound exegesis. Meanwhile, in systematic circles social trinitarianism became very popular, and its influence also penetrated evangelical circles.[18]

---

16. Charges have been made especially against Wayne Grudem and Bruce Ware. See, e.g., Wayne Grudem, "Biblical Evidence for the Eternal Submission of the Son to the Father," in *The New Evangelical Subordinationism?*, ed. Dennis W. Jowers and H. Wayne House (Eugene, OR: Pickwick, 2012), 223–61; Bruce A. Ware, *Father, Son, and Holy Spirit: Relationships, Roles, and Relevance* (Wheaton, IL: Crossway, 2004). For egalitarians who question this reading, see Kevin Giles, *The Trinity and Subordinationism* (Downers Grove, IL: InterVarsity Press, 2002); Giles, *Jesus and the Father* (Grand Rapids, MI: Zondervan, 2006); Millard Erickson, *Who's Tampering with the Trinity?* (Grand Rapids, MI: Kregel, 2009).

17. Those unfamiliar with the debate know that a sustained discussion broke out on the Internet starting June 3, 2016. I list only some of the initial salvos and conclude with a resource for further exploration. Liam Goligher, "Is It Okay to Teach a Complementarianism Based on Eternal Subordination?," June 3, 2016, http://www.mortificationofspin.org/mos/housewife-theologian/is-it-okay-to-teach-a-complementarianism-based-on-eternal-subordination; Goligher, "Reinventing God," June 6, 2016, http://www.mortificationofspin.org/mos/housewife-theologian/reinventing-god; Carl Trueman, "Fahrenheit 381," June 7, 2016, http://www.alliancenet.org/mos/postcards-from-palookaville/fahrenheit-381; Wayne Grudem, "Whose Position on the Trinity Is Really New?," June 9, 2016, http://cbmw.org/public-square/whose-position-on-the-trinity-is-really-new; Carl Trueman, "A Rejoinder to Wayne Grudem," June 9, 2016, http://www.mortificationofspin.org/node/40085; Bruce Ware, "God the Son—at Once Eternally God with His Father, and Eternally Son of the Father," June 9, 2016, http://www.reformation21.org/blog/2016/06/god-the-son-at-once-eternally-g.php; Carl Trueman, "A Surrejoinder to Bruce Ware," June 9, 2016, http://www.mortificationofspin.org/node/40084. For a bibliography of the debate up to July 20, 2017, see http://www.booksataglance.com/blog/thirtieth-updated-edition-trinity-debate-bibliography/.

18. For a thorough discussion of the person of Christ, see Stephen J. Wellum, *God the Son Incarnate: The Doctrine of Christ*, Foundations of Evangelical Theology (Wheaton, IL: Crossway, 2016).

Times have changed. Postmodernism has affected both exegesis and theology. Confidence in the historical-critical method has waned, and it is being fiercely challenged on many fronts. The notion that we are more objective than our ancestors has also been called into question. When it comes to the Trinity, Lewis Ayres's work has pulled scholars back in the Nicene direction, showing that the East and West were united in a pro-Nicene understanding of the Trinity.[19] Younger evangelical scholars have grown up in a different world than the previous generation, for believers are now a distinct minority, and rationalistic modernism is in retreat. Younger scholars are interested in reaching back to those who have preceded them, seeing in the exegesis and theological reflection of their forebears, especially in the early creeds, truths that have stood the test of time. The modernist experiment has been deemed a failure, and the sometimes naive confidence in objective biblical exegesis has eroded.

It is fascinating to see how younger evangelicals in particular have questioned some mature evangelical scholars with respect to the Trinity, saying that the latter make statements that seem to be at odds with the Nicene and Chalcedonian Creeds. Younger evangelical scholars are mining the wisdom of our ancestors, and they tend to trust the exegetical reflections of those who formulated the creeds. Older scholars who grew up in a different era may be puzzled by the breach that has arisen between them and the younger generation. Younger scholars, of course, need to beware of simply citing the creeds and neglecting careful exegesis. It sometimes feels as if the exegesis that fits the tradition is adopted without a careful reflection on the biblical text.

In any case, the charge that Wayne Grudem and Bruce Ware are guilty of heresy is clearly mistaken, since they explicitly support the notion that the Father, the Son, and the Spirit equally share the one divine essence. The charges against Grudem and Ware come with respect to entailments regarding the doctrine of the Trinity. It is one thing to disagree with the entailments of the views proposed by Grudem and Ware, but it is quite a different matter to identify their views as heretical. One of the dangers in the Reformed community is a kind of

---

19. Lewis Ayres, *Nicea and Its Legacy: An Approach to Fourth-Century Trinitarian Theology* (Oxford: Oxford University Press, 2004). See also the excellent exposition of the Trinity by Gilles Emery, *The Trinity: An Introduction to Catholic Doctrine on the Triune God*, trans. Matthew Levering (Washington, DC: Catholic University of America Press, 2011).

fundamentalism that insists on universal agreement regarding every dimension and detail of a doctrine. Charitable disagreement is salutary, but some who are quick to cry heresy are in danger of becoming cantankerous. The doctrine of the Trinity is complex and ultimately beyond our understanding. There is room for legitimate disagreement and give and take within the boundaries of orthodoxy. Some computers are becoming overheated, and the orthodox bona fides of Grudem and Ware should be recognized, even if there are disagreements with some of their formulations.

All of this brings us back to 1 Corinthians 11:3. How should we understand this verse? I think the verse relates to functional authority, to the *ad extra* relation between the Father and the Son. If we look at the text closely, it is interesting that the word "Christ" is used. The reference to the Christ points to Jesus's earthly ministry, to the incarnation and not to his eternal sonship as the second person of the Trinity. The focus, then, is *ad extra* and economic instead of *ad intra* and immanent. On the other hand, what we see in the economic Trinity reflects what is true of the persons of the Trinity in their personal relations to one another. The Father is always the Father, the Son is always the Son, and the Spirit is always the Spirit. The Father sends, and the Son willingly goes; and the Spirit proceeds from both the Father and the Son. When it comes to the personal relations among the members of the Trinity, the Father sends the Son, and the Son gladly and willingly submits himself to the Father's will for our salvation, thus reflecting in the economy an eternal ordering or *taxis*.[20]

The words of Stephen Wellum are apropos:

> In summary, then, we can say regarding the divine *ad intra* relations that the Father has priority not in nature but in mode of subsistence in the divine nature; the Son depends upon the Father not in nature but in personal filiation; the Spirit proceeds from the Father and the Son not in nature but in personal spiration. Regarding the *ad extra* economy, the entire Godhead acts in unity, but the Father initiates and acts through the Son and in the Spirit; the Son

---

20. The Second Council of Constantinople in AD 553 affirmed that the Father, Son, and Spirit share the same nature, substance, and authority. See Emery, *The Trinity*, 83. See also his discussion on 92–93, 166.

obeys the Father and works in the Spirit; the Spirit executes the acts of the Father and Son in power.[21]

Looking at one verse, of course, can hardly settle the issues at stake here, and scholars continue to disagree about what this verse means. We should also ask the following question, however. If the verse constructs a parallel between God's relation to Christ and the relationship of men to women, how should we formulate what is being said with respect to the relationship between men and women? Most complementarians would agree that the relationship between men and women in the Scriptures is clear enough, whatever we make of the Trinitarian implications of this verse. Still, the headship of the Father over the Son (the functional submission of the Son), grounds the relationship between men and women. Some have used the term "subordination" here, and that understandably makes people nervous, since it recalls ancient heresies where the Son was deemed to be of lesser worth or dignity than the Father. The scriptural and confessional testimony is that the Son is of the same nature with the Father and coequal with him, and that the Father doesn't have any attribute that is not fully shared by the Son and the Spirit. Hence, it is probably better not to use the word "subordination," since it is liable to be misunderstood. Nevertheless, "functional subordination" is really just another way of talking about functional submission. And to speak of functional subordination doesn't call into question the equality the Son has as the second person of the Trinity, as long as we recognize that we are talking about the personal relations between the Father and the Son.

A word needs to be said about 1 Corinthians 15:28 at this juncture, since it relates to our discussion. We read in that verse that the Son will subject himself (*hypotagēsetai*) to the Father. Does this text actually refer to an eternal submission of the Son that should

---

21. Wellum, *God the Son Incarnate*, 430. Wellum goes on to say:

Given this divine-filial relation, we can better make sense of such texts as John 14:28 (cf. 1 Cor. 15:27–28), which speak of the *priority* of the Father in relation to the Son. Scripture teaches that the Father enjoys *personal* priority in the *taxis* (order) of the triune life, but not ontological superiority. The church has captured this truth by describing the Father as the *fons divinitatis*. The Father is the source of the Godhead not in generating the deity/nature of the Son (and the Spirit) but in the priority of his personal relation to the Son and Spirit. All that the person of the Son (and Spirit) has is received from the person of the Father. The full equality and deity of the Son (and Spirit) is not diminished by the Father's personal priority, because all share fully and eternally in the divine nature. (432n30)

be understood in terms of the immanent Trinity? And would such a reading point us to a different interpretation of 1 Corinthians 11:3? Several lines of argument point to a negative answer. First, the paragraph refers to Christ's resurrection, and emphasizes his resurrection as a *man* (1 Cor. 15:20–21). Second, the contrast with Adam in the text (15:21–22) demonstrates that Jesus is conceived of as the last Adam here. Third, the reign of Christ is linked to his resurrection and to the fulfillment of the covenant promises made to Abraham, David, and the prophets (15:20–24). In other words, Jesus reigns as the Son of David. Yes, of course, he is also the Son of God. We aren't going Nestorian here, but the emphasis in the text is on his humanity. Fourth, the deliverance of the kingdom to God and the destruction of death, then, are accomplished through Jesus Christ as the crucified and risen one (15:24–26). Of course, the victory over sin and death can be accomplished only by One who is fully God and fully man (15:1–11), but the subjection of the Son in 1 Corinthians 15:27–28 should not be read as an ontological subjection but as functional subordination. As the Davidic King and the Messiah, he hands over the kingdom to God and submits himself to him. Still, the reality is complex. By virtue of his equality with God, he also reigns equally and forever with the Father (Rev. 11:15–19).

That brings us back to our question. If the submission in 1 Corinthians 11 and 15 is functional, how does that relate to complementarianism? The parallel still stands, but there are continuities and discontinuities. We have an analogy between the Trinity and male-female relationships, but not an exact parallel. We are not surprised to discover that there is discontinuity because the relationship of the incarnate Son (the second person of the Trinity) to his Father can't be completely analogous to any human relationship, given the uniqueness of the relationship between the Father and the Son. Still, an analogy is drawn. Jesus is the God-man, and as the eternal Son of God, he shares every attribute that belongs to the Father. And yet as the eternal Son, he voluntarily and gladly submits the Father. So, too, the call for wives to submit to husbands and for male leadership in the church doesn't call into question the essential dignity, value, and worth of women, just as Christ's functional submission doesn't contradict his essential unity with the Father.

One final comment seems to be in order, though we lack a definitive word on the matter addressed here. The submission to male leadership is confined to this present age. We have no evidence that the church structures present now will continue in the age to come. We know that marriage comes to an end as an institution (Matt. 22:30). Hence, the structures and institutions of this present evil age relative to men and women are temporary.

Conclusion

Three dimensions of 1 Corinthians 11:3 have been investigated in this essay. First, I argued that men and women in general are in view, though at times Paul slides over to a discussion of wives and husbands. Second, the word *kephalē* in context refers to the authority of men over women. The notion isn't that all men have authority over all women, for Paul reflects on authority when the church gathers for worship. Third, the relationship between God's headship of Christ and the headship of men over women was explored. We have both continuities and discontinuities since the doctrine of the Trinity cannot be mapped precisely onto male-female relations. The reference here is to the economic Trinity, but at the same time Paul sees the *ad-extra* relationship of God to Christ as an analogy for male-female relationships.

11

The Value of Literal
Bible Translation

Peter J. Williams

What Is Literal?

"Literal" is a vague term. Bible translations are typically seen as ranging on a spectrum from the very literal, such as Aquila's Greek translation of the Old Testament or *Young's Literal Translation of the Holy Bible*, through to the paraphrastic, such as *The Message* or *The Living Bible*. Between these would be the King James Version at the more literal end of the spectrum and the English Standard Version (slightly less literal), the Christian Standard Bible (partly literal), the New International Version (explicitly following a functional equivalence model), and the New Living Translation (rather paraphrastic).

Thinking of translations as existing on such a spectrum is a helpful generalization but must only be taken as a starting point. The reality is, of course, more complex. Brunn has pointed out that such a categorization hides the fact that sometimes a translation seen as less literal renders particular things more literally than one of the supposedly more literal translations. For instance, the KJV renders Greek δηνάριον as "penny," while the ESV, NASB, and NIV render it "denarius."[1] Given the number

---

1. Dave Brunn, *One Bible, Many Versions: Are All Translations Created Equal?* (Downers Grove, IL: InterVarsity Press, 2013), 126. Scripture quotations marked NIV in this chapter cite the 2011 edition.

of issues involved in a translation of the entire Scriptures, it is extremely unlikely that one translation will *always* be more literal than any other.

When considering literalism one might explore several different things, including the degree to which the translators "segment" the source text into smaller components for which they seek to have a one-to-one equivalent, or the degree of consistency with which they render a word. In this essay, I will not seek to provide a definition of literalism—not because I think it unhelpful to do so,[2] but because I think the usefulness of the term "literal" is precisely in its ability to encompass a range of phenomena and describe the character of a translation in a way that is helpful despite the many counterexamples of nonliteral translations within generally literal versions.

There are too many different types of data within a Bible translation as a whole to be able to give exact and comprehensive comparative statistics on how much more or less literal one translation is than another. All such comparisons will be selective. One can make exact comparisons in narrow areas or try to take a comprehensive view of all the data, but one cannot do both. Nevertheless, we can meaningfully say that one translation is generally more literal than another in the sense that it more often seeks to align smaller units of the original text with smaller units in the translation and is more often consistent in doing so.

My aim here is to make some quantitative and qualitative comparisons of translations and to extol the virtues of the more literal translations, even while acknowledging that no translation method is free of problems. I am not thereby suggesting that other sorts of translations have no place in society, the church, or personal study. My aim is rather to say that for the sake of the global spread of the gospel, we need more focus on literal translation, not less. This point is, of course, independent of the question of how well particular translations execute their translation philosophies.

Moving Away from Literal Translation

Two related factors feed into how we translate Scripture: (1) what we believe the Scriptures are; (2) what we believe translation is. Starting with the former, it is important to note that Scripture is not just God's Word but also his *words*. Jesus in Matthew 4:4, quoting Deuteronomy 8:3, strikingly identifies the Old Testament Scriptures with words that

---

2. A good basic analysis of the different aspects of literalism can be found in James Barr, *The Typology of Literalism in Ancient Biblical Translations*, Mitteilungen des Septuaginta-Unternehmens (Göttingen: Vandenhoeck and Ruprecht, 1979).

have come out of God's mouth. Though God has no physical mouth, the words in sequence found in Scripture are connected to God as their author every bit as much as verbal sequences that come from the mouth of a human. Moreover, Matthew 4:4 and Deuteronomy 8:3 say that these are what humans need to live by.

There is, however, an interesting relationship between the Hebrew of Deuteronomy and the Greek of Matthew. Deuteronomy says that humanity is to live עַל־כָּל־מוֹצָא פִי־יְהוָה (lit. "upon everything coming out of the mouth of YHWH"), and Matthew reads ἐπὶ παντὶ ῥήματι ἐκπορευομένῳ διὰ στόματος θεοῦ (lit. "upon every *word* coming out through the mouth of God"). Thus the very statement of Jesus shows that translation need not be literal as some would class literalism. Nevertheless, both the Hebrew and the Greek use a word rendered "every" (sometimes rendered "all"), which focuses human attention on the level of individual words. Christ himself showed that other sorts of translation could be legitimate. But, in doing this, Christ also gave us a focus on individual words as coming in sequence from God. These words are what we are to live by, and their value to humans is in fact infinite. God commends his Word to us as the only thing of ultimate value for humans. We cannot separate God's words from God himself since, although God's words are not the same as God, they are the only way we know him as our God, and the only way we know his Son and the salvation that he has provided. Those words, which are said to come out of God's mouth, should be our overwhelming obsession.

This raises a question: If we are obsessed by the verbal sequences that come from God and these are of infinite value, do we want access to precise knowledge of those sequences or not?

Second, we may ask what translation is. It seems clear that perceptions of what translation is have changed over time, and when we consider Bible translation specifically, we see a definite shift within the twentieth century. Over time it seems that translations have been designed far less to cater to the needs of people obsessed with the verbal sequences uttered by God. It is possible to show this shift using quantitative studies of translation technique. Here we consider four particular measures of literalness:

1. Translation of the Hebrew word הִנֵּה ("behold") by some formal equivalent.[3]
2. Translation of the Hebrew word יָדַע ("know") in the sense of "have sexual union with" by a word meaning "know."

---

3. This test was applied to Numbers and Judges.

3. Translation of the Hebrew word הוֹלִיד or the Greek word γεννάω ("beget") in genealogies by a verb of similar meaning.[4]
4. Translation of Hebrew construct phrases where the first element is cognate with the second—for example, "king of kings," "lord of lords," "heaven of heavens," "song of songs"—by a phrase involving repeated vocabulary.

These four measures of literalness have been applied to a range of translations in eleven European languages divided into three broad categories: (1) Protestant translations from before 1800; (2) Catholic translations; (3) post-1950 translations that are not specifically Catholic. The eleven languages are Czech, Dutch, English, Finnish, French, German, Hungarian, Italian, Portuguese, Spanish, and Swedish.[5] One could certainly criticize the choice of translations investigated. There are many gaps in the selection made, but enough data are available for some clear patterns to appear as seen in table 1, where percentages of literal renderings are given.

Table 1. Four measures of literalness in translations

	Protestant pre-1800	Catholic	Post-1950
Test 1 "behold"	87.4%	29.8%	35.1%
Test 2 "know"	89.1%	72.5%	36.1%
Test 3 "beget"	97.0%	100.0%	51.0%
Test 4 cognate genitives	92.1%	94.2%	71.4%

4. This test was applied to Genesis 5 and 11 and Matthew 1.
5. I am extremely grateful to S. R. Millar for extensive research assistance behind this entire section. The translations considered are: Czech: Kralická 1593; Český ekumenický překlad 1979; Překlad 21 2009; Dutch: Statenvertaling 1637; Moretus 1599; Het Boek 1987; English: KJV 1611; Douay-Rheims 1752; ESV 2001; NIV 2011; Finnish: "Vuoden 1776 raamattu" 1776; Uusi kirkkoraamattu 1992; French: Bible Martin 1744; La Bible de Louvain 1550–1608; Nouvelle Edition de Genève 1979; Bible du semeur 2000; German: Luther Bibel 1545; "Ulenberg Bible" 1630; Schlachter 2000; Hungarian: Vizsoly 1590; Káldi 1626; Magyar Bibliatársulat 1975; Italian: Diodati 1607(1649); Antonio Martini 1759; Nuova riveduta 2006; Conferenza Episcopale Italiana 2008; Portuguese: Almeida 1753; Pereira 1790; O Livro 2000; Spanish: "Biblia del Oso" 1569; Biblia de Petisco y Torres Amat 1825; Reina-Valera 1995; Nueva traducción viviente 2010; Swedish: Karl XII's Bibel 1703; Svenska Folkbibeln 1998; Levande Bibeln 2000.

It is striking that the Catholic translations have a deep interest in literally rendering terms of generation. The Catholic translations are also less interested in literally rendering the word "behold." However, in general we see a clear pattern whereby the pre-1800 Protestant translations are generally more literal than the Catholic ones and are overwhelmingly more literal than the modern ones.[6]

However, these data undermine part of the narrative being told in relation to some modern Bible translations. This is how the current preface to the NIV puts it:

> One of the main reasons the task of Bible translation is never finished is the change in our own language, English. Although a basic core of the language remains relatively stable, many diverse and complex linguistic factors continue to bring about subtle shifts in the meanings and/or connotations of even old, well-established words and phrases.

At one level, I agree with every word of this. English is constantly changing in subtle ways. However, let us consider this in relation to something like the Hebrew particle הִנֵּה, "behold." These data show that language change alone is not a sufficient explanation of why the pre-1800 translations differ from many post-1950 ones. After all, it is scarcely plausible to believe that all eleven European languages considered used to have an idiomatic equivalent of הִנֵּה, and all went through the same process of losing that equivalent over the last several centuries. It is true enough that the English word "behold" is rather dated. We do not generally conjugate the term or say "I beheld." However, "look" and "see" are perfectly common verbs today that could equally well be used. Therefore we should not cite the archaic feel of the English "behold" as an explanation for why a formal equivalent of הִנֵּה has often been dropped in these various languages. At least this cannot solely be put down to an avoidance of archaism. What else is going on is that there has clearly been a change of *attitude* toward translation. People more recently do not seem to think that having an equivalent of the Hebrew word הִנֵּה is worth paying the price of having a translation sound like a translation.

---

6. The modern translations were taken as a group, but include some literal ones. If they were removed, the contrast would be even more extreme.

This relates to the point that Lawrence Venuti makes in his classic work *The Translator's Invisibility*. Referring to the idea that translation should be "fluent" (i.e., sound like it is natural language and not a translation), Venuti writes, "Under the regime of fluent translating, the translator works to make his or her work 'invisible,' producing the illusory effect of transparency that simultaneously masks its status as an illusion: the translated text seems 'natural,' that is, not translated."[7] It thus seems that it is the questionable aim of some translators to present their work as if it is not a translation, which motivates them to adapt the text to the audience's expectations that terms such as "see," which are current but not found as frequently in the target language, will be dropped in the interest of sounding more fluent.

A second set of data confirm that what we are dealing with is substantially a change in attitude rather than a change in language. This set of data considers the nature of notes in four English translations of the Bible: the KJV, ESV, NIV, and GNT. The original KJV had notes on the outer margins, whereas the other translations use footnotes. When we consider the content of these notes, we see a startling development. In the KJV the first note that we encounter is in Genesis 1:4, where the main text reads "and God divided the light from the darkenesse." Here the KJV translators provide a note saying. "Hebr betweene the light and betweene the darkenesse," obviously referring to a more literal rendering of the Hebrew behind the last five words of their translation. This note is representative of many notes in the KJV but is, in terms of our own culture, rather remarkable. It is hard to imagine the producers of a modern translation bothering to inform their readers that such was the literal rendition of the Hebrew. So little would appear to us to be at stake. However, when we investigate KJV notes, we see that great importance is set on providing the readers with literal renderings of the original. The results of a complete investigation of the Pentateuch, Isaiah, and the New Testament yield the categorization of notes shown in table 2.[8]

---

7. Lawrence Venuti, *The Translator's Invisibility: A History of Translation*, 2nd ed. (London: Routledge, 2008), 5.
8. Again, I am grateful to S. R. Millar for compiling these data.

Table 2. The nature of notes in four English translations

	What the Notes Do	Quantity	Proportion
KJV	Give a more literal rendering of the original	1027	46.07%
	Give an alternative rendering of the original	1098	49.26%
	Convey the difficulty in expressing the original	1	0.04%
	Make the original easier to understand	92	4.13%
	Other	11	0.49%
	Total	2229	
ESV	Give a more literal rendering of the original	529	29.03%
	Give an alternative rendering of the original	658	36.11%
	Convey the difficulty in expressing the original	31	1.70%
	Make the original easier to understand	287	15.75%
	Other	317	17.40%
	Total	1822	
NIV	Give a more literal rendering of the original	178	13.72%
	Give an alternative rendering of the original	536	41.33%
	Convey the difficulty in expressing the original	33	2.54%
	Make the original easier to understand	322	24.83%
	Other	228	17.58%
	Total	1297	
GNT	Give a more literal rendering of the original	2	0.32%
	Give an alternative rendering of the original	244	39.35%
	Convey the difficulty in expressing the original	41	6.61%
	Make the original easier to understand	164	26.45%
	Other	169	27.26%
	Total	620	

The most noticeable shift has been away from the KJV's tendency to give more-literal renderings of the original. The NIV has the most of these among the modern translations, while the GNT scarcely has any. Use of these notes to give alternatives is surprisingly steady at between 36 percent and 50 percent in all translations. Growth areas have been notes that seek to make the text easier to understand and notes that cannot be classified under these headings.

In interpreting the significance of these shifts, we can note that reduction in notes giving more-literal renderings of the original and growth in notes making the text easier to understand are in some sense linked. Both mark a change in translation from being centered on the source text—but providing a window, for those who want it, into the source text—toward being less interested in the source text and more focused on serving the reader. We may say that there has been a change in *textual orientation*. Translators have focused more on making the task of Scripture reading easier at exactly the same time there has been unprecedented growth in literacy and levels of education. Surely, one might think, if education and literacy are on the rise, the public will be willing to read *harder* translations than before. Ironically, the reverse seems to be the case.

Our quantitative comparisons so far have only been with translations made since the advent of printing. They show a shift in some modern translations from the types of Protestant translation that arose after the Reformation. Arguably, at the time of the Reformation, when matters of scriptural detail might be the topic of public debate, translations as paraphrastic as the NLT or NIV would have received little, if any, acceptance. I will now seek to illustrate both the advantages of literal Bible translations and the shift that has taken place relative to the earliest Bible translations with reference to one short narrative.

The Advantages of Literal Translation: Elisha and the She-Bears

I want to show, by means of 2 Kings 2:23–24, the great value that a literal translation can have, and how less literal ones will present problems for which they offer no solutions. The passage is the famous one about Elisha and the two bears that maul forty-two children. We begin by considering two modern Bible translations.

> From there Elisha went up to Bethel. As he was walking along the
> road, some boys came out of the town and jeered at him. "Get out
> of here, baldy!" they said. "Get out of here, baldy!" He turned
> around, looked at them and called down a curse on them in the
> name of the LORD. Then two bears came out of the woods and
> mauled forty-two of the boys. (NIV)

> Elisha left Jericho and went up to Bethel. As he was walking along
> the road, a group of boys from the town began mocking and mak-
> ing fun of him. "Go away, baldy!" they chanted. "Go away, baldy!"
> Elisha turned around and looked at them, and he cursed them in
> the name of the LORD. Then two bears came out of the woods and
> mauled forty-two of them. (NLT)

While both translations are rather paraphrastic here, the verbal resem-
blance between them is uncanny. Several features of these translations
deserve highlighting. First, we notice that in both translations Elisha
"was walking along" the road, whereas the Hebrew clearly has the
verb עָלָה meaning "going up." A consequence of this is that both translations distinguish "went up" earlier in the verse from "was walking"
later in the verse, even though they are the same verb.

Second, we see that the young people are described as "boys" in
both translations of verse 23 and in the NIV of verse 24, where the
NLT lacks a full noun. This is somewhat interesting given that both
translations have made considerable efforts to ensure that elsewhere
generic terms are translated in a way that allows for females to be understood as included. The term in verse 24 is certainly generic, and the
term in verse 23 may at least be understood as generic. A reader of the
NIV or NLT will conclude that only males were mauled.

Third, whereas the Hebrew term describing the children in
verse 24 has no further descriptor, in verse 23 it appears with an adjective. The expression נְעָרִים קְטַנִּים might be rendered literally "small lads
(and lasses)" in my British context. That is not in itself a sufficiently
elegant translation to be used in public, but it reflects the ambiguity
inherent in the word נַעַר, which could be used of someone from infancy
to early adulthood, and which in the plural could almost certainly
include females. The descriptor "small" is obviously intended to steer

readers' understanding of the term to the younger end of the range.[9] A reader of the NIV or NLT might conclude that the children are somewhat older than the Hebrew is leading us to believe.

Fourth, we notice that the young people twice call out, "Get out of here" (NIV) or "Go away" (NLT). However, the same verb was already translated "went up" and "was walking" and is certainly a verb of upward motion. The young people are therefore telling someone walking up a hill to "go up," a fact to which we will return.

Fifth, whereas the Hebrew is explicit that the bears are female, this information is dropped from the NIV and NLT. Perhaps it was not perceived as important.

As we consider these translations, we read that a man of God is insulted by a group of boys, who are then mauled by bears. None of the adaptations in these translations seem to make for significantly greater readability, but perhaps the most significant one is that the verb of ascent has been replaced three times by a verb of motion without ascent. The verb "go up" repeated by the group of youths is translated as a verb of departure, presumably on the basis that asking someone to go away often accompanies disdain. The modern translators have thus surmised that the Hebrew verb is idiomatic and does not in this case particularly denote ascent.

The problem with this inference is that it totally ignores the context, where the verbs "go up" and "go down" are theme words, as the following review will show.

The book of 2 Kings has begun with Ahaziah falling down through a lattice. He sends to enquire of Baal-zebub whether he will recover, but God sends Elijah to intercept his messengers with the repeated message "you shall not *descend* from the [sick] bed to which you have *gone up*" (1:4, 6, my lit. trans.). The repetition of the message serves to emphasize it and to make the unusual phraseology stand out. A king who has fallen and then gone up onto a bed will not be able to come down.

Continuing these thoughts, we next encounter Elijah sitting on top of a hill and the king sending fifty troops for him with the message "come down." We sense an irony. The king has begun the book in an upper room and fallen (2 Kings 1:2). On the other hand, Elijah has

---

9. The rhetorically loaded parallel where Solomon applies the same expression to himself in 1 Kings 3:7 to stress his inexperience could suggest that at a stretch it might apply to someone no longer in his minority.

begun the book low down. That is why he is told to "go up" to meet Ahaziah's messengers (1:3). Now he is up high and the king is telling him to "come down" (1:9). Elijah replies that if he is a man of God, "let fire come down from heaven and consume you and your fifty" (1:10). This happens; "fire came down" (1:10). The king again sends fifty, with another captain who repeats the same call to "come down," adding "quickly" (1:11) to intensify the command. He and his fifty meet the same fate (1:12), and the verb "come down" thus occurs twice more. The final captain of fifty has the sense to "go up" (see 1:13) and, recounting to Elijah how fire has already come down (1:14), he begs Elijah to spare his life, without asking him to come down. God now tells Elijah to "go down" (1:15). Clearly the passage is showing that no one other than God should be commanding a man of God to "go down." Elijah "went down" (1:15) and repeats again the message to Ahaziah that he will not "come down" from the bed to which he has "gone up" (1:16). It is hard to miss the emphasis on these terms.

Unfortunately the NIV obscures this emphasis. Despite the narrative repetition, it translates Elijah's message as "You will not leave the bed you are lying on" (2 Kings 1:4; similarly 1:6, 16). The NLT is remarkably similar: "You will never leave the bed you are lying on" (1:4; also 1:6, 16).

The next chapter, 2 Kings 2, begins with an account of Elijah being taken up into heaven. Again, the vertical dimension of motion is at the center of focus. God is going to take Elijah up (hiphil of עָלָה in 2:1) and indeed he "goes up" (see 2:11).

Against this backdrop it is hard to see the taunt of the young people in Bethel as totally unrelated. We might have a range of interpretations, seeing them as telling Elisha to "go up" miraculously as Elijah had, or mocking him as he toils up the hill, seemingly without great power. We might see the similarity and contrast with Elijah, who was told to "come down." But however we focus, a literal translation gives us the tools to make these comparisons, whereas a paraphrastic one does not.

If we consider a couple of more literal translations of 2 Kings 2:23–24, we see this at once:

> He went up from there to Bethel, and while he was going up on the way, some small boys came out of the city and jeered at him, saying, "Go up, you baldhead! Go up, you baldhead!" And he turned

around, and when he saw them, he cursed them in the name of the Lord. And two she-bears came out of the woods and tore forty-two of the boys. (ESV)

And he went up from thence unto Bethel: and as he was going up by the way, there came forth little children out of the city, and mocked him, and said unto him, Go up, thou bald head; go up, thou bald head. And he turned back, and looked on them, and cursed them in the name of the Lord. And there came forth two she bears out of the wood, and tare forty and two children of them. (KJV)

The principal difference between these two translations is the gender of the children. The KJV is gender neutral and the ESV gender specific. The Hebrew in verse 23 could be taken either way.[10]

In the NIV the boys are cursed for insulting the man of God. In the ESV and KJV it is possible to read them as being cursed not only for insulting the man of God but also for making mockery of what has happened to Elijah. In this way the more literal translations repay study. If we expect readers in a culture only to read the Bible once or to read it fairly superficially, then it would make sense to give them a translation that is fairly easy to read and does not need to be read again and again. But if we truly believe that the words that come out of God's mouth are more precious and necessary for life than the food we eat, this would be a strange attitude.

We now look at the detail that these bears were she-bears. She-bears are known for one particular thing in the Bible, and that is the image of the ferocity of a she-bear robbed of her cubs (2 Sam. 17:8; Prov. 17:12; Hos. 13:8).[11] We may get a hint in this passage of the irony of the creatures associated with their own bereavement bereaving others of their offspring. The likelihood of this interpretation being correct is enhanced when we consider how bereavement and childlessness are

---

10. The question of social probability must be asked. Is it likely that a group of children larger than forty-two (since the forty-two are only a subset of the children) and loitering outside the city would be all male? While this possibility cannot be excluded, it seems less likely. The curse in Lev. 26:22 is not gender-specific, and therefore it seems more probable to me that the group contained boys and girls.

11. The Hebrew word דֹב on its own can refer to either a male or a female bear, and even with a female may take a masculine adjective. The bears in these references are believed to be female on the basis of the role they play, whereas in 2 Kings 2:24 their sex is established by the verb. All three occurrences are translated in the Latin Vulgate with *ursa*, which, although it can in some circumstances refer to a bear generically, here seems specifically to mean a she-bear.

themes in all the surrounding chapters (2 Kings 1:17; 3:27; 4:18–20). In fact 2 Kings 2:23–24 is presented as the fulfillment of the curse in Leviticus 26:22, which says that if Israel is disobedient, it will be robbed of its children by wild animals.[12]

Literal Translations in Continuity with Previous Translations

It is not just that literal translations have the pragmatic advantages that they allow more detailed study and repay rereading. They are also in greater continuity with the translations of the past.

We see this by considering four of the earliest translations of our passage in relation to four particular characteristics:

1. Do they use the same verb of ascent for all four cases of the Hebrew word meaning "go up"?
2. Do they use a term for the children that could include females?
3. Do they characterize the children with an adjective meaning "small"?
4. Do they characterize the bears as female?

The earliest is the translation of our passage into Greek that appears in Codex Vaticanus. It uses ἀναβαίνω, "go up," for all four occurrences of the verb. The terms for children could include females. The first phrase, παιδαρια μεικρα, specifically includes the adjective μεικρός (classical, μικρός), meaning "small." However, the bears are not marked as female.

The next translation is the Syriac Peshitta. It uses the verb *sleq*, "go up," in all four instances. The term for children could include females, and the first occurrence has an adjective for "small." The bears are clearly female.

Targum Jonathan uses the same verb for all occurrences of "go up," the same verb as occurred in the Syriac. The children are described as *yān(ĕ)qîn*, a gender-generic term that, at least in etymology, refers to those who are not yet weaned. It adds to this a term for "small." The bears are, again, female.

---

12. Brian P. Irwin, "The Curious Incident of the Boys and the Bears: 2 King 2 and the Prophetic Authority of Elisha," *TynBul* 67 (2016): 23–35. Note also that the root *škl*, "bereave" is common to 2 Sam. 17:8; Prov. 17:12; Hos. 13:8; and Lev. 26:22. It also occurs strikingly immediately preceding our passage in 2 Kings 2:21. There seems little doubt, therefore, that the appearance of specifically female bears is significantly related to the theme of bereavement.

Finally, the Latin Vulgate uses the verb *ascendere* in all four occurrences, describes the children as *pueri parvi*, an expression that certainly includes a word for small (*parvus*) and a word *puer*, "boy," which more probably than not in its plural form at the time of translation could include females. The bears are *ursi* (plural of *ursus*), definitely male, but this feature was probably inherited from the Greek, whose translator was less accurate.[13]

We see here that the KJV and ESV offer some improvements on the Greek and Latin translations by specifying the gender of the bears. The ESV, NIV, and NLT are more exclusive on the question of the gender of the children than any of the preceding translations.

Most importantly of all, however, all the older translations and the ESV keep the consistent verb "go up" throughout the passage. This, alongside the tendency of these translations to render the same verb literally elsewhere (e.g., 2 Kings 1:4), allows readers to make a lot more sense of the passage and to see its connection with its context.

Conclusions

From the preceding discussion I would conclude that some more-recent translations, among which are the NIV and NLT, stand in considerable discontinuity with both the translations of the Reformation and the earliest translations of the Old Testament into Greek, Aramaic (including Syriac), and Latin.[14] This shift, while it may be justified by appeals to theoretical models of translation, can reasonably be interpreted as a substantial shift in the conception of the task of Bible translation itself. In short, the translations that have shifted away from historic literalism expect people to be much more casual in their Bible study than would have been the case at the time of the Reformation. In the case of the translations of the passage involving Elisha and the she-bears, the NIV and NLT offer much less reward for serious study, arguably leaving the passage more problematic than it was in the more literal translations.

13. It should be remembered that the Greek translator probably had no predecessors, whereas later translators could often refine the work of predecessors. This makes a significant difference to the levels of accuracy achieved.

14. The most paraphrastic Greek translation made in the early centuries of the church was that of Symmachus, which would by today's standards be classed as literal. The Aramaic Targums are sometimes wrongly classified as paraphrases, but even these involve much quantitative literalism and imitation of Hebrew syntax, alongside expansionary exegetical material, which does not easily come under the heading of "translation."

Moreover, the more paraphrastic a translation is, the more unguided intellectual work a translator has to do. Literal translation can, of course, be problematic, but the mistakes with literal translations are generally made by the readers, not by the translators. However, the more a person reads of a literal translation, the fewer interpretative mistakes he or she is likely to make. This is not the case with "thought for thought" translations.[15] The art of completely recasting the meaning of a phrase in a source language by a phrase in the target language is one of immense complexity. On the other hand, the task of the literal translator, substituting words and structures in the target language for those in the source language, tends to be significantly simpler.[16] A literal translator is likely to retain an allusion to a parallel passage even without noticing the parallel, whereas a "thought for thought" translator is more likely to lose the allusion unless he or she has noticed it. "Thought for thought" translations, therefore, are much more liable to translator error, and in this short passage about Elisha and the she-bears one can see a cluster of significant errors carried out by teams of experts whose language skills would have to be deemed very high relative to most Bible translation teams in the world.

This raises a further question of the relationship between our doctrine of human fallibility (morally and practically) and the task of Bible translation. If the words of Scripture so often involve a rich tapestry of meanings, as suggested by New Testament exegesis of the Old Testament, as well as by Patristic, Rabbinic, and Reformation interpretations, the larger the segment of source text one decides one can process and represent by a segment in the target language, the more room for human error there is.

It is possible to argue that, historically, whenever the Bible has been at the center of a culture, there has been a demand for a literal translation. Even if, as in the Syriac church, the first generation of translations was less literal, as Christianity took a stronger hold on the culture over time, translations became successively more literal.[17] Arguably,

---

15. Including functional equivalence, dynamic equivalence, or, to use Jerome's expression, *sensum de sensu* translations.

16. A factor not really considered here is the "distance" between the structure of the source and target languages. In global terms Greek and English are not very different, both being part of the Indo-European group. Even Hebrew and English are far less different than many pairs of languages. Obviously, small unit-for-unit equivalence is much easier the closer the languages.

17. S. P. Brock, "Toward a History of Syriac Translation Technique," in *III Symposium Syriacum 1980*, ed. R. Lavenant, Orientalia Christiana Analecta 221 (Rome: Pontificio Istituto Orientale, 1983), 1–14.

therefore, as we wish the Scriptures to be more and more at the center of our own cultures, our desire should be to study them ever more closely in their original languages or at least in literal Bible translations, and we should expect increased appetite for literal Bible translations to precede, accompany, and follow real church growth.

It has been a pleasure to have Wayne Grudem as a friend over many years. Not least of my privileges has been to sit alongside Wayne in the Translation Oversight Committee of the English Standard Version and to be united in our passion for translating the Word of God as clearly and literally as we can.

PART 3

*PASTORAL
MINISTRY*

12

Thoughts on Leadership

The Servant Leader's True Distinctives

Darryl DelHousaye

In leadership philosophy, the servant leader concept has maintained currency since the 1960s, when Robert Greenleaf began talking about servant leadership as the true function of power and authority.[1] It's clear that there has been a movement away from a self-enhancing, dictatorial kind of leadership toward a growing interest in people as a leader's greatest asset. This is good news. Servant leadership has even become a prominent paradigm in the secular realm.

But as the twenty-first century makes greater demands on both secular and church leaders—and as Western culture accelerates its departure from a Judeo-Christian foundation toward pluralism and spiritual curiosity—the best and truest aspects of servant leadership are less understood and appreciated. That loss is rooted in the prevailing cultural view that absolutes can be safely discarded in favor of expediency, and that perception is reality.

Pastors and church leaders are not exempt from these trends. To be servant leaders in the twenty-first century, they must seek more than

---

1. Robert K. Greenleaf, *Servant Leadership* (New York: Paulist, 1977), 3.

ever to be genuine disciples of Jesus Christ. Adequately addressing the demands upon today's leaders will require greater attentiveness to the way of thinking Jesus had in mind two thousand years ago when he said, "Whoever wishes to become great among you shall be your servant" (Matt. 20:26).[2]

What is the essence of servant leadership? The antithesis to servant leadership—autocratic control through coercive power—is a stubborn contender among leadership models and can be observed in both secular and church leadership. Though largely disavowed in the literature of both realms (as irrelevant to a postmodern culture and inappropriate for the church), it tenaciously persists as an implicit model within the realm of leadership studies. Of equal concern is the thread of leadership theory that views people as a means to leadership, rather than the object of sacrificial service. This is clearly at odds with what Jesus taught and exemplified.

The profusion of leadership philosophies and methodologies can be confusing for those who desire to become Christlike leaders with a capable understanding of the difference between the healthy and unhealthy authorities Jesus referred to in the New Testament. Rather than turning to current philosophies and methodologies for help, those in leadership need only consult God's Word to gain a picture of true servant leadership. If genuine Christian servant leadership is to be understood and practiced in the way Jesus confirmed and modeled it, our thinking on the subject should be filtered through the biblical concepts for the design of leadership.

We find clarity on this through the study of seven biblical terms prominently related to leadership. Here we can identify distinctives that characterize the true servant leadership Jesus revealed. They represent seven things servant leaders must know about themselves. The seven terms are *power, authority, rule, headship, servant, example,* and *humility.*

Power

In the New Testament, the Greek word for power, *dynamis,* is used 118 times and conveys the meaning of strength or force, as well as

---

2. Scripture quotations in this chapter, unless otherwise indicated, are from the New American Standard Bible, ©1995 by The Lockman Foundation.

ability and capability. It denotes a capacity to carry out something—physically, militarily, politically, or spiritually.[3] The word is used to refer to either a natural or a supernatural ability to exercise power—the natural ability of man or the miraculous power God uses to accomplish his will.

This New Testament word, *power*, describes abilities one possesses to influence people and things. These abilities may be physical strength, mental acuteness, social charm, spiritual faith, or any other characteristic that can bring about *influence* in accomplishing one's desire.

Power is that force of influence over someone or something that can bring about desired change. It is meaningless to talk about leadership unless the leadership can make a real difference in people's lives, for leadership's essence is influence—the practical aspect of power. Where there is no influence, there is no leadership.

Power is a force possessed and thus should be a force carefully stewarded. The leader's abilities, natural or miraculous, must be identified and sharpened in their effectiveness to influence the lives of people.

Those who finds themselves in positions of leadership must carefully steward this responsibility as a gift from God. Any power of influence that a person possesses should not be denied or set aside, but rather used for the glory of God, not the glory of man. To this end, Paul admonishes believers to take a sober look at the giftedness they have been given: "For through the grace given to me I say to everyone among you not to think more highly of himself than he ought to think; but to think so as to have sound judgment, as God has allotted to each a measure of faith" (Rom. 12:3). The Christian leader understands the nature of this calling and the miraculous gifts he has been given.

The greatest threat to a servant leader's heart is the craving for power. There is no doubt that power in the wrong hands can have devastating repercussions. This was apparently John's issue with Diotrephes, "who loves to be first" (3 John 9).

The night before Jesus was put to death on a cross, he called his disciples together in an upper room. Significantly, this One who claimed more power than any earthly king, ruler, or rabbi alive had just washed his disciples' feet. He told them, "You call Me Teacher and Lord; and

---

3. Otto Betz, "Might," in *NIDNTT*, 2:606ff.

you are right, for so I am" (John 13:13). It was clear in the mind of Jesus who he was and what power he possessed, both natural and supernatural. He was their teacher because he knew more than they knew, and he was their Lord because he was (and is) God the Son. He was well aware of what he could do and what he had to offer them.

In regard to power, servant leaders must especially understand themselves. The beginning of leadership is to know one's person. The questions must be asked: Who am I? What do I stand for? What do I have to offer? To be credible, a leader must be able to identify what kind of influence (power) he or she can make available to others.

Power in this sense is defined as ability, whether strength, knowledge, experience, spiritual maturity, or any other quality that can influence others in positive ways that serves them. To deny its presence in some kind of mock humility would be both ludicrous and irresponsible. In true humility and with a sense of responsibility, the servant leader must proactively discover the area in which he is particularly gifted.

Possessing a philosophy of leadership is a great start, but a servant leader must consistently and competently execute this philosophy. His giftedness is that competence. He must know what he is doing and acquire the experience and training to do it well. He must believe that this is his giftedness, and he must persist in it, even in the face of adversity. When Paul comments in Romans that we are to "think so as to have sound judgment, as God has allotted to each a measure of faith" (Rom. 12:3), he's indicating that this "measure of faith" is the influence God has given to each of us, whether it be a natural talent or supernatural giftedness.

If you aspire to be a servant leader, ask yourself: What is my given "power"? What do I believe is my greatest contribution into the lives of others? Then find three people who can be objective, and ask them if they affirm the same influences in your life. If they have observed something different, listen to them, for "faithful are the wounds of a friend" (Prov. 27:6).

Authority

The New Testament makes a distinction between authority and power. For example, Luke tells us that Jesus has both power and authority over the forces of darkness (Luke 4:36). Whereas power is the ability to influence people and things, authority is the legitimate right to exercise that influence.

Authority often carries a negative connotation, especially for the emerging generation, because many persons in authority have violated trust. History shows a frequent partnership between authority and coercive force. Authority by design is not a bad thing; it's the abuse of authority that has made it an unpopular concept.

The New Testament distinction between power and authority is borne out by a study of the terms used. The principal word used for authority in the New Testament (as in Luke 4:36) is *exousia*.[4] Paul uses the same word when he says that the potter has the authority over the clay to make from the same lump whatever he chooses (Rom. 9:21). The word denotes the unrestricted possibility of freedom of action, or the right of action, and was used in regard only to people (never to natural forces).[5]

Exousia as "authority" is distinct from the power to actually enforce that authority. For example, whereas Jesus's *dynamis* had its foundation in his being God the Son, his *exousia* was founded in his being sent by the Father.[6] The power was there because of who he was; the authority was given because of what he was about to do.

We can safely deduce that the word *authority* carries the idea of freedom to choose and execute decisions. This exercise of power can be in accordance with knowledge (Mark 1:27) or with position (Matt. 8:9) and is used to describe the power exercised by rulers or others in high positions by virtue of their office.[7] This is the legitimate right to exercise power. The right may come from the personal influence one has or from one's position of influence. Power is thus the force of influence, whereas authority is the legitimate right to exercise that influence.

When Jesus said, "All authority has been given to Me in heaven and on earth" (Matt. 28:18), he was speaking in reference to the right to exercise the power given him by the Father because of what Jesus had accomplished on the cross. Thus we see that authority—as the ability to exercise one's influence upon the lives of others—is granted

---

4. This Greek word for authority is used 108 times in the New Testament.
5. Betz, "Might," 2:606–7.
6. Betz, "Might," 2:609.
7. Betz, "Might," 278.

by a higher power, as Jesus reminded Pilate. In essence it is delegated authority. The driving force behind this delegated authority was the intent of the one from whom the authority was given—the *dynamis* (power) behind the *exousia* (authority).

A servant leader understands the nature of the right he has been given to exercise influence in accomplishing the desires of the power behind him. The servant leader understands his position and the nature of the authority entrusted to him from God. Servant leadership cannot be exercised without full knowledge of that position and of the authority that has been entrusted to exercise it.

Jesus had a full understanding of what power he had to offer; he also had a full understanding of his position. He knew he had the right to exercise the power he possessed (John 5:19–23). It's clear that Jesus understood his authority before he commanded his followers to obey.

The study of authority reveals that a leader has the right to exercise power in pursuit of legitimate goals. A servant leader must have full knowledge of the freedom he has to make decisions to bring about change. Responsibility without freedom of authority most often results in frustration and failure. This is a crucial point. The right to lead is present when authority has been granted *and* is recognized by those under it.

Although formal authority may be delegated through an organizational structure or person in higher authority, the informal authority granted to a leader is equally important. People choose—even perhaps at a subconscious level—those whom they'll be influenced by. This is especially true of the emerging generation. Furthermore, though people may obey formal authority, they will not permit it to change them unless they believe their best interests are being served. Most people will willingly submit themselves to the influence of another only when they believe they're being offered something of significance, and when the person offering it has their trust.

A servant leader demonstrates an understanding of his or her authority by acknowledging that the right to influence others is really a right to serve them according to the will of God. This type of authority is freely granted to a leader.

As a servant leader, ask yourself: Am I in a place of influence where I can best help people with what I have to offer? Have I been given the "right" of influence so that I may have the freedom to exercise the giftedness I've been given?

Rule

In instructing his disciples about servant leadership in Matthew 20:25–28 (cf. Mark 10:42–45), Jesus begins with a reminder of typical secular rule:

> Jesus called them to Himself and said, "You know that the rulers of the Gentiles lord it over them, and their great men exercise authority over them. It is not this way among you, but whoever wishes to become great among you shall be your servant, and whoever wishes to be first among you shall be your slave; just as the Son of Man did not come to be served, but to serve, and to give His life a ransom for many."

Jesus communicates here the antithesis to servant leadership with two expressions: "lord it over" and "exercise authority over" (Matt. 20:25). The first of these is *katakyrieuō* (occurring also in Mark 10:42; Acts 19:16; 1 Pet. 5:3), a word with a clearly negative force. It implies an exercise of authority exclusively to one's own advantage and contrary to the interest and well-being of others. The second expression—"exercise authority over"—is *katexousiazō*, found in the New Testament only here in Matthew 20:25 and its parallel in Mark 10:42. It signifies the abusive exercise of authority to tyrannize someone.[8]

The abuse of leadership expressed by these terms has selfishness as the driving goal. In contrast, the servant leader understands the design behind his power and authority, and does not abuse the position in self-interest.

Servant leaders possess a willingness to sacrifice time and energy to support the achievement of others. Their focus is to help others accomplish their goals. They reflect the attitude expressed in the concluding words of Jesus in this passage: "The Son of Man did not come to be served, but to serve" (Matt. 20:28). As clearly evident throughout the Gospels, Jesus was never interested in abusing his power or authority to serve himself. We, too, must be careful not

---

8. William F. Arndt and Wilbur Gingrich, *A Greek-English Lexicon of the New Testament* (Chicago: University of Chicago Press, 1967), 422.

to lapse into the unintentional misuse of our position for selfish motives—an all-too-common phenomenon. When people feel used and manipulated to simply carry out someone else's agenda, they naturally lose both motivation and creativity, and bitterness will eventually grow in their hearts.

By contrast, the servant leader knows his purpose; he understands that to exercise power and authority is to serve, not to be served. Rather than using others, he makes himself available to them in useful, loving service.

As a servant leader, ask yourself: Is my leadership helpful to those under my care, or is it self-serving? Do others recognize that they're the focus of my attention? In what way does my leadership benefit those under it?

Headship

Peter referred to Christ as our "Chief Shepherd" (1 Pet. 5:4), and Jesus used the imagery of a shepherd to describe his own leadership. The intent of the metaphor was to describe the unique relationship he had with those who followed him. The duty of the shepherd is to care for his sheep, providing protection and nurture, seeking them out if they're lost, and knowing them by name.[9] All these elements—a position of authority, a task of protection, and a responsibility of support and care—are present in the concept of headship.

Whereas a hireling would abandon the sheep at any sign of danger in order to preserve his own life (John 10:12), the good shepherd lays down his life for them (John 10:11). This degree of love and responsibility, in contrast to being more interested in self-preservation, characterizes the servant leader. A leader who creates an environment where his authority provides protection and nurture will help cultivate successful lives for those under his or her influence.

We see this illustrated in God's design for family life. Paul says that "the head of every man is Christ," and "the head of a wife is her husband" (1 Cor. 11:3 ESV). Paul goes on to say that "the husband is the head of the wife, as Christ also is the head of the church" (Eph. 5:23).

---

9. John E. Skinner, *The Meaning of Authority* (Washington, DC: University Press of America, 1983), 6. Knowing sheep by their names is especially relevant and essential for shepherds in the Near East.

The husband's loving leadership is intended to portray Christ's loving and saving work for the church. Thus the responsibilities of husbands and wives are designed to serve as a living illustration of God's love for the church and the church's submission to Christ.

Paul's use of *kephalē* ("head") carried the primary meaning of "authority over," an authority that speaks of *responsibility*. The model for headship is illustrated in our heavenly Father's relationship with the Son, the Son's relationship with the church, and the husband's relationship with the wife (1 Cor. 11:3; Eph. 5:23; Col. 1:18). The responsibility in all these relationships includes two major provisions.

The first is *protection*. Protection develops from love. The heavenly Father loves the Son (John 3:35; 5:20; 10:17; 15:19). The Son of God loves the church, and the husband loves his wife (Eph. 5:25). John makes it clear that perfect love casts out fear because the object of love is so valued that it will be protected (1 John 4:18).

The Son is protected under the headship of the Father (John 7:30; 8:20, 54). Because of this protection, Jesus could entrust himself to the Father even during his crucifixion (1 Pet. 2:23). The church experiences protection from its Head, Jesus Christ. Jesus says he gives eternal life to those who are his, and "they will never perish; and no one will snatch them out of My hand" (John 10:28). Jesus, as Head of the church, will not let it be destroyed, for he makes this commitment: "I will build My church: and the gates of Hades shall not overpower it" (Matt. 16:18).

A careful reading of Paul's instruction to husbands in Ephesians 5:23–30 makes it clear that the wife is to be protected by her husband, who is to lay down his life for her as Christ did for the church. The husband is therefore to set her apart (sanctify her) and present her to himself in the same way: "in all her glory, having no spot or wrinkle or any such thing; but that she should be holy and blameless" (Eph. 5:27). This is protection. The husband is responsible for her care and thus should live with her in an understanding way (1 Pet. 3:7).

Besides an environment of protection, headship also provides *honor*. The Father honors the Son (John 5:23; Phil. 2:9–11); the Son honors the church (1 Pet. 1:7); the loving husband honors his wife (1 Pet. 3:7). The word *honor* (*timaō*) means to set value upon someone or something, to revere and to reward.[10] One feels honored

---

10. Arndt and Gingrich, *Greek-English Lexicon*, 824.

when one feels listened to. Listening is still one of the great tools of leadership.

To honor adds to a leader's effectiveness because it is received as reward, and reward is one of three motivations employed by the Lord in his dealing with mankind: love, fear, and reward. Too often, leadership forgets to model the Lord in the first and last of these three, settling for only the second. But the servant leader communicates appreciation of individuals' worth by rewarding them. In doing so, he honors them.

Headship creates a context for people to grow; they mature in an atmosphere of protection and honor. Headship is an act of love; its intention is to prize those one leads by nourishing their growth. It's the same care that the shepherd gives his sheep.

As a servant leader, ask yourself: How much do those under my leadership feel protected and honored? In what way am I fostering an environment that creates both safety and an appreciation of worth? What kind of soil have I provided my people to grow in?

Example

When Jesus explained why he had just washed his disciples' feet, he emphasized his leadership by example:

> Do you know what I have done to you? You call Me Teacher and Lord; and you are right, for so I am. If I then, the Lord and the Teacher, washed your feet, you also ought to wash one another's feet. For I gave you an example that you also should do as I did to you. Truly, truly, I say to you, a slave is not greater than his master, nor is one who is sent greater than the one who sent him. If you know these things, you are blessed if you do them. (John 13:12–17)

Jesus here uses the word *hypodeigma* for "example." Technically, *hypodeigma* is used to denote a model or pattern of something good to be followed (James 5:10) or of something bad to be avoided (Heb. 4:11; 2 Pet. 2:6).

The greatest force behind the authority of a servant leader is leading by example. Peter instructs elders to prove themselves as "examples to the flock" (1 Pet. 5:3). Paul admonishes Timothy to do the same (1 Tim. 4:12). Both Peter and Paul utilize the term *typos* to express the concept of example. *Typos* comes from the primary verb "strike," and speaks of the impression of a form—what an object leaves behind when pressed against another, such as a trace, a scar, the impression of a seal, a letter of the alphabet, a likeness.[11]

The same idea is conveyed in the New Testament by two other Greek words used by Paul: *summimētēs* (Phil. 3:17) and *mimeomai* (2 Thess. 3:7, 9). In these verses Paul issues a call to his readers to join with others in following his personal example. Paul viewed himself as a personal embodiment of an ideal that must be imitated (see also 1 Cor. 11:1). He confessed his own imperfection (Phil. 3:12); his example was not one of perfection but of excellence; his thought here could be stated this way: "Follow my lead in conduct and heart."

A servant leader knows and is concerned about how he is perceived by others because a positive perception is a key component of leadership. People value a leader's integrity (even those without integrity desire to see it in others). When it comes to servant leadership, there must be a continual pursuit for the highest integrity possible. The outcome of this is that our character will naturally become an example to others.

Credibility is mostly about consistency between words and deeds. People listen to the words and look at the deeds, then measure the congruence. A judgment of "credible" is handed down when the two are consonant.[12]

Integrity displayed by example is a compelling and indispensable instrument in the hand of an effective leader. When people see integrity in others, they're encouraged to act in the same way. Not only will they be motivated to follow, but the path to be traced will enable them to do so.

Even more importantly, through the example of godly leadership we glorify God in fulfilling the mandate of Jesus "Let your light shine before men in such a way that they may see your good works, and glorify your Father who is in heaven" (Matt. 5:16).

As a servant leader, ask yourself: What consistency is there between what I say I am and what I'm seen to be? What consistency is there between what I say and what I do? (For a good perception

---

11. Dietrich Muller, "Tupos," in *NIDNTT*, 3:904.
12. James M. Kouzes and Barry Z. Posner, *Credibility: How Leaders Gain and Lose It: Why People Demand It* (San Francisco: Jossey-Bass, 1993), 47.

check, ask those who are doing the perceiving to answer these questions for you.)

Servant

What is a servant? How does one have a servant attitude and yet carry out the responsibility of leadership?

When Jesus said, "Whoever wishes to become great among you shall be your servant, and whoever wishes to be first among you shall be your slave" (Matt. 20:26–27), he used the words *diakonos* ("servant," 20:26) and *doulos* ("slave," 20:27).

A *diakonos* was one who waited on another at a table, one who served, one who cared for or helped and supported another. Such a servant lived primarily to benefit others.[13] The servant mentality does not exclude reward, but the driving force behind it is the success of the person being served. This is why self-willfulness negates any picture of servanthood. People feel used when treated as servants. But the aim of true leadership is for them to feel served.

A *doulos*, as a slave, was a person of lower status than a *diakonos*. Freedom was a prized possession in ancient culture. To be independent of others without any accountability was the essence of freedom. At the opposite end of the continuum was the *doulos*, one who belonged by nature to another.[14] To be a *doulos* involved the abrogation of one's autonomy and the subordination of one's will to another. The slave's status as such was viewed with revulsion and contempt.

Jesus was well aware of the controversial thought he introduced by using the term *doulos*. Paul makes the point that Jesus took upon himself this very nature when he came to the earth, taking on the *morphē doulou* ("the form of a bond-servant," Phil. 2:7). This *morphē*, this form, had to do with one's nature. Jesus did not merely act like a servant; he took on the very nature of one. He understood his earthly role; his aim was not self-promotion but *other* promotion. Specifically, he came "to seek and to save that which was lost," and he was willing to be born in a stable and to die on a cross to accomplish this (Luke 19:10). *People* were his purpose.

---

13. Klaus Hess, "Serve," in *NIDNTT*, 3:544.
14. Hess, "Serve," 3:592.

Jesus emphasized to his followers that a leader is a *doulos*. Therefore someone who strives for personal glory is *not* a leader. When Jesus washed the feet of his disciples, what exactly was he doing? Washing the feet of those who'd spent the day on dusty roads in leather sandals was the responsibility of the lowliest of servants. When Jesus took on that role, he burned his point into his disciples' thinking. This was the example he intended to lay down for leadership (John 13:14–15).

A servant leader sees the powerful influence a servant can have in the lives of those he leads. When people know they're being served well by a servant leader, they'll permit their lives to be influenced by that leader.

This thinking counters the dark side of human nature. John Milton understood the motivation that lay behind Satan's rebellion against God as expressed in his epic poem *Paradise Lost*, where Satan declares, "Better to reign in hell, than serve in heaven."[15]

Most of us admire leaders who do not place themselves at the center, but rather place others there, and who say, "I'm here to make you successful!" These leaders focus attention on others, not themselves.

As a servant leader, ask yourself: How does my leadership provide for the growth and accomplishment of those I lead? How do I measure my achievement by the success of others? Would those I serve consider me one of the reasons for their achievement?

Humility

When Paul wrote about Jesus taking on a servant's form, it was in the context of a discussion on humility: "Do nothing from selfishness or empty conceit, but with humility of mind regard one another as more important than yourselves; do not merely look out for your own personal interests, but also for the interests of others" (Phil. 2:3–4). The word here for humility, *tapeinophrosynē*, means "not self-seeking." The "humility of mind" Paul speaks of here reflects the impelling drive of a servant leader. It's also the prescription against arrogance. James reminds us that "God opposes the proud, but gives grace to the humble" (James 4:6). Humility means fully understanding the simple reality that "God is God and I am not!"

---

15. John Milton, *Paradise Lost* (Danbury, CT: Grolier, 1978), bk. 1, p. 14.

How is humility recognized? Paul says in Philippians 2:3 that each Christian should "regard one another as more important than [himself]." This means viewing others not as smarter, wiser, more powerful, or nobler but as *more important*. This may traumatize our ego, but true humility is actually helping others to surpass oneself.

Paul's further instruction to "not merely look out for your own personal interests, but also for the interests of others" (2:4) indicates that Christians should include others' interests as part of their own (it is not a call to ignore one's own interests). This is the essence of servant leadership.

Jesus described himself as "gentle and humble in heart" (Matt. 11:29), using there the same word (*tapeinos*) that James uses in contrasting humility with prideful arrogance (James 4:6). *Tapeinos* is used in the sense of lowliness. In that same verse in Matthew, Jesus tells us, "Take My yoke upon you and learn from Me" (Matt. 11:29). A yoke was not an implement of burden but a device for instruction. A younger, less experienced ox would be yoked up to an older and more experienced one. As the wise older ox went about his routine of work, the younger ox would either learn the way of his elder or end up with a terrible pain in the neck.

Humility is a preference for treating others as more important than oneself. The humble mind is displayed by an attitude of wanting not to be revered or served but to focus attention on the success of others. A commitment to that success is not to think less of oneself but actually to not be thinking about oneself at all. When ego is set aside, a whole new dimension of leadership is unleashed. The preference of a servant leader is to *make great* those he leads.

As a servant leader, ask yourself: In my leadership, am I thinking, *how can I make others great?* How eager are you to take all you have to offer and use it to bring about the success of those around you?

Feeling Served

In summary, when people feel valued, inspired, invested in, protected, honored, supported, respected, advised, challenged, and rewarded—they feel *served*. When they feel served, they're experiencing the essence of servant leadership, for they're under the care of a shepherd who truly follows in the shepherding steps of Christ, our Chief Shepherd.

Addendum: That "Cup" of Suffering

Jesus called me to practice servant leadership, and for the most part it has been a good thing. But I have found from time to time it has created pain. Instead of being viewed as a leader, I have been mistakenly taken for being weak and powerless. There have been times when I have over-empowered others, then been betrayed by them.

Servant leadership is basically loving as a leader and letting the influence of love have its effect on others. But is this effect always successful? What is the "cup" of suffering Jesus mentions in Matthew 20? Jesus would later ask for it to be removed from him as he prayed in the garden (Matt. 26:39). After that night people turned against Jesus and crucified him.

Why would God permit this? Why would people not respond to servant leadership with love and respect? Moses was described in Numbers 12:3 as the most humble man, and what happens? Korah rebels against him in Numbers 16.

Paul's relationship with Hymeneas and Alexander deteriorated, according to 1 Timothy 1:18–20, as did his relationship later with Demas and others in 2 Timothy 4:9–16. That's why Paul warns young Timothy to give himself to faithful men who will in turn be faithful to teach others (2 Tim. 2:2). Not all have learned servant leadership.

Here's the lesson for us: love exposes flaws in others. As they are empowered by love, so their flaws are empowered and exposed. What flaws?

- arrogance
- competitiveness
- envy
- ambition

Most are acquainted with an Attila the Hun approach to leadership (lording over and exercising authority over) and call it strong leadership. And when they don't see it in you, they just might think you are weak and take advantage of you. Some people will not recognize servant leadership for what it is and will lose respect for it and for you.

Should we then abandon this approach? We need to take a long view. Eventually some will come to recognize who truly loved them, and the respect will return. We can rest assured that servant leadership was designed by Jesus Christ, and we must trust him for the results of this influence on the lives of others.

13

"Not in Vain"

Elliot Grudem

"Grudem, Grudem."

Once I started seminary in 2000, the question became commonplace.

"You're not related are you?"

The follow-up was also fairly standard.

"What was *that* like? What was it like to grow up as Wayne Grudem's son?"

As I write this, I've been Wayne Grudem's son for forty-three years. My answer is standard: "Fairly normal, I think."

I remember playing football with my dad and brothers most evenings after dinner. I don't remember many formal theological questions. We spent more time laughing around the dinner table (often) than we did talking through a catechism (never). Application of Scripture to life was done through conversation between a father and son, not by reading pages in a book.

I've known him as a dad—in all the good, imperfect, hard, and full-of-blessing ways that are part of a human father's relationship with his children—much, much more than as a prominent theologian or Bible scholar.

For all that, I'm eternally grateful.

The Lord gives us glory and honor (Ps. 8:5). Any glory or honor I can bestow on my dad pales in comparison to what the Lord gives him. Yet, as I think about what it means to be my father's son, three themes come up again and again. My dad has a deep love for God's Word. He places a high value on doing God's work. These come from a heart that loves to praise God—with both his words and his work.

Somewhere around my sixth year we memorized Psalm 8 together. There are stories of me repeating portions of Luke 2 for the family on Christmas Day around age three, but I don't remember doing that. Psalm 8—for me—is the first passage of Scripture we memorized together.

It's through Psalm 8 that I'll talk more about those three themes: praise to God, work for God, and love for God's Word.

Praise from the Heart

"Here comes the smile followed by Grudem" was how J. I. Packer once described my dad's arrival at a meeting. The description fits well. Dad loves to smile. Though the onset of Parkinson's disease means smiling takes more work, he considers it well worth the effort. Jesus said it's "out of the abundance of the heart" that our mouths speak (Luke 6:45). In my dad's case, it also smiles and sings.

Dad loves to sing. He is often heard singing hymns around the house. As a family, we sang hymns at Thanksgiving, Christmas, and other times we gathered together, using hymn sheets on colored paper Dad created for each occasion. When his friends or students gathered in our home, they often sang together. He asked one of his students to lead a time of singing at the second wedding reception he and my mom threw for me and my wife in my hometown. Contemporary praise songs and hymns of the faith take up most of the space on his iPod (along with the nearly twenty-four-hour audio version of Thomas Sowell's *Basic Economics*, which he uses as a way to redeem his commute). Ask any of his former students what they remember about my dad's classes, and it won't take long for them to talk about the hymns they sang each time they gathered. Each chapter in his *Systematic Theology* ends with a hymn.

My dad isn't a musician. He sings loudly and with great conviction. Though he can carry a tune, he isn't asked to sing solos or lead people in song. And yet he keeps singing.

Any of the first eleven chapters of Romans might seem the obvious choice as the first chapter of the Bible a Reformed-leaning theologian with a PhD in New Testament would memorize with his son. Dad chose Psalm 8. He did so, I think, because he loves to praise God in song, and the psalmist gives us reason to do that. I think he also chose it because of what he believes about theology.

"Systematic theology at its best will result in praise," he wrote in *Systematic Theology*.[1] He explains further: "The study of theology is not merely a theoretical exercise of the intellect. It is a study of the living God, and of the wonders of all his works in creation and redemption. We cannot study this subject dispassionately! We must love all that God is, all that he says and all that he does."[2] I think Psalm 8 is a great place to start a theological journey. Like all the Psalms it has a way of taking the truth about God and humans and moving that truth from the mind and to the heart, from facts to love, from knowledge to praise.

Theology at its best will result in praise—"Oh, the depth of the riches and wisdom and knowledge of God!" (Rom. 11:33). To get there, it must also start with praise—"For from him and through him and to him are all things. To him be glory forever. Amen" (Rom. 11:36). For as John Frame taught both me and my dad, "God reveals His best secrets to those who love Him best."[3]

Psalm 8 is a praise hymn. Bruce Waltke and James Houston explain well how the psalm fits praise-hymn form:

> Praise psalms celebrate *I AM's* greatness and goodness, his lordship over the cosmos as its Creator, his commitment to Israel as its covenant-keeping God who saves them to fulfill their mission to rule the earth. . . . Psalm 8 does not disappoint these expectations, wielding the two notions of God's great deeds in creation and history into a unique unity of profound reflection and of incomparable beauty.[4]

Psalm 8:1 lifts our eyes high to the great transcendent God:

1. Wayne Grudem, *Systematic Theology: An Introduction to Biblical Doctrine* (Leicester, UK: Inter-Varsity Press; Grand Rapids, MI: Zondervan, 1994), 42.
2. Grudem, *Systematic Theology*, 37.
3. John M. Frame, *The Doctrine of the Knowledge of God* (Phillipsburg, NJ: Presbyterian and Reformed, 1987), 323.
4. Bruce K. Waltke and James M. Houston, *The Psalms as Christian Worship: A Historical Commentary* (Grand Rapids, MI: Eerdmans, 2010), 255–56.

O Lord, our Lord,
>how majestic is your name in all the earth!
You have set your glory above the heavens.

God's glory is over the heavens. His majestic name is recognized throughout the earth.

Charles Spurgeon expounds on Psalm 8:1:

>Unable to express the glory of God, the Psalmist utters a note of exclamation. O Jehovah our Lord! We need not wonder at this, for no heart can measure, no tongue can utter, the half of the greatness of Jehovah. The whole creation is full of his glory and radiant with the excellency of his power; his goodness and his wisdom are manifested on every hand.[5]

As our eyes move down the hymn, they move from above the heavens to wonder over the "moon and the stars" (Ps. 8:3), to humankind (Ps. 8:4), to the rest of creation God put under our feet (Ps. 8:7–8):

All sheep and oxen,
>and also beasts of the field,
the birds of the heavens, and the fish of the sea,
>whatever passes along the paths of the seas.

A quick glance outside at all God created gives us many reasons to praise God, for "the glorious One, has endowed the earth with glory. A hymn of praise is sometimes the only way man can express his amazement with God's glorious rule."[6]

God is not just transcendent; he's also immanent. He created with his fingers (Ps. 8:3). He is Yahweh. He is in an eternal relationship that he initiated with each one of his children (Ps. 8:1). He is also *Adonai*, our Ruler (Ps. 8:1). This great King—the Ruler of everything in the entire universe—crowns us with glory and honor (Ps. 8:5) and makes us vice-regents over all his creation (Ps. 8:6).

>Out of the mouth of babes and infants,
you have established strength because of your foes,
>to still the enemy and the avenger. (Ps. 8:2)

---

5. Charles H. Spurgeon, *The Treasury of David*, vol. 1. (McLean, VA: MacDonald, n.d.), 79.
6. Willem A. VanGemeren, "Psalms," in *Psalms, Proverbs, Ecclesiastes, Song of Songs*, ed. Frank A. Gaebelein et al., EBC 5 (Grand Rapids, MI: Zondervan, 1991), 110.

This is an amazing expression of God's power. The vulnerable (infants) are contrasted with powerful enemies. "God is able to build up a people of weakness as a force to oppose his enemies."[7]

Derek Kidner summarizes the reasons Psalm 8:1–2 give us to praise God: "The God whose glory fills the earth is *our* Lord: we are in covenant with Him. His praise is chanted on high, yet acceptably echoed from the cradle and the nursery."[8] And, I would add, from the lips of a father who takes great joy in teaching his young son to praise God like he does.

Work and Dominion

In Psalm 8, we are not only given reasons to praise God; we are also told of the dignity he gives each one of us. The psalmist asks,

> What is man that you are mindful of him,
>   and the son of man that you care for him? (Ps. 8:4)

God's mindfulness and care of us are seen in the glory and honor he gives us (Ps. 8:5). It's also seen in the dominion God gave us over his creation (Ps. 8:6).

> You have given him dominion over the works of your hands;
>   you have put all things under his feet.

This is an echo of the command given Adam and Eve in the garden to subdue the earth and have dominion over it (Gen. 1:28). "Psalm 8 is Genesis 1:26–28 set to music."[9]

With the authority comes a command to work that is present in Psalm 8 and even more clearly stated in Genesis 1:26–28. That command was clearly echoed in our home. From an early age, my brothers and I were taught the dignity of the cultural mandate. We heard Proverbs like this:

> The sluggard says, "There is a lion in the road!
>   There is a lion in the streets!"
> As a door turns on its hinges,
>   so does a sluggard on his bed. (Prov. 26:13–14)

---

7. George H. Guthrie, "Hebrews," in *Commentary on the New Testament Use of the Old Testament*, ed. G. K. Beale and D. A. Carson (Grand Rapids, MI: Baker Academic, 2007), 944.
8. Derek Kidner, *Psalms 1–72* (Leicester, UK: Inter-Varsity Press, 1973), 66.
9. Waltke and Houston, *Psalms as Christian Worship*, 272.

We worked. Family meetings often involved the splitting up of tasks. Allowance came as payment for our work around the house. My brother's spoken protest against work when he was quite young— "I hate work!"—is an oft-told part of our family narrative.

I continue to watch my dad work as he seeks to serve "the purpose of God in his own generation" (Acts 13:36). He is spurred on by Paul's words, "See that you fulfill the ministry that you have received in the Lord" (Col. 4:17). So Dad continues to work with all his might, knowing "there is no work or thought or knowledge or wisdom in Sheol" (Eccles. 9:10).

His work ethic was instilled in him by his father, who came of age during the Great Depression and discovered hard work was necessary to survive. My grandfather's advice—do what you want, just be the best at what you do—has informed the way my dad sought to honor the Lord with his work. The bit of aimlessness my grandfather experienced in early retirement encouraged my dad to press into his work with an even greater diligence before Parkinson's robs him of his ability to write.

He's taken great pleasure in his work. He's reaped its rewards as he demonstrated the truth of Proverbs 22:29:

Do you see a man skillful in his work?
He will stand before kings;
he will not stand before obscure men.

Being given dominion over the earth, he wrote, "implies that God expected Adam and Eve and their descendants to explore and develop the earth's resources in such a way that they would bring benefit to themselves and other human beings."[10]

Dad has found great joy as he's benefitted from and enjoyed the dominion others have taken in turning trees into paper and other natural resources into ink. His childlike wonder at technological advancements is accompanied by a celebration of those advancements because they represent a subduing of the earth and having dominion over it. This understanding allows him to rightly and consistently thank the Lord

---

10. Wayne Grudem, *Politics—according to the Bible: A Comprehensive Resource for Understanding Modern Political Issues in Light of Scripture* (Grand Rapids, MI: Zondervan, 2010), 325.

for the benefits he receives from technology. Every technological advancement can be traced back to humans exercising their God-given dominion by utilizing God-created resources on earth to benefit themselves and others.

God-given dominion extends beyond what we can produce with our hands. There is an intellectual aspect to it as well. The ability to read and study theology, to compile what the Bible says about a specific topic, and to communicate it in a way that is understandable is exercising intellectual dominion. It is a uniquely human activity. It's not something that the rest of creation—that which God placed under our feet (Ps. 8:6–8)—can or is expected to do. The research and writing my dad continues to do gives expression to Psalm 8:6: "You have given him dominion over the works of your hands."

My dad's work also honors God because it reflects God's characteristics, especially his mental attributes (knowledge, wisdom, and truthfulness).[11] God made humans "a little lower than the heavenly beings" (Ps. 8:5). This is "a paraphrase of the Genesis creation account" where God said he made us in his own image.[12] In his work Dad reflects the image of his Creator, showing others what God is like.

In addition, if all work is an expression of our God-given dominion, my dad's writing in a wide variety of areas (theology, the church, business, politics, economics, and ethics) is an attempt to help others exercise dominion in their specific calling in a way that lines up with what the Scriptures teach, and therefore honors God.

My dad loves to work, and he loves his work. The ability to work and to enjoy that work is a gift from God. "Everyone should eat and drink and take pleasure in all his toil—this is God's gift to man" (Eccles. 3:13). Dad's work honors the One who made and gifted him to do it (Ps. 8:5), commanded and empowered him to do it (Ps. 8:6), and cares enough about him to give him work to do (Ps. 8:4).

Love for the Word

His work has focused and always will focus on the whole of Scripture. My dad loves the Bible. He firmly believes there is no higher authority, for there is no other collection of God's words. As he wrote:

11. Grudem, *Systematic Theology*, 190–97.
12. Waltke and Houston, *Psalms as Christian Worship*, 267.

The Bible *alone* is the Word of God written. There are no other written words of God anywhere else in the entire world. And the Bible *in its entirety* is the Word of God written. Every single bit of this book in the original documents has a fundamentally different character from every other bit of writing in the entire world.[13]

A number of years ago we were visiting Tyndale House, a biblical research library in Cambridge, England, that my father utilized to write his PhD dissertation and other books and articles. It has served and continues to serve as a community for Bible scholars. They benefit both from the excellent library and from the interaction with peers.

As we walked into the common room, Dad said, "I wonder if it's still here." "It" was a Greek New Testament. It was still there. He left it in the break room fifteen years prior with this inscription: "To be kept in Tyndale House lounge for use in discussions when all else fails and someone finally decides to find out what the text actually says."

So it is no surprise that he had me memorize Scripture instead of the Westminster Shorter Catechism. There is tremendous value in a catechism, but there's greater value in God's Word. It's why he read from the Bible to my brothers and me each night before we went to bed, without exception, even if we had friends over who didn't care much for what the Bible taught. It's why he quoted from Scripture to make a point or answer a question instead of giving us a book to read. It's why we continue to receive the various editions of the English Standard Version of the Bible each year for Christmas presents.

Scholarship and writings and catechisms all have value. But Scripture is of primary importance.

My dad rarely talks about how many copies any of the books he worked on have sold, with one exception. He frequently tells me about sales of the ESV. I think that's because it is the project he worked on that he cares about more than any other. It's the one he loves more than any other (Scripture). It's the book—the one without his name on it, the one he didn't write—that will still be around long past his death. His work with the ESV may be his longest-lasting legacy.

13. Wayne Grudem, "Do We Act As If We Really Believe That 'The Bible Alone, and the Bible in Its Entirety, Is the Word of God Written'?," *JETS* 43, no. 1 (March 2000): 5.

When I was in high school, one of my dad's students complained to me about how challenging Trinity Evangelical Divinity School's English Bible exam was. I asked him for examples of the questions on the exam. I answered all of them correctly. I share this not to promote myself as some Bible prodigy (I spent more time studying baseball than the Bible at that age) but instead to show the regular, repetitive exposure we had to Scripture in our home.

Dad's advice to me as a young preacher was this: try to get your congregation to look at the Bible as often as you can while preaching. His reason was that he wanted to make sure they were more focused on God's words than on my words.

When I stood for ordination in the Presbyterian Church in America, the concern among the presbytery following my examination was that while I knew my Bible really well, they weren't sure I was Presbyterian enough. Dad laughed and congratulated me when he heard that (and not because of the Presbyterian part).

While my dad believes creeds, catechisms, sermons, and theology books have great value (he's devoted his whole career to helping the church figure out what the whole Bible says about certain topics), he doesn't believe they have the same value as Scripture itself.

In 1999, he gave the presidential address at the annual meeting of the Evangelical Theological Society. He encouraged some of the members to devote their lives to "seeking out the whole counsel of God from Scripture, focusing on positive, constructive Biblical syntheses that will build up the Church."[14] Each phrase in that encouragement is important, for together they are a great summary of the specific work my dad believes God gave him to do—focus on the whole of Scripture, not just one section, and do your work for the whole church, not just the academy.

There are many things Dad could do. He has a PhD from the University of Cambridge and studied under C. F. D. Moule, one of the great New Testament scholars of the last century. Yet he chose to do his best work for the whole church, not just the academy, knowing that it wouldn't gain the praise of the scholars at his alma mater. In that same address, he told about the time he showed Professor Moule a first draft of his *Systematic Theology*:

---

14. Grudem, "Do We Really Believe?," 23.

I held the book in my hand and said to him, "Professor Moule, I don't think that you think this kind of thing can be done. But I'm trying to do it anyway." And I handed it to him. He looked at the table of contents, saw the topics being treated, paged through it and saw how I was trying to synthesize the teaching of all of Scripture on these various topics, and with a twinkle in his eye he handed it back to me and he said, "You're right, I don't think it can be done. But I hope you enjoy doing it!"[15]

What Professor Moule did not know was that earlier that year my dad experienced a turning point in his academic career. He was on sabbatical, back in Cambridge, England, and working on the first book, other than his dissertation, that would be published—a commentary on 1 Peter for the Tyndale New Testament Commentary series. After completing the first chapter, he read what he wrote. He was troubled by what he read. He realized he was writing it to earn the approval of those who deemed him worthy of a PhD in New Testament eight years earlier. While non-evangelical academics might admire that scholarship, the majority of the global church would struggle to understand what he wrote.

So he ripped up what he wrote and started again, this time writing in a way that would benefit the whole evangelical church around the world, the church he deeply loved. That commitment to writing and teaching about the whole of Scripture for all the church started with his commentary on 1 Peter and continues to this day.

Mindful of Him

Memorizing Psalm 8 was extremely beneficial to me as child. Having access to the whole of Scripture gave me greater insight into the psalm and gives me a greater reason to praise God for his tender care of me.

Psalm 8, by itself (without the New Testament), stands as a wonderful hymn of praise to God the Creator. His mindfulness of us is felt when things go well. But when it seems like his enemies are winning, and creation is pitted against us, when we suffer, we can read the psalm like Qoheleth, hoping that "God will bring every deed into judgment, with every secret thing, whether good or evil" (Eccles. 12:14). We can

---

15. Grudem, "Do We Really Believe?," 20.

join faithful Israel in believing that will be true, but longing for God to reveal exactly how he will work that out. For, "a messianic interpretation of Ps. 8 . . . is not evident in the Jewish literature."[16]

In Psalm 8:4 the psalmist asks,

> What is man that you are mindful of him,
>   the son of man that you care for him?

He wonders why God would care about us enough to give us such a prominent position in all creation.

In light of Jesus, the phrases "mindful of him" and "care for him" take on newer and greater meaning that is far beyond what the psalmist could imagine. It's so great, the angels continue to stare at it and marvel over it (1 Pet. 1:12).

Jesus is the ideal man, the final man, the forerunner who was made a little lower than the angels and is now crowned with glory and honor. Paul's use of Psalm 8 in 1 Corinthians 15, as well as the writer to the Hebrews's use in Hebrews 2, expands the meaning of "man" in Psalm 8:4–6 from only created humans to include the God-man Jesus Christ. In Christ, God took on flesh and suffered and died. Jesus didn't stay dead. He rose from the dead, victorious over it. So now, for those who belong to Christ, what is true of Christ is true of them. Paul's use of Psalm 8:6 in 1 Corinthians 15:27 "is an explicitly christological use of the OT, with the OT notion of corporate representation as its presumption; Christ represents his people."[17]

The same idea is put forth in Hebrews 2:5–9, which also uses Psalm 8 to make this point. In that passage, Christ is explained to be "the eschatological last Adam."[18] Jesus, "in his solidarity with human beings, was able to bring about the ultimate fulfillment of the psalm's intention."[19] In the person of Jesus "we see him who for a little while was made lower than the angels" (Heb. 2:9) so he could suffer and die for those he calls his own. He died "so that by the grace of God he might taste death for everyone" (Heb. 2:9).

16. Roy E. Ciampa and Brian S. Rosner, "1 Corinthians," in *Commentary on the New Testament Use of the Old Testament*, ed. G. K. Beale and D. A. Carson (Grand Rapids, MI: Baker Academic, 2007), 745.
17. Ciampa and Rosner, "1 Corinthians," 746.
18. Guthrie, "Hebrews," 946.
19. Guthrie, "Hebrews," 946.

Now exalted, Christ is crowned with glory and honor. Those who belong to him now share in that glory and honor. He took their punishment; they get his victory and glory and honor.

The writer further explains the implications for us: "Since therefore the children share in flesh and blood, he himself likewise partook of the same things, that through death he might destroy the one who has the power of death, that is, the devil, and deliver all those who through fear of death were subject to lifelong slavery" (Heb. 2:14–15).

The New Testament unpacking of Psalm 8 gives us great hope.

> What we see is the continuing struggle between the wicked and the righteous, between the rebel and the saint. Both the kingdom of God and the kingdom of Satan are expanding as wheat and tares, as good fish and bad fish. . . . The Pioneer of our faith, as Son of God and as son of man, has extended humankind's dominion over sin and death. Jesus Christ began dominion over all things, including sin and death, and his followers are bringing that dominion to its full realization. The full realization of humankind's manifest destiny is still a thing in the future, but details of its further course and its completion are already beginning to stand out clearly even in the present age as the faithful conquer under their resurrected, ascended, and exalted Head, who pioneered their faith.
>
> As Christians step onto the stage of life they wear the victor's crown over all things through their faith in Jesus Christ who conquered even death. To the triune God belongs all the glory. He works in his viceregents both to will and to do his good pleasure in establishing his rule over all things, including sin and death.[20]

The unpacking of Psalm 8 through the whole of Scripture leaves us with a greater hope and a greater reason to praise God. This gives us an even greater incentive to do the work God has for us to do.

Labor of Love, Not in Vain

Psalm 8 tells us about God and about ourselves. Therefore, it is a great place to start a theological journey. As John Calvin famously starts his *Institutes of the Christian Religion*, "Nearly all the wisdom we

---

20. Waltke and Houston, *Psalms as Christian Worship*, 274–75.

possess, that is to say, true and sound wisdom, consists of two parts: the knowledge of God and of ourselves."[21]

After people find out Wayne is my father, they often say something like this: "Please thank your dad for his work." Sometimes the "work" is a specific book or article. Other times it's a class he taught in seminary or at a church. And other times it's the care he and my mom showed them in a time of need.

Often ministerial or scholarly work is done with little feedback and little recognition. You work with people for a set time or on a specific project and never see or hear from them again. Sometimes you see others make great progress in their sanctification; more often you catch a glimpse of growth and have to trust that God really will complete the good work he started (Phil. 1:6). Ministry through writing is even tougher. You don't see the people reading your book. You hear more from critics than from those who are helped by your writing.

Recognition for the dominion we express through our work is a gift of grace. It's guaranteed in the new heavens and new earth.

> They shall build houses and inhabit them;
>   they shall plant vineyards and eat their fruit. (Isa. 65:21)

By God's grace we get to see a bit of the fruit of our labor during our time on this earth.

Most ministry is rightly done in obscurity. The stories I most appreciate about my dad are those not told here, which few will ever know. I think that's very appropriate. In those cases, his Father sees, understands, appreciates, and affirms. That is always enough.

Even so, I don't think it's wrong to desire or enjoy recognition (to see the fruit of your labor). Proverbs 27:2 encourages us to receive praise from another:

> Let another praise you, and not your own mouth;
>   a stranger, and not your own lips.

Jesus tells of God thanking us for our work and affirming it (see, e.g., Matt. 25:21; Luke 17:8–10). Paul often speaks of the rewards we will receive from God in eternity in recognition of our work (see,

---

21. John Calvin, *Institutes of the Christian Religion*, ed. John T. McNeill, trans. Ford Lewis Battles (Philadelphia: Westminster, 1960), 1.1.1.

e.g., Rom. 2:6; 1 Cor. 9:24–25; Eph. 6:8). It is always a gift of grace when God brings a bit of eternity into our present.

We don't need the recognition or affirmation. In serving God, "we are unworthy servants; we have only done what is our duty" (Luke 17:10). In Christ, we already have the Father's full affirmation and love: "See what kind of love the Father has given to us, that we should be called children of God; and so we are" (1 John 3:1). And yet our Father, who loves to give good gifts to his children, allows us to receive recognition and affirmation.

At the end of 1 Corinthians 15, Paul spells out a wonderful present-day implication of God putting all things in subjection under Jesus's feet. It's a tremendous affirmation for "the work of the Lord" we all do. The affirmation is this: keep working hard, knowing that "in the Lord your labor is not in vain" (1 Cor. 15:58).

This is an echo of what Isaiah says will be true of our work in the new heavens and new earth: "They shall not labor in vain" (Isa. 65:23). The word translated "labor" in 1 Corinthians 15:58 and in the Septuagint translation of Isaiah 65:23 is *kopos*. Some commentators translate *kopos* "wearisome toil."[22]

Paul considers this "wearisome toil" necessary for kingdom work. *The Theological Dictionary of the New Testament* explains this: "A final and distinctive NT use of kop- is for Christian work in and for the community. This is found most frequently . . . in Paul, and it seems to have been then adopted by the community. . . . Paul uses kop- not only for his own work but also for the missionary and pastoral work of others."[23] Ceslas Spicq explains this further, using terms that describe both Paul's ministry and the ministry of every other worker who follows Paul as he follows Jesus:

In the NT, *kopos/kapiao*, "work hard," means (1) constant, exhausting manual labor; (2) the fatigue of long, incessant missionary wanderings; (3) blows, wounds, and suffering endured in the course of stonings and riots; (4) slanders and insults by enemies, the humiliations of imprisonment; (5) the difficulties of governing

22. Archibald Robertson and Alfred Plummer, *A Critical and Exegetical Commentary on the First Epistle of St. Paul to the Corinthians*, 2nd ed. (Edinburgh: T. & T. Clark, 1929), 380.
23. Gerhard Kittel, *Theological Dictionary of the New Testament*, 10th ed., 10 vols. (Grand Rapids, MI: Eerdmans, 1977), s.v. *kópos, kopiáō*.

and exercising apostolic authority; (6) the preparation of sermons, speeches given in the open air, the editing of epistles; (7) care for all the churches and for each soul . . . who will or will not be saved on the steep path except through costly endurance and violence. . . . There is no Christian life, no apostolic ministry, without rough, preserving labor.[24]

It wouldn't take long to fill a very large room with former students, pastors, church members, lay leaders, missionaries, ministry leaders, friends, and neighbors who would all say, enthusiastically and in unison, that they are living proof that in the Lord my dad's labor (*kopos*) is not in vain.

And then there's Mom, Oliver, Alexander, and I—and our families. And we would all affirm the same. Our affirmation would not be because of Dr. Wayne Grudem's writing or scholarship or teaching. We appreciate that, but that's not the way we know him. To us he is a husband and father and father-in-law and grandfather. Yes, we sometimes roll our eyes at another family hymn sing. Yes, we differ on a few secondary issues about what the Bible teaches. Yes, there are things that we as husbands and fathers do differently than he did. But we love him. We appreciate him. And we know Jesus better because of him.

And so we gratefully say: God is mindful of you. He cares for you. He gave you dominion over his creation, and you executed that dominion well. Everything is in subjection to Jesus. He is crowned with glory and honor. He sent the Holy Spirit to be at work within you. The Holy Spirit gives you insight into the Scriptures and empowers your work, including that of a husband, father, father-in-law, and grandfather.

It's because of the work of the triune God and your faithful work that we all affirm—loudly and enthusiastically and with great conviction—that with us, your labor is not in vain.

---

24. Ceslas Spicq, *Theological Lexicon of the New Testament*, 3 vols. (Peabody, MA: Hendrickson, 1995), 2:329.

14

The Doctrine of Scripture and the Shape of the Sermon

Kent Hughes

Over the years, I have come to know Wayne Grudem quite well. In fact, he is a good friend. My association with Dr. Grudem goes back to about 1980 when I sat in a room in Danvers, Massachusetts, while he and John Piper and others hammered out "The Danvers Statement on Biblical Manhood and Womanhood." Next, Wayne and I were involved in administrating the Council on Biblical Manhood and Womanhood in its early years. And then, providentially, we both served for seventeen years on the Translation Oversight Committee of the English Standard Version, and spent hundreds of hours of intense discussion over the biblical text. Also, both Wayne and I have served on the board of directors of Crossway for decades. So I am intimately aware of his immense scholarly abilities, his "Energizer Bunny" tenacity in pursuing and arguing his point, his utter integrity, and his passion and love for Christ, Christ's church, and his holy Word.

When the editors of this Festschrift honored me with a request to contribute an essay on the doctrine of Scripture and the shape of the sermon, I readily accepted because those two subjects have been in my thoughts through decades of expository preaching.

This chapter assumes what I have always believed about Scripture, namely, that it is wholly inerrant, totally sufficient, and massively potent. My intention here is not to defend this view but to demonstrate how one's doctrine of Scripture must interface with the shape of the sermon.

The Doctrine of Scripture

When Moses finished writing the Torah, the words of the law, he commanded the Levites to take the scroll and lay it beside the ark of the covenant. He then directed the elders of the tribes to assemble the people before him, and sang what we now call the "song of Moses."[1] When Moses finished his paean, he concluded with an epilogue that ended with these words: "Take to heart all the words by which I am warning you today, that you may command them to your children, that they may be careful to do all the words of this law. For it is no empty word for you, but your very life" (Deut. 32:46–47). Moses's declaration that the words of the book of the law were Israel's *very life* informed Israel's regard for the holy Scriptures for the next millennium and beyond.

We see this in Psalm 19, where the psalmist begins by celebrating the fact that we live in a worded world:

The heavens declare the glory of God,
    and the sky above proclaims his handiwork.
Day to day pours out speech,
    and night to night reveals knowledge. (19:1–2)

And then the psalmist further declares of God's *written* words,

More to be desired are they then gold,
    even much fine gold;
sweeter also than honey
    and drippings of the honeycomb. (19:10)

Next, in extended concert with this, Psalm 119 celebrates the life-giving sufficiency of God's Word in a 176-verse, 22-stanza Hebrew acrostic poem, singing that the Word of God is everything from A to

1. Deut. 32:1–43.

Z (*aleph* to *tav*). Kevin DeYoung writes of Psalm 119, "Surely it is significant that this intricate, finely crafted, single-minded love poem—the longest in the Bible—is not about marriage or children or food or drink or mountains or sunsets or rivers or oceans, but about the Bible itself."[2] Every faithful child of the old covenant considered God's Word the center of his or her very life.

When we look to the new covenant, we find Jesus, the second Moses, resisting Satan's temptations by quoting God's words to Moses from Deuteronomy 8:3, "Man shall not live by bread alone, but by every word that comes from the mouth of God" (Matt. 4:4). Thus, the Son of God, in his great hour of need, depended upon the Word of God, declaring, in essence, that it is our very food.

So we see that the first Moses tells us that the Word is our very *life*, and the second Moses, that it is our very *food*. This sweeping regard for the sufficiency of God's Word implicitly argues for its verbal, plenary inspiration, underlined by Jesus's subsequent declaration, "For truly, I say to you, until heaven and earth pass away, not an iota, not a dot, will pass from the Law until all is accomplished" (Matt. 5:18). As earlier noted, it is not within the scope of this essay to defend these doctrines, but I hope to demonstrate that if a pastor holds that the Scriptures are his very life and food, as did both the first Moses and the second, it will profoundly shape his exposition of the Word of God.

Scripture's Perfections

The opening lines of the Torah that Moses directed to be laid by the ark (Gen. 1:1–2) are redolent with the perfections of the inspired Word. The late Hebrew University professor Umberto Cassuto pointed out that "the structure of the days of creation is based on a system of numerical harmony, using the number seven."[3] He wrote, "The work of the Creator, which is marked by absolute perfection and flawless systematic orderliness, is distributed over seven days: Six days of labour and a seventh day set aside for the enjoyment of the completed task." And then he made these observations: The words "God" (*Elohim*), "heavens" (*samayim*), and "earth" (*eretz*), which are the three nouns of the opening verse, "In the beginning, *God* created the *heavens* and

---

2. Kevin DeYoung, *Taking God at His Word* (Wheaton, IL: Crossway, 2014), 12.
3. Umberto Cassuto, *A Commentary on the Book of Genesis* (Jerusalem: Magnes, 1989), 12.

the *earth*," are repeated in this creation account in multiples of seven. "God" occurs thirty-five times (five times seven), "heavens" twenty-one times (three times seven), and "earth" twenty-one times. In addition to this, in the Hebrew original the first verse has seven words, and the second fourteen words. The seventh paragraph (the seventh day) has three sentences, each of which has seven words, and contains in the middle phrase, "the seventh day." Cassuto concludes: "This numerical symmetry is as it were, the golden thread that binds together all the parts of the section and serves as a convincing proof of its unity."[4] So Genesis 1 is remarkable literature as to its arrangement, its correspondences and symmetries, and its literary-numerical perfection.

Indeed, this is true for all of Genesis. The controlling theme of Genesis is God's desire to *bless* all the world as we read sequentially at the beginning, in the middle, and at the end of Genesis. At the beginning of primeval history, we read of divine blessing: "And God *blessed* them. And God said to them, 'Be fruitful and multiply and fill the earth and subdue it, and have dominion over the fish of the sea and over the birds of the heavens and over every living thing that moves on the earth'" (Gen. 1:28). At the beginning of patriarchal history, God said to Abram, "And I will make of you a great nation, and I will *bless* you and make your name great, so that you will be a *blessing*. I will *bless* those who *bless* you, and him who dishonors you I will curse, and in you all the families of the earth shall be *blessed*" (Gen. 12:2–3). At the conclusion of the book of Genesis, we see Jacob blessing each of the twelve patriarchs, as Moses summarizes: "All these are the twelve tribes of Israel. This is what their father said to them as he *blessed* them, *blessing* each with the *blessing* suitable to him" (Gen. 49:28). Genesis is imbued with marked literary and theological perfection!

The literary and theological perfections extend through all the narratives of Genesis. For example, Genesis 2:4 begins a new section in the primeval history of the world. The six days of forming and then filling the earth left a dazzling, complete creation under the benign rule of Adam and Eve. Upon the seventh day (the number of perfection), "God rested from all his work that he had done in creation" (Gen. 2:3). And because there was no evening or morning that day, he still rests. Up to this point in the story, Moses has used only one designation for God, the

---

4. Cassuto, *Genesis*, 12.

name *Elohim*. And he has used it with studied care some thirty-five times (five times seven, the number of perfection). *Elohim* is the appropriate word for the majestic portrayal of God as Creator of the universe, signifying the omnipotent Deity. The thirty-five repeated uses of this name are metered praise for the perfect creation of the perfect Creator.

Later, in chapter 4, when we come to the account of Cain's murder of Abel, we see that Moses has exercised the same exquisite literary care in telling the story. Within verses 1–17, the name "Abel" and the designation "brother" both occur seven times. The name of the protagonist "Cain" occurs fourteen times. And whereas in 1:1–2:3 (the first *toledot*) the name "God" (*Elohim*) occurs thirty-five times, from 2:4 to the end of chapter 4 (the second *toledot*) the words "God," "the Lord," or "the Lord God" occur a total of thirty-five times. The careful Hebrew scholar Gordon Wenham observes: "The last verse of chapter 4, 'At that time people began to call on the name of the Lord,' thus contains the seventieth mention of deity in Genesis."[5] Thus there is vast intentionality amid the words and shape of this narrative as it instructs us about the essential nature of all mankind.

Theological Inspiration

This said, there is a theological depth and cohesion throughout all Scripture, which functions on the analogy of the human brain as it informs and coordinates the body. Geerhardus Vos, in his inaugural address as professor of biblical theology at Princeton Theological Seminary, declared:

> In the Bible there is an organization finer, more complicated, more exquisite than even the texture of muscles and nerves and brain in the human body; that its various parts are interwoven and correlated in the most subtle manner, each sensitive to the impressions received from all the others, perfect in itself, and yet dependent upon the rest, while in them and through them all throbs as a unifying principle the Spirit of God's living truth.[6]

Vos voiced this high view of Scripture as stemming from his understanding about how all of it is redolent with Christ. The Bible contains

---

5. Gordon J. Wenham, *Genesis 1–15*, WBC (Waco: Word, 1987), 96.
6. Geerhardus Vos, *Inaugural Address* (New York: Anson D. F. Randolph, 1894), 40.

many genres—narrative, prophetic, apocalyptic, wisdom, poetry, epistle, gospel, and acts—to name a few. Literary critic Leland Ryken states that the number of literary genres in the Bible "readily exceeds 100."[7] Having preached through many of the genres, I can say that the literary, theological, and Christological perfections continue to amaze. The more a man exposits the Word, the more amazed he becomes at the living wonders of God's words (Heb. 4:12; 1 Pet. 1:23).

I say all of this because the awareness that the text is divinely inspired and divinely shaped means that the preacher must give due consideration to the biblical shape of his sermon if he is to honor God.

Verbal Inspiration

Jesus Christ's mind encompassed the full range of the Scriptures of the Old Testament and was saturated with them. And more, he lived in full submission to the Scriptures he knew so well. Adolf Schlatter comments: "Jesus saw his entire life calling in the Scripture—it was not marginal but absolutely central to his life. . . . His whole will was consumed with this: to do what each commandment commanded. Here is the one man—the first in history—who not only knew the Word but did it."[8] The mind of Christ was infused with the words of the Old Testament. Jesus's declaration that not one iota or dot of the law would pass away until all is accomplished (verbal inspiration) was informed by his perfect knowledge of the Scriptures. Correspondingly, Jesus employed the wording of the Scriptures as the final authority in his teaching, as evidence by his repeated challenges "Have you not read?" and "Have you never read?" and "What did Moses command you?"

Jesus's explicit belief in the verbal inspiration of the Scriptures is memorably demonstrated in his use of God's famous declaration to Moses at the burning bush—"I am the God of your father, the God of Abraham, the God of Isaac, and the God of Jacob" (Ex. 3:6)—to embarrass some resurrection-denying Sadducees by noting the present tense of the verb used in God's declaration: "I *am*," not "I *was*" (cf. Luke 20:37–38). Thus, Abraham, Isaac, and Jacob have been raised. Resurrection is implied in one little word! Get it, Sadducees?

---

7. Leland Ryken, *Preach the Word: Essays on Expository Preaching* (Wheaton, IL: Crossway, 2011), 42.
8. Frederick Dale Brunner, *Matthew: A Commentary*, vol. 1, *The Christbook, Matthew 1–12* (Dallas: Word, 1987), 167, quoting Adolf Schlatter, *Das Evangelium nach Matthaus*, 61.

Plenary Inspiration

Plenary means "full" or "complete" and has been used to indicate that all the words of Scripture are God's words. Here I am extending its logic because if all the words of Scripture are inspired, then the very form of the discourse, poetry, narrative, history, prophecy, and parable is inspired.

In the largest sense, the shape and theme of each of the books of Scripture are inspired just as we have seen, for example, in the book of Genesis with its divisions into primeval history and patriarchal history and its welling theme, or "melodic line,"[9] of blessing to Israel and the nations.

Within each book of the Bible there are natural divisions according to the genre employed. The primeval-history section of Genesis features five narratives that follow the same pattern: (1) sin, (2) speech, (3) grace, and (4) punishment. This is shown in table 3, which is based on the work of D. J. A. Clines.[10]

Table 3. Divisions within five Genesis narratives

	Sin	Speech	Grace	Punishment
1. The fall	3:6	3:14–19	3:21	3:22–24
2. Cain's murder of Abel	4:8	4:10–12	4:15	4:16
3. The sons of God marrying the daughters of men	6:2	6:3	6:8, 18ff.	7:6–24
4. The flood	6:5, 11f.	6:7, 13–21	6:8, 18ff.	7:6–24
5. The tower of Babel	11:4	11:6f.	10:1–32	11:8

---

9. David R. Helm, *Expositional Preaching: How We Speak God's Word's Today* (Wheaton, IL: Crossway, 2014), 47, explains:

A melodic line is a short sequence of notes that form a distinctive portion of a song. It may be part of the main melody that gets repeated and varied. Books of the Bible work in the same way. Each book has a melodic line, an essence that informs what the book is about. And each passage in the book, then, will serve that melodic line in some way. So in preaching, we might ask, what is the essence of my book? And how is my particular passage informing it and informed by it?

10. See D. J. A. Clines, "Theme in Genesis 1–11," *CBQ* 38, no. 4 (1976): 487–88. Clines explains that Gerhard von Rad initially observed a pattern of sin, mitigation, and punishment. Then Claus Westermann discerned another element, that of divine *speech*. Though he did not include it in the pattern, Clines does.

Preachers will find much help in understanding the recurrent outline as, for example, in the account of Cain and Abel:

- *Sin*—the first homicide (Gen. 4:8)
- *Speech*—to Cain by God (Gen. 4:10–12)
- *Grace*—to Cain, a divine mark (Gen. 4:15)
- *Punishment*—of Cain, exile from the Lord's presence (Gen. 4:16)

This is not to suggest that a preacher must teach these narratives deductively, under the same neat headings, but that understanding the divinely wrought structure will enhance the preaching of the Word.

Similarly, the patriarchal narratives, the generations of Abraham, Isaac, and Jacob (which includes the long narrative of his son Joseph), are finely wrought, each with a readily discernable theme and structure.

When we come to the New Testament, its narratives and parables demonstrate a similar plenary artistry and care. There was a time when form critics were dismissive of the Gospel of Mark with assertions like these: "Mark is not sufficiently master of his material to be able to venture on a systematic construction himself" (Rudolf Bultmann); "Mark was a clumsy writer unworthy of mentioning in any history of literature" (Étienne Trocmé).[11] These critics (blinded by their singular devotion to source criticism) saw Mark only as a jumble of unrelated pericopes and stories.

Today, this is not the case, because of the scholarship of James Edwards and others who have shown that Mark intentionally employed a literary technique—some nine times in his Gospel—popularly termed the "Markan sandwich." Mark begins with story A, introduces story B, then returns to and completes story A. Moreover, as Edwards explains:

> Mark sandwiches one passage into the middle of another with an intentional and discernable theological purpose. The technique is, to be sure, a literary technique, but its purpose is theological; that is, the sandwiches emphasize the major motifs of the Gospel, especially the meaning of faith, discipleship, bearing witness, and the

---

11. James R. Edwards, "Markan Sandwiches: The Significance of Interpolations in Markan Narratives," *NovT* 31, no. 3 (1989): 194.

dangers of apostasy. Moreover . . . the *middle of the story provides the key to the theological purpose of the sandwich*.[12]

The nine A-B-A sandwiches are as follows:[13]

1. Mark 3:20–35
2. Mark 4:1–20
3. Mark 5:21–43
4. Mark 6:7–30
5. Mark 11:12–21
6. Mark 14:1–11
7. Mark 14:17–31
8. Mark 14:53–72
9. Mark 15:40–16:8

The sixth sandwich, 14:1–11, is structured as follows:[14]

A Plot to kill Jesus (14:1–2)
   B Anointing of Jesus at Bethany (14:3–9)
A Judas's agreement to betray Jesus (14:10–11)

In briefest terms, an anonymous woman's lavish anointing of Jesus, (termed by the master as "a beautiful thing" [14:6] and a deed that would be told "wherever the gospel is proclaimed" [14:9]) is bracketed by dual betrayals. First by the murderous machinations of the religious establishment, and then by Judas's treachery. The striking woman, sandwiched by betrayal, becomes the dazzling ideal of faith and devotion. Mark, the writer of the Gospel, far from being a bumbling historian, is an author and theologian of immense subtlety.

The other Gospel writers also display remarkable skill in the shaping of their texts. An excellent example is the account of Zacchaeus in Luke 19:1–10. In the preceding context, Jesus says of the departing rich young ruler, "It is easier for a camel to go through the eye of a needle than for a rich person to enter the kingdom of God." Luke continues, "Those who heard it said, 'Then who can be saved?' But [Jesus] said, 'What is impossible with man is possible with God'" (18:25–27). Then, after foretelling his death in verses 31–34 and healing the blind beggar

---

12. Edwards, "Markan Sandwiches," 196.
13. Edwards, "Markan Sandwiches," 197–98.
14. Edwards, "Markan Sandwiches," 197–98.

in verses 35–43, Jesus encounters Zacchaeus, and we have a narrative that tells about how the impossible happens, how a filthy-rich little man goes through the eye of a needle by the grace of God and comes out whole. The Zacchaeus account ends famously, "For the Son of Man came to seek and save the lost" (19:10). The form of the Zacchaeus narrative is precise and beautiful:

1. *Sovereign initiative* (19:1–7): interior initiative, exterior initiative
2. *Sovereign transformation* (19:8): big divestment, big man
3. *Sovereign declarations* (19:9–10): declaration to Zacchaeus, declaration to the world!

Even an occasional letter written on the departure of a faithful servant, such as Paul's epistle to the Philippians, demonstrates plenary cohesion. The unifying theme of the letter can be stated as a call to live in unity amid the claustrophobic oppression of the little, self-consciously elitist Roman colony of Philippi. Within this tiny four-chapter letter are nineteen imperatives, and the initial imperative does not occur until nearly the end of the first chapter, where we read in 1:27, "Only let your manner of life be worthy of the gospel of Christ." The Greek verb is *politeuesthe* which is better translated "live as citizens" (implicitly, *of heaven*; cf. 3:20, *politeuma*) worthy of the gospel of Christ. This initial imperative controls all the discourse and theology that follow until the end of chapter 2. Therefore, six successive sermons can be preached under the series heading "How to Live Life as Citizens of Heaven Who Are Worthy of the Gospel of Christ" (Phil. 1:27–2:30).

1. Living Worthily in the World (1:27–30)
2. Living Worthily in the Church (2:1–4)
3. Living Worthily: Christ the Ultimate Example (2:5–11, several sermons?)
4. Living Worthily as Light in the World (2:12–18)
5. Living Worthily: Timothy's Example (2:19–24)
6. Living Worthily: Epaphroditus's Example (2:25–30)

And then, of course, there are the classic dominical passages (the *ipsissima verba* of Christ) that display an astonishing cohesion and symmetry, such as the Beatitudes, which introduce the Sermon on the Mount in Matthew 5:1–10. The Beatitudes are framed by an *inclu-*

sio, "for theirs in the kingdom of heaven" (5:10), which tells us that they are about the hearts of those who are in God's kingdom. The Beatitudes are arranged as eight consecutive spiritual H-bombs, concentrated theological epigrams that detonate with increasing effect, each standing upon the preceding statements, mounting a ruthless theological logic that assaults the soul with hammer-like power.

The logic is as follows: Those who are "poor in spirit" (5:3), who realize they have nothing within themselves to commend them to God, will naturally mourn over their sins and the sins of the world. This will in turn produce a meek and gentle spirit. And when the first three beatitudes are in place, one will hunger and thirst for righteousness. The presence of the preceding virtues will make one merciful and then pure in spirit. The effect of all of this is to be become a peacemaker, which means that one will be persecuted. The Beatitudes expose the true state of our hearts and call us to ever-higher planes of holy living. They are the postures of regeneration from the lips of God himself (see fig. 1).

Figure 1. Ascending steps within the Beatitudes

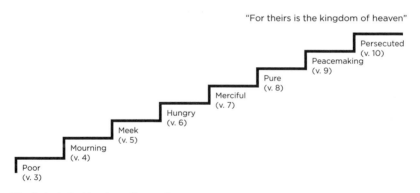

"For theirs is the kingdom of heaven"

Persecuted
(v. 10)

Peacemaking
(v. 9)

Pure
(v. 8)

Merciful
(v. 7)

Hungry
(v. 6)

Meek
(v. 5)

Mourning
(v. 4)

Poor
(v. 3)

"For theirs is the kingdom of heaven"

Having preached *lectio continua* for some fifty years, I am constantly amazed at the verbal and plenary inspiration of the Scriptures and am convinced that every word is inspired (every tense and connective), as is the shape of the text, whether it be narrative or history or poetry or prophecy or parable or compact dominical dicta, like the Beatitudes and the Lord's Prayer. I am convinced that every genre has its divinely shaped form and symmetries, and that the text's structure reveals the emphasis of the text. Therefore, the sermon must rest on the divinely given shape of the text.

The Shape of the Sermon

The goal of biblical exposition is to allow the sermon to function much as the text did on the original horizon. So the preacher must first understand what the text meant in Sinai, or Jerusalem, or Corinth, or Rome. The truth is that if preachers get the text right in its original context, it will come powerfully to today's horizon. Put another way, if preachers get it right in Corinth, it will play in Hong Kong, Paris, and Oshkosh. But the fact is that much of the trouble with contemporary preaching comes from preaching the biblical text without taking the trouble to make the necessary journey to and from the biblical horizon. However, when the preacher understands what the text meant on the original horizon as Paul or Luke wrote it, and how it addressed the hearers' sin in respect to their "Fallen Condition Focus" (FCF), to borrow Bryan Chapell's helpful term,[15] that will enhance the sermon's "punch" in today's horizon.

Fidelity to the original horizon and the FCF of the text requires submission to the words and shape of Scripture. The preacher's job is to say no more and no less than what the Scripture says—to preach "the whole truth and nothing but the truth" as it comes both in word and form—to preach "a Bible-shaped word in a Bible-shaped way."[16] The sermon's shape must be consonant with the inspired text's form and substance.

When expositing any text, regardless of genre, whether narrative or didactic, the preacher must read and reread the text, examining its context, words, grammar, and structure to determine what the unifying/integrating theme of the text is. This is regularly the hardest part of sermon preparation. My personal process is to clear my desk of

---

15. Bryan Chapell, *Christ-Centered Preaching: Redeeming the Expository Sermon* (Grand Rapids, MI: Baker Academic, 2005), 14, says that some read "the Fallen Condition Focus as just an oblique way of speaking about human felt needs. The main reason to ask why the Holy Spirit inspired any text is to expose what fallen aspect of the human condition needs to be addressed in order for God's glory to be properly recognized and honored. The FCF exposes the necessity of a divine solution to the human dilemma."

16. Sydney Greidanus, *The Modern Preacher and the Ancient Text: Interpreting and Preaching Biblical Literature* (Grand Rapids, MI: Eerdmans, 1989), 10, quoting Leander Keck, *Bible in the Pulpit*, 106.

everything but my English text and a machine copy of the Greek or Hebrew text and a legal pad. I then read my English text several times out loud, because the ear sometimes discerns what the eye misses. Besides, I think in English!

After noting my observations, which will include contextual and theological observations, redemptive-historical notes, cross references, applications, illustrations, questions, and stabs at the structure and theme, I take my copy of the text in the original, along with a concordance and grammatical aids, and begin to mark the text with colored pens, noting recurring connectives, vocabulary concordance, tenses, and key words (putative discourse analysis). Many times, I cannot tell what emerges first, the theme or the structure of the text, because the structure contains the theme. Next, I check my jottings with some critical commentaries—and sometimes find myself substantially corrected. But the mere work itself means that I have to think, and the labor is an ongoing education. When the theme and structure are determined, I craft the theme into a brief, simple sentence, and then construct an outline, which I fill in with some of the things I have listed along the way, including the insights of commentaries. Then I begin to write.

And it is here that I must decide in what form the sermon will be delivered, whether *inductive* or *deductive*. In every case, the form must be consonant with and serve the inspired text. If the text is narrative (and the majority of Scripture is narrative), I will most often preach it inductively, allowing the congregation to follow the storyline and to discover the meaning as the sermon progresses. As a rule, preaching a narrative deductively can "de-story" the text. This said, a narrative can be effectively preached in a deductive form by stating what the protagonist is going to learn, and then revealing it piece by piece. Genesis 39, the account of Joseph and Potiphar's wife, can be preached both inductively and deductively with good effect. A deductive form would state the theme of the text early by noting that the beginning and ending of the text say that God was "with" Joseph and he was "successful." The inductive form of the Joseph story would, of course, teach the same truth, but allow it to unfold with its natural drama so that the hearers discover the truth amid the texture of the narrative.

Apart from narrative texts, most sermons begin deductively, with the theme stated or implied in the introduction and then exposited according to the structure and flow of the text. The deductive method has intrinsic advantages. The sermon's outline is determined by the text. A faithful outline allows the congregation to follow the logic of the text and grasp the fullness of the unifying theme. It also enhances clarity. The deductive method serves the epistles and didactic sections of both testaments well.

The overall point of this essay is that, because both the words and the structures of the sacred text are fully inspired, a preacher must take great care as to the homiletic approach he employs. Specifically, the preacher must decide what form, inductive or deductive, best serves the text he is preaching. Many preachers may do that intuitively, or unconsciously, because they take great care to honor the genre they preach; some have never given it any thought. But it is incumbent upon all preachers to understand how the choice of homiletic form used to preach a text will either enhance or detract from its divinely intended effect, and thus to select the appropriate form.

Paul's charge to Timothy must inform all preachers: "Do your best to present yourself to God as one approved, a worker who has no need to be ashamed, rightly handling the word of truth" (2 Tim. 2:15).

Exquisite Care

The fact that the very words of Scripture, as well as its genre and forms, are inspired demands great care by the faithful expositor. This involves a number of steps by the preacher.

1. He must read and reread the text from the book he will preach. Personally, when I preached on the book of Philippians, I read it through forty consecutive times in the summer, as well as the Greek text. Doing this allowed me to discern the melodic line of the book, as well as its contours, and positioned me to do my own thinking on the text.

2. The preacher must prayerfully interpret the text in its context using the established canons of interpretation: lexical, grammatical, and syntactical. Only when this is done should he turn to the commentaries, employing two or three of the best sources available. When in

doubt, the commentary surveys of D. A. Carson[17] and Tremper Longman[18] will offer seasoned help.

3. During the process, the preacher must naturally seek to determine wherein the text is a revelation of Jesus Christ, and must make the appropriate intra-canonical connections. Here, good commentaries may be helpful, as well as works like *Commentary on the New Testament Use of the Old Testament*[19] and the *New Dictionary of Biblical Theology*.[20]

4. The preacher must then confirm the central, unifying theme of the text in a simple sentence. Along with this, the preacher must articulate the aim of his exposition.

5. This done, the preacher must outline his exposition, using the literary structure of the text as a guide, and decide whether an inductive or deductive form of exposition best serves the sacred text.

6. As the preacher writes his manuscript or outline, he must use clear language that effectively communicates in his own cultural context, employing only those stories and illustrations that truly illuminate the text.

7. The preacher must then submit himself to the inspired text, so that it permeates his soul, to the effect that he is sympathetic to the text and desires its truth to be active in his life.

8. When the preacher stands in the pulpit, in full dependence upon the Holy Spirit, the truth of God's Word will flow in authentic power from his heart and over his lips and out to his people.

17. D. A Carson, *New Testament Commentary Survey* (Grand Rapids, MI: Baker Academic, 2013).

18. Tremper Longman III, *Old Testament Commentary Survey* (Grand Rapids, MI: Baker Academic, 2013).

19. G. K. Beale and D. A. Carson, *Commentary on the New Testament Use of the Old Testament* (Grand Rapids, MI: Baker, 2007).

20. T. Desmond Alexander and Brian S. Rosner, *New Dictionary of Biblical Theology: Exploring the Unity and Diversity of Scripture* (Downers Grove, IL: InterVarsity Press, 2000).

15

Patiently Sowing God's
Word in Pastoral Ministry

C. J. Mahaney

It is with great pleasure that I submit this chapter to a volume dedicated to honoring my friend Wayne Grudem. I am deeply grateful for Wayne's friendship, and I have learned so much from his example, his writings, and his teaching. One enduring lesson has been Wayne's love for God's Word and his intentional application of God's Word to all of life for God's glory. This chapter is inspired by Wayne's example.

In 1882, Charles Spurgeon observed, "It is to be feared that the Psalms are by no means prized as in the earlier ages of the Church."[1] One can only imagine what Spurgeon would say if he were alive today. As a pastor writing mainly to fellow pastors here, I think he would wonder if we treasure the Psalms adequately and deploy them appropriately in our personal lives, our preaching, and our ministries.

Do you share Spurgeon's fear in relation to the Psalms? Are the Psalms prized in your church? Do the Psalms function in the daily and weekly life of your congregation? What about in your own soul

---

1. Charles H. Spurgeon, in C. Richard Wells, "Conclusion," in *Forgotten Songs: Reclaiming the Psalms for Christian Worship*, ed. C. Richard Wells and Ray Van Neste (Nashville: B&H Academic, 2012), 203n1.

and in your own ministry? Do you prize the Psalms personally and devotionally? Do you bring the Psalter with you into ministry as an indispensable tool?

The Psalms a Gift

J. I. Packer once said, "The older I get, the more the psalms mean to me."[2] Do you find that to be your experience? As the years pass, is your love for the Psalms deepening? Is your skill in interpreting and applying them maturing? Pastor, if we don't cherish the Psalms personally, if we don't value the Psalms pastorally, and if we don't preach the Psalms consistently, then it is highly unlikely that the churches we serve will prize the Psalms. Spurgeon's fear will be realized in our hearts and in our congregations. The opportunity lies before us to rediscover the Psalms and their value for us personally and pastorally. Consider with me just a few reasons why the Psalms are a unique gift from God to us.

First, *the Psalms inform our experience.* There is not an experience of triumph or trial that hasn't been captured in the Psalms. There is not an emotion you will feel that hasn't been described and articulated in the Psalms. When we come to the Psalms, we discover that we are not alone. The Psalms equip us to interpret our experiences rightly by understanding our circumstances in relation to God.

Second, *the Psalms shape our expression.* The Psalms give us words to express to God our hopes and fears, our joys and sorrows, our worship and pain. Because of the Psalms, there is no moment or season of your life, be it adversity or prosperity, where you will lack a divinely inspired song for your soul to sing. God has kindly provided us with soul-comforting, heart-strengthening, burden-lifting songs for every conceivable experience, from the dark pit of unrelieved suffering and depression in Psalm 88 to the boisterous celebration of God's greatness and grace in Psalm 150. When the Lord *gives*, the Psalms provide us with a divine perspective of his gifts and prod us to gratefulness. When the Lord *takes away*, the Psalms teach us to lament and trust. As we humbly submit to these words, we will, as one writer put it, "grow into these words," even if we don't presently feel these words. The Psalms become a potent means of spiritual growth. Most important,

---

2. J. I. Packer, in Wells, "Conclusion," 110.

the Psalms were the hymnbook of our Savior: this was his songbook, even on the cross. Ultimately these songs point to him.

Third, *the Psalms equip our ministry*. Pastoral ministry involves preparing God's people for both prosperity and adversity. The Psalms are uniquely designed to equip God's people to respond appropriately to grace and to suffer well. The Psalms direct our gaze to the sovereignty, wisdom, and goodness of God so that we can trust and obey in every circumstance.

The Psalms are a unique gift from God and must inform our personal lives and pastoral ministry. The Psalms are to be prized, cherished, loved, explored, contemplated, sung, and experienced. If we do not have a plan to ensure that those we love and serve prize the Psalms, they will find many reasons to neglect them. In his book *Forgotten Songs*, Richard Wells identifies some of these reasons:

> Of course, even apart from the malaise of biblical illiteracy, there are special reasons for neglect of the psalms. The language of poetry doesn't easily connect in a sound-byte culture. The psalms call for time, not tweets—time to read, ponder, pray, digest. It's easy to be too busy for the psalms. Then again, the strong emotions of the psalms make many modern people uncomfortable—which is ironic since our culture seems to feed on feelings. . . . On top of everything else, strange to say, the psalms are just so . . . well . . . God intoxicated. We are fascinated with ourselves, the psalms are fascinated with God.[3]

Let us not become pastors who are too busy for the Psalms, uncomfortable with the emotions of the Psalms, or more fascinated with ourselves than with God himself. As goes the pastor's appreciation of the Psalms, so goes the church's.

I want to draw your attention to a psalm I have found particularly helpful in pastoral ministry, Psalm 126. This psalm should inform a pastor's prayer for the church and labor in the church. This psalm has served me immensely in lean seasons of ministry: times when fruitfulness hasn't seemed readily evident, times when sermons haven't seemed particularly inspiring, times when I've tended to be more aware of deficiencies in the church than of evidences of grace,

---

3. Wells, "Conclusion," 203–4.

times when joy in ministry has been a distant memory rather than a present reality.

These few verses contain a reflection on God's saving activity (126:1–3), a request for deliverance (126:4), and a realization that sowing God's Word precedes the reaping of all manner of joy and fruitfulness (126:5–6). Let us reflect on Psalm 126 and find fresh encouragement for the challenges of pastoral ministry.

The Psalmist's Reflection (Ps. 126:1–3)

When the LORD restored the fortunes of Zion,
    we were like those who dream.
Then our mouth was filled with laughter,
    and our tongue with shouts of joy;
then they said among the nations,
    "The LORD has done great things for them."
The LORD has done great things for us;
    we are glad.

The psalmist begins this song with a reflection upon a time when the people of God were liberated from captivity and exile. Scholars—the smart guys who serve us well with their commentaries—debate among themselves as to the exact occasion of this psalm. But regardless of the historical context, what is indisputable is the significance of the liberation and the suddenness of the liberation. This psalm reflects both the painful experience of captivity and the dramatic deliverance.

Derek Kidner notes, "Whether Zion's [restoration] was from famine or siege, captivity or plague, it had been obviously miraculous and widely talked about. It remained a vivid national memory."[4] In his reflection on this vivid national memory, the psalmist draws our attention to the experience of those set free. His description of their experience is animated and noisy, characterized by serious joy: "We were like those who dream." It was so good that they wondered, *is it real or is it a mirage?*

Then our mouth was filled with laughter
    and our tongue with shouts of joy. (Ps. 126:2)

---

4. Derek Kidner, *Psalms 73–150: A Commentary on Books III–V of the Psalms*, Tyndale Old Testament Commentaries (Downers Grove, IL: InterVarsity Press, 1973), 439.

Even the Gentile nations noticed and remarked: "The LORD has done great things for them" (126:2). In the next verse, the psalmist summarizes the experience:

> The LORD has done great things for us;
>   we are glad. (126:3)

So glad, their mouths were filled with laughter.

What makes you laugh? You can tell a lot about a person by what makes him or her laugh. Often we laugh when we observe or hear something we don't expect, particularly if it is absurd. Allow me to demonstrate: Jason Gay is an author and writes primarily about sports for *The Wall Street Journal*. I often enjoy his writing. He can be insightful and funny. He once tweeted from a New York City coffee shop, "There's a guy in this coffee shop sitting at a table, not on his phone, not on a laptop, just drinking coffee, like a psychopath."[5]

Perhaps, like me, you laughed when you read this. What is funny about this tweet? Well, you weren't expecting him to identify this guy as a psychopath when all he was doing was drinking a cup of "joe" in a coffee shop. The ending was a surprise—an absurd conclusion. You didn't see it coming, so it made you laugh.

Now consider this: nothing was more unexpected, unanticipated, or undeserved than your deliverance from the captivity of sin by the grace of God through the gospel. There is nothing funny about the wrath of God, but those who understand what they have been saved from can't help but experience the kind of overwhelming joy that leads to spontaneous, holy laughter.

In light of God's holiness and our sinfulness, the gracious provision of the Son of God to die as the substitute for our sins was the most unexpected event and undeserved expression of mercy in all of history. If you haven't humbly and gratefully laughed before God in response to the grace that he has shown you through the gospel, then it's possible you haven't understood how unexpected your salvation was. Maybe you have forgotten how unlikely it was that you would become an object of mercy. Pastor, are you still amazed at the grace of God in your life? Do you still marvel at your conversion?

---

5. https://twitter.com/jasongay/status/646301750346010624.

Are you astonished at the "difference between your receivings and your deservings?"[6]

When the psalmist reflects on the experience of gracious, sudden, dramatic liberation from captivity by God, he describes the response of those who were freed. They erupted in unrestrained laughter and shouts of joy. They were humanly incapable of liberating themselves from captivity because of their sin, but God graciously took action—action they did not deserve. He intervened and set them free from their captors. Their fortunes were restored. Once again, they found reason for joy. Once again, they found an occasion to laugh.

There is a very real sense in which every Christian can relate to this experience, having been captive to sin and delivered from sin by the grace of God through the proclamation of Christ crucified and risen from the dead. Every Christian shares this experience.

Think about your conversion. Was it not a surprise? In light of God's holiness and our sinfulness, your conversion and my conversion were most unexpected. It is all too easy to spend our days reflecting on many other things while failing to reflect on this most important thing. We must not let our pastoral role, which is temporary, obscure our personal deliverance, which is eternal. Remember how the Bible describes our deliverance? I pray you have not grown so familiar with these words that you are no longer affected by them:

> And you were dead in trespasses and sins in which you once walked, following the course of this world, following the prince of the power of the air, the spirit that is now at work in the sons of disobedience—among whom we all once lived in the passions of our flesh, carrying out the desires of the body and the mind, and were by nature children of wrath, like the rest of mankind. [Here comes the unexpected—the unfathomable really.] *But God*, being rich in mercy, because of the great love with which he loved us, even when we were dead in our trespasses, made us alive together with Christ—by grace you have been saved. (Eph. 2:1–5)

This description of our liberation from the captivity and consequences of sin—the wrath of God—is most unexpected because it is

---

6. Arthur Bennett, ed., "The Mover," in *The Valley of Vision* (Carlisle, PA: Banner of Truth, 1975), 8.

most undeserved. The effect should be delirious happiness gushing forth in unbridled laughter and joyous shouts. Perhaps you don't associate your story of coming to Christ with laughter. But your conversion should make you laugh for joy because of its unexpected and undeserved nature. What other experience in life could possibly leave us more surprised and more delighted than our salvation in Christ?

Alec Motyer writes about this outbreak of joy, "So throughout this psalm laughter, singing and rejoicing often . . . are evidence of a salvation to which the recipients have contributed nothing but subsequent joy. We took no part in it. It was done for us—we woke up to find it was true."[7] Perhaps it is time to wake up again and remember that you took no part in it. It was done for you. You and I contributed nothing but "subsequent joy."

We must never tire of reflecting on the miracle of our conversion, the miracle of our liberation from captivity to sin—a liberation which we did not initiate, to which we could not contribute, and for which we can only give thanks. When is the last time you reflected on the mercy and miracle of your conversion? It is well known that seventeenth-century philosopher Blaise Pascal kept a handwritten account of his conversion sewn into his coat. In his book *Union with Christ*, Rankin Wilbourne explains:

> Pascal kept this parchment on his person for eight years, moving it from coat to coat, so that it was literally next to his heart wherever he went. Pascal knew that while God would never forget him (Isa. 49:15), he was prone to forget God. So he sewed a reminder into his life, a daily tutorial. . . . And if Pascal, a genius, needed a reminder sewn into his coat, then how much more do we need to sew reminders into our lives?[8]

My fellow pastor, how can you sew a reminder of your conversion into your daily life? How can you regularly review the grace that has been shown to you in order to delight in God and his grace? Think of where you would be today if you weren't converted by the grace of God. It is a miracle of mercy, and we must remind ourselves often

---

7. Alec Motyer, *Psalms by the Day: A New Devotional Translation* (Fearn, Ross-Shire, UK: Christian Focus, 2016), 375.
8. Rankin Wilbourne, *Union with Christ: The Way to Know and Enjoy God* (East Sussex, UK: Cook, 2016), 242–43.

because we are so prone to forget. This most important thing is so easily eclipsed by the daily demands of pastoral ministry.

In light of this mercy, we can experience true joy that erupts in joyous laughter. This happiness is a God-given gift to the pastor who feels overwhelmed by pastoral responsibilities. When you find yourself overwhelmed by the cares of ministry, it's possible that you've lost sight of this mercy. And notice the difference this reflection made in the prayer life of the psalmist. As he reflected on his experience of liberation from captivity, it energized him to pray for revival in the present.

The Psalmist's Request (Ps. 126:4)

> Restore our fortunes, O LORD,
>   like streams in the Negeb!

Reflection on the experience of deliverance from the past provokes the psalmist to pray for a fresh experience of God's mercy in the present. This prayer reflects the challenges of real life. Time has passed, and the experience of dramatic deliverance and its accompanying joy has faded. It is no longer a felt reality. The vividness of the memory, however, inspires the psalmist to pray that his good and gracious God would do it yet again. So the psalmist prays for God to restore his people's fortunes.

The psalmist prays for another sudden and dramatic work of God where dry land is suddenly filled with water and comes to life, like the streams in the Negeb. It is a prayer that captive hearts would be suddenly liberated and laughing. These words are strikingly similar to the language in verse 1, only here they've been crafted into a prayer. In his commentary on the Psalms, Kidner helpfully points out that the psalmist presents two images of revival and renewal in verses 4–6: "The two images of renewal (4b, 5–6) are not only striking: they are complementary. The first of them is all suddenness, a sheer gift from heaven; the second is slow and arduous, with man allotted a crucial part to play in it."[9] So revival and renewal can be both sudden and slow.

The ancient world was familiar with sudden changes: although the desert region of the Negeb was dry for much of the year, after a heavy downfall, the barren wasteland would bloom into a desert garden

---

9. Kidner, *Psalms 73–150*, 439.

overnight. The psalmist views his life and the life of God's people as a barren desert. His appeal is for God to act suddenly and to rain down torrents of transforming grace.

Our experience of mercy in the past can provoke our prayer and inspire our expectation for revival personally, in our city, across our country, and around the world. Our experience of mercy should inspire us to pray and not tire of praying for others to have the same experience. Our hope is that they will discover grace suddenly and unexpectedly, like the Negeb flowering overnight. But the psalmist knows that God doesn't always act swiftly. In the final two verses of Psalm 126, he describes a second image of renewal and revival. While verse 4 describes the desert breaking out in sudden and surprising blooms, verses 5 and 6 depict a process that is slow and arduous, with man allotted a crucial part to play in it through sowing. This is particularly relevant to pastoral ministry and makes all the difference.

The Psalmist's Realization (Ps. 126:5–6)

Those who sow in tears
    shall reap with shouts of joy!
He who goes out weeping,
    bearing the seed for sowing,
shall come home with shouts of joy,
    bringing his sheaves with him.

Here, the psalmist recognizes that he must not only pray; he must also sow. In the earlier image, the results were as sudden as they were undeserved. In this second image the psalmist uses to depict God's intervening grace, the results come only after the hard work of sowing and a lengthy period of waiting. These results are undeserved as well. Both images must inform our pastoral ministry. There are times when God works suddenly and unexpectedly, and it appears we make little or no contribution. Those are my personal preference. That is how I prefer to roll. But normally the fruit comes only after the hard work of plowing and sowing and watering and weeding and waiting. Normally the slow precedes the sudden. The slow prepares the way for the sudden. Verse 4 depicts an appeal for the sudden work of God. Verses 5 and 6 describe slow and arduous work, "with man allotted a crucial part to play in it."

Here, the psalmist draws his imagery from the world of agriculture. It is a world of sowing and waiting. Take note of this imagery. Remember that the metaphors of the Bible are drawn from the world of agriculture, not technology or business. For most of us, this is a world we are unfamiliar with. When I was young, I was too cool for the 4-H Club or Future Farmers of America, so now I'm at a disadvantage and my ignorance doesn't serve me. But if we are going to benefit from this imagery, our ministry must be informed and inspired by this metaphor.

There is nothing idyllic about this illustration. This work of sowing is backbreaking, and it can be heartbreaking. Did you notice that this hard work of sowing is often done with "tears"?

> Those who sow in tears . . .
> He who goes out weeping . . . (Ps. 126:5–6)

To be faithful in pastoral ministry is to be familiar with having tears in your eyes. John Piper helps us to understand and apply this with these words:

> This psalm teaches the tough truth that there is work to be done whether I am emotionally up for it or not, and it is good for me to do it. Suppose you are in a season of heartache and discouragement, and it is time to sow seed. Do you say, "I can't sow the field this spring, because I am brokenhearted and discouraged"? If you do that, you will not eat in the winter. Suppose you say instead, "I am heartsick and discouraged. I cry if the milk spills at breakfast. I cry if the phone and doorbell ring at the same time. I cry for no reason at all, but the field needs to be sowed. That is the way life is. I do not feel like it, but I will take my bag of seeds and go out in the fields and do my crying while I do my duty. I will sow in tears."[10]

The hard work of sowing God's Word, sowing the gospel, sowing through serving, is often done with tears. It's often done with a broken heart and tear-filled eyes. My fellow pastor, where do you need to sow, even if you are in a season of heartache and discouragement?

- It could be continuing to sow the reading of Scripture and preaching the gospel into your own heart even if—and especially when—joy is a distant memory rather than a present reality.

---

10. John Piper, *A Godward Life* (Colorado Springs: Multnomah, 1997), 89–90.

- It might be continuing to sow into your children. It's all too easy to grow weary and tired from the exhausting work of teaching and training and discipline, particularly when there are no immediate results and no indication of fruitfulness. (When our children were growing up, my wife, Carolyn, would banish discouragement from my soul and put fresh faith and resolve in my soul by reminding me, "Dear, you are sowing; stop looking for immediate fruit.")
- For you, faithful sowing might mean continuing to sow the gospel with the lost even if you can't remember the last time someone you shared the gospel with was converted.
- Often, sowing involves preparing yet another sermon even if you don't feel like it, even if those you serve don't seem particularly appreciative of your preaching and appear to be more animated and appreciative when there is a guest speaker.
- Continuing to sow might mean faithfully reaching out to guests at your church, even when your soul is weighed down by the lack of growth in your church, or after you've been informed that one of your best families is leaving the church.
- It means discipling men, even while knowing they will be sent out from your church and that another congregation will reap the fruit of your sowing.
- It can mean continuing to sow by serving and leading and not giving up even after you hear from other pastors about how their churches are prospering and growing.

Where do you need to sow, even through tears? What do you need to sow? Do you have a strategy for sowing? You should. Every farmer does, whether he feels like it or not. And in God's kindness, the psalmist doesn't simply inform us of the challenging work of sowing; he also provides us with hope for our tear-filled sowing!

If we could look the psalmist in the eye, we would not only see tears; we would also perceive hope. In his tearful sowing he is certain of the graciousness of God. He is certain of the promise of God. He is certain of the purpose of God. He is certain that those who sow—even in tears—shall reap! And when (not if) they reap, their tears will be replaced by shouts of joy!

Psalm 126 calls us to share in this certainty! We are to sow the gospel in our hearts and in our churches and in our communities with this certainty! Those who sow in tears, those who go out weeping, bearing the seed of sowing, shall reap with shouts of joy, shall come home with shouts of joy bringing their sheaves with them. James Montgomery Boice explained that this verse has "been taken as a proverb by countless generations of God's people as they have looked up from the difficulties of their present work expecting blessings from God."[11]

So let me encourage you to look up from the plow, look up from your desk, look up from your seemingly fruitless labor, look up and be strengthened by this promise. Keep sowing God's Word; keep sowing the gospel; keep serving, even with tears in your eyes. Keep praying and keep sowing and don't be surprised or dismayed that the work is hard and sometimes heartbreaking. Keep sowing because the way to reap with songs and shouts of joy is to sow the seeds of those future blessings with tears, certain of the reaping that is to come.

Sowing precedes reaping. The slow precedes the sudden. Tears precede joy.

John Piper has one more thing to say to us on this:

> So here's the lesson: When there are simple, straightforward jobs to be done, and you are full of sadness, and tears are flowing easily, go ahead and do the jobs with tears. Be realistic. Say to your tears: "Tears, I feel you. You make me want to quit life. But there is a field to be sown (dishes to be washed, car to be fixed, sermon to be written). I know you will wet my face several times today, but I have work to do and you will just have to go with me. I intend to take a bag of seeds and sow. If you come along then you will just have to wet the rows."
>
> Then say, on the basis of God's Word, "Tears, I know you will not stay forever. The very fact that I just do my work . . . will in the end bring a harvest of blessing. . . . I believe that the simple work of my sowing will bring sheaves of harvest." And your tears will be turned to joy.[12]

---

11. James Montgomery Boice, *Psalms*, vol. 3, *Psalms 107–150* (Grand Rapids, MI: Baker, 1998), 1113.
12. John Piper, "Talking to Your Tears," Desiring God, July 15, 1991, http://www.desiringgod .org/articles/talking-to-your-tears.

My fellow pastor, I commend you for continuing to sow in the midst of heartbreak and tears. Take heart: your tears will be turned to joy. A harvest awaits. And if you've been contemplating quitting because you are tired of sowing with no sign of reaping, I want to say to you, I understand, but that is not an option for you. In Charles Spurgeon's *Lectures to My Students*, there is one lecture I encourage pastors to read each month. It's entitled "The Minister's Fainting Fits." In fact, it might be wise to read it every week. Many times over the years, these words have put fresh faith, joy, and courage into my soul. I pray this will be your experience as Mr. Spurgeon cares for your soul with these words:

> The lesson of wisdom is, *be not dismayed by soul-trouble.* Count it no strange thing, but a part of ordinary ministerial experience. Should the power of depression be more than ordinary, think not that all is over with your usefulness. Cast not away your confidence, for it hath great recompense of reward. Even if the enemy's foot be on your neck, expect to rise and overthrow him. . . . Live by the day—ay, by the hour. . . . Care more for a grain of faith than a ton of excitement. . . . Be not surprised when friends fail you: it is a failing world. . . . Be not amazed if your adherents wander away to other teachers: as they were not your all when with you, all is not gone from you with their departure. . . . Be content to be nothing, for that is what you are. . . . Set small store by present rewards; be grateful for earnests by the way, but look for the recompensing joy hereafter. Continue with double earnestness to serve your Lord when no visible result is before you. Any simpleton can follow the narrow path in the light: faith's rare wisdom enables us to march on in the dark with infallible accuracy, since she places her hand in that of her Great Guide. Between this and heaven there may be rougher weather yet, but it is all provided for by our covenant Head. In nothing let us be turned aside from the path which the divine call has urged us to pursue. Come fair or come foul, the pulpit is our watch-tower, and the ministry our warfare; be it ours, when we cannot see the face of our God, to trust under the shadow of his wings.[13]

My friend, all is not over with your usefulness. Continue with double earnestness to serve your Lord when no visible result is before

13. Charles Spurgeon, *Lectures to My Students* (Grand Rapids, MI: Zondervan, 1954), 164–65.

you. You must not stop sowing. And if you've put down your bag of seed, I want to encourage you—even challenge you—to pick it up and get back to work. Let us resolve afresh to die sowing the seeds of the gospel. For we shall reap, if not in this lifetime, then surely in the one to come, when we hear the Chief Shepherd himself say, "Well done, my good and faithful servant; your labor was not in vain."

Conclusion

Finally, we can't read Psalm 126:5–6 without thinking of the ultimate fulfillment of these verses in the person and work of Jesus Christ on the cross. Jesus himself would have been familiar with this psalm and would have understood it as ultimately being fulfilled in himself. Imagine the Son of God reading and reflecting on this psalm, knowing it pointed ultimately to him.

In his Gospel, Luke reminds us of a particular moment as the Son of God drew near to Jerusalem knowing that the hour for which he had come, the hour of his death, was fast approaching: "And when he drew near and saw the city, he wept over it saying, 'Would that you, even you, had known on this day the things that make for peace!'" (19:41–42). He would then proceed to a hill called Calvary, where he would sow himself through his death. He was the seed that had to fall into the ground and die, resulting in massive fruit. He died, certain the Father would raise him from the dead. He died, certain he would come home with shouts of joy bringing his sheaves with him. The author of Hebrews reminds us to look to Jesus, "who for the joy that was set before him endured the cross" (Heb. 12:2). And in just a matter of weeks after his death, resurrection, and ascension, we read that in response to Peter's proclamation of the gospel, "there were added that day about three thousand souls" (Acts 2:41).

Jesus entered Jerusalem weeping, sowing his life through his death on the cross. It was all so unexpected and surprising—stunning really. And the fruit was all so unexpected, surprising, and stunning. The fruit included sinners like you and me. And so the only appropriate response in light of the unexpected mercy is one of laughter, singing, and shouts of joy, for it is all the Lord's doing, and it is marvelous in our eyes.

16

The Spirit, the Word, and Revival

Ray Ortlund

I rejoice to join with the other contributors to this volume in honoring our friend Dr. Wayne Grudem with a Festschrift devoted to the theme of Holy Scripture, which has been central to Wayne's faithful life and ministry these many years.

Jonathan Edwards summarizes the historical progress of God's redemptive work with this striking observation:

> It may here be observed that, from the fall of man to our day, the work of redemption in its effect has mainly been carried on by remarkable communications of the Spirit of God. Though there be a more constant influence of God's Spirit always in some degree attending his ordinances, yet the way in which the greatest things have been done towards carrying on this work always have been by remarkable effusions at special seasons of mercy.[1]

George Smeaton complements the positive statement by Edwards with a more controversial but, in my opinion, equally valid assertion:

---

1. Jonathan Edwards, "A History of the Work of Redemption," in *The Works of Jonathan Edwards*, ed. Edward Hickman, 2 vols. (London, 1834; repr., Edinburgh: Banner of Truth, 1979),1:539.

No more mischievous and misleading theory could be propounded, nor any one more dishonouring to the Holy Spirit, than the principle . . . that because the Spirit was poured out at Pentecost, the Church has no need, and no warrant, to pray any more for the effusion of the Spirit of God. On the contrary, the more the Church asks the Spirit and waits for His communication, the more she receives.[2]

Our Lord's words in John 6:63 can align us with the long-standing ways of God for richly blessing his people, including our generation. Jesus said, "It is the Spirit who gives life; the flesh is no help at all. The words that I have spoken to you are spirit and life."

The Spirit, Generously Given

On that great Pentecost Sunday in the book of Acts, the apostle Peter said of the risen Jesus, "Being therefore exalted at the right hand of God, and having received from the Father the promise of the Holy Spirit, he has poured out this that you yourselves are seeing and hearing" (Acts 2:33). The people there did not have to "take it by faith." It was obvious to believers and unbelievers alike that something real was happening. What the crowds didn't understand, until Peter explained it, was that this experience was the heavenly glory of Jesus coming down through the outpouring of the Holy Spirit.

The risen Christ does not give us his Spirit grudgingly. John Stott conveys the magnitude of his generosity: "The whole Messianic era, which stretches between the two comings of Christ, is the age of the Spirit in which his ministry is one of abundance. Is not this the significance of the verb 'pour out'? The picture is probably of a heavy tropical rainstorm."[3]

The risen Lord *outgushes* with the Holy Spirit to make his glory, till now above, a felt experience here below. Jesus Christ is too great to remain a mere theory, even an orthodox theory. The Spirit comes down with abundant power to awaken us to Jesus as a gloriously captivating reality.

---

2. George Smeaton, *The Doctrine of the Holy Spirit* (repr., Edinburgh: Banner of Truth, 1974), 288–89.
3. John R. W. Stott, *The Message of Acts: The Spirit, the Church and the World* (Downers Grove, IL: InterVarsity Press, 1990), 73.

In Nashville, where I serve, a full-size replica of the Parthenon stands as a landmark in Centennial Park. At night it is bathed by flood-lights and quite spectacular. But no one walks up to the floodlights and says, "What amazing lights those are." People look at the building il-luminated by the floodlights and say, "How glorious the Parthenon is!" And so it is with the Holy Spirit floodlighting Jesus in the darkness of this world. Jesus said of the Spirit, "He will glorify me" (John 16:14). And the apostle Peter, filled with this Holy Spirit, said on that Pente-cost Sunday, "Men of Israel, hear these words: *Jesus of Nazareth . . .*" (Acts 2:22). The Holy Spirit turns the concepts of the gospel into vivid existential clarity that dispels our natural darkness.

The Flesh, No Help

But if that is so, and it is, then why do we not receive this experience more frequently and more fully? One part of the answer must be, sadly, that we are disinclined to the ways of the Spirit. That is *why* Jesus said, "The flesh is no help at all."

We do not believe that. We are self-assured people. We see ourselves as effective in life and ministry. We can plant churches, start move-ments, organize campaigns, all of which are good, in their way. But all good things accomplished with the help that the flesh provides leave the world as it is. We might feel better about ourselves for what we have done. But still, the Enemy comes in like a flood, and people are swept away without even understanding what is happening to them. So Jesus gave us these uncompromising, unsettling words in John 6:63, to help us think in terms of what only he can do. We are therefore intrigued by our Lord's strong assertion, with its hint of admonition: "It is the Spirit who gives life; the flesh is no help at all."

Naturally, we would not disagree with our Lord. As a matter of theological affirmation, his statement is clearly unarguable. But at a practical level, we need to be reminded often of the weakness and fu-tility of the flesh. Geerhardus Vos redirects our confidence toward the Spirit of God when he writes of

> the tremendous irresistible power with which the Spirit makes his
> impact and produces his results in every sphere of operation. . . .
> The fundamental note in his activity was that of divine, unique
> forth-putting of energy. In the Old Testament this can be tested

> easily; one passage for many may suffice: "Now the Egyptians are men, and not God; and their horses flesh, and not Spirit," Isaiah 31:3. But, according to this statement "flesh" is the direct opposite of "Spirit" for no other reason than that *its* characteristic is inertia, lack of power, such as can only be removed by the Spirit of God. The two terms are not only correlatives but are mutually exclusive.[4]

That enduring reality is why all grandiosity in ministry fails, as it should. It is inertia disguised as energy. Only the Spirit can display the glory of Jesus with saving power. If our generation is to experience Jesus as the true King of Glory, then we must honestly admit our weakness and realign our hearts moment by moment with the ministry of the Holy Spirit as our only hope.

One Hope, Two Dangers

Our Lord's claim in John 6:63, therefore, leads us to a solemn awareness that we must do the Lord's work in the Lord's way for our work really to be the Lord's work.[5] We might have thought we could choose between two categories: doing the Lord's work versus doing the Devil's work. But the truth is that we are always choosing between three categories:

1. Doing the Lord's work in the Lord's way, for his glory
2. Doing the Lord's work in our own way, for our glory
3. Doing the Devil's work

Our natural self-assurance will never warn us about how these three approaches interrelate. The great divide is not between options 2 and 3—doing the Lord's work in our own way versus doing the Devil's work. The great divide is between options 1 and 2—doing the Lord's work in the Lord's way, for his glory alone, versus doing the Lord's work in our own way, for our glory, for our self-display, for us to be impressive. John the Baptist articulated the humility essential to our being involved in what is truly of the Lord: "He must increase, but I must decrease" (John 3:30). None of us would say, "Jesus must decrease, and I must

---

4. Geerhardus Vos, *The Pauline Eschatology* (repr., Grand Rapids, MI: Baker, 1979), 300, emphasis original.

5. I gratefully acknowledge my debt to Francis A. Schaeffer, "The Lord's Work in the Lord's Way," in *No Little People: Sixteen Sermons for the Twentieth Century* (Downers Grove, IL: InterVarsity Press, 1974), 61–75.

increase." But we might feel within, without even realizing it, "Jesus and I can increase together. I'll be big about this. After all, I owe him a lot." All self-exaltation is of the flesh, and the flesh is no help at all. There is no power in the flesh, but only inertia. The Spirit shines to floodlight the glory of Jesus only.

Or we might think that the difference between doing the Lord's work in the Lord's way and doing the Lord's work in our own way is only a matter of degree and emphasis and nuance. We might think that the Lord's work in the Lord's way is an upgrade on the Lord's work in our own way. But it is not a difference of degree; it is a difference of kind. Doing the Lord's work in our own way is not, say, a 5 on a scale of 1 to 10, while doing the Lord's work in the Lord's way is an 8 or 9, or even a 10 on a good day. No, doing the Lord's work in our own way is betrayal. It is a stab in the Lord's back. It is using his real glory to enhance our own false glory. That is not a 5 on the scale. It is not a 1. It is evil. Doing the Lord's work in our own way for our own glory and doing the Devil's work are the same.

If this is so, then is there any higher priority in every generation than to stop and pray and consider what it means to do the Lord's work in the Spirit *to the exclusion of the flesh*? Many important matters press upon us all. But what is more important than that?

In the cultural upheaval and intensity of our times, our nation does not need more "successful" churches and ministries making an impact by deploying whatever trendy methods will generate buzz and lure people in and reinforce our already self-exalting lifestyles. When Paul warned the elders in Ephesus about leaders who cultivate a personal following—"to draw away the disciples *after them*"—Paul called those self-serving leaders "fierce wolves . . . speaking twisted things" (Acts 20:29–30). Any ministry with the wrong kind of attractive power, however much that ministry might be admired, with thousands of people flocking in—that kind of ministry is a total disaster brilliantly disguised as a massive success. If we have to choose—and inevitably every one of us does have to choose—it is better to fail in the weakness of the Spirit than succeed in the power of the flesh. Why? Because even a failure in the Spirit will still play some key role in the real battle being fought in the heavenlies in this generation. But a ministry making it big by the strategies of the flesh makes itself irrelevant to the real cause of Christ in the world today. It is concealing his true glory just as effectively as any adult bookstore, and maybe more so. How could it be otherwise? "The mind that is set on the flesh is hostile to God, for it does not submit to God's law; indeed, it cannot" (Rom. 8:7).

Peter illustrates how we can lose our way. When he tried to persuade Jesus to bypass the cross, the Lord said to him, "Get behind me, Satan" (Matt. 16:23). How did Peter, the lead disciple, go so shockingly wrong? Jesus explained: "You are not setting your mind on the things of God, but on the things of man." Peter did not have to set his mind on the things of Satan in order to become useful to Satan; all he had to do was set his mind on the things of man—on understandable human things, like survival. It is easy to play into Satan's hands. Even Peter did so.

What's more, in the immediately preceding paragraph in Matthew's Gospel, Peter had borne witness to Jesus as the Christ, the Son of the living God. And Jesus explained to him, "Flesh and blood has not revealed this to you, but my Father who is in heaven" (Matt. 16:17). How disturbing, then, that Peter went right on to speak under the opposite influence—Satan himself. The unsettling insight we gain here is that acting in the flesh rather than in the Spirit is a Christian problem. It is a continuing problem for people who know Jesus by real divine grace. But Peter did not perceive the difference between the illumination of the Father and the darkness of Satan. Jesus had to tell Peter what was really going on. Peter did not consciously decide for Satan. All he had to do was proceed with the intuitive thoughts of man, the instincts of the flesh, without allowing himself to be overruled by the humbling of the cross. If we are not consciously redirecting ourselves into the counterintuitive ways of the Spirit, the Lord might say to us as, in fact, he said to none other than Peter, "You are a hindrance to me" (Matt. 16:23).

To promote the cause of Christ in the flesh rather than the Spirit, to do the Lord's work with the covert purpose of floodlighting our own talents and importance—that is being distracting and even destructive with what feels promising and exciting and impressive. To do the Lord's work in the Spirit for the glory of Jesus is costly deep within. There is a cross we must embrace. But it is glorious to serve the Lord in the power of the Lord for the glory of the Lord. He himself is in it, and he is our resurrection life.

In the Bible Belt, where I live, we are still conservative enough that we accept God-talk, even Jesus-talk. The great divide in the Bible Belt is not between Christianity and secularism. The great divide is between the real Jesus and our false Jesuses. We in the American South like Jesus and want to keep him around because we have redefined him. We have invented our own Jesus Junior, who always forgives us, never judges us, guarantees us a place in heaven, and is small enough to fit conveniently into the margins of our crowded weekend schedules. He knows his place, and he never makes demands, since he is all about "grace." But our pet Jesus is a projection of our own self-idealization and an utterly false religion. Any Jesus who never confronts sin cannot be the Jesus who died for sin. And any ministry that obscures his true glory is actively advancing the dis-hallowing of his holy name and assisting the advance of full-scale secularism. All we have to do to become a hindrance to him is think of him with the thoughts of man—that is, our own thoughts.

Taking Our Lord's Words to Heart

We therefore come to our Lord's words in John 6:63 with all the more attentive reverence: "It is the Spirit who gives life; the flesh is no help at all. The words that I have spoken to you are spirit and life." Each phrase deserves careful consideration.

"It is the Spirit who gives life; the flesh is no help at all." Jesus already drew this contrast in his conversation with Nicodemus: "That which is born of the flesh is flesh, and that which is born of the Spirit is spirit" (John 3:6). Why is that so? Because "nothing can carry us beyond the limits of its own realm."[6] We accept that we are actively engaged in the display of the glory of Jesus through our ministries of the gospel. But our involvement is not causational, nor must our participation be limited to the realm of our own capacities. "The Spirit gives life" (2 Cor. 3:6). We are saved "by the washing of regeneration and renewal of the Holy Spirit" (Titus 3:5). According to the Nicene Creed of AD 325, the Holy Spirit is "the Lord and Giver of life."

What sets Christianity apart from all false religion everywhere is not only God's grace in justification but also God's power in regeneration

---

6. B. F. Westcott, *The Gospel according to St. John* (repr., Grand Rapids, MI: Eerdmans, 1973), 109.

and sanctification and service and revival and comfort and guidance and illumination and all the ongoing ministries of the Spirit. The finished work of Christ on the cross and the endless powers of the Holy Spirit—that is unique to Christianity and a continual adjustment even for us Christians. Moment by moment, real Christianity is coming down to us from beyond all this world and dependent upon nothing in this world. It is not primarily management but primarily miracle. The Holy Spirit, the Lord and Giver of life, comes down to create the atmosphere of heaven in the world today, so that more people can experience Jesus and come to him and be saved and flourish forever.

In the experience of the early church, on Pentecost Sunday, "suddenly there came from heaven a sound like a mighty rushing wind" (Acts 2:2). The suddenness caught the people by surprise, with no buildup, no working up of people's emotions. The sound came from heaven, not from anything on earth. It came as an undeniable reality, observable by all. The Holy Spirit was giving life, as only he can. And why are we told this? God put the account of Acts 2 in the Bible because he wants to put the power of Acts 2 in our lives and our churches, to make Jesus more real to us than we ourselves can ever make him. Jesus said, "But you shall receive power when the Holy Spirit has come upon you, and you will be my witnesses" (Acts 1:8). The risen Lord breathed upon the disciples and said, "Receive the Holy Spirit" (John 20:22). He said, "You are clothed with power from on high" (Luke 24:49). He said, "Apart from me you can do nothing" (John 15:5). We can do much without Jesus; but we cannot do the work of Jesus without Jesus and his Spirit. The apostle Paul understood his own ministry as so dependent upon and so filled with divine power that he summed up his life work as "the ministry of the Spirit" (2 Cor. 3:8).

The only real glory we will ever experience in all this world comes down from above. Paul had to help the Corinthians see that: "The natural person does not accept the things of the Spirit of God, for they are folly to him, and he is not able to understand them because they are spiritually discerned" (1 Cor. 2:14). Well-meaning unregenerate people in our churches cannot understand what we are talking about, because they do not experience Jesus at a spiritual level. He is only a concept, an ethical ideal. Until the Spirit awakens them, they will always expect the wrong things from us. We who lead can feel the pressure of that. But we should never retool our ministries so that people who reject Jesus will still accept us. There is no glory in human popularity; but there is great glory in the cross of Jesus. The Holy Spirit will always make sure of that, until the second coming of Christ.

Harold O. J. Brown, in *The Sensate Culture*, helps us understand how we can be squeezed into the mold of our shallow culture:

> Because its purpose is entertainment, and because people are more easily amused by the comical and ridiculous than by the noble and edifying, sensate art readily resorts to comedy, farce, satire and ridicule. In order to avoid boring the viewer or hearer, it [sensate culture, that is, the flesh] constantly changes, always looking for something new and exciting. . . . "It stands and falls by its external appearance, [making] lavish use of pomp and circumstance, colossality, stunning techniques, and other means of external adornment."[7]

Incarnational contextualization of the gospel should be modest. The Word became flesh, like us, not like a Super Bowl half-time extravaganza. No one takes hype seriously enough to stake his or her life on it. Many might like it. They might pay to go see it. But it does not change them. After the momentary excitement, it leaves them as they were before. And that is our opportunity as Christians. Any church with modest resources has all the potential for the breakthrough power of the early church. Simplicity and honesty are advantages, because that is where the Spirit moves for the glory of Someone Else.

Even thoughtful unbelievers understand the importance of honest realism. An article at the Gibson guitar website recalls an unusual moment in late-1960s rock music:

> Of all the albums that formed the soundtrack to 1967's "Summer of Love," *The Doors* is the one least tethered to its time. More importantly, The Doors' self-titled disc remains one of the greatest debuts in rock history. . . . To this day, few albums sound more inspired. "We stayed away from trendy clichés . . . ," producer Paul Rothchild said in the Jim Morrison biography, *Break On Through*.

---

7. Harold O. J. Brown, *The Sensate Culture: Western Civilization between Chaos and Transformation* (Dallas: Word, 1996), 39, quoting Pitirim A. Sorokin, *The Crisis of Our Age*, 2nd ed. (Oxford: Oneworld, 1992), 28–29.

"I asked the band if they wanted to be remembered in 20 years, and they said, Yes. I told them that, in that case, we couldn't use any tricks. It had to stay honest and it had to be pure."[8]

I have to believe that the servants of the living God can be at least as shrewd as Jim Morrison and the Doors.

Faking it in the flesh, with appearances that exaggerate and falsify our reality, is a perennial temptation in ministry. But it accomplishes nothing life-giving, nothing that lasts, nothing that *Christ* will ever say is of Christ. *The flesh is no help at all.* It is far more hopeful to say today what Charles Haddon Spurgeon said so long ago:

> We must confess that just now we have not the outpouring of the Holy Spirit that we could wish. Many are being converted, but we are, none of us, labouring as our hearts could desire. Oh, that I could feel the Spirit of God in me, till I was filled to the brim. . . . We seek not for extraordinary excitements, those spurious attendants of genuine revivals, but we do seek for the pouring-out of the Spirit of God. There is a secret operation which we do not understand; it is like the wind, we know not whence it cometh nor whither it goeth; yet, though we understand it not, we can and do perceive its divine effect. It is this breath of Heaven which we want. The Spirit is blowing upon our churches now with his genial breath. Oh, that there would come a mighty rushing wind that would carry everything before it, so that even the dry bones might be filled with life and be made to stand up before the Lord, an exceeding great army. This is the lack of the times. May this come as a blessing from the Most High![9]

Where then do we turn? *How* do we seek this blessing from the Most High in such a way that he would consider himself truly sought?

"The words that I have spoken to you are spirit and life." Here our Lord explains how he gets his life-giving Spirit into us. He does it by his words. J. C. Ryle paraphrases the force of our Lord's statement in his typically convincing way:

---

8. http://www.gibson.com/News-Lifestyle/Features/en-us/the-doors-0721.aspx.
9. C. H. Spurgeon, in *Lectures Delivered before the Young Men's Christian Association in Exeter Hall from November 1858 to February 1859* (London: James Nisbet, 1859), 168–69.

It is the words of Christ brought home to the hearts of men by the Spirit, which are the great agents employed in quickening and giving spiritual life to men. The Spirit impresses Christ's words on a man's conscience. These words become the parent of thoughts and convictions in the man's mind. From these thoughts spring all the man's spiritual life.[10]

Moreover, Westcott observes the emphatic function of the pronoun *I* in our Lord's assertion, such that Jesus, as opposed to any prophet before him, including Moses, is the focal point.[11] His words of grace for the undeserving and of resurrection for the dead are his own appointed means of renewal.

Interestingly, Jesus does not refer to "the *word* that I have spoken to you," the overall gist of his message, which might settle into our minds as vague generalities. But Jesus insists on "the *words*," the actual sayings with their specificity and definiteness. Earlier in John 6 Jesus fed the five thousand. They loved that. They thought, *This guy can do anything. We can eat for free every day!* So they wanted to make him king. But Jesus refused. Then he told them something about real eating and drinking: "Unless you eat the flesh of the Son of Man and drink his blood, you have no life in you" (6:53). But they did not like those words. He sounded like a cult leader. If only he had put it another way, with different words, maybe they would have gone along with him. But he said it the way he did to make clear the way into the only life that is truly life. He chose his words not to block the way but to open it up. So Peter declared in verse 68, "You have the words of eternal life." Jesus had to speak in surprising ways, because, to us, real life is surprising. We must make many midcourse corrections, realigning with his words and ways continually.

We thrive not primarily on the general ideas of the Bible but on its actual sayings, one verse at a time, with its nouns and verbs and prepositions and conjunctions. The *words* are where we drill down into the life that comes from the Spirit.

Personally, the moments in my own life when I have been most savingly changed have been marked by careful attention to the words of

---

10. J. C. Ryle, *Expository Thoughts on the Gospels: John 1:1 through John 10:9* (Grand Rapids, MI: Zondervan, n.d.), 416–17.
11. Westcott, *St. John*, 110.

the Lord. For example, I will never forget the first time I read the words of Romans chapter 9 with detailed attention. I had always avoided Romans 9. I was afraid of it. But this time I was reading it carefully because I had to, as a course assignment. Moreover, I was reading the Greek text, so it was slow going, one word at a time. And verse 18 snuck up on me. I did not see it coming. I did not have time to duck. The words leapt out at me: "So then he has mercy on whomever he wills, and he hardens whomever he wills" (Rom. 9:18).

I was stunned. I could not deny what the words were saying. For the first time in my life I stopped feeling big, with a small God at the margin of my existence playing a support role in my drama. To my own surprise, I felt joyfully small before a great God high above me as a mighty Savior, and I wanted to get down low before him in worship. Suddenly there came from heaven a mighty rushing wind of change into my heart through the words of the Lord. It was of the Spirit. And it proved to be a permanent change, redefining my reality from then on. But I did not plan this. I did not cause it. I did not even want it. The words came and found me and ambushed me, surprising me with a gift of new life from far beyond myself, a gift I did not even know existed. Only the Spirit puts us down on our faces before the Lord with reviving power. Our self-exalting flesh never does that.

The words of the Lord get us past the glib pre-understanding we bring to the Bible. They penetrate to the deepest core of our being as his appointed delivery system for his Spirit and his life. In all our ministry efforts, therefore, what the Spirit will surely bless with newness of life are the words of the Lord, with the power of the Lord, for the glory of the Lord. As Jeremiah said so long ago,

> Your words were found, and I ate them,
>   and your words became to me a joy
>   and the delight of my heart. (Jer. 15:16)

That is the Holy Spirit reviving the church from generation to generation, until the work is done and our Lord returns.

It is the Spirit who gives us life; the flesh is no help at all. The words that he has spoken to us are Spirit and life.

17

The Glory of God as the Ground of the Mind's Certainty and the Goal of the Soul's Satisfaction

John Piper

My aim in this chapter is to show the relationships between the *Word* of God, the *glory* of God, the *satisfaction* of the human soul, and the *certainty* of the human mind.[1]

And the main point is that, in and through the *Word* of God—the Bible—the *glory* of God becomes the *ground* of the mind's certainty, and the *goal* of the soul's satisfaction.

Or to put it another way: In the Bible, the glory of God reveals itself to be inescapably *real* to the mind, and incomparably *rewarding* to the heart. Nothing could be more true, and nothing could be more precious. Undeniable truth, unsurpassed treasure.

This has an amazing implication, and I'll state it four ways:

---

1. This chapter began as a sermon delivered under the same title in Rock Hill, South Carolina, October 9, 2015, accessed at https://www.desiringgod.org/messages /the-glory-of-god-as-the-ground-of-the-mind-s-certainty-and-the-goal-of-the-soul-s-satisfaction.

1. The quest for *truth* and the quest for *joy* turn out to be the same quest.
2. The path to unshakable *conviction* and the path to unending *contentment* are the same path.
3. *Knowing* for sure and *rejoicing* forever happen by the same discovery of the glory of God in the Word of God.
4. The way you *know* for sure what is *true* and the way you find your supreme treasure are the same, namely, by seeing the glory of God in the Word of God, especially in the saving work of the Son of God, Jesus Christ.

The Goal of the Soul's Satisfaction

I have devoted most of my life to trying to understand and proclaim and live the relationship between God's glory and our happiness. In God's providence, this is partly because of the way I grew up, and partly because the ultimate goal of God in creating and redeeming the world is really written on the human heart. Every human heart!

Deep down, under the repressions of sin, is written: *You were made for the glory of God. You were made to reflect the worth of your Maker. And you were made to do this by being more satisfied in him than in anything else.* Every person knows, deep down, that we magnify the worth of what we enjoy most. And we know that God is most to be magnified. God is worth more than anything else. And therefore God is to be enjoyed more than anything else. This is written on the heart of every person.

But sin—the bondage to self-exaltation, instead of God-exaltation—has torn the single fabric of our happiness and God's glory apart. And neither of them can come to a proper expression without the other.

So when I was growing up, I knew two things beyond the shadow of a doubt. One, because of what my parents taught me and what I saw in the Bible, and the other, because of what I saw in my own soul and could not deny. On the one hand, I knew that God intended for me to glorify him. My father loved the glory of God, and 1 Corinthians 10:31 was woven into my mind with clarity and certainty: "Whether you eat or drink, or whatever you do, do all to the glory of God."

And on the other hand, I knew I wanted to be happy. And I knew this was not a choice I was making. I didn't choose to want to be happy.

When I pondered who I was, at the bottom of my being, I was a wanter, a desirer, a craver. My heart was—and is—a desire factory. And I know now what I didn't know then, namely, that this is the way human beings were created by God. This is not a result of the fall. This is not sin. This is part of what it means to be human. Humans are designed by God to desire—to seek and find happiness, to long for and discover joy, to want and attain full and lasting satisfaction. Namely, happiness in God, joy in God, satisfaction in God.

But when I was growing up, I couldn't put the two together: God's demand for glory and my craving for happiness. For some reason, these two always seemed to be at odds. It seemed that I would have to choose—as if that were possible—between being happy and glorifying God. There were subtle messages that seemed to say: *Are you willing to lay down your desires and choose God's will?* And there are Bible verses that sound just like that. Like 1 Peter 4:2, "[You should live] the rest of the time in the flesh no longer for human passions but for the will of God." And Mark 8:34, "If anyone would come after me, let him deny himself and take up his cross and follow me."

And so the thought that God never intended his greatest glory and our greatest happiness to be alternatives either didn't occur to me or didn't take root the way it should have. The thought that somehow God might be glorified in me by my being happy in him wasn't part of my conscious faith.

And then, when I was about twenty-two years old, everything began to change. Three waves of new insight broke over me. It was terrifying and exhilarating. And changed the rest of my life. I would not be writing this without them.

First, I saw that the pursuit of God's glory not only was supposed to be my ultimate goal, but also was God's ultimate goal. From cover to cover the Bible showed God doing everything he does for his glory—to uphold and display and communicate his own greatness and beauty to the world.

> For my name's sake I defer my anger;
> > for the sake of my praise I restrain it for you,
> > that I may not cut you off.
> Behold, I have refined you, but not as silver;
> > I have tried you in the furnace of affliction.

For my own sake, for my own sake, I do it,
> for how should my name be profaned?
My glory I will not give to another. (Isa. 48:9–11)

This raised the stake of my pursuit of the glory of God as high as imaginable. I was being called to join God in God's self-exaltation.

The second wave that broke over me was the discovery that my desires were not too strong but too weak, and that the remedy for my early perplexity was not getting rid of desires but glutting them on God.

I saw this first in C. S. Lewis while standing in Vroman's Bookstore on Colorado Avenue in Pasadena, California, reading the first page of "The Weight of Glory":

> The New Testament has lots to say about self-denial, but not about self-denial as an end in itself. We are told to deny ourselves and to take up our crosses in order that we may follow Christ; and nearly every description of what we shall ultimately find if we do so contains an appeal to desire. If there lurks in most modern minds the notion that to desire our own good and earnestly to hope for the enjoyment of it is a bad thing, I submit that this notion has crept in from Kant and the Stoics and is no part of the Christian faith. Indeed, if we consider the unblushing promises of reward and the staggering nature of the rewards promised in the Gospels, it would seem that Our Lord finds our desires not too strong, but too weak. We are half-hearted creatures, fooling about with drink and sex and ambition when infinite joy is offered us, like an ignorant child who wants to go on making mud pies in a slum because he cannot imagine what is meant by the offer of a holiday at the sea. We are far too easily pleased.[2]

This was amazing to me. Then I began to see it all over the Bible.

> As a deer pants for flowing streams,
> > so pants my soul for you, O God.
> My soul thirsts for God,
> > for the living God.
> When shall I come and appear before God? (Ps. 42:1–2)

---

2. C. S. Lewis, "The Weight of Glory," in *The Weight of Glory and Other Addresses*, ed. Walter Hooper (New York: Simon and Schuster, 1996), 25–26.

Then I will go to the altar of God,
    to God my exceeding joy. (Ps. 43:4)

Delight yourself in the LORD,
    and he will give you the desires of your heart. (Ps. 37:4)

Serve the LORD with gladness!
Come into his presence with singing! (Ps. 100:2)

Rejoice in the Lord always; again I will say, rejoice. (Phil. 4:4)

This mandate from God to enjoy God is not marginal. It is central and pervasive. Being satisfied in God is not icing on the cake of Christianity. It is the essence and the heart of Christianity. Christianity is not a religion of willpower and decisions to do things we don't want to do. It is a supernatural new birth of the human heart to want God more than we want anything else. Desires for God are not peripheral. They are demanded and they are essential.

And then came the third wave—the insight that God being glorified and my being satisfied are not in competition. They are not even separate. They both come about in the same act: God is most glorified in us when we are most satisfied in him. I saw this with the help of Jonathan Edwards, where he said,

God glorifies Himself toward the creatures also in two ways: 1. By appearing to . . . their understanding. 2. In communicating Himself to their hearts, and in their rejoicing in . . . the manifestations which He makes of Himself. . . . God is glorified not only by His glory's being seen, but by its being rejoiced in. When those that see it delight in it, God is more glorified than if they only see it. His glory is then received by the whole soul, both by the understanding and by the heart.[3]

Then I saw it in Philippians 1:20–21: "It is my eager expectation and hope that I will not be at all ashamed, but that with full courage now as always Christ will be honored in my body, whether by life or by death. For to me to live is Christ, and to die is gain." How is

3. Jonathan Edwards, *The Works of Jonathan Edwards*, vol. 13, *The "Miscellanies," Entry Nos. a–z, aa–zz, 1–500*, ed. Thomas A. Schafer (New Haven, CT: Yale University Press, 1994), 495 (no. 448).

Christ honored or magnified in Paul's body? Whether by life or death! How by death? For to me to die is gain! Why? Because we go to be with him. Which means Christ is magnified—shown to be magnificent—when I am so satisfied in him that when death takes from me every earthly possession, I say: *Gain.* Christ is most magnified in me when I am most satisfied in him, especially in the moments of suffering and death.

And I have spent the last fifty years now trying to work out the implications of that truth—which I call Christian Hedonism. The truth that the pathway to glorifying God and to satisfying the soul are the same path. If you try to separate them, you will not glorify God, and you will not find lasting happiness.

The Ground of the Mind's Certainty

Now suppose someone says, at this point, "You've staked an awful lot on the Bible. How do you know it's true? You treat it as God's Word. Why? How do you know it's God's Word?"

And here is the amazing thing, and the point of this chapter. That question does not take us in a different direction than we have been going so far. On the contrary, as I said at the beginning,

1. The quest for *truth* and the quest for *joy* turn out to be the same quest.
2. The path to unshakable *conviction* and the path to unending *contentment* are the same path.
3. *Knowing* for sure and *rejoicing* forever happen in the same discovery of the glory of God in the Word of God.
4. The way that God has planned for us to *know* for sure what is *true* and the way he planned for us to find our supreme treasure are the same, namely, by seeing the glory of God in the Word of God, especially in the saving work of the Son of God, Jesus Christ.

I wrote a book about this called *A Peculiar Glory: How the Christian Scriptures Reveal Their Complete Truthfulness.* And the way the Scriptures reveal their complete truthfulness is by embodying, in their words and their meaning, the self-authenticating glory of God, so that whoever has eyes to see can see it and know that this is the Word of

God. The glory of God is really there. It is not in the eye of the beholder. It is objectively in the Word of God. If the veil is lifted from the eyes of the heart (Eph. 1:18), we see it and we know, just as we know that the sun has risen.

And so it turns out that in the Word of God the glory of God is both the *ground* of the mind's certainty and—as we have seen—the *goal* of the soul's satisfaction. The glory of God shows itself to be inescapably *real* to the mind—there's no denying it—and incomparably *rewarding* to the heart. When your eyes are opened, nothing could be more true, and nothing could be more satisfying. Both in one seeing of the glory of God! God intends for us to know the truth of the Bible by means of seeing the glory of God in it.

Ever since I first got serious about the question of how we know the Bible is true, it has seemed to me that the most urgent question is not how to provide arguments that convince modern atheists (Sam Harris, Richard Dawkins, Christopher Hitchens), but rather how it is that an uneducated, Muslim villager in the bush of Nigeria or a preliterate tribesman in Papua New Guinea can know that the message of the Bible is true so that, three weeks after hearing and believing it, he has the courage to die for his conviction—and not be a fool.

That, to me, is a far more urgent question than how to answer secular skeptics.

And I believe God's answer to that question is that his divine glory, especially the glory of God's interwoven majesty and meekness, climaxing in Christ, pervades the Bible and shows it to be God's reliable Word.

Here are a few sightings or analogies of how the peculiar glory of God is meant to bring us to the truth of God's Word.

Jonathan Edwards saw the issue clearly and pointed the way. From 1751 to 1758, Edwards was pastor of the church in the frontier town of Stockbridge, Massachusetts, and was a missionary to the Indians. His concern for Indian evangelization extended back into his pastorate at Northampton. And you can see this in these comments from *Religious Affections*, written about ten years earlier:

> Miserable is the condition of the Houssatunnuck Indians and others, who have lately manifested a desire to be instructed in

Christianity, if they can come at no evidence of the truth of Christianity, sufficient to induce them to sell all for Christ, in any other
way but this [path of historical reasoning].⁴

The mind ascends to the truth of the gospel but by one step, and
that is its divine glory. . . . Unless men may come to a reasonable
solid persuasion and conviction of the truth of the gospel, by the
internal evidences of it, . . . by a sight of its glory; it is impossible
that those who are illiterate, and unacquainted with history, should
have any thorough and effectual conviction of it at all.⁵

So Edwards is arguing that the path to a well-grounded conviction
of the truth of the gospel, and of the Scriptures that tell that story, is a
path that the Nigerian villager and the Papuan tribesman can follow.
It is the path of seeing the glory of God in the Word of God.

*A second sighting of how God's glory authenticates the Word of
God is the analogy with the glory of God in nature.* Psalm 19:1 says
that "the heavens declare the glory of God." And Romans 1:19–21 says,

What can be known about God is *plain to them*, because God has
shown it to them. For his invisible attributes, namely, his eternal
power and divine nature, have been *clearly perceived*, ever since the
creation of the world, in the things that have been made. So they are
without excuse. For although *they knew* God, they did not honor
him as God or give thanks to him, but they became futile in their
thinking, and their foolish hearts were darkened.

This means, then, that if God holds us accountable to seeing his
glory by means of the created world, how much more will he hold us
accountable to seeing his glory by means of his inspired Word.

My guess is that very few of us have stumbled over the claim that
the heavens tell the glory of God. Not the glory of the heavens. The
glory of God! Do you see it? Do your physical eyes become the lenses
through which your spiritual eyes—what Paul calls "the eyes of your
hearts" (Eph. 1:18)—see not just nature, but the very glory of the God
of nature? If so, you have an idea of what I am talking about, because

4. Jonathan Edwards, *The Works of Jonathan Edwards*, vol. 2, *Religious Affections*, ed. John E.
Smith (New Haven, CT: Yale University Press, 1959), 304.
5. Edwards, *Religious Affections*, 299, 303.

the same thing happens in the Scriptures. The Scriptures reveal themselves to be the Word of God the way nature reveals itself to be the world of God.

A third sighting of how God's glory authenticates the Word of God is the analogy with the glory of God in Jesus Christ, the God-man. God expected people in Jesus's day to see the glory of God in him and know that he was the Son of God because of that sight.

> And the Word became flesh and dwelt among us, and we have seen his glory, glory as of the only Son from the Father, full of grace and truth. (John 1:14)

> Philip said to him, "Lord, show us the Father, and it is enough for us." Jesus said to him, "Have I been with you so long, and you still do not know me, Philip? Whoever has seen me has seen the Father. How can you say, 'Show us the Father'?" (John 14:8–9)

Many people looked at God incarnate and did not see God. And many people hear God's Word and do not hear God. But the Son of God was there (with real, self-evident, objective, divine glory) for those who had eyes to see, and the Word of God is here (with similar divine glory) for those who have ears to hear. The glory of God in Christ was missed by many. And the glory of God in the Word is missed by many. But neither is deficient.

I think God will say to many people, *Have you heard my inspired Word and not heard me? Do you not know the glory of my voice?* The divine glory of God's inspired Word is as clear and compelling as was the divine glory of the incarnate Word.

One final sighting—the most important one—of how God's glory authenticates the Word of God is the way the glory of God vindicates the gospel. Paul says in 2 Corinthians 4:4, "The god of this world has blinded the minds of the unbelievers, to keep them from seeing *the light of the gospel of the glory of Christ*, who is the image of God." The gospel—the story of how God came to save sinners—emits a light to the eyes of the heart: the "light of the gospel of the glory of Christ." Christ's self-authenticating glory shines through the gospel. And God shatters the blindness in verse 6: "God, who said, 'Let light shine out of darkness,' has shone in our hearts to give the light of the knowledge of the glory of God in the face of Jesus Christ."

That is what happens in the creation of a Christian. We are given eyes to see the glory of God.

Conclusion

And so when we become Christians—being born again—God reveals to us in the gospel both the *ground* of the mind's certainty and the *goal* of the soul's satisfaction. He opens our eyes to see that the glory of God is both inescapably *real* and incomparably *rewarding*.

In one miracle moment the sight of his glory implants solid *conviction* and sweet *contentment*. The quest for the fountain of truth and the fountain of joy—the foundation of certainty and the fountain of satisfaction—is over. They are the same fountain—the glory of God. In the light of that glory we know for sure, and we rejoice forever.

18

Transgender Identity
in Theological and
Moral Perspective

Owen Strachan

In centuries past, the faith has faced many challenges from without, pressures that, in truth, the church still faces across the world.[1] Pressure to conform doctrine to state strictures. Secular attacks from atheists new, old, and middle-aged. In a word, persecution.

Such challenges are not new. In the eighteenth century, skeptics cast aspersions on the miracles of Scripture. In the nineteenth century, Unitarianism turned the lights out in many American churches, demoting Jesus from God to sacred teacher. In the twentieth century, liberal Protestants undermined the inerrancy of the Bible, rendering it a mystical but flawed book.

In the twenty-first century, the church finds itself in a major anthropological struggle. Nowhere does our culture more oppose biblical teaching than in our doctrine of humanity. This has numerous referents,

---

1. This chapter is adapted from Owen Strachan, "The Clarity of Complementarity: Gender Dysphoria in Biblical Perspective," *JBMW* 21, no. 2 (April 25, 2017), https://cbmw.org/topics/complementarianism/the-clarity-of-complementarity-gender-dysphoria-in-biblical-perspective/.

but few are more controverted than the matter of "gender identity."[2] In such times, the church faces a remarkable question, one unthinkable to previous generations: Is embracing the identity of the opposite sex an amoral or moral act? Some voices today argue primarily from psychological grounds that it is. In this chapter, I will respectfully counter this view and show that in order to minister grace and compassion to sinners like us who experience gender dysphoria, we must fundamentally approach it in light of a comprehensive theological-moral perspective.

My primary conversation partner here is professor Mark Yarhouse, whose book *Understanding Gender Dysphoria* (InterVarsity, 2015) offers much food for thought.[3] Yarhouse is ahead of his movement in addressing his subject; I am thankful for his pioneering efforts as a Christian leader, and for his evident compassion for the frail and struggling. I do, however, have some concerns with Yarhouse's model. I will articulate these concerns and offer a doctrinally charged response to his view. My ultimate goal, as with any true teacher of the Word of God, is not that a given position be vindicated, but that the Christ who transforms sinners will once more take center stage in the church. As we shall see, his redemption knows no bounds, his truth knows no prescribed limits, and his gospel is no respecter of persons.[4]

Engaging Yarhouse's Model

The matter at hand requires quick definitional work. To experience "gender dysphoria" means that we feel as if our biological sex does not match up with our true identity. To embrace a "transgender" identity means that we formally recognize our identity as different from our biological sex. To "transition" means that we take the physical steps necessary to complete this formal recognition—think of the various measures Bruce Jenner used to own the identity of "Caitlyn" Jenner.

---

2. Few have been more influential than Judith Butler in shaping the now-common cultural view that our gender is a "social construct" (see Butler, *Gender Trouble and the Subversion of Identity* [London: Routledge, 1990]). French writer Simone de Beauvoir famously voiced an early version of this view by arguing that a child is not born a woman but becomes one (de Beauvoir, *The Second Sex* [New York: Bantam, 1952], 249).

3. Mark Yarhouse, *Understanding Gender Dysphoria: Navigating Transgender Issues in a Changing Culture* (Downers Grove, IL: InterVarsity Press, 2015).

4. I am grateful for the wisdom of Wayne Grudem and other voices—John Piper, Bruce Ware, Albert Mohler, J. Ligon Duncan, Mark Dever, and numerous other leaders—on the issues covered here. Dr. Grudem's ministry has shaped me in a considerable way, and I am grateful for his uncompromising promotion of biblical truth and divine wisdom. It was my joy to serve with Wayne at the Council on Biblical Manhood and Womanhood, 2012–2016.

Yarhouse defines these matters in his text before laying out the three basic approaches to gender dysphoria. (1) The conservative evangelical approach is situated in an "integrity framework" that calls struggling people back to the sure coherence of God's design.[5] (2) The "disability framework," by contrast, sees "gender incongruence as a reflection of a fallen world in which the condition is a disability, a nonmoral reality to be addressed with compassion." (3) The "diversity framework" celebrates and even encourages individuals to embrace a different gender identity. Yarhouse notes that he sees "value in a disability framework" that views dysphoria as "a nonmoral reality."[6] The church should "reject" the view that "gender incongruence is the result of willful disobedience," for this places "the blame on the person navigating gender identity concerns."[7]

The matter of shame is a controlling concern; Yarhouse indicates that people who experience dysphoria struggle greatly with shame due to the church's expectations. In chapter 3, Yarhouse will share that he does not believe that counselees choose gender dysphoria—they have just experienced it, though the ultimate "cause is still unknown."[8] He encourages those dealing with dysphoria to consider a range of responses. He notes:

> Different behaviors or dress may not be ideal, but the person identifies the least invasive way to manage their dysphoria so that it does not become too distressing or impairing. This places such management on a continuum from least to most invasive and recognizes that hormonal treatment and sex reassignment could be the most invasive.[9]

Thus we see that Yarhouse allows for "management" of dysphoria such that those experiencing it may undertake actions such as cross-dressing.[10]

Yarhouse holds out three basic possibilities for people who experience gender dysphoria: (1) resolving it in accordance with their biological sex, (2) engaging in cross-dressing behavior intermittently to manage dysphoria, and (3) adopting the cross-gender role through

5. Yarhouse, *Gender Dysphoria*, 46.
6. Yarhouse, *Gender Dysphoria*, 53.
7. Yarhouse, *Gender Dysphoria*, 54.
8. Yarhouse, *Gender Dysphoria*, 61.
9. Yarhouse, *Gender Dysphoria*, 123–24.
10. See also Yarhouse, *Gender Dysphoria*, 144.

possible hormonal treatment or sex-reassignment surgery.[11] This three-fold response grid should have our full attention. According to Yarhouse, the church should avoid "rigid stereotypes" that reflect "cultural concerns" more than "biblical concerns."[12] Congregations that adopt such stereotypes risk "not being hospitable" due to their focus on "conveying biblical truths to those on the inside."[13] Indeed, the stakes are high. If the church does not warm to an "integrated framework," Yarhouse believes that "speaking solely with reference to the integrity framework will increasingly isolate evangelicals from a cultural context in which the diversity framework is emerging as most salient."[14] In the end, "Christians can benefit from valuing and speaking into the sacredness found in the integrity framework, the compassion we witness in the disability framework, and the identity and community considerations we see in the diversity framework."[15]

By this point, several things are clear. First, Yarhouse believes that gender dysphoria necessitates compassionate Christian treatment. Second, he recognizes that the Scripture teaches, at least to some degree, that manhood and womanhood are God-designed realities, and that redemption is needed for broken sinners. Third, he believes that individuals experiencing gender dysphoria may choose various means of navigating their personal experience. This includes cross-dressing and even gender-reassignment surgery. Fourth, he views the actual experience—and resultant choices—of gender dysphoria as nonmoral; it is not the result of "willful disobedience."

Yarhouse has given us much to respond to, and his substantive material requires a biblical-theological answer. What follows is an attempt at such a Scripture-shaped response. We will look at five key biblical sections.

A Synthesis of Biblical Texts on the Sexes
God Makes Humans "Male and Female" in Genesis 1 and 2
Genesis 1 is not merely informative for understanding God's plan and expectations for humanity. It is also formative. The Lord creates

---

11. Yarhouse, *Gender Dysphoria*, 153.
12. Yarhouse, *Gender Dysphoria*, 155.
13. Yarhouse, *Gender Dysphoria*, 156.
14. Yarhouse, *Gender Dysphoria*, 160.
15. Yarhouse, *Gender Dysphoria*, 161.

two sexes on the sixth day. The apex of his creation is the man and the woman.

> So God created man in his own image,
>> in the image of God he created him;
>> male and female he created them. (1:27)

Genesis 2 fills out our understanding of this divine work, as it portrays the Lord making the man from the dust of the ground and the woman from the rib of the man (Gen. 2:7, 21). There is much to unpack here, but for our purposes, the Lord is showing us that manhood and womanhood are the products of his superintelligence and his desire to be glorified by unity (one human race) in diversity (two sexes). The Trinity itself is the ultimate ground of this concept (Gen. 1:26–27). The human race is an intentional reflection of the divine symbiosis. We must therefore see manhood and womanhood not as randomly developed evolutionary outcomes, but rather as the very intention of God from the beginning of our world. Commenting on this material in Genesis, Ray Ortlund says it well: "It is God who wants men to be men and women to be women; and He can teach us the meaning of each, if we want to be taught."[16]

Genesis 1:26–28 shows us that manhood and womanhood are essential properties with essential duties. The first couple cannot, for example, fulfill the dominion mandate of this passage without living in marital union. They *must* act as a man and a woman in their God-created marriage; they have the joyful duty of being "naked and not ashamed" in one-flesh union (Gen. 2:24–25).[17] The man and the woman have no way to fulfill this mission without full-fledged recognition of their distinctive designs, their complementary physiology.[18]

---

16. Raymond C. Ortlund Jr., "Male-Female Equality and Male Headship: Genesis 1–3," in *Recovering Biblical Manhood and Womanhood: A Response to Evangelical Feminism*, ed. John Piper and Wayne Grudem (Wheaton, IL: Crossway, 1991), 99.

17. See Andreas and Margaret Köstenberger, *God's Design for Man and Woman: A Biblical-Theological Survey* (Wheaton, IL: Crossway, 2014), 31. The authors helpfully note that "God delegated to humanity as male and female the power to rule and to procreate. He put humans on the earth to take care of it for him, requiring them to reproduce as male and female."

18. Modern evangelicals have not availed themselves enough of the witness of the natural order—including the witness of the God-made body. But there is a thread within the evangelical tradition recognizing natural design. John Calvin, for example, gives voice to the "order of creation" as the grounding for marriage (Calvin, "Genesis 2:18," in *Commentary on Genesis*, ed. Alister McGrath and J. I. Packer, Crossway Classics [Wheaton, IL: Crossway, 2001], 38). A good deal more scholarly work is needed to link evidentiary wisdom and special revelation, with the order rightly arranged, and the Word of God being the authority of authorities.

Manhood and womanhood as essential realities are the grounds for the survival and growth of humanity, the enactment and sustenance of marriage, and the faithful pursuit of the *missio Dei* in its early form: populating and ruling the earth *coram Deo*.

The Fall of Genesis 3 Represents an Attack on God's Plan for the Sexes

All sin is rooted in the real historical fall of Adam and Eve as recorded in Genesis 3:1–13. I will not interrogate this passage at length, but we can note one major truth of this passage: Satan, acting as the serpent, seeks nothing less than the overturning of the created order that the Lord has established. He, a creeping thing, takes dominion over the woman, whom God made from the man's body. The Lord has signaled to Adam, by making the woman from his flesh, that Adam has the responsibility to protect and lead his wife, even as the Lord has made his leadership role in the marriage plain by having Adam name Eve (Gen. 2:23). Yet Adam, in the moment of testing, fails to step in and crush the serpent's head. He passively receives the forbidden fruit from his wife, and then, when called by God to account for his double failure—the failure to obey and the failure to lead—he blames both God (who made the woman) and the woman (Gen. 3:12). So the fall is a successful attack by Satan on the sexes and God's design for them.[19]

Here is the ground, within marriage, of all manly abuse, of all womanly insubordination and, outside of marriage, of every other form of sin (Gen. 3:16–19). Here is the ground of all disobedience and creaturely rejection of the Creator and his intentions for creation. All the sin and brokenness that we taste in this cursed world is a result of the fall. All gender dysphoria, transgender instincts, and cross-dressing impulses stem from the fall, and none from the wisdom of God.[20] Because of

---

19. As Denny Burk insightfully points out, "The apostle Paul indicates that it was indeed the undoing of this order that was the basis for the fall of humanity into sin (1 Tim. 2:13–14)" (Burk, *What Is the Meaning of Sex?* [Wheaton, IL: Crossway, 2013], 166).

20. Heath Lambert articulates this well: "Total depravity means that every aspect of our human existence has been touched. In our inner man, our conscience, will, intellect, and emotions have been corrupted. In our outer man our bodies are given over to decay, weakening our ability to obey and tempting us to sin" (Lambert, *A Theology of Biblical Counseling: The Doctrinal Foundations of Counseling Ministry* [Grand Rapids, MI: Zondervan, 2016], 224). This does not mean, of course, that every effect of the fall in our lives is directly the result of our sin, as Lambert makes clear. It does mean that, as Christians, we know decisively why we malfunction and fail to glorify God as human beings.

this historical testimony, Christians—and Christians alone—know why
people go through confusion, pain, and rejection regarding their personal identity. All such broken behavior and thinking begins here, in a
darkened Eden. Take away this terrible scene, and you can describe and
diagnose gender dysphoria, but never truly understand and redress it.

God Forbids Cross-Dressing in the Old Covenant Law

The point at which the Scripture most addresses the matters covered
by Yarhouse comes in the Deuteronomic discussion of various non-
Israelite practices.[21] The people of God, we see in Deuteronomy 22,
are called to be a set-apart people in big and small ways. One of the
markers of God-fearing Israelites is that they will wear clothes appropriate to their sex: "A woman shall not wear a man's garment, nor
shall a man put on a woman's cloak, for whoever does these things is
an abomination to the LORD your God" (Deut. 22:5). Yarhouse recognizes that this verse has import—of some kind—for the discussion
surrounding gender dysphoria. He comments here, "The passages from
Deuteronomy are certainly important, and we can see different ways
in which we might understand them." He continues by both softening
and backing up this observation: "We can also see that even where we
might demonstrate some restraint and caution, we see a reaffirmation
of gendered distinctiveness that Christians would want to understand
and support."[22]

I do not know all that Yarhouse might mean by sounding out "different ways" in which this prohibition could be understood. It is true,
in my view, that we are not bound by the old covenant law. That
aside, the will of God regarding ancient cross-dressing could not be
clearer.[23] To embrace such a practice is to commit an "abomination"
against God.[24] This behavior is clearly immoral in light of the biblical

---

21. Jeffrey Tigay introduces a possible tie to ungodly Amorite sexuality in his discussion of this passage: "Pertinent to the suggestion that it was a pagan practice is a Babylonian adage, according to which a person who is apparently an Amorite says to his wife, 'You be the man and I'll be the woman,'" a fascinating possibility (Jeffrey H. Tigay, *Deuteronomy*, The JPS Torah Commentary [Philadelphia: Jewish Publication Society, 1996], 200).

22. Yarhouse, *Gender Dysphoria*, 31–32.

23. Robert Bratcher and Howard Hatton suggest that the prohibition could include "anything that pertains to a man: this seems to include other things besides clothes, such as adornments and weapons" (Robert G. Bratcher and Howard A. Hatton, *A Handbook on Deuteronomy*, UBS Handbook Series [New York: United Bible Societies, 2000], 366).

24. See the illuminating words of Jason DeRouchie here: "Idolatry gives glory to someone other than YHWH; witchcraft looks to means other than God's word to discern his will or what will

testimony referenced earlier. Because in Genesis 1–2 God created the sexes and gave them a plan for glorifying his name and subduing the earth—a mission that can only proceed by the sexes living according to God's design—it is wrong for the sexes to blur lines that God himself has drawn.[25]

Separating Deuteronomy from Genesis 1–2 leaves Deuteronomy without meaning. Connecting the two texts, however, brings fresh light. God created men to present themselves as men and women to present themselves as women. The Israelites glorified their Maker by their personal presentation. Jason DeRouchie says it well: "Those born boys are to live and thrive as boys, and those born girls are to live and thrive as girls. When corrupt desires want to alter this course, one must choose with God's help the path that magnifies the majesty of God best, and that path is defined in Deuteronomy 22:5."[26] The teaching of Deuteronomy endures and instructs even today.

Jesus Affirms the Goodness of Man and Woman in Matthew 19

In a discussion of divorce (Matthew 19), Jesus reinforces the ancient view of the sexes. In his divine logic, to understand divorce, one must understand marriage; to understand marriage, one must understand the sexes. So we see in this text:

> And Pharisees came up to him and tested him by asking, "Is it lawful to divorce one's wife for any cause?" He answered, "Have you not read that he who created them from the beginning made them male and female, and said, 'Therefore a man shall leave his father and his mother and hold fast to his wife, and the two shall become one flesh'? So they are no longer two but one flesh. What therefore God has joined together, let not man separate." (Matt. 19:3–6)

happen in the future, and dishonest gain diminishes the value of God's image in others. We must conclude, therefore, that something about transgender expression and gender confusion directly counters the very nature of God" (Jason S. DeRouchie, "Confronting the Transgender Storm: New Covenant Reflections from Deuteronomy 22:5," *JBMW* 21, no. 1 [Spring 2016]: 65).

25. Eugene Merrill notes the problem of "mixtures" in this broader passage, suggesting that God wants creation to function as he intends it to function. "Another linkage between the verse [Deut. 22:5] and its context is the chiasm connecting vv. 5–8 with 9–12: dress (v. 5), animals (vv. 6–7), house (v. 8), field (v. 9), animals (v. 10), dress (vv. 11–12). There is thus a strong tie-in between death and mixtures, that is, between the expositions of the sixth and seventh commandments. The sin in improper mixtures is brought out in the laws of purity that follow (22:9–23:18)" (Eugene H. Merrill, *Deuteronomy*, vol. 4 of *The New American Commentary* [Nashville: Broadman & Holman, 1994], 297–98).

26. DeRouchie, "Transgender Storm," 64.

Too often, Genesis 1–2 matters little for evangelicals when it comes to sorting out our practical anthropology. But these chapters matter greatly for Jesus, the Lord of the church. The creational design for the sexes is marriage (a lifelong covenant most believers will enter). Marriage, however, depends on men being men and living out God's plan for them, and women being women and living out God's plan for them. If we wanted to use modern terms here, Christ—not shockingly—holds an "essentialist" or "integrity" perspective on the sexes. Marriage is not whatever we make of it, just as the sexes are not whatever we perceive them to be. The sexes and marriage are fixed and formed by God.[27]

This passage has great import for understanding gender dysphoria. We are not free to remake marriage, Jesus teaches; we are not free to remake the sexes, for marriage depends upon the essentialist foundation of two sexes. This text does not speak directly against the inborn instinct to cross gender boundaries, but it does help to build a foundation, a backdrop, by which to reason our way to a biblical perspective on "gender identity" and gender dysphoria. Those looking to the teaching of Christ himself for a softening of old covenant theology find none; instead, Jesus not merely underlines the ancient witness but adds the fullness of his doctrine-norming authority to it.

Here we should add that the apostle Paul will build on Christ's testimony in Ephesians 5:22–33. The imaging of the Christ-church relationship in earthly covenantal union depends upon a fixed understanding of manhood and womanhood. Only one man and one woman are able to fulfill God's ultimate intention for marriage, namely, the portrayal of the divine salvific drama. You cannot support Ephesians 5, and the eschatological realization of Revelation 21, without a correspondent man-woman union. By contrast, the same-sex activity prohibited in texts like Romans 1:22–27 depends upon a blurring of the sexes. There is an indissoluble connection between owning our God-given sex and entering a God-made union.

From numerous corners of Holy Scripture, we learn that it is vital that we embrace an essentialist vision of the sexes. The very glory

---

27. David P. Nelson says it well: "Jesus based his teaching on divorce and the sanctity of marriage on God's purpose in creation and also affirmed that marriage is, by definition, the union of a man and woman" (Nelson, "The Work of God: Creation and Providence," in *A Theology for the Church*, ed. Daniel L. Akin [Nashville: B&H, 2007], 265).

of God and plan of God rest on this sturdy and beautiful bedrock. From such an understanding, we may help sinners like us experiencing gender dysphoria to understand just how much the Lord wants us to savor the goodness of his design—and just how troubling and sinful it is to reject, to not inhabit for any reason, the vision of manhood and womanhood he unfolds in the story of his people.

Paul Calls Men and Women to Represent Their Given Sex in 1 Corinthians 11

I once heard Alistair Begg say that he feared Song of Solomon like no other text. Many preachers do. Another text that modern preachers might edge away from is 1 Corinthians 11:1–16, a biblical passage filled with countercultural insights. In this section of Scripture, the apostle Paul affirms an order to earthly marriage that is dependent upon the order and functioning of the Godhead (1 Cor. 11:3). He also teaches that men and women are to present themselves in distinct ways so that the divine plan of Genesis 1–2 may be upheld:

> For a man ought not to cover his head, since he is the image and glory of God, but woman is the glory of man. For man was not made from woman, but woman from man. Neither was man created for woman, but woman for man. That is why a wife ought to have a symbol of authority on her head, because of the angels. Nevertheless, in the Lord woman is not independent of man nor man of woman; for as woman was made from man, so man is now born of woman. And all things are from God. Judge for yourselves: is it proper for a wife to pray to God with her head uncovered? Does not nature itself teach you that if a man wears long hair it is a disgrace for him, but if a woman has long hair, it is her glory? For her hair is given to her for a covering. (1 Cor. 11:7–15)

This passage has sparked much discussion, and rightfully so. It is material to our purposes, for it shows us that the new covenant vision of the sexes is precisely the same as the old covenant vision, in that it accords with essentialism. Men and women are not the same. They are united as God's creation but distinct from one another. A husband is called to be the head of his wife even as God is the head of Christ in verse 3. Men are to honor the Lord by showing the distinctive glory of their God-given sex. The glory of a woman is her "long hair" in a way that is not true for a man.

Writing in the *Calvin Theological Journal*, Branson Parler comments on the latter part of this section:

> 1 Corinthians 11:14–15 can and should be understood as stemming from the same moral logic that undergirds the biblical prohibition of same-sex sexual activity, namely, the creational difference of male and female. When Paul names same-sex sexual activity as a sin, he does so because God created humans as male and female, [and] when Paul argues that hair length ought to properly differentiate male and female, he does so because God created humans as male and female.[28]

This is quite right. It matters for handling gender dysphoria rightly. Paul clearly taught that men and women are called to own their God-given sex in order to glorify their Maker by the power of Christ in them. We do not know, of course, the specific hair length that the apostle desires in his teaching on differentiation between the sexes. We feel some cultural tension here. But we must be careful not to press too quickly the "First-Century Teaching Only" button here.[29] An apostle of the new covenant cut in Christ's blood reinforces the kind of sex distinctions found in the formation of humanity and the teaching of the old covenant.[30] It is to the glory of God that men and women display the distinctiveness of each sex.[31] This is a matter of obedience; it is also a matter of joyful, satisfied, God-blessed Christian living.

---

28. Branson Parler, "Hair Length and Human Sexuality: The Underlying Moral Logic of Paul's Appeal to Nature in 1 Corinthians 11:4," *Calvin Theological Journal* 51 (2016): 135.

29. I concur with Mark Taylor on this point. He argues that "Paul's use of the intensive construction ('nature itself') and his prior appeal to the created order in 1 Cor. 11:7–10 suggest that mere human convention is not Paul's meaning here" (Mark Taylor, *1 Corinthians*, vol. 28 of *The New American Commentary* [Nashville: B&H, 2014], 265–66).

30. See Anthony Thiselton on this point: "Gender differentiation relates to that which God wills, decrees, and expresses in creation or in the creation order" (Anthony C. Thiselton, *The First Epistle to the Corinthians: A Commentary on the Greek Text*, NIGTC (Grand Rapids, MI: Eerdmans, 2000), 836–37).

31. Craig Blomberg asserts regarding verses 7–10: "For a Christian man to appear gay or pagan dishonors God; for a woman to appear lesbian or unfaithful dishonors her husband. Obviously husbands also dishonor their wives and wives dishonor God when they act in these inappropriate ways, but if an authority structure is implicit in this passage, Paul's less inclusive wording becomes understandable." This is sound. (Craig Blomberg, *1 Corinthians*, The NIV Application Commentary [Grand Rapids, MI: Zondervan, 1994], 211–12).

Synthesis and Takeaways

In the foregoing, I have attempted to build out the beginnings of a biblical-theological framework by which to understand gender dysphoria, gender identity, and transgenderism. We must undertake sure work, particularly in an age when many evangelicals have learned, however unwittingly, a hermeneutic of silence regarding such inquiries: the Scripture does not definitively address these matters; better to stay quiet and let the psychological experts speak.

We have to take a different stance here. Those who know the Lord have no greater authority than the Bible. We must affirm with full confidence the sufficiency of Scripture for all of life and godliness (2 Tim. 3:16; 2 Pet. 1:3). Because of this, the Christian pastor, working together with scholars and wise guides, is equipped to deal with all matters that bear on life and godliness, and the Scripture is what equips him to do so. R. Albert Mohler Jr. speaks to our role in this tumultuous time: "We are called to be the people of the truth, even when the truth is not popular and even when the truth is denied by the culture around us."[32]

We are a people of the truth, and we thus have hope to offer sinners of every kind. As we have seen, the Bible speaks to gender dysphoria, to the duty to own our God-given sex, and thus by extension to the fallen reality of the person who suffers from gender dysphoria. While making clear that such individuals require deft pastoral care that takes full stock of the complex human person, we must set our mark by this: the church of the Lord Jesus Christ has *the* means of helping people through these matters. It is the gospel of grace. We undertake what the Puritans used to call "the cure of souls" by the Word and the gospel. The good news of Christ is "the power of God unto salvation" and thus the means by which sinners of every kind, bearing every burden a cursed world lays upon their backs, may taste wholeness, forgiveness, and redemption to the uttermost (Rom. 1:16).

In many situations, including the problem of gender dysphoria, it may be hard to find the precise cause and origin of our feeling that we do not fit our bodies. Skilled pastors and counselors will work hard and graciously to identify the roots of our suffering, but they will also help people see that there is a wildness that runs in our hearts, a *desperate*

---

32. R. Albert Mohler Jr., *We Cannot Be Silent: Speaking Truth to a Culture Redefining Sex, Marriage, and the Very Meaning of Right and Wrong* (Nashville: Thomas Nelson, 2015), 183.

wickedness that extends not merely to behavior but also to "defiling passion" (2 Pet. 2:10). As fallen beings, we may not even know we are sinning against God and dishonoring his design, but if we are missing the mark he has set for us, we are sinning nonetheless.[33]

Gender dysphoria and sexual confusion may well be the result of unasked-for events and acts. According to Lawrence Mayer and Paul McHugh, "non-heterosexuals are about two to three times as likely to have experienced childhood sexual abuse."[34] We thus take great care not to blame any suffering individuals for trauma done to them. What we are responsible for, however, is helping suffering men and women handle their desires, feelings, affections, instincts, and appetites. Every pastor, every minister of the gospel of Christ, is fully equipped by the Word of God to see sin-tossed sinners remade and transformed.

This is rigorously practical. From a variety of backgrounds and sin patterns, counselees may also want to cross-dress, to identify with the opposite sex in some unbiblical and unnatural way. From the smallest such inclination (a fleeting desire running through our minds) to the greatest (undergoing a medical "transition" to take on an opposite-sex identity), we must know and preach and counsel that all such expressions run counter to the plan and wisdom of God. Embracing and nurturing such ungodliness will only bring trouble and pain.[35] We are not free by Scripture to encourage and allow individuals experiencing gender dysphoria to cross-dress, to take on an opposite-sex identity, and to surgically "transition" out of our natural bodies. Here I must break, and break strongly, with Yarhouse.[36]

---

33. See Owen Strachan, "A Referendum on Depravity: Same-Sex Attraction as Sinful Desire," *Journal for Biblical Manhood & Womanhood* 20, no. 1 (Spring 2015): 24–34; Denny Burk and Heath Lambert, *Transforming Homosexuality: What the Bible Says about Sexual Orientation and Change* (Phillipsburg, NJ: P&R, 2015).

34. See Lawrence S. Mayer and Paul R. McHugh, "Executive Summary," in "Sexuality and Gender: Findings from the Biological, Psychological, and Social Sciences," *The New Atlantis*, Fall 2016, https://www.thenewatlantis.com/publications/executive-summary-sexuality-and-gender.

35. The chaos unleashed by owning a "transgender" identity is fierce, even deathly, for many. For example, the likelihood of suicide skyrockets for youths who lean into their gender dysphoria. See Paul McHugh, "Transgender Surgery Isn't the Solution," *Wall Street Journal*, June 12, 2014, http://www.wsj.com/articles/paul-mchugh-transgender-surgery-isnt-the-solution-1402615120. McHugh is the former psychiatrist-in-chief for Johns Hopkins Hospital and a nationally renowned specialist. For a longer investigation, see Mayer and McHugh, "Sexuality and Gender," http://www.thenewatlantis.com/publications/introduction-sexuality-and-gender.

36. I should point out that some people are born with the condition called "intersex," meaning that they possess from birth genitalia of both sexes. With others, I read this condition as a symptom of the fall, not as a normative state. For wisdom regarding care and counseling for individuals in such situations, see Burk, *What Is the Meaning of Sex?*, 169–76.

I come to this position not because of censoriousness but because of hope. To repent of all our ungodly inclinations and desires is not to bury hope in the ground. To repent in the manner I have just outlined is the very genesis of hope. It is the beginning of newness. It is the first step in a long walk of obedience powered by the grace of Christ. It is essential material for those who experience gender dysphoria. The journey of every man or woman to the celestial city will vary, and we all must navigate our own ups and downs on the way to the new Canaan, to lasting and permanent wholeness. But we must unmask as no wisdom at all the cultural wisdom that tells us we cannot change. To tell people that they cannot change and cannot overcome their flesh by Christ's power is to feed them a lie. There is nothing more hopeless than the view that we cannot surmount our struggles or overcome our natural desires. There is nothing less true for the Christian.

As stated above, gender dysphoria may proceed from a range of fallen experiences and behaviors. Though we should carefully and compassionately probe the backgrounds and narratives of those who face it, we should also recognize that finding the root may prove difficult in some cases. Wherever we can, we unspool what people are experiencing. We ask good and searching questions; we listen well; we show empathy; we help our friends see that we are fallen just as they are. But our counsel to people who struggle with gender dysphoria is not merely psychological or emotional. It is preeminently biblical, moral, and theological. To resist God's good design, to move out of step with God's gift of our sex, is to dishonor and disobey God. It is only when sinners like us hear this that they can begin to heal, for they may step out of the darkness of sin and walk in the light of Christ.

Conclusion

In our day, the church must go back to Scripture. We must know that Scripture equips us to lend gospel aid to people who experience gender dysphoria. It is compassionate—profoundly compassionate—to do so. The cross-dresser of ancient Israel needed to hear God's word about this behavior. The Corinthians enticed to bend their gender in Paul's day needed to return to the clarity of God's design. The men and women told they will find healing and wholeness in the cyclone of gender confusion need us to speak warmly and firmly in our time. They need the clarity of complementarity; they need the gospel of transforming grace.[37]

In the end, it is not that transgenderism is a radical behavior. It is that it is not radical enough. God wishes to remake us not to a degree but in full. This is transformation the world cannot understand, and the sinner can scarcely believe.

---

37. For more on the biblical vision of the sexes, see Owen Strachan and Gavin Peacock, *The Grand Design: Male and Female He Made Them* (Fearn, Ross-Shire, UK: Christian Focus, 2016).

19

Scripture, the Image of God, and the Sinner

Reflections on Discipleship and Care of Souls

K. Erik Thoennes

Wayne Grudem is a godly man who deeply loves Christ. Over the twenty-two years I have known him, I have seen that this love and godliness are direct results of his strong commitment to the authority of the Bible worked out in a Spirit-empowered way in his daily life. Among many examples I could give, I would like to highlight the first time his godliness made a lasting impression on me.

It happened during the first session of a PhD seminar at Trinity Evangelical Divinity School. It was in my first class with Dr. Grudem, which was called Leadership in the Church. As we tried to put together the paper-presentation schedule for the semester, we were at an impasse. We, the students, were in survival mode, and there was little cooperation or willingness to be flexible with our schedules. After about fifteen or twenty minutes of getting nowhere, Dr. Grudem decided we needed to pray. During that time of prayer, our hearts began to rest in God, and the semester game plan came together beautifully. In the midst of a rigorous academic environment, a God-dependent, unselfish tone was set that lasted for the entire semester.

Our professor taught us great content that semester, but who he was made the most lasting impression. He helped us to be better scholars, but more importantly, he showed us how to become better Christians. What was it that led Dr. Grudem to stop and pray like this? I am sure the Spirit was guiding him, but I am also confident that the Spirit was using a passage like Philippians 4:6 to motivate him to stop for prayer: "Do not be anxious about anything, but in everything by prayer and supplication with thanksgiving let your requests be made known to God." He saw that his students were feeling anxious and ungrateful, and that we were unproductive, so he initiated turning our hearts toward God in prayer.

This was a great example to me of the need to see the spiritual component even in mundane things like scheduling presentations. Our lives are not mostly burning bushes and parted seas. Even for missionaries on the front lines, our lives look more like tending sheep in the wilderness and waiting patiently for God to free us from sin and sorrow. Therefore, as we wait, work, rest, sit in traffic, change diapers, and grow in our longing to see Jesus, we depend on his Word to be an anchor for our souls.

I have seen God's Word anchor Wayne Grudem's soul, enabling gratitude and joy even as he has endured health challenges that both he and his wife, Margaret, have encountered. The Spirit and the Bible have guided him to graciousness when he has been unfairly criticized. The promises of Scripture have given him hope and perspective when death and tragedy have struck his family. The teaching of the Bible has led him to love his wife as Christ loves the church, to raise his children in the nurture and instruction of the Lord, and to watch his life and doctrine closely. The guidance of the Bible has led him to live a life of integrity that is beyond reproach. Theology and ethics have been far more than an academic exercise for Wayne Grudem.

The ultimate goal in Christian ministry is making disciples for the glory of God. At the very heart of disciple making is Spirit-empowered activity, guided by the clear and authoritative teaching of Scripture. Without the Spirit, we are like a car without an engine; without Scripture, we are like a car without a steering wheel. One is useless, the other is dangerous. A biblically grounded understanding of human nature is essential for Christian ministry to be God-honoring and truly effective. Practical principles driven by pragmatic values will not get us to thoroughly Christian discipleship. The Bible must be our guide.

In honor of Dr. Grudem, and for the glory of God, what follows is my attempt to lay out central biblical truths about human beings that should guide Christians in our disciple-making endeavors. The care of souls must be grounded in God's definition of human beings. Only then will we understand the reasons for our existence, the cause of our greatest problems, and how those problems are solved. If you do not know what something is, you will never be able to care for it well. Our understanding of ministry must begin with a right understanding of God, humans, sin, and redemption. Good theology leads to good anthropology, which sets the stage for good ministry.

We Are Created by God for His Glory

"In the beginning, God created the heavens and the earth" (Gen. 1:1). The first thing we learn about God and the Bible is that he is the Creator of everything, and the first thing we learn about ourselves is that we are created (Gen. 1:26–31; cf. 2:7; 5:1–2; Matt. 19:4). Father, Son (Col. 1:16), and Spirit (Gen. 1:2) were all equally involved in creation. Nothing is more important than understanding this fundamental distinction between God and his creation. He is the infinite, all-powerful, all-wise, Creator of all, and we are utterly dependent on him for our very existence. Forgetting this distinction leads to forgetting our dependence on and accountability to God. Exalting ourselves above our Creator is at the heart of idolatry and the horrific evil it unleashes.

Throughout the Bible, when God is recognized as Creator, worship is the response.

> Oh come, let us worship and bow down;
>   let us kneel before the LORD, our Maker! (Ps. 95:6)

When we see his amazing power, wisdom, beauty, and knowledge displayed in creation (Ps. 19:1), the only correct response is to bow down before him in praise (cf. Neh. 9:5–6; Ps. 139:13–16). In the Bible, God is frequently set apart from idols because he is Creator.

For all the gods of the peoples are worthless idols,
   but the LORD made the heavens. (1 Chron. 16:26; cf. Acts
      14:15)

We were created primarily to know and glorify God. He did not create humanity out of any need within himself. He, the one "who made the world and everything in it, being Lord of heaven and earth, does not live in temples made by man, nor is he served by human hands, as though he needed anything, since he himself gives to all mankind life and breath and everything" (Acts 17:24–25). Our service and worship should never be motivated by any thought of meeting perceived needs God has.

Who has given to me, that I should repay him?
   Whatever is under the whole heaven is mine. (Job 41:11; cf.
      Ps. 50:9–12)

God has no unmet needs, but he nevertheless desires to be glorified through the joy we take in him. More than anything else, we are created for an all-satisfying relationship with our Creator. The only thing worth boasting about is that we understand and know God (Jer. 9:23–24), and eternal life is found in knowing the Father through the Son (John 17:3).

When we delight in God and obey his commands, he is glorified through our lives.

Everyone who is called by my name,
   whom I created for my glory,
   whom I have formed and made. (Isa. 43:7; cf. Eph. 1:11–12)

Glorifying God in simple daily faithfulness can bring joy to his heart.

You shall be a crown of beauty in the hand of the LORD,
   and a royal diadem in the hand of your God.
You shall no more be termed Forsaken,
   and your land shall no more be termed Desolate,
but you shall be called My Delight Is in Her,
   and your land Married;
for the LORD delights in you,
   and your land shall be married.

For as a young man marries a young woman,
   so shall your sons marry you,
and as the bridegroom rejoices over the bride,
   so shall your God rejoice over you. (Isa. 62:3–5; cf. Zeph. 3:17)

God's delight in our delight in him should be our greatest motivation. We should not be driven primarily by the psychological, social, or relational benefits of obedience. Those are not the highest motives. Our greatest goal is to honor the One who made us. That is how we are most fulfilled and flourish as human beings.

The doctrine of creation provides the essential foundation for discipleship and soul care. As we minister to others, we must see them through God's eyes. We must help others to mature in light of God's revelation about who they are. The primary implications of the doctrine of creation for discipleship and soul care are as follows:

1. *Purpose.* As human beings, we desperately want to know that our lives have meaning and purpose. Without intentional divine creation, we cannot have such a *telos.* But when we understand that we are made by God for his glory, our lives are flooded with eternal significance.

2. *Dependence.* When we realize that we owe our very existence to God, any thought of human autonomy disappears. There is no such thing as a self-made man. Not a molecule, heartbeat, or breath is ours apart from God's creating and sustaining power. As we seek to help others grow, we need to point them to the One to whom they owe their very lives.

3. *Accountability.* Because God made us, we answer to him for the way we spend our lives (1 Cor. 10:31). We are to steward everything we have, and everything we are, in a way that pleases him and expresses our gratitude. Our bodies, money, relational ability, creativity, sense of humor, sexuality, and everything else we have belong to him, and we will answer to him for the way we use his gifts.

4. *A big view of God.* When we consider the glories of creation and that God spoke them into existence with the word of his power, it increases a healthy fear of him and an appropriate *smaller view of ourselves* (Isa. 2:22; Rom. 9:20).

5. *A positive view of everything.* Genesis 1:31 says, "And God saw everything that he had made, and behold, it was very good. And there was evening and there was morning, the sixth day." Because

God determined that his creation was very good, this should lead us to take great pleasure in all of creation, knowing that God "richly provides us with everything to enjoy" (1 Tim. 6:17b). There should be no boredom or negative views of the world that God made. This positive view of creation is the best reason I have ever heard for a liberal arts education. No matter what we study, whether physics, biology, art, history, psychology, political science, or music, it should all inspire worship of the God who made it all. We should be in a continual state of wonder at the God who made waterfalls, dogs, apples, sunsets, the cell, the braided rings of Saturn, and, most of all, men and women in his image.

6. *A better understanding of God's work in redemption.* When the New Testament describes God's redeeming work, it draws from the creation language of Genesis: "For God, who said, 'Let light shine out of darkness,' has shone in our hearts to give the light of the knowledge of the glory of God in the face of Jesus Christ" (2 Cor. 4:6; cf. 5:17; Eph. 2:10). When we realize that our Redeemer is our Creator, it gives us great confidence in his desire and ability to redeem us.

7. *Hope.* Because the God who transforms us is the same God who made us, we should have unbridled hope in his ability to transform even the most hardened sinner. No one is beyond his reach. This means that even when we get discouraged about our own seeming lack of growth, we continually hope in his power to change us. And we know he is more than able to change those to whom we minister. We should never despair, even when there seems to be little evidence of transformation in those we lead. God is able to soften the hardest heart and bring sight to the blind. We also have great hope that God will one day make *all* things new. One day all sickness, sin, suffering, weariness, anxiety, boredom, and apathy will be gone (Revelation 21). We have cosmic hope, personal hope, and hope for ministry. "And let us not grow weary of doing good, for in due season we will reap, if we do not give up" (Gal. 6:9).

8. *A philosophy of ministry.* When we know that God's glory is our goal in everything, it frees us from slavishly following the latest trends, and from the fear of man. In ministry, our driving questions will always be "Will God be pleased with this?" and "What will bring the most glory to him?" This way, mere popularity and worldly definitions of

success will not drive our ministries—seeking God's glory will. "So, whether you eat or drink, or whatever you do, do all to the glory of God" (1 Cor. 10:31).

We Are Made in the Image of God

"Then God said, 'Let us make man *in our image, after our likeness*'" (Gen. 1:26). There is nothing more important or distinctive about human beings than that we are made in the image and likeness of God (Gen. 1:26–31; 5:1). Without exception, from conception to death, all human beings are created in God's image. This is what sets us apart from everything else in creation and is the fundamental source of human dignity. To say that we are made in God's image means that "we are like him and represent him."[1] Within this definition is an inherent limitation. To say that something is *like* something else means it is not that thing. So, before we run to extremes of human deification with image-of-God teaching, we should recognize that we are not God. This is why Calvin said that "we are not to consider that men merit [honor and love] of themselves but to look upon the image of God in all men, to which we owe all honor and love."[2] But there is also a stunning amplification of the worth of the human when we say that we alone were made in the image and likeness of God. We are the zenith of creation, designed to live as God's created analogy.

It is vital that we define ourselves by our essence, what we are, rather than by our function, what we do. What we do flows from who we are, but we must anchor our definition of humans to the image of God. It is *humans as humans*, not some element or ability in us, that constitutes the divine image. Manifestations of the image of God are to be enjoyed and celebrated, but all humans are sacred and are to be treated with dignity, even if they are not reflecting the image of God well.

Even after the fall, we remain in God's image, and this becomes the primary basis for biblical ethics. Not one story in the news today is unaffected by how one defines a human being. One's views on abortion, sexuality, economics, politics, sports, pornography, the environment, international relations, terrorism, fracking, euthanasia, and food are all

---

1. Wayne Grudem, *Systematic Theology: An Introduction to Biblical Doctrine* (Leicester, UK: Inter-Varsity Press; Grand Rapids, MI: Zondervan, 1994), 442.
2. John Calvin, *Institutes of the Christian Religion*, ed. John T. McNeill, trans. Ford Lewis Battles (Philadelphia: Westminster, 1960), 3.7.6.

profoundly affected by one's definition of a human being. After the fall, capital punishment is instituted in the Mosaic Law for the murderer, with this explanation:

> Whoever sheds the blood of man,
>   by man shall his blood be shed,
> for God made man in his own image. (Gen. 9:6)

In the New Testament, the image of God remains the foundation for how we treat others: "No human being can tame the tongue. It is a restless evil, full of deadly poison. With it we bless our Lord and Father, and with it we curse people who are made in the likeness of God. From the same mouth come blessing and cursing. My brothers, these things ought not to be so" (James 3:8–10). The image of God in humanity stands behind the two greatest commandments: "And [Jesus] said to him, 'You shall love the Lord your God with all your heart and with all your soul and with all your mind. This is the great and first commandment. And a second is like it: You shall love your neighbor as yourself. On these two commandments depend all the Law and the Prophets'" (Matt. 22:37–40). The same verb "love" is required of us toward God and neighbor. This is because of the similarity between God and neighbor. Insofar as all human beings are like God, they deserve love and respect. "If anyone says, 'I love God,' and hates his brother, he is a liar; for he who does not love his brother whom he has seen cannot love God whom he has not seen. And this commandment we have from him: 'whoever loves God must also love his brother'" (1 John 4:20–21).

If we do not have this kind of theological definition of human beings, we are left with merely functional ways of defining persons. We then need to rely on the findings of social scientists' for definitions, and we are reduced to our capabilities within relative and subjective categories.[3] This way of defining human beings reduces our worth to categories like IQ, self-awareness, and happiness. Functional definitions of humans logically lead to deeply troubling conclusions, like those of Princeton bioethicist Peter Singer. He says, for example:

---

3. Some of the influential efforts among social scientists to define humans took place in the early 1970s around the time of Roe v. Wade: for example, Joseph Fletcher, Situation Ethics; "Indicators of Humanhood: A Profile of Man," Hastings Center Report 2, no. 5 (November 1972); and "Four Indicators of Humanhood: The Enquiry Matures," Hastings Center Report 4, no. 6 (December 1974).

I have argued that the life of a fetus is of no greater value than the life of a nonhuman animal at a similar level of rationality, self-consciousness, awareness, capacity to feel, etc., and that since no fetus is a person no fetus has the same claim to life as a person. Now it must be admitted that these arguments apply to the newborn baby as much as to the fetus. . . . If the fetus does not have the same claim to life as a person, it appears that the newborn baby does not either, and the life of a newborn baby is of less value than the life of a pig, a dog, or a chimpanzee.[4]

More recently, the well-knowm atheist Richard Dawkins said on social media that "it would be immoral to bring it [a baby with Down Syndrome] into the world if you have the choice." Would-be parents who learn their child has the condition have an ethical responsibility to "abort it and try again." This "is very civilised" because "these are foetuses diagnosed before they have human feelings." The important question in the abortion debate "is not 'is it "human"?' but 'can it suffer?'"[5]

Thank God, we are not limited to functional expressions of our humanity to define us. Those who hold to a biblical definition of human beings value the enduring dignity of all people as equally bearing the divine image.

We have the perfect example of humanity in the person of Christ. Jesus ultimately shows us how the image of God is intended to be displayed in humanity. This display is seen primarily in his perfect fellowship with the Father, perfect obedience to the Father's will (John 15:10), and selfless love for others: "Greater love has no one than this, that someone lay down his life for his friends" (John 15:13). Jesus perfectly fulfilled his intended purpose: "Although he was a son, he learned obedience through what he suffered. And *being made perfect*, he became the source of eternal salvation to all who obey him" (Heb. 5:8–9).

The implications of the image of God and humanity could not be more significant for discipleship and soul care. As those made in God's image, we belong to him. When Jesus was questioned by the religious leaders about paying taxes to Caesar, he told them that if Caesar's image was on their money, then they should give to Caesar

---

4. Peter Singer, *Practical Ethics* (Cambridge University Press, 1979), 122–23.
5. "Richard Dawkins: 'immoral' to allow Down's syndrome babies to be born," Twitter, August 21, 2014, http://www.telegraph.co.uk/news/health/news/11047072/Richard-Dawkins-immoral-to-allow-Downs-syndrome-babies-to-be-born.html?mobile=basic.

what belonged to him. But then Jesus's stunning conclusion was that we should give to God whatever belongs to God (Mark 12:13–17). Jesus and his hearers were well aware of the teaching of Genesis 1 that all humans are image bearers. Discipleship is surrendering our lives to the One in whose image we are made. We do this by following the pattern that Jesus gives from his life: "Whoever says he abides in him ought to walk in the same way in which [Jesus] walked" (1 John 2:6; cf. 1 Pet. 2:21). When we follow in the steps of Jesus, we experience true humanity that is in right relationship to God. We will then experience the abundant life for which God created us (John 10:10).

We Are Body and Soul

Another very important aspect of Christian anthropology that applies to discipleship and the care of souls is that God made us body and soul. While there is some debate among theologians about whether the Bible intends a distinction between soul and spirit, the nonnegotiable biblical teaching is that there are at least two constituent parts in the human makeup—material and immaterial.[6] The goodness of creation in humanity includes both spiritual and physical aspects. There is a tragic separation of body and soul in death, yet resurrection reunites our souls and bodies, so that we can live in eternity as God intended for us.

Although the Bible makes a distinction between body and soul, the overall emphasis it gives is a holistic, unified understanding, so we do not ever think that the ideal state as a disembodied one.[7] This means that as we seek to help others grow in conformity to Christ, we need to pay attention to both the spiritual and physical aspects of ourselves. As C. S. Lewis expressed through the character Screwtape, "Whatever their bodies do affects their souls."[8] Growth in Christ includes using our bodies in ways that help to shape the state of our spiritual lives—as Paul says, "praying at all times in the Spirit, with all prayer and supplication. To that end *keep alert* [in body and spirit] with all perseverance, making supplication for all the saints" (Eph. 6:18). Our efforts to grow spiritually are worked out as embodied creatures. We

---

6. See Anthony A. Hoekema, *Created in God's Image* (Grand Rapids, MI: Eerdmans, 1986), 203–26.

7. See Elizabeth Hall and Erik Thoennes, "At Home in Our Bodies: The Implications of the Incarnation for Embodiment and Counseling Psychology," *Christian Scholars Review* (Fall, 2006).

8. C. S. Lewis, *The Screwtape Letters* (New York: Collier, 1961), 20.

should never think, for instance, that our bodily position makes no difference when we pray or worship. Getting on our knees or lifting our hands can have a helpful effect on our souls

Caring for our bodies can make us more alert spiritually (1 Kings 19:5–8), and being spiritually healthy can positively affect our physical health (Prov. 17:22). We should not have an overly spiritualized holiness that leads to a disdain for the body and values the spiritual over the physical. Nor should we neglect the spiritual aspects of our makeup, as if the physical is all there is. This is one of the reasons God takes sexual sin so seriously. Many in our culture believe that sex is a merely physical thing, but like everything else in our lives, there is a spiritual component as well, and there is a sacredness to all of life.

We Are Men and Women

> So God created man in his own image,
>> in the image of God he created him;
>> male and female he created them. (Gen. 1:27)

One of the most important aspects of humanity, according to God's good design, is that God made us male and female. Gender and sexuality have become increasingly controversial issues in recent years, but for those committed to the divine inspiration and ultimate authority of Scripture, God's good intention in making men and women equal in worth and dignity but distinct as male and female is an essential part of the wonder and joy of creation (Gen. 1:31).

One of the main reasons God made us male and female was to display his character and glory. To disregard God's intention for gender *equality* in creation is sinful rebellion against God. There is no created superiority or inferiority between men and women in the Bible. "There is neither Jew nor Greek, there is neither slave nor free, there is no male and female, for you are all one in Christ Jesus" (Gal. 3:28). But to disregard God's intention for gender *distinction* in creation is also sinful rebellion against God. Our roles and relational distinctions are grounded in the nature of the triune God and are intended to reflect his character (Rom. 1:24–27).

The God who inspires Scripture is our Creator who knows what is best for us. The ordered design of men and women that is seen in marriage reflects the order within God himself: "But I want you to understand that the head of every man is Christ, the head of a wife is her husband, and the head of Christ is God" (1 Cor. 11:3). Here we see that the unity and distinction within the Trinity is reflected in the relationship between the husband and wife in marriage. Man without woman was not the best display of God's nature in creation, and therefore God said, "It is not good that the man should be alone; I will make a helper fit for him" (Gen. 2:7). This lack of goodness is often reduced only to the idea that Adam must have been lonely and unproductive without Eve. While that is true, I believe the most important reason for humanity as both male and female is the unified yet distinct way the sexes together image and glorify God.

Jesus affirmed gender distinctions and unity grounded in creation. When asked about divorce, he went back to Genesis 2 and gave his understanding of God's good intentions in creation when he made man and woman:

> He answered, "Have you not read that he who created them from the beginning made them male and female, and said, 'Therefore a man shall leave his father and his mother and hold fast to his wife, and they shall become one flesh'? So they are no longer two but one flesh. What therefore God has joined together, let not man separate." (Matt. 19:4–6)

In these three verses, we can see that Jesus trusted the creation account in Genesis as true history; that he viewed the Bible as his ultimate authority in discussions of objective, true morality; and that he believed marriage between a man and woman to be ordained by God in creation. If someone says he loves Jesus, he also must love the Bible that Jesus trusted, and hold to the view of marriage and sexuality that Jesus held.

Marriage is created and defined by God and is a sacred union between one man and one woman. This covenant is intended for life and points beyond itself to God's covenant love and faithfulness in Christ. Men and women are designed by God to be equal and yet wonderfully distinct. This unity and distinction is most vividly seen in marriage. Marriage is created to display the transforming effects of the gospel and to lead people to Christ. Quoting Jesus, Paul wrote, "'Therefore a man shall leave his father and mother and hold fast to his wife, and the two shall become one flesh.' This mystery is profound, and I am saying that it refers to Christ and the church" (Eph. 5:31–32; cf. Matt. 19:4–6; 1 Tim. 2:1–15; 1 Pet. 3:1–8).

What are the implications of manhood and womanhood for discipleship in the care of souls? While there are fundamentally similar ways that men and women grow in Christ, there is also specificity in this according to God's design in making us men and women.[9] Distinct roles for men and women are part of God's created design, and, although distorted by the fall, they are to be expressed in relationships between men and women, especially in the church and family. Masculinity is a God-given role and instinct for men to provide, protect, and initiate in their relationships with women, and femininity is a God-given role and instinct for women to encourage and support this leadership role in men. This relational dynamic is most clearly seen in marriage and the local church, but it also exists in less-defined ways in male-female relationships generally. These instincts and ways of relating will include practical differences in how we function together, but they primarily are seen in the *degree* of responsibility men have and the relational *dynamic* between men and women.[10]

I recently took my sons to see a stirring display of artifacts from the *Titanic*. One of the most powerful aspects of the drama that unfolded on the ship the night it sank was the implementation of the rule that women and children should take the seats on the lifeboats before men. John Jacob Astor was one of the richest men in the world at the time and was returning home from an extended honeymoon with his wife, Madeline, who was five months pregnant. He helped his young wife climb through a window of the promenade deck and escorted her onto lifeboat 4. He then stayed behind with the rest of the men. His body was found and returned to New York, where he was buried at Trinity Cemetery. He never got to meet his son.

This example of manly unselfish bravery made a lasting impression on my eleven- and twelve-year-old sons. I pray they develop into young men who take the lead in selflessly laying down their lives for others, especially for the women they know. And I hope my two young daughters grow to

---

9. See David Talley, "Gender and Sanctification: From Creation to Transformation, A Comparative Look at Genesis 1–3, the Creation and Fall of the Man and the Woman, and Ephesians 5, the Sanctification of the Man and the Woman in a Redemptive Marriage Context," *JBMW* 8, no. 1 (Spring 2003): 6–16.

10. These definitions of masculinity and femininity are my effort to provide some clarity to the nature of gender distinctions that should be found between men and women.

love and encourage this kind of Christlike leadership in the men in their lives. The church should be a place where men and women care for each other with a beautiful equality of dignity and worth, but with distinction of relational dynamics in roles as well. We should not check our gender at the door as we think about growing as disciples. God will be most pleased and glorified when we live according to what he has created us to be.

We Are Sinful

When we forget that God made us and that we are not our own, we believe the lie of Eden and think we can determine good and evil for ourselves. This leads to everyone doing what is right in his own eyes, and evil reigns. I am writing these words on the day when fifty-eight people were killed and over five hundred injured at a concert in Las Vegas. As many lack the words to explain this unspeakable evil, we can look to the Bible for those words, and for the solution. Sin is always irrational and destructive, but at its core it is rebellion against our Creator, and it causes unspeakable heartache.

In the midst of great evil, however, there often are also great displays of human compassion and courage. Stories of brave first responders continue to be told, stories of ordinary people running toward the danger, rather than away, to help people in distress. On 9/11 the world watched in horror as terrorists flew planes into the World Trade Center, and we watched with amazement as unselfishness, kindness, and bravery were also on display as people sought to help their fellow man. Murderous hate and unselfish compassion—great good and great evil—all live in the human heart. Understanding this tension between the goodness of humanity rooted in the image of God and the badness of humanity rooted in our sinful natures is vital to understanding the human condition. Without understanding this tension, we will either neglect our capacity for goodness or ignore our inescapable inclination to evil. We will then seek the wrong solutions and live unwisely. Good parenting, politics, ministry, government, education, counseling, and marriage all need to be based in an accurate understanding of this great tension in humanity.

Sin is any lack of conformity, active or passive, to the moral law of God (which reflects his character). This may be a matter of act, thought, inner disposition, or state.[11] The most important thing about this defini-

---

11. Grudem, *Systematic Theology*, 490.

tion is that it is God-centered. We often think that the main problems of sin are the ways it hurts us. Practical, psychological, social, and relational effects of sin often concern us more than the effect of our sin on God. We must define sin in a God-centered way. It is rebellion against him, and he hates it. Most of all, sin is a worship problem. You will find no better definition of sin than this description in Romans 1:18–25:

> For the wrath of God is revealed from heaven against all ungodliness and unrighteousness of men, who by their unrighteousness suppress the truth. For what can be known about God is plain to them, because God has shown it to them. For his invisible attributes, namely, his eternal power and divine nature, have been clearly perceived, ever since the creation of the world, in the things that have been made. So they are without excuse. For although they knew God, they did not honor him as God or give thanks to him, but they became futile in their thinking, and their foolish hearts were darkened. Claiming to be wise, they became fools, and exchanged the glory of the immortal God for images resembling mortal man and birds and animals and creeping things.
>
> Therefore God gave them up in the lusts of their hearts to impurity, to the dishonoring of their bodies among themselves, because they exchanged the truth about God for a lie and worshiped and served the creature rather than the Creator, who is blessed forever! Amen.

Exchanging God's glory for our own is the essence of idolatry and leads to all the problems in the world. Sin is a particular kind of evil. It is moral evil expressed by moral agents who choose to disobey God and usurp his rightful authority. It exists in our very nature, our hearts as well as specific external actions. "For out of the heart come evil thoughts, murder, adultery, sexual immorality, theft, false witness, slander" (Matt. 15:19; cf. Ex. 20:17; Heb. 13:5). Sin is always and ultimately related to God and is profoundly personal and relational.

> Wash me thoroughly from my iniquity,
>   and cleanse me from my sin!
>
> For I know my transgressions,
>   and my sin is ever before me.

Against you, you only, have I sinned
　　and done what is evil in your sight,
so that you may be justified in your words
　　and blameless in your judgment.
Behold, I was brought forth in iniquity,
　　and in sin did my mother conceive me. (Ps. 51:2–5; cf. Rom.
　　　　5:10; James 4:4)

A holy God cannot, and should not, be ambivalent about idolatry. Rather, he intensely hates sin and responds with anger and judgment to all sin and rebellion.

God is a righteous judge,
　　and a God who feels indignation every day. (Ps. 7:11; cf. Deut.
　　　　12:31; Pss. 5:4–6; 11:5; Prov. 6:16–19; Rev. 6:16–17)

Those who align themselves with God and his ways will also hate sin with godly hatred. "Let love be genuine. Abhor what is evil; hold fast to what is good" (Rom. 12:9). All who love children will hate child abuse and vehemently oppose the abuser. Hatred of evil goes hand in hand with the love of good.

When we truly understand the pervasiveness of human depravity (Rom. 3:10–12) and how much God hates it, we then realize that the only solution is to flee to the mercy and grace of God found at the foot of the cross of Christ. We are completely unable to solve our great sin problem (Eph. 2:1–3), but Christ accomplished the perfect atonement by taking our place. "For our sake he made him to be sin who knew no sin, so that in him we might become the righteousness of God" (2 Cor. 5:21). More than anything else, discipleship and the care of souls are helping others to know God's amazing and transforming grace for them in Christ!

Conclusion

The authority of Scripture leads us to define and see ourselves the way our Creator does. Then we are able to understand our purpose, our problems, and their solutions the way God does. Only then are we able to minister to others in ways that really help them become who God created them to be. We are created in his image—body and soul, male and female—tragically fallen, and wonderfully redeemed by the God-man, Jesus Christ. If we pay attention to these key elements of what it means to be human, we will grow and minister according to the Scriptures. People will have their own definitions and agendas for how we should understand and help them, but loving them well will require defining and helping them in submission to God's Word. And his ways alone lead to abundant and eternal life.

> This God—his way is perfect;
> the word of the LORD proves true;
> he is a shield for all those who take refuge in him. (Ps. 18:30)

Appendix

Scripture Versions Cited

Unless otherwise indicated, Scripture quotations are from the ESV® Bible (The Holy Bible, English Standard Version®), copyright © 2001 by Crossway, a publishing ministry of Good News Publishers. Used by permission. All rights reserved.

Other Scripture versions cited include the following:

Scripture quotations marked ASV are from the American Standard Version of the Bible, 1901.

Scripture quotations marked CSB have been taken from the Christian Standard Bible®. Copyright © 2017 by Holman Bible Publishers. Used by permission. Christian Standard Bible® and CSB® are federally registered trademarks of Holman Bible Publishers.

Scripture quotations marked GNT are from the Good News Translation, Copyright © 1992 by American Bible Society.

Scripture quotations marked HCSB® are taken from The Holman Christian Standard Bible®. Copyright © 1999, 2000, 2002, 2003, 2009 by Holman Bible Publishers. Used by permission. HCSB® is a federally registered trademark of Holman Bible Publishers.

Scripture references marked JB are from The Jerusalem Bible. Copyright © 1966, 1967, 1968 by Darton, Longman & Todd Ltd. and Doubleday & Co., Inc.

Scripture quotations marked KJV are from the King James Version of the Bible.

Scripture quotations marked NASB are from The New American Standard Bible®. Copyright © The Lockman Foundation 1960, 1962, 1963, 1968, 1971, 1972, 1973, 1975, 1977, 1995. Used by permission.

Scripture references marked NEB are from The New English Bible © The Delegates of the Oxford University Press and The Syndics of the Cambridge University Press, 1961, 1970.

Scripture references marked NIV are taken from The Holy Bible, New International Version®, NIV®. Copyright © 1973, 1978, 1984, 2011 by Biblica, Inc.™ Used by permission. All rights reserved worldwide.

Scripture references marked NJB are from The New Jerusalem Bible, copyright © 1985 by Darton, Longman & Todd, Ltd., and Doubleday, a division of Random House, Inc. Reprinted by permission.

Scripture references marked NKJV are from The New King James Version. Copyright © 1982, Thomas Nelson, Inc. Used by permission.

Scripture references marked NLT are from The Holy Bible, New Living Translation, copyright © 1996, 2004. Used by permission of Tyndale House Publishers, Inc., Wheaton, IL, 60189. All rights reserved.

Scripture references marked NRSV are from The New Revised Standard Version. Copyright © 1989 by the Division of Christian Education of the National Council of the Churches of Christ in the U.S.A. Published by Thomas Nelson, Inc. Used by permission of the National Council of the Churches of Christ in the U.S.A.

Scripture references marked RSV are from The Revised Standard Version. Copyright ©1946, 1952, 1971, 1973 by the Division of Christian Education of the National Council of the Churches of Christ in the U.S.A.

Writings of Wayne Grudem

Entries are chronological by years and arranged alphabetically within the same year. Translations into multiple languages have not been included. Evangelical Theological Society papers and other informal writings have also been omitted.

1970s

"Alphabetical Reference List for Old Testament Apocrypha and Pseudepigrapha." *Journal of the Evangelical Theological Society* 19, no. 4 (Fall 1976): 297–313.

"A Response to Gerhard Dautzenberg on 1 Cor. 12.10." *Biblische Zeitschrift* 22, no. 2 (1978): 253–70.

"1 Corinthians 14.20–25: Prophecy and Tongues as Signs of God's Attitude." *Westminster Theological Journal* 41, no. 2 (Spring 1979): 381–96.

1980s

The Gift of Prophecy in 1 Corinthians. Washington, DC: University Press of America, 1982. Reprint, Eugene, OR: Wipf & Stock, 1999.

"Scripture's Self-Attestation and the Problem of Formulating a Doctrine of Scripture." In *Scripture and Truth*, edited by D. A. Carson and John D. Woodbridge, 19–59. Grand Rapids, MI: Zondervan, 1983.

"Keys of the Kingdom." In *Evangelical Dictionary of Theology*, edited by Walter Elwell, 604–6. Grand Rapids, MI: Baker, 1984.

"Does Κεφαλή ('Head') Mean 'Source' or 'Authority over' in Greek Literature? A Survey of 2,336 Examples." *Trinity Journal* 6, no. 1 (Spring 1985): 38–59. Also published as an appendix in *The Role Relationship of Men and Women*, by George W. Knight III, 49–80. Rev. ed. Chicago: Moody Press, 1985.

"Christ Preaching through Noah: 1 Peter 3:19–20 in Light of Dominant Themes in Jewish Literature." *Trinity Journal* 7, no. 2 (Fall 1986): 3–31.

"Prophecy—Yes, but Teaching—No: Paul's Consistent Advocacy of Women's Participation without Governing Authority." *Journal of the Evangelical Theological Society* 30, no. 1 (March 1987): 11–23.

The First Epistle of Peter. Tyndale New Testament Commentaries. Leicester, UK: Inter-Varsity Press; Grand Rapids, MI: Eerdmans, 1988.

The Gift of Prophecy in the New Testament and Today. Westchester, IL: Crossway, 1988.

"Why Christians Can Still Prophesy." *Christianity Today* 32, no. 13 (September 16, 1988): 29–35.

"How an Economic System Can Be Compatible with Scripture." In *Biblical Principles and Economics: The Foundations*, edited by Richard Chewning, 27–52. Colorado Springs: NavPress, 1989.

"Should Christians Seek the Gift of Prophecy Today?" In *Tough Questions Christians Ask*, edited by David Neff, 79–92. Wheaton, IL: Victor, 1989.

1990s

"Investing in What Lasts." In *The Midas Trap*, edited by David Neff, 55–63. Wheaton, IL: Victor, 1990.

"The Meaning of Κεφαλή ('Head'): A Response to Recent Studies." *Trinity Journal* 11, no. 1 (Spring 1990): 3–72. Republished in *Recovering Biblical Manhood and Womanhood: A Response to Evangelical Feminism*, edited by John Piper and Wayne Grudem, 425–68. Wheaton, IL: Crossway, 1991.

"What Should Be the Relationship between Prophet and Pastor?" *Equipping the Saints* (Fall 1990): 7–9, 21–22.

"Charity, Clarity, and Hope." Coauthored with John Piper. In *Recovering Biblical Manhood and Womanhood: A Response to Evangelical Feminism*, edited by John Piper and Wayne Grudem, 403–22. Wheaton, IL: Crossway, 1991.

"He Did Not Descend into Hell: A Plea for Following Scripture Instead of the Apostles' Creed." *Journal of the Evangelical Theological Society* 34, no. 1 (March 1991): 103–13.

Recovering Biblical Manhood and Womanhood: A Response to Evangelical Feminism. Coedited with John Piper. Wheaton, IL: Crossway, 1991.

"Does God Still Give Revelation Today?" *Charisma* (September 1992): 38–42.

The Vineyard's Response to The Standard. Anaheim, CA: Association of Vineyard Churches, 1992.

Power and Truth: A Response to the Critiques of Vineyard Teaching and Practice by D. A. Carson, James Montgomery Boice, and John H. Armstrong in "Power Religion." Anaheim, CA: Association of Vineyard Churches, 1993.

"Should Christians Expect Miracles Today? Objections and Answers from the Bible." In *The Kingdom and the Power: Are Healing and Spiritual Gifts Used by Jesus and the Early Church Meant for Today?,* edited by Gary Greig and Kevin Springer, 55–110. Ventura, CA: Regal, 1993. Republished in *Strangers to Fire: When Tradition Trumps Scripture,* edited by Robert W. Graves, 225–60. Woodstock, GA: The Foundation for Pentecostal Scholarship, 2014.

"What Is the Real Meaning of a 'Word of Wisdom' and a 'Word of Knowledge'?" *Ministries Today* (January–February 1993): 60–65.

Systematic Theology: An Introduction to Biblical Doctrine. Leicester, UK: Inter-Varsity Press; Grand Rapids, MI: Zondervan, 1994.

"The Perseverance of the Saints: A Case Study from Hebrews 6:4–6 and Other Warning Passages of Hebrews." In *The Grace of God and the Bondage of the Will.* Vol. 1, *Biblical and Practical Perspectives on Calvinism,* edited by Thomas R. Schreiner and Bruce A. Ware, 133–82. Grand Rapids, MI: Baker, 1995. Republished in *Still Sovereign: Contemporary Perspectives on Election, Foreknowledge, and Grace,* edited by Thomas R. Schreiner and Bruce A. Ware, 133–82. Grand Rapids, MI: Baker, 2000.

Ed. *Are Miraculous Gifts for Today? Four Views.* Counterpoints: Bible and Theology. Grand Rapids, MI: Zondervan, 1996.

"What's Wrong with 'Gender Neutral' Bible Translations?" *Journal for Biblical Manhood and Womanhood* 1, no. 3 (June 1996): 3–5.

"The Nature of Divine Eternity: A Response to William Craig." *Philosophia Christi* 20, no. 1 (Spring 1997): 55–70.

What's Wrong with Gender-Neutral Bible Translations? Libertyville, IL: Council on Biblical Manhood and Womanhood, 1997.

"Willow Creek Enforces Egalitarianism: Policy Requires All Staff and New Members to Joyfully Affirm Egalitarian Views." *CBMW News* 2, no.5 (December 1997): 1, 3–6.

"A Response to Mark Strauss' Evaluation of the Colorado Springs Translation Guidelines." *Journal of the Evangelical Theological Society* 41, no. 2 (June 1998): 263–86.

Bible Doctrine: Essential Teachings of the Christian Faith. Edited by Jeff Purswell. Grand Rapids, MI: Zondervan, 1999.

2000s

"Do We Act As If We Really Believe That 'The Bible Alone, and the Bible in Its Entirety, Is the Word of God Written'?" *Journal of the Evangelical Theological Society* 43, no.1 (March 2000): 5–26.

The Gender-Neutral Bible Controversy: Muting the Masculinity of God's Words. Coauthored with Vern S. Poythress. Nashville: Broadman & Holman, 2000. Updated as *The Gender-Neutral Bible Controversy: Is the Age of Political Correctness Altering the Meaning of God's Words?* Coauthored with Vern S. Poythress. Fearn, Scotland: Mentor, 2003.

"Prophecy, Prophets." In *New Dictionary of Biblical Theology*, edited by T. Desmond Alexander and Brian S. Rosner, 701–10. Downers Grove, IL: InterVarsity Press, 2000.

The Holy Bible, English Standard Version (ESV). Translation Oversight Committee member. Wheaton, IL: Crossway, 2001.

"The Meaning of Κεφαλή ('Head'): An Evaluation of New Evidence, Real and Alleged." *Journal of the Evangelical Theological Society* 44, no.1 (March 2001): 25–65. Also published under the same title as a chapter in *Biblical Foundations for Manhood and Womanhood*, edited by Wayne Grudem, 145–202. Foundations for the Family. Wheaton, IL: Crossway, 2002.

"Upon Leaving: Thoughts on Marriage and Ministry." *Trinity Magazine* 2 (Summer 2001): 20–21.

Ed. *Biblical Foundations for Manhood and Womanhood.* Foundations for the Family. Wheaton, IL: Crossway, 2002.

"Key Issues in the Manhood-Womanhood Controversy." In *Building Strong Families*, edited by Dennis Rainey, 29–88. Foundations for the Family. Wheaton, IL: Crossway, 2002.

"The Myth of Mutual Submission as an Interpretation of Ephesians 5:21." In *Biblical Foundations for Manhood and Womanhood*, edited by Wayne Grudem, 221–32. Foundations for the Family. Wheaton, IL: Crossway, 2002.

Pastoral Leadership for Manhood and Womanhood. Coedited with Dennis Rainey. Wheaton, IL: Crossway, 2002.

Business for the Glory of God: The Bible's Teaching on the Moral Goodness of Business. Wheaton, IL: Crossway, 2003.

"When, Why, and for What Should We Draw New Boundaries?" In *Beyond the Bounds: Open Theism and Undermining of Biblical Christianity*, edited by John Piper, Justin Taylor, and Paul Kjoss Helseth, 339–70. Wheaton, IL: Crossway, 2003.

Evangelical Feminism and Biblical Truth: An Analysis of More Than One Hundred Disputed Questions. Sisters, OR: Multnomah, 2004. Reprint, Wheaton, IL: Crossway, 2012.

"Should We Move beyond the New Testament to a Better Ethic? An Analysis of William J. Webb, *Slaves, Women and Homosexuals: Exploring the Hermeneutics of Cultural Analysis.*" *Journal of the Evangelical Theological Society* 47, no. 2 (June 2004): 299–346.

The TNIV and the Gender-Neutral Bible Controversy. Coauthored with Vern Poythress. Nashville: Broadman & Holman, 2004.

"Are Only *Some* Words of Scripture Breathed Out by God? Why Plenary Inspiration Favors 'Essentially Literal' Bible Translation." In *Translating Truth: The Case for Essentially Literal Bible Translation*, coauthored with Leland Ryken, C. John Collins, Vern S. Poythress, and Bruce Winter, 19–56. Wheaton, IL: Crossway, 2005.

Christian Beliefs: Twenty Basics Every Christian Should Know. Edited by Elliot Grudem. Grand Rapids, MI: Zondervan, 2005. Also published under the same title by Leicester, UK: Inter-Varsity Press, 2005 and 2010.

"Response to *Who's Afraid of the Holy Spirit?*" In *Who's Afraid of the Holy Spirit? An Investigation into the Ministry of the Spirit of God Today*, edited by Daniel B. Wallace and M. James Sawyer, 279–85. Dallas: Biblical Studies Press, 2005.

Why Is My Choice of Bible Translation So Important? Coauthored with Jerry Thacker. Louisville: Council on Biblical Manhood and Womanhood, 2005.

Evangelical Feminism: A New Path to Liberalism? Wheaton, IL: Crossway, 2006.

"Right and Wrong Interpretation of the Bible: Some Suggestions for Pastors and Bible Teachers." In *Preach the Word: Essays on Expository Preaching in Honor of R. Kent Hughes*, edited by Leland Ryken and Todd Wilson, 54–75. Wheaton, IL: Crossway, 2007.

"Biblical Ethics: An Overview." Contributor. In *ESV Study Bible*. Wheaton, IL: Crossway, 2008.

Gen. ed. *ESV Study Bible*. Wheaton, IL: Crossway, 2008.

Study notes on Luke. Contributor. In *ESV Study Bible*. Wheaton, IL: Crossway, 2008.

Foreword to *Should Christians Embrace Evolution? Biblical and Scientific Responses*, edited by Norman Nevin, 9–10. Nottingham, UK: InterVarsity Press, 2009.

"Why It Is Never Right to Lie: An Example of John Frame's Influence on My Approach to Ethics." In *Speaking the Truth in Love: The Theology of John Frame*, edited by John J. Hughes, 778–801. Phillipsburg, NJ: P&R, 2009.

2010s

"Pleasing God by Our Obedience: A Neglected New Testament Teaching." In *For the Fame of God's Name: Essays in Honor of John Piper*, edited by Sam Storms and Justin Taylor, 272–92. Wheaton, IL: Crossway, 2010.

Politics—according to the Bible: A Comprehensive Resource for Understanding Modern Political Issues in Light of Scripture. Grand Rapids, MI: Zondervan, 2010.

Gen. ed. *ESV Student Study Bible*. Wheaton, IL: Crossway, 2011.

"The Government's Role in Market Regulation and Economic Inequality." *Christian Lawyer* 7, no. 3 (Winter 2011): 29–31.

Making Sense of Series. Seven parts from *Systematic Theology* reissued in separate volumes. Grand Rapids, MI: Zondervan, 2011.

"Property Rights Inherent in the Eighth Commandment Are Essential for Human Flourishing." Coauthored with Barry Asmus. In *Business Ethics Today: Stealing*, edited by Philip J. Clements, 119–34. Philadelphia: Center for Christian Business Ethics Today, 2011.

"What Is at Risk for Business If We Lose a Christian Worldview?" Coauthored with Barry Asmus. In *Business Ethics Today: Foundations*, edited by Philip J. Clements, 115–27. Philadelphia: Center for Christian Business Ethics Today, 2011. Also published in *Biblical Perspectives on Business Ethics: How the Christian Worldview Has Shaped Our Economic Foundations*. Coauthored with Charles Colson, Peter Lillback, Philip Ryken, Barry Asmus, Philip J. Clements, Mac McQuiston, and Ron Ferner. Philadelphia: Center for Christian Business Ethics Today, 2012.

"Biblical Evidence for the Eternal Submission of the Son to the Father." In *The New Evangelical Subordinationism? Perspectives on the Equality of God the Father and God the Son*, edited by Dennis W. Jowers and H. Wayne House, 223–61. Eugene, OR: Pickwick, 2012.

"The English Standard Version (ESV)." In *Which Bible Translation Should I Use? A Comparison of Four Major Recent Versions*, edited by Andreas J. Köstenberger and David A. Croteau, 40–77. Nashville: B&H Academic, 2012.

Introducing Scripture: A Guide to the Old and New Testaments. Coedited with C. John Collins and Thomas R. Schreiner. Nottingham, UK: Inter-Varsity Press; Wheaton, IL: Crossway, 2012.

Understanding Scripture: An Overview of the Bible's Origin, Reliability, and Meaning. Coedited with C. John Collins and Thomas R. Schreiner. Nottingham, UK: Inter-Varsity Press, 2012.

Understanding the Big Picture of the Bible: A Guide to Reading the Bible Well. Coedited with C. John Collins and Thomas R. Schreiner. Wheaton, IL: Crossway, 2012.

Voting by the Bible: The Economic and Foreign Policy Issues. Grand Rapids, MI: Zondervan, 2012.

Voting by the Bible: The Social Issues. Grand Rapids, MI: Zondervan, 2012.

The Poverty of Nations: A Sustainable Solution. Coauthored with Barry Asmus. Wheaton, IL: Crossway, 2013.

"Public Hope: How Can This 'Good' Be Achieved?" In *Good News for the Public Square: A Biblical Framework for Christian Engagement*, edited by Timothy Laurence, 91–116. London: The Lawyers' Christian Fellowship, 2014.

"Doctrinal Deviations in Evangelical-Feminist Arguments about the Trinity." In *One God in Three Persons: Unity of Essence, Distinction of Persons, Implications for Life*, edited by Bruce A. Ware and John Starke, 17–45. Wheaton, IL: Crossway, 2015.

Fifty Crucial Questions: An Overview of Central Concerns about Manhood and Womanhood. Coauthored with John Piper. Wheaton, IL: Crossway, 2016.

"Free Grace" Theology: Five Ways It Diminishes the Gospel. Wheaton, IL: Crossway, 2016.

"Do Global Corporations Exploit Poor Countries?" Coauthored with Barry Asmus. In *Counting the Cost: Christian Perspectives on Capitalism,* edited by Art Lindsley and Anne R. Bradley, 277–304. Abilene, TX: Abilene Christian University Press, 2017.

Redeeming the Life of the Mind: Essays in Honor of Vern Poythress. Coedited with John M. Frame and John J. Hughes. Wheaton, IL: Crossway, 2017.

Theistic Evolution: A Scientific, Philosophical, and Theological Critique. Coedited with J. P. Moreland, Stephen C. Meyer, Christopher Shaw, and Ann K. Gauger. Wheaton, IL: Crossway, 2017.

Christian Ethics: An Introduction to Biblical Moral Reasoning. Wheaton, IL: Crossway, 2018.

Contributors

Gregg R. Allison (PhD, Trinity Evangelical Divinity School) is professor of Christian theology at the Southern Baptist Theological Seminary.

Darryl DelHousaye (DMin, Western Seminary) is president of Phoenix Seminary.

John DelHousaye (PhD, Fuller Theological Seminary) is associate professor of New Testament at Phoenix Seminary.

Lane T. Dennis (PhD, Northwestern University) is president and CEO of Crossway, Wheaton, Illinois.

John M. Frame (DD, Belhaven College) is professor of systematic theology and philosophy emeritus at Reformed Theological Seminary in Orlando, Florida.

Elliot Grudem (MDiv, Reformed Theological Seminary) is founder and president of Leaders Collective in Raleigh, North Carolina.

John J. Hughes (ThM, Westminster Theological Seminary) is director of academic development for P&R Publishing.

Kent Hughes (DMin, Trinity Evangelical Divinity School) is professor of practical theology at Westminster Theological Seminary.

C. J. Mahaney is senior pastor of Sovereign Grace Church of Louisville, Kentucky.

Ray Ortlund (PhD, University of Aberdeen) is pastor of Immanuel Church in Nashville, Tennessee.

John Piper (DTh, University of Munich) is founder and teacher of DesiringGod.org and chancellor of Bethlehem College & Seminary.

Vern S. Poythress (PhD, Harvard University; DTh, University of Stellenbosch) is professor of New Testament interpretation at Westminster Theological Seminary.

Jeff T. Purswell (MDiv, Trinity Evangelical Divinity School) is director of theology and training for Sovereign Grace Churches and dean of the Sovereign Grace Pastors College.

Leland Ryken (PhD, University of Oregon) is emeritus professor of English at Wheaton College.

Thomas R. Schreiner (PhD, Fuller Theological Seminary) is James Buchanan Harrison Professor of New Testament Interpretation at the Southern Baptist Theological Seminary.

Sam Storms (PhD, University of Texas) is pastor of Bridgeway Church in Oklahoma City, Oklahoma.

Owen Strachan (PhD, Trinity Evangelical Divinity School) is associate professor of Christian theology and director of the Center for Public Theology at the Midwestern Baptist Theological Seminary.

K. Erik Thoennes (PhD, Trinity Evangelical Divinity School) is professor of theology and chair of undergraduate theology at Biola University/Talbot School of Theology and pastor of Grace Evangelical Free Church in La Mirada, California.

Bruce A. Ware (PhD, Fuller Theological Seminary) is T. Rupert and Lucille Coleman Professor of Christian Theology at the Southern Baptist Theological Seminary.

Peter J. Williams (PhD, University of Cambridge) is principal of Tyndale House, Cambridge, England.

General Index

sufficiency of, 15, 41–42, 55–56, 80,
81–83, 327
transformative power of, 42–43
as Trinitarian communicative
agency, 34, 36–40, 51
verbal inspiration of, 193, 270, 275
as the Word of God, 54–55, 64, 217
secondary causes, 43
self-assurance, 297
selfishness, 247
self-knowledge, 238, 262
sensate culture, 302
sensum de sensu translations, 230n15
sermon
inductive or deductive, 277–78, 279
outline of, 279
shape of, 276–78
Sermon on the Mount, 192, 274
servanthood, 246–47
servant leadership, 235–49
seven (number of perfection), 267–68
sex, spiritual component of, 341
sex-reassignment surgery, 319, 328
shaliah (messenger), 111
shame, and gender dysphoria, 318
shepherd imagery, 242
Silva, Moisés, 13
similes, 186
simplicity, 302
sin
as bondage to self-exaltation, 307
defined in a God-centered way,
344–46
as irrational and destructive, 344
pervasiveness of, 346
Singer, Peter, 338–39
singing hymns, 251
slave, 246–47
Smeaton, George, 294–95
social trinitarianism, 210
sola Scriptura, 15, 55, 64, 99, 102
Son
ad intra relations, 212
authority of, 41
and creation, 108
eternal generation of, 103n14
as the eternal image of God, 69–70

eternal submission of, 100, 105–6,
112, 213–14
eternal subordination of, 18
functional subordination of, 213
as the image of the Father, 72, 75
as mediating creation, 69
name of, 102–3
protected by the headship of the
Father, 243
roles of, 104–12
sent by Father, 105, 110–12
Son as Word, 67–68
Song of Moses, 145
Song of Solomon, 325
sonship, 144
soul, satisfaction of, 306, 307–11, 315
soul care, 42n18
source, "head" as, 200, 202, 205–6
source criticism, 272
Sowell, Thomas, 251
sowing, in pastoral ministry, 288–93
speech act theory, 34, 35–36, 47
Spicq, Ceslas, 263–64
spiritual experience, 168
spiritual gifts
and Christian life, 176
diversity of, 169–71, 172
and edification, 177–80
and the gospel, 167–69, 180
pursuit of, 175–77, 180
and the unity in the church, 171–73,
180
Spurgeon, Charles Haddon, 253, 280,
281, 292, 303
Stonehouse, Ned B., 13, 14
Stott, John, 295
strong and the weak, 172n20
suffering, 249
symbols, in the Bible, 186
Symmachus, 229n14
Syriac Peshitta, 228
Systematic Theology (Grudem), 15,
18, 19, 22, 23, 34, 35, 40, 44, 99,
164–65, 251–52, 258–59

Targum Jonathan, 228
Taylor, Mark, 326n29
teachers, 179

Scripture Index